AFPC®
STUDY TEXT

Paper G70

Investment Portfolio Management

UPDATES ARE AVAILABLE ON OUR WEBSITE
www.bpp.com/afpc
(see page (v) for more details)

BPP Professional Education
July 2005

First edition 1999
Seventh edition July 2005

ISBN 0 7517 2341 X (previous edition 0 7517 1709 6)

British Library Cataloguing-in-Publication Data
A catalogue record for this book
is available from the British Library

Published by

BPP Professional Education
Aldine House, Aldine Place
London W12 8AW

www.bpp.com

Printed in Great Britain by KKS Printing
The Printworks
12-20 Rosina Street
London
E9 6JE

Contents

Page

Contents

Page

INTRODUCTION TO THIS STUDY TEXT

This Study Text has been written to cover the syllabus for G70: *Investment Portfolio Planning*.

Each *chapter* of the Study Text is divided into *sections* and contains:

- A list of topics covered, cross-referenced to the syllabus
- An introduction to put the chapter in context
- Clear, concise topic-by-topic coverage
- Examples and questions to reinforce learning, confirm understanding and stimulate thought, with answers at the end of the chapter
- Exam focus points with hints on how to approach the exam
- A roundup of the key points in the chapter
- A quiz (with answers at the end of the Study Text)

Practice examination

At the end of the Study Text, you will find a full practice examination. You should attempt this before you sit the real examination.

Updates to this Study Text

To cover changes occurring in the period up to the publication of the next edition of this Study Text, we provide free **Updates**.

Possible changes to be covered in Updates include:

- Syllabus changes, which normally take effect from January

- Changes in legislation, which for AFPC may be examined three months after they become legally effective.

To obtain and print out your free **Updates,** go to our website at **www.bpp.com/afpc.**

If you do not have Internet access please telephone our Customer Service Team on 020 8740 2211 to request a free printed copy of Updates.

SYLLABUS

Introduction

The following is the syllabus for the G70 *Investment Portfolio Management* paper of the Advanced Financial Planning Certificate®, as published by the Chartered Insurance Institute®. The syllabus is examined on the basis of English Law and practice. The syllabus printed here will be examined in 2005. See page (v) for details of our syllabus Updates.

Objective

To develop in the candidate the ability to:

- Describe investment markets and the main types of financial investments
- Explain how investment markets are affected by economic, technological and political conditions
- Explain the theory and the practical implications of investment risk and portfolio theory
- Evaluate the success of investment strategies and asset allocation models
- Describe the regulatory requirements for investment portfolio management
- Apply knowledge and skills to practical situations
- Synthesise different aspects of the syllabus and apply them to given scenarios

Assumed knowledge and application skills

It is assumed that the candidate already has the knowledge gained from a study of the relevant elements of units of papers 1, 2 and 3 of the FPC or equivalent qualification. The candidate is also assumed to have a basic knowledge of statistical methods and financial mathematics and is advised to have studied for G20 *Personal investment planning* before attempting this unit, since it builds on the knowledge gained from G20.

		Covered in Chapter
1	**The economic environment**	
1.1	The key political and social factors which affect investment markets	1

Candidates should be able to

- Describe in outline the main political and social factors which affect investment values and returns

1.2	Economic and financial factors which affect financial markets	1

Candidates should be able to

- Describe the main economic and financial factors which affect investment values and returns, including economic growth trends, the effects of inflation and deflation, productivity of labour and capital, technological change, sectional, regional, national and world business cycles, international trade, capital movements, exchange rates, money supply, interest rates, inflation and demographic changes, types of unemployment, monopolies and perfect competition, demand and supply curve, Phillips curve

1.3	How political, social, economic and financial factors affect investment markets	1

Candidates should be able to

- Describe how these factors can affect the development and behaviour of financial institutions and markets
- Explain these issues in relation to the UK and make comparisons with other markets (UK, Japan, Europe) and also emerging markets

 (vi)

1.4   The role of governments in investment markets   1

Candidates should be able to

- Describe in outline the role of governments in determining monetary and fiscal policy, interest rates, public sector finance, government borrowing, regulation of financial markets and other businesses

1.5   Central banks and the banking system   1

Candidates should be able to

- Outline the functions of central banks and the banking system and their relationship to bond markets

2   Direct financial investments

2.1   **Cash investments**   2

Candidates should be able to

- Describe the main classes of cash investments including deposits, certificates of deposit, Treasury bills
- Distinguish between the main types of cash investment and be able to contrast cash investments with other main categories of investments, such as fixed interest securities and equities
- Describe the risks and returns of cash investments
- Describe methods of analysing cash investments
- Explain the main issues with respect to investment in different currencies

2.2   **Fixed interest investments**   3

Candidates should be able to

Explain and distinguish between:

- The main types of fixed interests investment including gilts, both fixed interest and index-linked (including the basic function of strips and repo markets)
- Debentures and loan stock
- Convertibles and preference shares
- Foreign government bonds
- Local authority bonds
- UK and overseas corporate bonds
- Eurobonds

They should be able to

- Explain their uses and applications
- Describe fixed interest markets and how fixed interest securities are issued and redeemed
- Describe the structure and use of the yield curve
- Interpret yield curves
- Evaluate how economic, political and other developments may affect fixed interest investments
- Explain how yields are calculated
- Describe the risks and returns of fixed interest investments
- Distinguish between financial risks and credit risks
- Explain the relevance of credit rating
- Explain duration and modified duration

(vii)

2.3   **Equity investments**

Candidates should be able to

- Describe the characteristics of different equity investments including market ratings, size, sector classifications, financial strength and extent of cyclical influences
- Demonstrate how shares are valued including Gordon's growth model, dividend yield, price earnings ratio, net asset value, borrowing, liquidity and cash flow
- Explain the basic mechanics of mergers and take-overs, privatisations, demutualisations and management buy-outs and how mergers and acquisitions are financed and analysed
- Describe the main features of venture capital markets
- Explain the operation of the new issues market, scrip issues, rights issues, splits and how these affect investors and investment decisions
- Describe the risks and returns of equity investments

2.4   **Derivatives**

Candidates should be able to

- Describe the main kinds of derivatives: futures, options (including warrants), hedge funds and their main investment characteristics, how they are traded and their use in investment management including the role of warrants in the issue of new investment trusts
- Explain the risk involved including counterparty risk
- Assess the potential risks and rewards of derivatives
- Demonstrate how investment managers can use derivatives to stimulate markets and to increase or reduce risk in portfolios

Covered in
Chapter

4   Other investments

4.1   **Unlisted securities**   10

Candidates should be able to

- Describe and evaluate the risks involved in investment in unlisted securities

4.2   **Venture capital trusts, enterprise investment schemes, enterprise zone buildings**   10

Candidates should be able to

- Describe the main tax features, principal rules and risks involved in venture capital trusts, enterprise investment schemes and enterprise zone buildings

4.3   **Physical assets and commodities**   10

Candidates should be able to

- Describe and evaluate the main risks and costs of buying and selling physical assets (including works of art and commodities) as well as investing in commodity futures and options
- Compare the risks and returns of investing in these assets in relation to equity investments

4.4   **Property**   10

Candidates should be able to

- Describe the basic issues surrounding both commercial and residential property investment and property markets, including the main participants (institutions, tenants, developers, planners, investors), direct and indirect holdings, valuations, investment characteristics
- Compare the risks and returns of property investment in relation to equity and fixed interest investment

5   Interpretation of financial data

5.1   **Accounts and accounting principles**   11

Candidates should be able to

- Interpret company accounts in the investment context
- Explain the requirements for company accounts

5.2   **How financial data underpin investment decisions**   11

Candidates should be able to

- Explain how accounts and annual reports are relevant to investment decisions and the limitations of such information
- Compare different company profiles
- Describe the use of accounting ratios which will be helpful in making investment decisions
- Describe research methodology and different types of information sources   13

Covered in
Chapter

8 Fund management services

8.1 Portfolio investment management

14

Candidates should be able to

- Explain the roles of investment managers and advisers for the main types of institutional and private clients in relation to different markets, investment objectives and legal constraints, different risk, profit, growth and income needs
- Describe the main features of portfolio investment management services
- Distinguish the roles and responsibilities of portfolio managers and compare discretionary and advisory services and requirements for reporting to clients on a regular basis
- Evaluate different charging structures and their impact on investment decisions

8.2 Management of direct investments, unit trusts, offshore funds, fund of funds, pooled investments, OEICs, ICVCs, investment trust and life assurance products

14

Candidates should be able to

- Describe the features of management services as they apply to direct investments, unit trusts, offshore funds, fund of funds, pooled investments, OEICs, ICVCs, investment trusts, life assurance products and multi-managers
- Compare the relative merits of investing in these different structures and vehicles

8.3 Pensions

14

Candidates should be able to

- Describe the investment requirements of individual pension arrangements including Self Invested Personal Pension (SIPP), Small Self Administered Scheme (SSAS), Individual Pension Accounts (IPA) and unit-linked pensions generally
- Recommend appropriate strategies for pension funds where fund withdrawal facilities are used

8.4 Personal Equity Plans (PEPs)/Individual Savings Accounts (ISAs)

14

Candidates should be able to

- Evaluate how PEPs/ISAs fit into overall portfolio planning and determine when switches are appropriate

8.5 Fund supermarkets and wrap accounts

14

Candidates should be able to

- Describe and evaluate the features of funds supermarkets and wrap accounts

8.6 Legislative requirements

14

Candidates should be able to

- Outline the proposed changes to the legislative regimes for pensions and their potential impact on investment strategies

9   Performance assessment and financial calculations

9.1   **Time value of money**   15

Candidates should be able to

- Describe the principle of the time value of money and carry out
  simple compound interest and related calculations including
  effective rate of interest

9.2   **Benchmarks and indices**   15

Candidates should be able to

- Describe the broad principles of financial index construction,
  distinguishing between those indices used in the main investment
  markets both in the UK and overseas
- Show how financial indices are used in assessing portfolio
  performance

9.3   **Qualitative data and quantitative statistical data: measurement of**   15
           investment performance and returns of equity, fixed interest and
           other investment portfolios

Candidates should be able to

- Use qualitative data and quantitative statistical data for the
  measurement of investment performance
- Calculate rates of return and distinguish between time-weighted
  and money-weighted returns
- Evaluate the uses and limitations of performance measurement
- Calculate Sharpe ratios

9.4   **Investment criteria, switching**   15

Candidates should be able to

- Establish and evaluate criteria for the selection of investment
  managers, pension funds, insurance funds, unit trusts and
  investment trusts
- Describe and justify criteria for making switching decisions
  between investments
- Define appropriate performance benchmarks

9.5   **Risk indicators**   15

Candidates should be able to

- Appraise critically statistical information about measures of
  volatility including Beta factors and other indicators of risk

THE EXAMINATION PAPER

The examination is in three sections, which together carry 200 marks in total.

(a)   Section A consists of several compulsory short answer questions to test knowledge across the syllabus. (Total 45 marks).

(b)   Section B consists of a single Case Study questions requiring the display of analytical and application skills. (Total 75 marks).

(c)   Section C consists of three questions. You must answer any two. The questions require discussion based answers. (Total 80 marks).

LEGISLATION

The examination is based on the legislative position **three months** before the date of the examination.

How up-to-date is your BPP study material?

This Study Text is up-to-date as at 1 June 2005. Legislation and syllabus changes affecting the exam from June 2005 up to the time of publication of the next edition of this Study Text will be covered by our free **Updates**. See page (v) for details.

Part A

The economic environment

Chapter 1

THE ECONOMIC ENVIRONMENT

Chapter topic list	Syllabus reference
1 Key economic concepts	1.2
2 Political, economic and social factors	1.1, 1.2
3 How political, social and economic factors affect markets	1.3
4 The role of government	1.4
5 Central banks and the banking system	1.5

Introduction

An **investor's return** from an investment portfolio is **influenced** by various local and global economic and financial factors. Decisions made by governments and those participating in markets can impact on the **investment environment** in various ways.

Key economic concepts which the syllabus requires you to cover include **demand and supply curves**, **monopolies** and **perfect competition**, types of **unemployment**, and the relationship between **unemployment and inflation**.

1   KEY ECONOMIC CONCEPTS

Demand and supply

1.1   A market involves **the buyers and sellers of a good** who influence its **price**. Markets can be worldwide, as in the case of oil, wheat, cotton and copper for example. Others are more localised, such as the housing market in a particular area, or the market for second-hand cars. We are all broadly familiar with the idea that markets are subject to the forces of **demand** (from potential customers) and **supply** (by producers or providers of a service).

1.2   **Demand** for a product is the quantity of that good that potential purchasers would buy, or attempt to buy, if the price of the good were at a certain level.

1.3   The relationship between demand and price can be shown graphically as a **demand curve**. The demand curve of a single consumer or household is derived by estimating how much of the good the consumer or household would demand at various hypothetical market prices. A **market demand curve** is a similar curve, drawn from a demand schedule, expressing the expected total quantity of the good that would be demanded by **all consumers together,** at any given price.

1.4   A **supply curve** can also be created both for an individual supplier and for all firms which produce the good. A supply curve is constructed in a similar manner to a demand curve (from a schedule of supply quantities at different prices) but shows the quantity suppliers

BPP
PROFESSIONAL EDUCATION

are willing to produce at different price levels. It is an **upward sloping curve from left to right**, because greater quantities will be supplied at higher prices.

1.5 The **price mechanism** brings **demand and supply** into equilibrium and the equilibrium price for a good is the price at which the volume demanded by consumers and the volume that firms would be willing to supply are the same. This is also known as the **market clearing price** since at this price there will be neither surplus nor shortage in the market.

1.6 These ideas can be illustrated by drawing the market **demand curve** and the market **supply curve** on the same diagram (Figure 1).

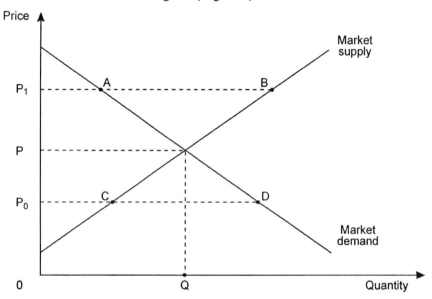

Figure 1 Market equilibrium

1.7 At price P_1 in the above diagram, there is an excess quantity that suppliers want to produce over the quantity demanded at that price, equal to the distance AB. Suppliers would react as unsold stocks accumulate.

(a) They would cut down the current level of production in order to sell unwanted stocks (de-stock).

(b) They would also reduce prices in order to encourage sales.

1.8 The opposite will happen at price P_0 where there is an excess of demand over supply shown by the distance CD. Output and price would increase. Faced with an excess of demand, manufacturers would be able to raise their prices. This would make supplying the good more profitable and supply would increase.

1.9 At price P the amount that sellers are willing to supply is equal to the amount that customers are willing to buy. Consumers will be willing to spend a total of $(P \times Q)$ on buying Q units of the product, and suppliers will be willing to supply Q units to earn revenue of $(P \times Q)$. P is the **equilibrium price**.

1.10 The forces of supply and demand push a market to its equilibrium price and quantity. Note carefully the following key points.

(a) If there is no change in conditions of supply or demand, the **equilibrium price will prevail** in the market and will remain stable.

(b) If price is not at the equilibrium, the market is in **disequilibrium** and supply and demand will push prices towards the equilibrium price.

(c) Shifts in the supply curve or demand curve will change the equilibrium price (and the quantity traded).

Perfect competition and monopoly

1.11 **Perfect competition** is a theoretical market structure in which no supplier has an advantage over another. Perfect competition acts as a useful theoretical benchmark, although no actual market is completely 'perfect'.

   (a) We can use it to judge or predict what firms might do in markets where competition shows some or most of the characteristics of being perfect

   (b) We can also contrast the behaviour of firms in less perfect markets, such as **monopoly**.

1.12 **Characteristics of perfect competition**

   - There is a large number of buyers and sellers in the market.
   - Firms are 'price takers', unable to influence the market price individually.
   - Producers and consumers act rationally and have the same information.
   - The product is homogeneous: one unit of the product is the same as any other unit.
   - There is free entry of firms into and free exit of firms out of the market.
   - There are no transport costs or information gathering costs.

1.13 In **perfectly competitive** markets, firms are price takers: they must take whatever price is available in the market, and cannot influence that price individually themselves. Therefore, firms' decisions are concerned with what output level will maximise profits. In imperfect competition, firms can influence the market price, and so their decisions are about what price to set as well as what volumes of output to produce. Pure **monopoly** is an extreme form of imperfect competition.

1.14 In a **monopoly**, there is only one firm, the sole producer of a good or service which has no closely competing substitutes.

1.15 A firm's monopolistic position may result from some natural factor which makes it too costly for another firm to enter the industry. For example, in the domestic water supply industry it will normally be too costly for a second firm to lay a second water supply system to compete for part of the business of an existing sole supplier: the sole supplier enjoys a **natural monopoly**. In other cases, a monopoly may be formed by mergers of a number of firms in an industry. However formed, **monopoly** can only exist if potential competitors are kept out of the market by **barriers to entry**. For a monopoly, the total market supply is identical with the single firm's supply and the average revenue curve in monopoly is the same as the total market demand curve.

1.16 In **perfect competition**, a firm should not be able to earn excess ('supernormal') profits in the long run because they would be 'competed away' by new entrants to the industry. A monopoly firm can however earn **supernormal profits**, because there are **barriers to entry** which prevent rivals entering the market.

Unemployment

1.17 The **rate of unemployment** in an economy can be calculated as the number of persons who are unemployed, as a percentage of the total workforce. The number of unemployed at any time is measured by government statistics. If the flow of workers through unemployment is constant, then the size of the unemployed labour force will also be constant.

BPP
PROFESSIONAL EDUCATION

1.18 Unemployment can lead to the following problems.

    (a) **Loss of output.** If labour is unemployed, the economy is not producing as much output as it could. Thus, total national income is less than it could be.

    (b) **Loss of human capital.** If there is unemployment, the unemployed labour will gradually lose its skills, because skills can only be maintained by working.

    (c) **Increasing inequalities in the distribution of income.** Unemployed people earn less than employed people, and so when unemployment is increasing, the poor get poorer.

    (d) **Social costs.** Unemployment brings social problems of personal suffering and distress, and possibly also increases in crime such as theft and vandalism.

    (e) **Increased burden of welfare payments.** This can have a major impact on government fiscal policy.

1.19 Unemployment may be classified into categories.

Category	Comment
Frictional	It is inevitable that some unemployment is caused not so much because there are not enough jobs to go round, but because of the *friction* in the labour market (difficulty in matching quickly workers with jobs), caused perhaps by a lack of knowledge about job opportunities. Frictional unemployment is temporary, lasting for the period of transition from one job to the next.
Seasonal	This occurs in certain industries, for example building, tourism and farming, where the demand for labour fluctuates in seasonal patterns throughout the year.
Structural	This occurs where long-term changes occur in the conditions of an industry. A feature of structural unemployment is high regional unemployment in the location of the industry affected.
Technological	This is a form of structural unemployment, which occurs when new technologies are introduced. (a) Old skills are no longer required. (b) There is likely to be a labour saving aspect, with machines doing the job that people used to do. With automation, employment levels in an industry can fall sharply, even when the industry's total output is increasing.
Cyclical or demand-deficient	It has been the experience of the past that domestic and foreign trade go through cycles of boom, decline, recession, recovery, then boom again, and so on. (a) During recovery and boom years, the demand for output and jobs is high, and unemployment is low. (b) During decline and recession years, the demand for output and jobs falls, and unemployment rises to a high level. Cyclical unemployment can be long-term, and a government might try to reduce it by doing what it can to minimise a recession or to encourage faster economic growth.

1.20 Seasonal employment and frictional unemployment will be short-term. Structural unemployment, technological unemployment, and cyclical unemployment are all longer term, and more serious.

1.21 A government can try several options to create jobs or reduce unemployment.

(a) **Spending more money directly on jobs** (for example, hiring more civil servants or teachers)

(b) **Encouraging growth** in the private sector of the economy. When aggregate demand is growing, firms will probably want to increase output to meet demand, and so will hire more labour.

(c) **Encouraging training in job skills.** A government can help to finance training schemes, in order to provide a 'pool' of workers who have the skills that firms need and will pay for.

(d) **Offering grant assistance to employers** in key regional areas

(e) **Encouraging labour mobility** by offering individuals financial assistance with relocation expenses, and improving the flow of information on vacancies

1.22 Other policies may be directed at **reducing real wages to market clearing levels** (in accord with demand and supply).

(a) Abolishing **closed shop** agreements, which restrict certain jobs to trade union members

(b) Abolishing **minimum wage regulations**, where such regulations exist

Unemployment and inflation

1.23 The problems of unemployment and inflation were very severe for many countries in recent years. It has been found that boosting demand to increase the level of employment can cause a higher rate of inflation. However, **growth in unemployment** can also be associated with a **rising rate of inflation**.

1.24 In 1958 *A W Phillips* found a statistical relationship between unemployment and the rate of money wage inflation which implied that, in general, **the rate of inflation falls unemployment rose and vice versa.** A curve, known as a **Phillips curve**, can be drawn linking inflation and unemployment (Figure 2).

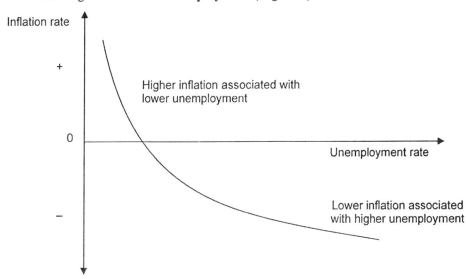

Figure 2 Phillips curve

1.25 Note the following two points about the Phillips curve.

(a) The curve crosses the horizontal axis at a positive value for the unemployment rate. This means that zero inflation will be associated with some unemployment; it is not possible to achieve zero inflation and zero unemployment at the same time.

(b) The shape of the curve means that the lower the level of unemployment, the higher the **rate of increase** in inflation.

1.26 The existence of a relationship between inflation and unemployment of the type indicated by the Phillips curve suggests that the government should be able to use demand management policies to take the economy to acceptable levels of inflation and unemployment.

1.27 This re-emphasises the argument of **Keynesian** economists that, in order to achieve full employment, some inflation is unavoidable. If achieving full employment is an economic policy objective, a government must therefore be prepared to accept a certain level of inflation as a necessary evil.

1.28 However, the Phillips curve relationship between inflation and unemployment broke down at the end of the 1960s when Britain began to experience **rising inflation at the same time as rising unemployment**.

1.29 The **monetarist** concept of a stable equilibrium implies that with zero price inflation, there is a natural optimal level of unemployment, and a rate of economic growth and balance of trade position from which the economy will not deviate. Monetarism focuses on economic stability in the medium to long term, which can only be achieved by abandoning short-term demand management goals.

2 POLITICAL, SOCIAL AND ECONOMIC FACTORS

Political factors

2.1 The **investment returns** produced by a company are **dependent** on its ability to **generate profits** and to **grow**. In turn, the legal framework and labour market within which it must work will influence these. This legal framework is largely determined by politics and will affect a company on different levels: nationally, regionally and globally. **Politics** can influence the labour market, but **demographics**, the distribution of a population by age and sex, can ultimately limit production. **Social** factors, such as the levels of education and the extent to which populations can migrate, also influence productivity.

2.2 At a **political** level, the following key factors can affect investment markets.

- Currency agreements
- Industry regulation
- Interest rates
- International trade agreements
- International treaties or conflicts
- Government spending
- Taxation
- Zoning and planning regulations

2.3 These factors can have an impact through the following.

- **Commercial property prices**
- The **balance of trade**
- Economic **cycles**
- Economic **growth**
- **Exchange rates**
- **Labour** markets

2.4 At a **national** level, issues such as subsidies, grants and enterprise zones can make a significant difference to production, profit levels and employment. The level of **local** taxes (the business rate or Council Tax) can affect the costs of businesses and hence their profitability. Decisions made at the local government level can affect the size and nature of local businesses.

2.5 At the **regional** level, the influence of European legislation can affect individual businesses and business areas, while the establishment of separate assemblies for Scotland, Wales and Northern Ireland means that the business environment can be affected by political decisions applicable to those separate regions, for example, by way of increased or even reduced taxation. **Subsidies** for various industries, grants, zoning and taxation will all affect the investment returns of shares in various sectors differently.

2.6 **Globally,** the political environment has a significant impact on investment. The 'bear market' of 1998 resulted from **political instability** in the Far East, spreading to Russia and on to Western economies. **Armed conflicts** across the globe and incidents such as the terrorist attacks in the USA of September 2001 can also have a **destabilising effect** on various investments and the greater the chance that the conflict will spread, the greater the effect on investment markets.

Question 1.1

Without looking at the text above, list the main factors that politicians can alter that will impact on investment markets.

Business cycles

> **KEY TERM**
>
> The term **business cycle** refers to the tendency of levels of business activity to rise and fall, and then rise again, in a cyclical way.

2.7 Business cycles can be caused by the **delay in the effectiveness of political measures** to boost, or reduce, productivity. A reduction in interest rates might be brought about by government in order to improve the country's ability to export goods, as it will tend to bring with it a relative reduction in the value of the currency. This will be accompanied with a lower cost of borrowing, giving companies the opportunity to expand. The rapid expansion can be bad for the economy, leading to 'overheating' and the requirement to slow down the economy.

2.8 One of the ways to do this is to raise interest rates. However, this can cause a combination of increasing the value of the currency, leading to reduced exports, and an increased cost of borrowing and finance. If not handled carefully this could lead in turn to **recession**.

2.9   There are **political** considerations here. Governments could attempt to time such cycles so that they can be seen in the best possible light at election time. The down side of the cycle also represents an opportunity to blame a previous government for financial mismanagement.

Social factors

2.10   In addition to political factors, there are a number of **social factors** that affect investment markets.

Social factor	Effects on investment market
Distribution of **age** of the population	An **increasing population** with a high proportion of **young people** normally represents an **increasing workforce** and with it a possible increase in productivity, as in the case of the so-called 'emerging economies' in China and the Far East. The potential for increasing productivity attracts investors from around the world, providing the financial structure is there to fuel the expansion. This helps to promote a spiral of growth and investment, allowing companies to expand rapidly. The shares of those companies start to be in demand as they provide spectacular increases in capital value.
	In the many economically advanced countries, the numbers of young individuals is reducing in relation to older members of the population. This change brings with it increased costs for healthcare and the provision of pensions. At the same time, the younger working population needs to support these increasing costs through higher taxation. In order to support themselves and to improve their standard of living, people will invest significant sums directly into the investment markets and indirectly via pension plans. The end result is large amounts of money being invested, increasing the demand for investments and in many cases pushing up share prices. In the late 1990s, equity markets were often supported by the sheer volume of cash pouring in from pension funds and other investment sources.
Size of the working population	In the UK, this remains relatively constant. This effectively **limits the supply of labour** and hence the ultimate level of production. In contrast, the working populations of the emerging economies are rapidly increasing, boosting their potential levels of economic activity.
Level of **education** of the workforce	Skill levels determine the type of goods that can be produced. Economies with low skill levels will not have the ability to produce high technology goods. In turn, this will affect the ability of the economy to compete and expand, as more traditional manufacturing is restrictive in this respect. Having a poorly educated workforce could mean that levels of safety are lower and pollution levels higher, leading to production at lower financial cost, but at a significantly higher social cost. Education levels will also affect the demands of the consumer. These factors vary from region to region and will affect investment markets differently in different countries.
Availability of **training**	Training allows a workforce to be more versatile and move into new markets more quickly. This has a positive effect on production and economic growth.

Social factor	Effects on investment market
Trade unions	**Trade unions** have traditionally been seen as a dampener of economic growth and hence of the investment returns of the companies in which they are active. Constant demands for increased salaries, lower hours and improved working conditions can only usually result in an increase in production costs. This reduces the company's ability to compete and the investment returns provided to its shareholders. In the 1980s, the Trade Union Act 1984, the Wages Act 1986 and a number of Employment Acts were passed, eroding the power of the trade unions in the UK.
Migration of the workforce	Where a country or region is **short of labour**, production and economic growth will be limited. One way around this is to encourage migrant labour. This is normally a low-cost way of boosting productivity and economic prosperity, but brings a number of new problems with it.

Question 1.2

List social factors that affect investment markets.

Economic factors

2.11 **Economic factors** that influence investment markets include:

- Economic growth
- Economic cycles (the business cycle)
- Inflation
- Technology
- World trade

Let us examine each of these in turn.

Economic growth

> **KEY TERM**
>
> **Economic growth** is most often defined as the annual rate at which the **Gross Domestic Product (GDP)**, or the total value of the goods and services produced in a country during an annual period, increases.

2.12 For an economy to **grow**, it needs **capital** and a **good supply of appropriately qualified workers**. Countries with high rates of growth will tend to show impressive increases in the value of the shares on their stock markets. Those with lower rates of growth may continue to grow steadily, but do not have the capacity for such rapid expansion.

2.13 Economies that are growing **rapidly** will be dependent on the **supply of capital** from investors to maintain the growth. When this supply of capital in the form of equity or loans is not available, the rates of growth can slow or even stop. Investments in such economies can carry a **high risk** that they may suddenly reduce in value or become worthless. Investors

BPP PROFESSIONAL EDUCATION

will be looking for a premium on top of their returns to allow for the greater risk. **Fixed interest stocks** will be expected to provide a suitable margin over other local interest rates to cover this. **Equities** will be expected to produce substantial increases in capital values, although there is usually less requirement for dividends. Companies are expected to re-invest their profits to produce more growth.

2.14 In countries where the birth rate is high, there will be a rapidly **expanding working population**. This can fuel economic growth, where there is sufficient capital to take advantage of it. As an economy becomes more developed, the birth rate starts to fall, so the working population expands more slowly. This will affect the country's economic output and growth will slow, but as the workforce becomes better educated, they are capable of handling higher technology allowing greater productivity and fuelling further growth. It is typical for maturing economies to have a slowing rate of growth. A good example of this is in Japan which had economic growth in excess of 5% per annum in the past. This had fallen to 2.5% by 1990 and, at the time of writing, Japan, which had been in recession (negative growth) for some time, appears to be entering a new phase of growth.

Question 1.3

What are the two main requirements for rapid economic growth?

Economic cycles (the business cycle)

2.15 Just as levels of business are cyclical within an industry so are the economies of individual countries. The global economy from 1999 to early 2003 will be recorded as a time of **economic downturn** with signs of recovery from mid 2003. Economic upturns were predicted in 2000, 2001 and 2002, but did not materialise, demonstrating the unpredictability of the economic cycle. In mid-2005, the future course of the economy cannot be predicted easily.

KEY TERM

Recession is generally defined as a reduction in year on year GDP for two successive quarters.

2.16 **Financial markets** are affected by the economic cycle in a number of ways.

Phase in the economic cycle	Effect on financial markets
The 'up phase' (recovery)	• The value of goods and services produced increases. • The profitability of companies improves, boosting the value of their shares. • Companies will borrow more to allow themselves to expand. • The returns from equities in income and capital terms are good. • Interest in fixed interest stocks is reduced as investment strategies favour equities. • Interest rates may be raised to 'cool down' the economy.

Phase in the economic cycle	Effect on financial markets
The 'peak' (boom)	• The rate of growth in the economy is starting to slow down. • Returns from equities in income and capital terms begin to level out and may reduce. • Equities prices and the level of dividends may fall. • Investment strategies will start to favour fixed interest stocks over equities.
The 'down phase' (recession)	• The value of goods and services produced is decreasing. • The profitability of companies reduces and this may be reflected in share prices. • Dividends may reduce, or may continue to be paid from retained profits. • Companies which borrowed to fuel growth will now suffer through having to pay interest out of reduced or non-existent profits. • Company failures cause further concern over the vulnerability of bank lending and the shares of banks may decline in value. • Diminishing returns from equities will encourage investment strategies which favour fixed interest stocks. • Interest rates may be reduced to stimulate the economy.
The 'trough' (slump)	• The value of goods and services produced stabilises and later shows the first signs of improvement. • Equity prices may rise in anticipation of an increase in company profits.

2.17 Not all equities match the ups and downs of the economic cycle. Some precede it, others lag behind it and others still are '**counter-cyclical**'. Some are '**non-cyclical**', not following the economic cycle at all. The utilities sector tends to be resistant to business cycles, as it provides goods and services that will be required whatever the rest of the business climate is doing.

Inflation

2.18 Prices of the goods that consumers buy will vary from month to month.

KEY TERM

Inflation is a persistent rise in the general level of prices.

2.19 In its mildest form, inflation does not cause too many problems, but when it accelerates it can cause severe problems by **undermining** the **value of currency** and the **confidence of investors**. This causes problems for both fixed interest and equities markets.

2.20 **Fixed interest investments** provide protection for the capital of investors. The money invested is returned, but this ignores the effect of inflation. Where inflation is high, the capital returned will be worth less in real terms. Unless the interest returns on the stocks are high, the net effect of such an investment is a loss in real terms.

2.21 **Equities** tend to be part of an inflation cycle. As prices rise, wage demands from workers rise. Therefore the cost of producing goods increases leading to higher wage expectations and further price rises, and the cycle starts again. During times of high inflation, equity prices can rise substantially. However the level of real growth when inflation has been allowed for will be much lower.

2.22 **Business problems caused by inflationary conditions**

- The constant need to re-price goods adds to the overheads

- Inflation reduces the ability to enter into long-term contracts because of the lack of certainty on profit levels

- Where inflation in a country is out of step with inflation in other countries, the increased price of goods can make the country's goods and services less competitive

- Increased wage demands and the possibility of unionised workforces taking industrial action can hit a company at a time when it is already vulnerable

2.23 Where a business is unprepared for problems like these, it can come under severe pressure and may fail. Both situations will fuel recessionary influences in the financial markets.

Question 1.4

How will fixed interest stocks be affected when inflation rates rise?

Deflation

2.24 Deflation in economic terms is a situation in which the price of goods and services fall. A major deflation in this century occurred during the Great Depression in the 1920s and 1930s. Since then, governments have avoided deflation wherever possible, although deflation has occurred persistently in Japan in recent years.

2.25 Many businesses and individuals will have experienced and dealt with inflation and the problems associated with it, but up until the start of the new millennium there seemed very little real prospect of deflation in Western economies. However, by the end of 2001, Japan had been suffering deflation for some time and a series of interest rate cuts in America, Europe and the UK appeared to be moving other economies closer to this position. A cover story in the *Economist* even suggested that it is deflation and not inflation that could be the greatest concern for the world economy. These fears have mostly now subsided.

2.26 One of the main causes of deflation is excess production of goods and services. Where the consumer has a choice, there is a compelling argument for them to choose the lowest price where the quality is the same. This cycle is self-sustaining; a company that has spent money bringing its goods and services to the market needs to sell them to meet its costs, even where this is done at a loss.

2.27 **Business problems caused by deflationary conditions**

(a) The time delay between manufacture and sale leads to reduced profits, or losses

(b) The constant need to reprice goods and services adds to the cost of selling goods and a reduction in profit

(c) The consumer is less inclined to buy goods at today's price when tomorrow's price could be lower

(d) Lower consumer demand puts pressure on the profitability of companies, for whom staff are often a major cost, these companies lay off staff and the unemployed have low incomes and therefore buy less, further exacerbating the problem

2.28 **Investment problems caused by deflationary conditions**

(a) Pressure on company profits reduces dividends and capital value of shares

(b) Deflation is usually accompanied by lowering interest rates - this tends to reduce the yields on gilts and fixed interest stocks, but can result in an increase in their capital values

(c) The use of lowering interest rates to increase consumer demand can ultimately lead to a situation in which deposit investors are charged interest, ie they get a negative return on their investment

Controlling deflation

2.29 One way to control deflation is through the Government printing more money. However, few Governments still have the ability to do this. For a number of reasons (including the temptation for Governments to just start printing money), the control of this has been passed to a politically independent central bank, with a clear remit to keep price inflation under control. It was not generally envisaged that they would need to control deflation.

2.30 This does not mean it is impossible to use monetary policy to control the situation. Most governments appear to be in agreement that the solution is to stimulate consumer demand, for example by cutting interest rates, to effectively get them to 'buy' the country out of the situation. It would also be possible to increase government spending to help in this process, but any concerted effort would probably require an increase in taxes in some form, something that might be unpopular with savers losing money, employees losing jobs and businesses failing.

Technology

2.31 **Technological changes** will also influence financial markets.

(a) There will be increased production and productive efficiency, so that prices can reduce in real terms (for example media and communications products).

(b) Better goods can be produced, increasing demand and creating it in new areas, such as Broadband, digital and flat screen televisions and monitors.

(c) Increasing technology provides better communications, informing people of products available in other countries, and hence developing new markets and new demand.

2.32 Where a company fails to keep pace with **changes in technology**, it could become less competitive. Companies that embrace new technology can increase production and market share rapidly, and the shares of such companies can be attractive to investors.

2.33 As an industry in its own right, technology has experienced dramatic growth. Over the past 10 years shares in technology-based companies have shown growth rates far in excess of the rest of the market. However, there is a substantial amount of risk attached to such shares, as new processes and new technology move so quickly that a previously competitive company can be left behind. Also, the potential seen in a company for boosting equity prices may never come to fruition, a situation that applies to many shares in Internet technology companies. It is fears such as these that caused significant falls in the value of technology shares during 2000.

Question 1.5

Why does improved technology increase the demand for products?

World trade

2.34   All financial markets can be affected by **world trade conditions**.

KEY TERM

Globalisation is the process resulting in an increasing world market in goods and an increasing integration in world capital markets.

2.35   It is therefore ever more important for governments to consult with their trading partners. Capital now flows freely around the world, which can have a destabilising effect on local economies. Increased co-operation between governments is required to co-ordinate **macroeconomic policies** to avoid such capital movements.

2.36   World trading conditions improved significantly after the end of the Second World War by the establishment of **GATT** (General Agreement on Tariffs and Trade). The organisation negotiated **reductions in tariffs** on the movements of goods and the breaking down of 'protectionist' policies that have, in the past, been **barriers** to trade. The Uruguay Round, started in 1986 and ending in 1994, led to GATT becoming the **World Trade Organisation (WTO)** in early 1995. Changes to the makeup of the organisation provide an increasing involvement for developing countries, to reflect their importance in the global economy.

2.37   Globalisation means that the world has largely become an open market, but there are some disadvantages. The extent to which the **financial systems of the world are integrated** means that all countries are now affected to a greater or lesser extent by their neighbours. This is demonstrated by the **stock market falls** in 1987, 2000 and in September 2001, when local instabilities affected stock markets world-wide.

Financial and monetary factors

2.38   **Financial and monetary factors** in the economy that influence investment markets are:

- Exchange rates
- Interest rates
- Money supply
- Levels of taxation

Let us examine each of these in turn.

Exchange rates

2.39   In order for world trade transactions to be freely made, the currency of a country must be readily convertible. Currencies are exchanged on the **foreign exchange ('forex') market**, which comprises the traders who buy and sell currencies on behalf of individuals, companies, banks and other institutions. The supply of, and demand for, the currency will determine its value. However, governments may intervene in this process via their central banks.

2.40 There are broadly three exchange rate policies.

Exchange rate	Method
Floating exchange rates	The rate of exchange is determined by the supply and demand for that currency within the market without government intervention.
Fixed exchange rates	The rate of exchange is fixed by the government at a set level by the intervention of the country's central bank in the forex markets. The central bank will support the exchange rate by buying or selling the currency. Where this becomes impossible, a revaluation or devaluation of the currency can take place.
Managed exchange rates	A managed exchange rate is one where the currency is not allowed to float completely freely, as the central bank will intervene to a greater or lesser extent. It is sometimes referred to as a 'dirty float', ie the currency has not been allowed to float 'cleanly'. It is effectively a compromise between a floating and fixed rate exchange.

Relative advantages and disadvantages of floating and fixed exchange rate systems

System	Advantages	Disadvantages
Floating exchange rates	Floating exchange rates automatically compensate for an imbalance in balance of payments. Balance of payments control will cease to be a constraint on a government's internal economic policy. Governments do not require large reserves to defend the currency.	Leads to uncertainty over the current and future exchange rates acting as a barrier to trade Encourages speculation in the currency which can lead to further fluctuations Can compensate for a lack of discipline in the control of the economy, that ultimately can cause inflation
Fixed exchange rates	Exchange rates are known, providing certainty for foreign trade. Encourages discipline in the control of an economy. Can lead to a reduction in speculation on a currency.	Government economic policy is constrained by exchange rates. Speculators may view a fixed rate as unsustainable and speculate on a devaluation by selling the currency, which in itself can put pressure on to devalue the currency. Under a fixed exchange rate, large reserves are required to protect the currency if it comes under pressure.

2.41 Financial markets can be seriously affected by exchange rates. Certainty over levels of exchange can impact on the willingness of a company to commit to long-term contracts. This in turn affects profitability and hence the share price and levels of dividend.

2.42 As part of a **floating rate mechanism**, it is possible for exchange rates to increase or reduce rapidly. When exchange rates for the domestic currency are high, domestic manufactured goods will seem more expensive than those produced elsewhere, making them less competitive. This will **affect the investment returns** from companies who rely on exports. **Low exchange rates** will make exporters more competitive.

2.43 Imports will become **cheaper** when the domestic currency strengthens. This low cost will increase demand for foreign goods in the UK, having a number of effects. The balance of payments will move against the country concerned and cause other economic problems. Importers and distributors of foreign goods will benefit from the situation, but producers for the domestic market encounter competition from cheap imports. A weaker currency, on the other hand, will improve the balance of payments position and increase the relative cost of foreign goods, reducing the profits for importers and distributors. Competition for domestically produced goods will then also reduce. According to **purchasing power parity theory,** in the long run exchange rates should reflect prices in different currency zones, so that the sterling price of an item bought in the UK should be equivalent to the dollar price of the same item bought in the USA. In the reality, in the short run, the purchasing powers of different currencies differ significantly.

2.44 Supporters of the **Euro** argue that joining the single currency would provide stability for trade in the Euro zone for the UK. The risks to companies and individuals arising from exchange rate movements within the Euro Zone would be removed.

The ERM

2.45 The Exchange Rate Mechanism (ERM) was a managed flexible exchange system operating in Europe. The UK entered the system in October 1990. Individual currencies within the ERM were allowed to float within a predetermined band either side of the agreed central rate.

2.46 Over time, markets became convinced that the UK government was unable to maintain Sterling at the agreed rate. On the 16 September 1992, speculators sold Sterling, convinced that it could not be held at its minimum value. Interest rates were increased from 10% up to 12% and then to 15%, but the UK government failed to maintain the value of Sterling. It eventually suspended its membership of the ERM, returned to a floating rate.

The Euro

2.47 The successor to the ERM was the adoption of a single currency for the majority of countries in the European Economic Area. This provides stability for exchange inside the area without the need for an exchange rate mechanism and the cost of maintaining it. The **Euro** floats freely on currency markets.

Question 1.6

Which currency exchange system is more susceptible to speculation, fixed or floating rate? Why is this?

Interest rates

2.48 Interest rates can act directly, as **fixed interest stocks** and the returns they provide are directly dependent on interest rates. If interest rates rise, the return from fixed interest stocks falls relative to deposits and other investments. Therefore the prices of stocks fall until they represent a reasonable return. For traders in such stocks, this represents an opportunity to buy and sell and make money on the turn. For long-term investors, this effectively reduces their income returns relative to interest rates available elsewhere.

2.49 Where **interest rates fall**, the opposite situation occurs. The investment returns from stocks begin to look greater relative to the market and prices increase. In these circumstances the long-term investor will benefit as well as the traders.

2.50 Interest rates will also impact directly on the **equity markets**. Increased interest rates means a higher cost of borrowing for companies. This has a number of consequences.

- Higher costs of borrowing
- Reduced profitability
- Less capital available for investment
- Reduced dividends

2.51 In the worst case scenario, companies can go into liquidation. This can put pressure on creditors, who along with suffering the above also have to cope with bad debts. When interest rates are reduced, the opposite happens.

2.52 Interest rate changes can also affect investment markets **indirectly**. If interest rates rise and firms start to struggle, investors may switch to fixed interest stocks. This has a double effect of avoiding losses in equities and fixing the investment at a higher interest rate in the fixed interest stocks. When interest rates fall again, this will be realised as a capital gain, which will in many cases be tax-free.

2.53 Interest rate levels have an effect on exchange rates. As interest rates rise relative to other countries, investments flow into the UK. This increases the value of a currency with a floating exchange rate. However, as discussed in the previous section, increased exchange rates can cause problems for UK companies in both foreign and domestic markets.

Question 1.7

How do fixed interest stock prices vary with interest rates?

Money supply

2.54 Money supply and interest rates are the **two main tools** of monetary policy for a government, employed to control the supply of money via the Bank of England.

2.55 In turn, **money supply** and the **methods for controlling it** can affect the investment markets directly or indirectly. An example of this is the issue of **gilts**, which can be used to **reduce the money supply** because individuals and institutions will wish to reflect the new issues in their portfolios. This will tie up more money in investments which reduces the money supply. However, if the supply of gilts is too great, it will reduce the demand and hence the price of gilts. Reducing the amount of gilts available will have the opposite effect. Either way, gilts may become relatively more or less attractive than equities.

2.56 Indirectly the **reduction in money supply** will, via the banks, **reduce the level of lending**. This will in turn reduce a company's ability to expand reducing equity values and dividends. Increase in the money supply will release more liquidity for the banks, making more money available for lending. Companies can use the money to expand, increasing equity values and dividends.

Levels of taxation

2.57 The absolute level of taxation influences an investor's ability to invest, by dictating the proportion of income available for investment. Typically, investments will benefit business either directly, by being invested in equities, or indirectly, by being invested by other institutions into equities. Money left on deposit provides lending institutions with further liquidity to enable them to lend money on to businesses.

2.58 **Investment in companies** can be encouraged by **schemes with tax incentives.** ISAs, EISs and VCTs all encourage investment in companies to a greater or lesser extent. This can stimulate equity markets and provide a source of capital for companies who are looking to expand and may not have funds available elsewhere.

Question 1.8

How does a tax incentive on an investment affect investment markets?

3 HOW POLITICAL, SOCIAL AND ECONOMIC FACTORS AFFECT MARKETS

3.1 The **development and behaviour of financial institutions** is shaped by the political, social and economic factors to which they are exposed.

Effect of political factors

3.2 The level of control imposed by a government will directly influence the development of the financial institutions and investment markets.

(a) With a **market-based economy**, financial institutions are created and grow in response to the need for capital. Investors with excess capital look to invest their money for a return. The financial institutions give them a return by lending the money on to businesses that will pay them interest. Part of this goes to the original investor, the rest is retained as profit.

(b) With a **centrally planned economy**, the level of control imposed by the government is complete. Financial institutions are created as part of the system, but are not influenced by the market. No individual actually makes a profit out of the transaction as the government performs the distribution of wealth.

There is much variation within these two extremes.

3.3 The level of government control will depend on the political party in power. Typically a government biased to the 'the right' will embrace market values, so the **shareholder model of company ownership** (where individuals and institutions own the shares of companies) will prevail. The shares they own are chosen for their potential to provide an investment return which is, in turn, linked to the demand for the goods and services that they supply. **Market forces** will dictate that the consumer will buy the products and services they want and this reflects in the **investment return** of the company. Companies whose products are in demand will expand and others will contract, change direction or go out of business.

3.4 A government biased to the left will place a different emphasis on company ownership ranging from full governmental ownership to the **stakeholder model of ownership** instead of ownership purely by shareholders. In these societies, share ownership is much reduced and can be non-existent. Capital markets in such countries will be smaller as there is little need to raise money on the open market.

3.5   In the UK and the USA, the shareholder model of ownership prevails, with large proportions of the population owning shares directly and indirectly through pooled investment. In Europe, the stakeholder model is more prevalent although share ownership in Europe has been on the increase with both the German and the French stockmarkets showing rapid increases in size and volume.

3.6   In Japan, where the financial system works on a similar system to the stakeholder model, there is a relatively **low level of share ownership**. Ownership of companies in Japan is largely via other companies in inter-related and complex groups known as Kieretsu. Japan has for some time been undergoing the slow break-up of the Kieretsu system.

3.7   **Emerging countries** tend to have more **limited share ownership**, with some of them still being tightly controlled by government. However, share ownership in such nations is increasing rapidly to provide the capital to complement the increasing levels of labour. In combination, this is a powerful fuel for business expansion.

Question 1.9

What are the two main 'models' of company ownership and briefly how does each work?

Social factors

3.8   **Social factors can influence investment markets** in a number of different ways. In Western countries, populations are ageing, with each generation living 10 years more on average than the previous one. This brings a number of new problems, including the need for such individuals to provide for themselves. State pensions tend to be limited to subsistence levels, so any person requiring income above this must provide it from their **own resources**. This is producing an **increasing supply of capital for investment**, which is having a number of effects. The demand for shares and fixed interest stocks has been sustaining the market at relatively high levels. As the average age of the population increases, this effect will be more pronounced as more and more save in the expectation of living longer.

3.9   Typically, there is a marked difference in the economic growth of mature and emerging economies. The **growth in emerging economies** is caused by the presence of large and increasing supplies of **labour**. **Education** is also having a profound effect and is increasing productivity further. As it increases, the economy's ability to make use of technological advances improves. The rapid growth of such economies needs significant amounts of capital as fuel and the globalisation process can provide this with capital markets throughout the world becoming connected. Money can flow to the areas where it is needed, providing it will make a good profit. To get even more capital to fuel expansion, financial institutions use the process of **'securitisation'**.

KEY TERM

Securitisation is the process of raising money on the back of an income stream. This removes the need for collateral in the business, used to support traditional lending, or provides security where all existing assets already form collateral.

3.10 Mature economies such as the UK, Europe and US will tend to have a **limited labour market**. The effect of this is relatively low unemployment and a very large proportion of working women. Education levels are already relatively high and there is limited potential to increase economic growth by improving education. As such, one of the few tools available to increase growth is the widespread use of technology.

3.11 Japan is a good example of a **recently matured economy**, which has more recently been experiencing similar problems to the Western economies. In contrast, the emerging nations of the Far East continue to expand rapidly.

Question 1.10

Why do emerging economies tend to grow at a much faster rate than mature ones?

Economic factors

3.12 Financial institutions have always been ready to lend to countries with good economic growth. However, many of the loans to these emerging markets from Western banks have had to be rescheduled. Criticism is being levelled at many of the institutions for allowing these emerging economies to get themselves into a **cycle of debt** whereby a large proportion of their gross domestic product (GDP) is being used to **repay capital** and **interest on loans**. Pressure is mounting to stop interest accruing on such loans at least and, at best, to write them off. In the meantime, however, the shares of such lending institutions have been prone to periodic bouts of weakness.

3.13 Globalisation has for some time been causing the economic cycles of **world economies** to converge and there is increased potential for a **worldwide recession**. Previously, international companies that operated in a number of economies were considered a haven in times of local economic trouble, due to diversification throughout different geographical areas, some of which may not be in recession.

3.14 **Inflation** in most developed countries is currently low and getting lower and this is in contrast to the last 30 years, where inflation has been an issue. Individuals with savings increasingly try to ensure that these do not decrease in real terms by turning away from deposits towards equities in all forms. **Low inflation** has been a feature of the late 1990s and early 2000s.

3.15 **Advances in technology** can produce staggering increases in production and, in most cases, can add value. Many investors understand this and the requirement for **technology stocks** has produced specialist stock markets such as NASDAQ in the USA. This remains a highly speculative investment area and is prone to occasional loss of confidence like that experienced globally at the beginning of 2000 and on into 2001. The NASDAQ stock exchange is a market specialising in hi-tech stocks which, over a very short period, became one of the world's largest stock markets. NASDAQ set up a similar market in Europe, NASDAQ Europe (formerly EASDAQ), but this was closed in 2003, in the wake of the collapsed internet stocks 'bubble'.

3.16 **Trade agreements** and **international co-operation** have led to significantly increased international investment and generally have a very positive effect on all markets. In the 1980s and early 1990s such a spread of investment was useful to avoid losses in more localised investment areas. This will continue to be the case in a normal trading environment but down turns increasingly act on all markets simultaneously. Recession across world markets causes many countries to reassess **international co-operation**. For example, after the downturn of 1998 plans to quickly rectify the situation by a co-ordinated response were discussed by the seven richest countries in the world, known as G7 (Japan, the US, Germany, France, Canada, Italy and the UK).

Question 1.11

What is globalisation and what impact is it having on world markets?

Financial factors

3.17 **Exchange rates** can have a direct effect on investments held in currencies other than sterling. Changes in the relative values of the currencies will cause a **direct change** in the value of the investment in sterling terms. This factor must be taken into account when considering investments denominated in currencies other than sterling.

3.18 Exchange rates can also **indirectly influence** financial markets. In the recent past, Sterling has been valued relatively highly against other currencies making exports more expensive and so reducing demand. This affected all UK exporters. Conversely, imports were cheaper, encouraging consumers to spend their money on imports rather than domestically produced goods. The combined effect was a cause of concern in UK equity markets.

3.19 **Interest rates** are set by the **Monetary Policy Committee** (MPC) of the Bank of England at its series of regular meetings. Giving this control to an independent committee has the effect of tightening fiscal policy by ensuring that politicians do not manipulate interest rates for the short-term goal of improving popularity. However, there can be other consequences. The MPC does not have to worry about popularity and is primarily concerned with **controlling inflation**. In addition to influencing inflation rates, the level of interest rates also affects **exchange rates**. The higher the interest rates, the more money flows into the UK and the higher the exchange rates are relative to other countries.

3.20 The UK **inflation target** is determined by Government. With the introduction of the new harmonised European inflation measure, the **Consumer Prices Index (CPI)** in 2003, the CPI replaced the RPI as the basis of the inflation target. The target is now set at a CPI of below 2%.

3.21 It is the job of the Treasury to implement interest rate changes by dealing in the 'Repo' market. The trading of this gilt derivative in volume can be used to alter interest rates generally.

3.22 **Money supply** is a further financial factor affecting the markets. As the money supply is increased, consumer spending also increases. This stimulates growth in the production of goods and services, bringing with it increased profits for the companies concerned. If money supply is reduced, consumer spending is reduced, resulting in decreased profits for many companies.

3.23 Overall, **levels of taxation** will have a **direct impact** on **investment markets**. Lower taxation levels mean there is a greater capacity for people to both spend and save. The spending increases the demand for goods and the profitability of companies, and the saving will directly or indirectly supply money to companies to grow. The net effect is stimulation of financial markets. However, taxation is a **complex issue**. Taxes can be direct or indirect and the way in which taxes are raised can stimulate different parts of the economy. Taxes on specific products such as alcohol and petrol can impact on demand for those specific products. **Removal of taxes on savings** can also encourage individuals to save. The introduction of Personal Equity Plans in 1987 provided the appropriate encouragement for thousands of individuals to start investing in the stock market, directly via equities and indirectly via pooled investments. This action provided a direct stimulus to the UK markets and continues to do so even as PEPs have been replaced by Individual Savings Accounts and has been reinforced by the maintenance of the £7,000 ISA limit which applies until 2009/10. The loss of the ability of ISAs and PEPs to reclaim dividend tax credits from 2004 may well reverse some of these effects.

Question 1.12

What is the impact of high exchange rates in a country?

4   THE ROLE OF GOVERNMENT

4.1   The **level of control** a government takes over financial markets will have a significant impact on how the markets operate. In the UK, the government currently embraces market values and exerts relatively little control over the markets. In other countries, the stakeholder model of company ownership typically means that government control will be tighter.

4.2   The **controls** exerted by the government on UK markets are largely indirect via **self-regulators** under the overall supervision of the Financial Services Authority, the overall regulator of the financial services industry. It is the job of the regulator to ensure that transactions in the markets are properly conducted to ensure the **safety of investors**. Where problems arise, the level of government control will tend to tighten.

4.3   The government may take action on mergers and acquisitions which could result in **reduced competition** in the market place, especially with privatised utility companies where competition is already scarce. In these instances, the government will intervene directly to **block** a merger or acquisition or introduce controls in a particular market place. Reduced competition interferes with the market's ability to regulate itself.

4.4   Governments control the economy via **monetary or fiscal policy**. In turn, actions taken to implement this policy will impact on investment markets.

Monetary policy

KEY TERM

Monetary policy is concerned with the value, supply and cost of money in the economy. The main objective is to **stabilise prices** and to maintain the **purchasing power of money**.

4.5   Uncertainty about inflation is damaging to the proper functioning of the economy. With a stable general price level, consumers can make suitable decisions as to whether to save or borrow, invest or consume. The future for businesses is also more predictable and they can make better decisions as to the levels of borrowing they are comfortable with and the levels of production that are most suitable for the market. Monetary policy acts on inflation and action taken will either be **inflationary** or **deflationary** in effect. In principle, inflationary policies stimulate the markets and deflationary policies dampen them down.

4.6   There are five main aspects of monetary policy.

- Interest rates
- Monetary base control
- Exchange rate controls
- Direct controls on lending
- Reserve ratio control

Question 1.13

How does monetary policy stabilise prices and maintain the purchasing power of money?

Interest rates

4.7 The main tool of monetary policy is **interest rates**. Attempts to control the supply of money at source have proven ineffective in the past, so control of money by changing the demand for it is the most popular method for most countries. When **interest rates increase,** it is more expensive to borrow and savings produce higher returns, so the demand for money is **reduced** and this is a deflationary influence. **Reduced interest rates** increase the demand for money by making it cheaper to borrow and less rewarding to save and this is **inflationary**.

4.8 The effect of interest rate changes can produce **rapid changes** in the economy. In the UK in 1988, inflation was rising rapidly and the economy was showing clear signs of **overheating**. The Bank of England raised interest rates sharply in a **tightening of monetary policy**. The effect of this was to make businesses cut back on investment plans. Mortgage costs increased, and with it, consumer spending. The economy cooled so rapidly that a **recession** developed in 1990/91. Although this shows how effective interest rate policy can be in **controlling an economy**, it also demonstrates how **monetary policy** should be used **in conjunction** with **fiscal policy** to help spread the effect uniformly across the economy.

4.9 In the UK of the late 1990s, the use of interest rates as a form of monetary control caused additional problems, due to the fact that, as a currency, the interest rates for sterling were considerably out of line with other countries particularly those tied in with the Euro. This caused an influx of investors for UK deposits, which increased the demand for Sterling. This increase in demand increased the exchange rate and made exports less competitive and imports more competitive.

Question 1.14

How does a change in the interest rate control money in the economy?

Monetary base control

4.10 Control over **'base money'** (the banking system's holdings of balances at the Bank of England, and notes and coins) can influence monetary policy. However, such an approach would cause difficulties because of the variability in demand. Such controls have unwelcome effects on liquidity and on the volatility of interest rates in the short-term markets, without necessarily yielding any more practical or effective means of monetary control than current methods provide.

Exchange rate controls

4.11 Where exchange rates are **directly controlled,** this can influence **inflationary** and **deflationary pressures** in a country. Few countries exercise such controls as they bring with them a raft of other economic problems, not the least of which is that it discourages international trade. Many countries allow their currency to **float freely** on the foreign exchange and influence monetary policy by interest rates and control of money supply.

4.12 A lesser effect can be achieved by **linking a currency** with others as part of an **agreed exchange rate** system. This allows all the countries within the system to work together to influence exchange rates.

Direct controls on lending

4.13 **Direct controls** on lending or credit are often suggested as an alternative to reliance on interest rates to implement monetary policy. Such controls introduce **rigidities** into the financial system and **reduce competition**. Modern, deregulated and sophisticated international financial markets do not require such controls. Few monetary authorities worldwide rely on credit controls; most have either ended them or are in the process of doing so.

Reserve ratio control

4.14 In some countries, banks are required to place a proportion of their **liabilities** as **deposits** (often non-interest-bearing) with the central bank.

KEY TERM

The level of this deposit calculated as a proportion of a bank's total lending is known as the **Reserve Ratio** which can be used to create **liquidity shortages**.

4.15 When the deposits are non-interest bearing, they also affect the size of the margin above money market rates that the banks need to charge on loans to their customers. From the borrower's perspective, the effect is the same as an increase in interest rates. In the UK, liquidity levels tend to be controlled by the Treasury bill issue. An increase in the reserve ratio is sometimes perceived as a tax on banks and as such is unpopular. Recently, the reserve ratio for banks in the UK has been set at 0.35% of liabilities and is on a non-interest bearing basis. This has no monetary policy purpose: the intention is to secure the income and resources of the Bank, and the ratio is reviewed from time to time in the light of that requirement alone. The Bank of England has the facility to call for special deposits, if required. These would be interest bearing, but the bank has not made use of these facilities since 1979.

Fiscal policy

KEY TERM

Fiscal policy is mainly concerned with **taxation and government spending,** each of which will have an impact on the economy.

4.16 In the UK in the 1950s and 1960s, fiscal policy was considered the **main mechanism** by which inflation could be controlled. More recently, monetary controls and specifically interest rates have taken over.

4.17 The following are aspects of **fiscal policy**.

- Taxation
- Public sector borrowing
- The national debt
- Public spending

Taxation

4.18 The **total level of taxation** is important for a number of reasons. The level of the tax burden will directly affect the **amount of money** an individual has to spend. Consumer spending creates demand for goods, which stimulates manufacturing, distribution and service industries and, hence, financial markets. Governments can **increase taxation** to **cool down** an economy or **lower tax** to **stimulate it**. However, the level of taxation directly affects the amount of money available for the government to spend which, if insufficient, will need to be borrowed.

Question 1.15

How does a tax reduction stimulate the economy?

Public sector borrowing

> **KEY TERMS**
>
> Where a government receives less in taxes than it spends, a budget deficit is produced. The government will need to borrow the money to make up the difference. The level of borrowing required to make up the difference is known as the **Public Sector Net Cash Requirement**.
>
> If more money comes in than goes out, there is a **Public Sector Debt Repayment**.

4.19 The Public Sector Net Cash Requirement can be met from a number of different sources.

Source	Method
The issue of notes and coins	The government can **sell securities** to the Bank of England in exchange for a new issue of notes and coins, which the government can then spend. This finds its way into circulation, increasing money supply, which can in itself stimulate demand in the economy.
Borrowing from the banking sector	The government can **borrow** money from the banking sector itself on a short or long-term basis. Short-term lending is satisfied by the sale of treasury bills which reduces the deposits held by banks with the Bank of England with the overall effect of increasing money supply.

Source	Method
Borrowing from public and financial institutions outside the banking sector	The government can borrow from the public directly, and indirectly via financial institutions investing the savings and pension money of private individuals. This is done by the sale of Gilts or National Savings securities. From the money supply perspective, this action tends to be neutral, as deposits in financial institutions are transferred to the government with no net increase in money supply.
Borrowing from abroad	Borrowing from abroad increases the money supply in the UK as the money borrowed by the government is spent in the UK.

The national debt

4.20 This is the **accumulated debt** from a series of budget deficits. In the UK, the debt is held mainly by UK citizens and institutions, but some 10-15% is held abroad. The trend in most Western economies is to **reduce the national debt** by a regime of reductions in public spending. This can be supplemented by the privatisation of public companies to further reduce debt. Many Western economies are forecasting overall budget surpluses over the next five to ten years. In the UK, the sale of the new mobile phone licences raised over £20 billion and did help to wipe out the government debt. A reduction in economic growth since, combined with the costs associated with the war in Iraq has turned this situation around and government debt is currently increasing.

Public spending

4.21 As part of fiscal policy, **public spending** is a method in its own right of controlling the economy. Public spending **increases money supply** and can be used to **stimulate the economy**. It will, in many cases, have a greater influence on the economy than tax cuts. One billion pounds of public spending will mostly be spent in the UK on British goods, providing a direct lift for British industry. Tax cuts on the other hand will stimulate demand for goods, but the tendency is to stimulate the demand for all goods. This will include imports as well as those produced domestically.

Question 1.16

Why does government spending have a greater impact than reduced taxation?

5 CENTRAL BANKS AND THE BANKING SYSTEM

5.1 All countries have a **central bank,** whose key role is to issue notes and coins and to **regulate** the banking system. Central banks ensure that the banking system is kept as stable as possible by being a 'lender of last resort'. They will effectively lend to banks with liquidity problems so that the needs of the depositors are met.

Country	Bank name
UK	Bank of England
Germany France	European Central Bank
Japan	Bank of Japan
USA	Federal Reserve

5.2 Central banks may have the task of regulating the banking system so as to avoid bank failures. In the UK, this responsibility was passed from the Bank of England to the Financial Services Authority in 1997.

5.3 A further role of central banks is to **implement the monetary policy** of the government. The level of independence with which this is done varies from country to country. In the UK, the Bank of England up until May 1997 was restricted to simply implementing the wishes of the government. Since that time, the responsibility has fallen to the Monetary Policy Committee, which acts independently of the government. The Governor of the Bank of England chairs the committee of nine members, four of which are appointed by the Chancellor of the Exchequer.

5.4 In contrast, other countries (such as Germany and the USA) allow their central banks different levels of independence, with the typical model being a council of individuals from regional banks throughout the country making the decisions. The Bank of Japan is given autonomy to implement monetary policy to maintain price stability, which it believes is 'essential to laying the foundations for sustainable and balanced economic growth'.

The European Central Bank

5.5 The European currency, the **Euro**, is administered by the European Central Bank. This is an independent central bank with the role of ensuring financial stability in countries covered by the Euro. The bank delegates its actual operation to the constituent central banks in the countries with the Euro.

Question 1.17

When a country is a member of a controlled exchange rate mechanism, what additional tasks must a central bank perform?

Chapter roundup

- Investment markets are affected by the following factors:
    - **Political** (at national, regional, local and global levels)
    - **Social** (age distribution, size of workforce, education and skill levels, training, trade unions, migration)
    - **Economic** (growth, the business cycle, inflation, technology, globalisation)
    - **Financial** (exchange rates, interest rates, money supply, taxation)
- How these factors affect investment markets is a complex matter.
- Governments play a huge role in balancing the interaction of all factors as they affect financial markets, using:
    - **Monetary policy**
    - **Fiscal policy**
- **Central banks** generally regulate the borrowing system and play a major role in implementing the government's monetary and fiscal policies.

Quick quiz

1   How would you define a recession?

2   How can the level of technological development of a country affect the pace of growth?

3   How does globalisation benefit investors in developed countries?

4   What are the possible effects of a strong currency?

5   What are the potential market influences as a result of an ageing and wealthier population?

6   How would you describe the model of share ownership in the United States?

7   Why does the economic growth of emerging economies happen at a greater pace than with the more established ones?

8   Who sets interest rates in the UK?

9   How are the values of currencies determined on the Foreign Exchange?

10 What is fiscal policy?

11 What is meant by the reserve ratio?

12 What is the effect on money supply of the Bank of England borrowing money from abroad?

The answers to the questions in the Quick Quiz can be found at the end of this Study Text. Before checking your own answers against them, you should look back at this chapter and use the information in it to correct your answers.

Answers to Chapter Questions

1.1   • Currency agreements
      • Industry regulation
      • Interest rates
      • International trade agreements
      • International treaties or conflicts
      • Government spending
      • Taxation
      • Zoning and planning regulations

1.2   • The distribution of age of the population
      • The size of the working population
      • The level of education and training of the workforce
      • The availability of training
      • The presence of trade unions
      • Migration of the workforce

1.3   The main requirements are capital and a good supply of labour.

1.4   Higher rates of inflation will erode the capital values of the stocks held by investors and reduce the real returns from the coupon payments. For newly issued stocks, interest rates may need to be higher to overcome the effect of inflation on returns.

1.5   As technology improves the quality and range of goods also improves. This makes the goods more desirable and therefore increases demand.

1.6   A fixed rate system is more susceptible as the level of exchange is maintained by buying and selling the currency using reserves. If speculators perceive that a government does not have sufficient reserves to maintain the rate, they may sell the currency, forcing a devaluation. The speculators can make large amounts of money when this happens.

1.7 When interest rates rise, the returns from fixed interest stocks fall relative to deposits causing a reduction in their market price. When interest rates fall, holders of fixed interest stocks are effectively locked into the higher rates and the market price of the stock will rise.

1.8 The provision of tax incentives on investments in the form of exemption from income and Capital Gains Tax will make the investment more attractive. In turn, this will provide the incentive to invest in such schemes, creating demand in the relevant financial market.

Tax incentives also free up capital for spending on products and services. This in turn stimulates company profits and hence stock markets.

1.9 The two main models of company ownership are 'shareholder value' and 'stakeholder'. With the shareholder value model, individuals and institutions own companies via shares. The prime motivation for ownership is profit in the form of dividends and increases in capital. With the stakeholder model, individuals and companies own few shares. The motivation for ownership is influenced by other factors such as levels of employment.

1.10 With emerging nations, there is a rapidly growing workforce to support economic growth and there is good potential to improve education levels with the increases in production this can bring.

1.11 Globalisation is the free movement of capital around the world. The ability to move capital quickly is causing the cycles of world markets to converge and stock market movements to become increasingly inter-dependent.

1.12 High exchange rates cause an economy to cool down as exports become less competitive and domestically produced goods become more expensive relative to imports.

1.13 Monetary policy influences inflation to stimulate or cool down the economy. Actions will produce either inflationary or deflationary effects.

1.14 Changes in interest rate control money in the economy by influencing the demand for it. Increasing interest rates reduces the demand and reducing interest rates increases it.

1.15 Tax reductions stimulate the economy by releasing more money for consumers and industry to spend.

1.16 Government spending tends to purchase goods and services produced in the home country. Tax reductions will be partly spent on imported goods.

1.17 The central bank is required to implement monetary policy by intervention in the foreign exchanges to indirectly change interest rates.

PRACTICE QUESTION 1

Answer the following questions using bullet points and short sentences wherever possible. You should allow no more than one minute per mark.

(a) What are the main economic effects of raising interest base rates? (5)

(b) Explain the main responsibilities of a central bank. (5)

(c) What methods are available to the Bank of England to implement changes in interest rates?

(6)

Part B

Direct financial investments

Chapter 2

CASH INVESTMENTS

Chapter topic list	Syllabus reference
1 Characteristics of cash investments	2.1
2 Risk and return	2.1
3 Methods of analysis	2.1
4 Different currencies	2.1

Introduction

In this chapter, we will be looking at cash investments: their characteristics, risk and return, methods of analysis and the main issues relating to investments in different currencies. The return from a cash investment is totally in the form of income, typically paid as interest, with no increase in capital value. Banks, building society and other deposit takers offer such investments.

1   CHARACTERISTICS OF CASH INVESTMENTS

1.1   The main characteristics of cash investments are as follows.

(a)   The return on the investment is in the form of **interest**.

(b)   The interest can be at a **fixed or a variable rate**.

(c)   There is **no return in the form of capital growth**.

(d)   The **capital** will not lose its nominal value (although its purchasing power will inevitably be eroded by inflation).

(e)   The capital must be **available to** the investor within a **clearly defined period**.

(f)   The defined period may be fixed or may be a period of notice ranging from **immediate access to over a year**.

(g)   The investments will usually be **short-term** in nature.

Question 2.1

Why does a Local Authority bond not fall within the definition of a 'cash' investment?

1.2   The main **classes of cash investments** are as follows.

- Deposits
- Certificates of deposit
- Treasury bills
- Commercial bills

Deposits

1.3 **Deposits** generally fall into three categories.

- Instant access accounts
- Notice accounts
- Time deposits

1.4 **Instant access accounts** provide **immediate access** to funds via a passbook, cash card, or chequebook. Typically, interest rates paid will be **variable** and will tend to be lower than with notice or time deposits. Instant access accounts tend to be used where access to money is required at all times, such as a current account for an individual or business.

1.5 For investors with **mutual building societies** (one owned by its account holders), there are two main types of instant access account, **share accounts** and **deposit accounts**. With a share account, the account holder becomes a part owner of the business and as such may be entitled to a pay-out in the form of securities or cash in the event of the building society demutualising. The possession of a share account will normally qualify the account holder to vote on major decisions, including whether the society will demutualise now or in the future. Deposit accounts do not usually confer these rights.

1.6 **Notice accounts** differ from instant access accounts because of the requirement for the account holder to provide **a period of notice** to withdraw money. Some of these accounts will allow withdrawal within the notice period subject to interest penalties. Others do not. In the money markets, this type of account is called a **call account** and they tend to be used where money is not required immediately.

1.7 **Time deposits** are accounts that require the money to be left in for a **fixed period**. Typically, the longer the term, the higher the interest rate, but this may not always be the case. Long-term and short-term interest rates can often be quite different and this will be reflected with this type of investment. The investment is not normally accessible within the fixed rate period, although some deposit takers will release cash and charge an interest penalty. This type of account can be used when there is no immediate need for money.

1.8 At the request of the account holder, such deposits can be 'rolled over' continuously, until the customer instructs otherwise. In these circumstances, the money will be available at the end of the next period.

Certificates of deposit

1.9 It is possible for banks, companies and even governments to **raise money** by issuing **securities** known as **certificates of deposit**. This is, in effect, a short-term loan from a private or institutional investor. These deposits are financial instruments in their own right and are **tradeable** as securities. This type of security is classified with reference to the type of institution that issues them.

Question 2.2

Why does the ability to trade certificates of deposit compromise their description as a 'cash' investment?

1.10 Certificates of deposit are **time deposits** with a bank. They provide an investment return in the form of an agreed rate of interest for the period. The rate of return will normally be less than for an equivalent term deposit, but the holder can get access to their money by selling on the security. The rate of return on the certificate will be based on the **credit rating** of the issuer. As they can be traded on the open market, where their prices can vary, it is possible for the investor to suffer a **loss**. This can be avoided if the bills are held to maturity as the instrument will be redeemed at face value.

Treasury bills

1.11 **Treasury bills** are **short-term loan notes** issued by the **government**. Typically they will be for three months and pay no interest. The investment and return comes from purchasing the security at a discounted rate. At maturity, they can be redeemed at the full value providing a fixed return over the term.

1.12 Treasury bills are issued by the government and, as such, are very low risk investments. As tradeable securities on the open market, it is possible for an investor to suffer a loss. However, this can be avoided if the bills are held to maturity.

Commercial bills

1.13 **Commercial bills** are short-term **loan notes** issued by **companies**, on a similar basis to the Treasury bills. They work in a similar way, but will carry a greater risk. The company issuing the security underwrites the instrument and the rate of return will depend on the company's credit rating. The investor may suffer a loss if the bills are not held to maturity.

2 RISK AND RETURN

2.1 The **return on a cash investment** will vary with a number of different factors.

- The sum invested
- Current levels of inflation
- The level of investor protection
- The currency in which it is invested

2.2 With cash investments, the levels of interest available will **increase** with the **sum of money invested**. Investments in the money markets will yield a higher return than those invested in high street banks and building societies. The published money market rates payable will also increase depending on the size of the investment.

2.3 Cash is only as valuable as the products it can buy. **Inflation** will erode the purchasing power of cash over time, which can cause a problem for the cash investor. If rates of inflation exceed the interest rates available there will be a decrease in the value of cash in 'real' terms. National Savings & Investments Index-linked Savings Certificates remove **inflation risk** by guaranteeing a fixed level of investment return above the level of the Retail Prices Index over the term.

2.4 As well as the **risk of inflation** eroding the purchasing power of their capital, holders of cash investments face a **risk of default** by the financial institution (alternatively called **institutional risk**). The **Financial Services Compensation Scheme** protects deposits held with UK banks and building societies in case of an institution having financial difficulties. 100% of the first £2,000 and 90% of the next £33,000 is covered, giving a maximum of £31,700. If deposits are made in Sterling offshore, the level of protection will depend on local legislation. Jersey, Guernsey and the Isle of Man have levels of protection similar to the UK so interest rates will be similar, but other offshore centres offer higher levels of interest, but without the same level of investor protection. The level of **investor protection** on a cash product could affect the interest rates available.

Question 2.3

Why do deposits in countries with limited investor protection usually pay higher interest rates?

2.5 Cash investments can be made in **most currencies**. Where this is the case, the exchange rate presents an extra risk. For UK investors, investing in other currencies, there will be a wide range of interest rates available, some better than the UK, others worse. However, although the return on the investment in interest terms may be good, it will be the overall return when the currency is returned to sterling that matters. This will depend on the exchange rate movements of the currency relative to sterling. If sterling has weakened the return will be greater, if it has strengthened it will be less. For some investors, the opportunity to speculate on such movements is what makes cash investment more attractive.

Question 2.4

An individual holds sterling and makes a deposit into a US$ account. If the exchange rate changed from US$1.80 to the pound to US$1.90, would this increase or reduce the value of the investment on conversion back to sterling?

3 METHODS OF ANALYSIS

3.1 In order to compare the returns from cash investments with others, including fixed interest and equities, it is essential to ascertain the **actual returns** on the money invested. To do this it is necessary to look through the various factors that can confuse the issue.

Size of investment

3.2 Most accounts will pay **more interest** to investors with **larger sums of money**, and these rates vary between organisations. However, not all deposit accounts provide a fixed interest rate regardless of the amount invested. Most institutions offer a rate that increases with the size of the deposit held. When analysing the investment return on such accounts, it is essential that these factors be taken into account.

3.3 In addition to this, it is essential that investors check the levels of return on their accounts regularly. Building societies and banks will promote their latest accounts with their best interest rates, whereas the older accounts tend to become less competitive with time.

Accessibility

3.4 In many cases, **greater returns** are available for those who can tolerate **restrictions on accessibility**. Although it is important to ensure that the notice period or fixed term is appropriate, it is essential to survey the market as reduced accessibility does not always lead to better returns. When comparing such investments to fixed interest or **equities**, the level of accessibility is an important factor. Typically equities are only suitable for investments of five years plus, and **fixed interest investments** can be profitable over the shorter term, but both are subject to the vagaries of the market place in which they are traded.

When choosing accounts with limited accessibility, it is important to ascertain whether early withdrawal is possible and the **penalty charges** that may be incurred in this event.

Real interest rates

3.5 The **return on an investment** will **vary** with the way the interest is calculated. Interest rates for deposit accounts and other cash investments in the UK will normally also quote an **Annual Equivalent Rate (AER)** in addition to the nominal interest rate.

When an interest rate is quoted, the **frequency** and **method of payment** of interest will affect the **real rate of return**. A bank account offering a nominal interest rate of 8% where interest is paid twice a year would give an AER of 8.16%. Another account offering 8% nominal on a monthly basis would return 8.3%.

Question 2.5

Which would give a greater real return, an account paying 5% per annum once a year, or one which pays 4.9% per annum on a monthly basis?

Taxation

3.6 **Interest on deposit accounts** will be paid **net** of 20% tax as savings income via UK building societies or banks. For a basic or lower rate taxpayer, this satisfies the requirement for tax at the basic rate (22%). However, if the individual concerned is a non-taxpayer and completes the Inland Revenue form R85 the income can be paid **gross**. Lower rate (10%) taxpayers benefit from simplified methods of reclaiming the difference. Other accounts will pay gross automatically, such as those held offshore, with stockbrokers, merchant banks, and deposits in the money markets. In addition to these, there are tax-exempt deposit investments such as the TESSA-only ISA (existing accounts only) and cash ISA and certain National Savings & Investments products, eg their **Fixed Interest** and **Index Linked Savings Certificates**. The returns actually received by investors from deposit investments will be affected by the tax status of both the investment and the investor.

3.7 When comparing **deposit investments** with fixed interest or equities, the way in which the return is paid will have a significant impact on the return. A higher rate taxpayer will pay higher rate tax on the whole of the return from a deposit account. The same person investing in a zero dividend split capital investment trust may be able to offset part or all of the investment return against their annual capital gains tax exemption.

Question 2.6

One bank account offers a gross interest rate of 6% whereas another account offers 5% net. Which has the greater gross return?

Fluctuations in returns

3.8 **Deposit accounts** in the UK enjoy a relatively **high level of stability** in their investment returns. Investment returns on accounts will vary with changes in base rates of interest, but overall they are reasonably predictable. Investing in fixed term and notice accounts can help to remove these differences.

3.9   In contrast, **equity investments** experience great fluctuations in the level of income and the amount of capital returned. **Fixed interest investments** will provide a known fixed capital return and a fixed income if held to maturity. If they are traded, both of these factors may vary.

4   DIFFERENT CURRENCIES

4.1   Cash investments can be made in the UK or **offshore** in any freely exchangeable currency. However, in these circumstances, the currency itself behaves like any other freely tradeable security and can experience **wide fluctuations**. Accounts denominated in different currencies will normally pay interest, but the reasons for investing in other currencies can vary. For some, the opportunity to get better interest rates in other currencies will be the attraction, for others it will be the ability to combine cash investment with ability to speculate on the movements in exchange rates.

4.2   With investment in different currency there is always the risk that **exchange rates** will move and reduce the value of the investment in sterling terms. However, the converse may also be true increasing the return in sterling terms. Effectively, currency movements will affect the purchasing power of the money in the country in which the investor intends to spend it. Individuals who are paid in a different currency to the one they need to spend will often make deposits in the relevant currency to avoid this situation.

Chapter roundup

- **Cash investments** provide a return in the form of **interest** at a fixed or variable rate, not growth of capital.

- **Capital** must be available within a **clearly defined period**, which may be fixed or a period of notice.

- Capital is **not at risk**, but the investment is short-term in nature.

- Cash investments are usually:

  - **Deposits** (instant access, notice and time deposit accounts)
  - **Certificates of deposit**
  - **Treasury bills**
  - **Commercial bills**

- **Return** on a cash investment varies with:

  - The sum invested
  - Inflation
  - Level of investor protection
  - Currency of investment

- Analysing the **actual return** of a cash investment can be confused by:

  - The size of the investment triggering different interest rates
  - How accessible the capital is
  - How interest is calculated
  - Taxation
  - Fluctuations in returns over time

- Cash investments in a **foreign currency** carry the **additional risk**, or opportunity, of exchange rate fluctuations.

Quick quiz

1   What type of account would entitle an investor to a share in the proceeds in the event of the demutualisation of a building society?

2   What is a time deposit?

3   Is a certificate of deposit a risk-free investment?

4   What is the maximum investor protection in the UK on a deposit account?

5   What type of individual could be interested in a deposit account denominated in a currency other than sterling?

The answers to the questions in the Quick Quiz can be found at the end of this Study Text. Before checking your own answers against them, you should look back at this chapter and use the information in it to correct your answers.

Answers to Chapter Questions

2.1   With a local authority bond that is not held to maturity, the level of capital returned may be greater or less than that originally paid. Essentially the capital return from this investment means that the capital is at risk.

2.2   The ability to trade the securities means that a capital loss is possible.

2.3   The deposits pay a premium to attract investors despite the additional risk. The greater the risk, the greater the premium.

2.4   The investor would receive less sterling for each US$ than when the investment was made. Ignoring any interest that may have been paid, this would have lost money.

2.5   The real rate of return from an account paying 5% per annum would be 5%. An account paying 4.9% per annum on a monthly basis would give a real rate of return of 5.01%, marginally more.

2.6   An interest rate of 5% net is equivalent to 6.25% gross and will give the greater return in gross terms. $(5\% \times 100/80 = 6.25\%.)$

PRACTICE QUESTION 2

Mr Smith has a number of sterling cash investments. State the level of risk and type of investment return he would expect to receive from this type of investment. Explain how you would compare the returns between different investments of this type. (9)

Chapter 3

FIXED INTEREST INVESTMENTS

Chapter topic list	Syllabus reference
1 Characteristics of fixed interest investments	2.2
2 Uses and applications of fixed interest investments	2.2
3 Factors which affect fixed interest investments	2.2
4 Methods of analysis	2.2
5 Risk and return	2.2

Introduction

In this chapter, we will be looking at **fixed interest investments**. We will examine the factors that affect the investment returns from this type of investment and the way we measure these returns. Finally, we will examine the risks involved and the potential rewards.

1   CHARACTERISTICS OF FIXED INTEREST INVESTMENTS

KEY TERM

Fixed interest investments are financial instruments issued by a variety of institutions to raise capital. Central and local governments, international organisations, banks and building societies and companies, in the UK and abroad, issue them in a variety of currencies and in a number of different forms. The loans are repaid at an agreed time in the future and interest is paid, usually at a **fixed rate**, until this redemption. Within these parameters, this form of investment is diverse in character and form.

The issuer

1.1   **Fixed interest investments** are typically categorised by the type of institution issuing them.

- Governments
- International organisations
- Banks and building societies
- Companies

The following sections will examine instruments issued by each of these sources in more detail.

1.2 Here is a summary of fixed interest instruments.

Issuer	Instrument
British central government	**Gilts** When gilts were originally issued the edge of the certificate for the security was embossed with gold. This 'gilt-edge' denoted the quality of the loan stock and the name gilt is still used today, despite the lack of the 'gilt-edge' on current issues. These are low-risk instruments.
British local government	**Local authority bonds** Used by local authorities to borrow money to aid their own cash flow. Interest rates are normally slightly higher than for gilts to reflect higher levels of risk.
British companies	**UK corporate bonds** Used by British companies to borrow money in sterling.
Foreign governments, companies and international institutions	**Eurobonds** These securities are bonds underwritten by an international syndicate, which are sold in countries other than the country of the currency in which the issue is denominated. As such, they are subject to additional risk from currency fluctuations. They tend to be issued in bearer form. The main market for these instruments is in the UK.
Foreign governments, companies	**Bulldogs** These are issued in sterling and are mainly traded in the UK. The interest rates available will vary with the credit rating of the issuer.

Gilts

1.3 **Gilts** – UK Government securities – make up a large part of the UK bond market and are mainly classified by their term.

Term	Characteristics
Shorts	Run for less than seven years to redemption (or five years, as defined in some newspapers). Investors and institutions use them for short-term investment.
Mediums	Have 7-15 years (or 5 – 15) to redemption. Less popular than the other two classes, being a bit too long for short-term investment and not long enough for longer-term commitments. They are suitable for school fees provision, as the term is right and reduced demand can give them a better yield.
Longs	15 years or more to redemption. They are very popular for meeting long-term income commitments, such as those required for retirement.
Undated gilts	Have no specific date for redemption, or have become undated through the small print in the terms, for example, war loans. Interest will be paid until the government finally redeems them.

Question 3.1

What type of insurance based investment is underwritten by 'long' gilts?

1.4 Gilts may also be **classified by the size of their coupon**. They are normally divided into small, medium and large coupon stocks, as each will typically have a different application. The coupon is paid gross.

1.5 Some gilts provide their return in the form of a premium over the **Retail Prices Index (RPI)** for the term of the stock. With these, both the coupon and the redemption value of the stock are linked to the RPI and in this form can provide 'real' growth. They were introduced in 1981 at a time of particularly high inflation. They are considerably **less popular** than fixed yield gilts and are even less so at times of reduced inflation. They make up less than a quarter of the total gilt market.

STRIPS (Separate Trading of Registered Interest and Principal of Securities)

1.6 A bond's individual **income payments and final return of capital** can be split up and traded separately as individual instruments. Where this happens, the investments are known as gilt STRIPS. These new financial instruments can be used for a variety of different applications, such as the provision of a guaranteed fixed rate of income for income withdrawals under a pension, or fixed lumps of capital for school fees. The uses for these derivatives effectively make the market more attractive, increasing the demand for gilts. In turn, this demand reduces the coupon that the government needs to pay and hence the cost of it borrowing money.

1.7 The original concept for the **STRIPS** market came **from the USA,** where stripping is used to increase the demand for, and marketability of, bonds. The STRIPS provide a range of new financial instruments and the increased demand caused by them helps to **ensure liquidity** in the bond markets.

Question 3.2

If a gilt has five years to run to redemption, how many separate 'STRIPS' can it be turned into?

Repos

KEY TERM

A **repo** is a transaction whereby one party sells securities (eg government bonds) to another, agreeing to repurchase (repo) the securities at a future date at a pre-agreed price. In the UK, repo usually refers to gilts, but in the US where this transaction type originated, it is increasingly used with other marketable securities as well.

A repo is essentially a collateralised short-term loan of fixed interest securities

1.8 The British government uses the **repo market** as the main tool to alter interest rates and implement monetary policy. In addition to this, repos serve a further function: like STRIPS, they help increase the **liquidity of the gilt market**.

1.9 Wherever there is a **derivative** (discussed in more detail in Chapter 5), there will be a **speculator** willing to use it to speculate on a market. In the case of **repos**, they are used to **speculate on the gilts market.** This is done by purchasing stock and **immediately selling it,** with an agreement to repurchase the same stock on a set date in the future at an agreed price. The buyer of the original stock can use the money received from the sale to pay for it. When the stock is **repurchased** in the future, it will be at **an agreed premium** to the sale price. This is the premium or 'interest' paid by the speculator to have exposure to large quantities of stock without using large amounts of capital. In many cases, this will equate to a very competitive rate of interest on terms far better than borrowing the money elsewhere. Prior to repurchase, the stock itself acts as **collateral** for the transaction. If gilt prices rise, the investor will make a profit but, if they fall, that investor will make a loss. The original person purchasing the gilts will make a small profit every time.

Question 3.3

How can Repos be used for speculating on the Gilt market?

Local authority bonds

1.10 **Local authorities** have also sometimes issued bonds to finance their activities. The market in these instruments has contracted as a result of changes in the rules relating to their issue.

UK corporate bonds

1.11 **Larger companies** issue **bonds** to **borrow money** from investors **via the bond markets**. Some companies, particularly the large ones, will have credit ratings at least as good or even higher than banks. The yields given are linked to the credit worthiness of the issuer but will be **higher than gilts** to offset the increased risk. Prices tend to be **more volatile** than equivalent gilts and news about individual companies, and the economy as a whole, will have an impact. Interest is paid to investors gross.

1.12 The market for **top quality corporate bonds** is active and the higher the quality of the bond (based on the credit worthiness of the issue) the more active it will be. Lower quality stocks can occasionally suffer as a result of the market in them being significantly smaller and less liquid. The lower liquidity results in larger buying/selling price spreads.

1.13 Corporate bonds are further defined by the nature of the **underlying guarantees**.

Debentures

1.14 A debenture is a **loan secured** on the **assets of a limited liability company**. The company must pay the fixed level of interest before any dividends are paid to its own shareholders. Debentures can be backed by the general creditworthiness of a company, or by a 'floating charge' over company assets. Details of the security and the priority for payment are included in the **debenture trust deed** together with any limitations applied to the underlying security. It is these restrictions that set debentures apart from secured loan stock.

1.15 In the US, a debenture would normally be a loan backed by the general creditworthiness of the company. It is more common in the UK to have a **floating charge**.

Loan stock

1.16 **Loan stock** issued by a company can be written on a **secured or unsecured basis**. However, the conditions applicable will typically be less onerous than with a debenture. They will usually be given far lower priority for repayment should the company go into liquidation, representing a higher risk for the investor (the risk still being low overall). This is turn means that yields on the open market will be higher.

Permanent Interest Bearing Shares (PIBS)

1.17 Building societies issue a specific type of fixed interest stock called a **PIBS**. Where the building society has subsequently demutualised, they are called **perpetual subordinated bonds** (PSBs). The name comes from the fact that they are low down in the order for payment against other loans, often described as '**deeply subordinated**'. As part of the rules associated with this type of instrument, the issuer reserves the right to **withhold payments of interest** where they have insufficient income. Very few (if any) will default, but the risk premium on this type of investment makes the yield higher than other corporate bonds and gilts. The market in these investments is relatively illiquid resulting in larger buying/selling price spreads than with other similar investments.

Interest on PIBS is typically paid **twice yearly** gross.

Other loan instruments issued by companies

1.18 Companies can also issue other financial instruments that have some of the characteristics of fixed interest stock.

1.19 **Preference shares** are a class of equity (not corporate bonds) and do not normally carry voting rights. They have been included in this section because they do provide an investment return in the form of a **fixed return** based on the face value of the stock. These shares give rights superior to those of ordinary shares, such as **priority** in **receiving dividends** and priority in the case of the company being wound up. They do, however, rank behind other forms of loan stock. This makes them less secure and as a result they will normally give a higher yield. This subject will be covered in more detail when we look at equities.

1.20 **Convertibles** are **fixed interest bonds** that may be converted into a stated number of shares at a specific date in the future. **Debentures, loan stock** and **preference shares** can all be issued in this 'convertible' format. **Convertibles** give the holder the right to exercise the option either to **receive repayment** of capital, or **conversion** to one or more forms of equity. The decision will be influenced by the value of the equity offered on the **day of the conversion**. The characteristics of the convertible can make them considerably **more volatile** than other loan stock. As a rule they operate like fixed interest stocks earlier in their life but, as they get closer to their redemption dates, take on more and more of the characteristics of the **underlying equity**. This subject will be covered in more detail when we look at equities.

Question 3.4

Do convertibles behave more like fixed interest investments or equities?

1.21 **Deep discount bonds** issued by companies produce no interest. Their investment return is in the form of increased capital. They are issued at a discount and repaid at face value. Although only producing capital, some can give rise to an income tax charge for investors. As they produce no income, the capital values of these instruments are extremely sensitive to movements of interest rates in the market.

Eurobonds

1.22 **Eurobonds** are bonds **underwritten** by an international syndicate, and are sold in countries other than the country of the currency in which the issue is denominated. They are not governed by the jurisdiction of any one country. **Eurobonds** are usually **issued in bearer form,** which means that the right to an income or capital repayment belongs to the person presenting the certificate to the issuer.

1.23 The bonds can be issued in **many different forms,** but straightforward traditional Eurobonds are known as **'straights'.** No government regulates the market and it is relatively unrestricted, allowing issuers to try various inventive ideas. Bonds can be issued with a variety of **fixed** and **floating** and **capped** rates in **single or multiple currencies.** Of these variations, one of the most popular is the **Floating Rate Note (FRN).**

Bulldogs

1.24 A **bulldog** is a **foreign fixed interest security issue** made in London in sterling. A foreign government or corporation usually issues them to raise money in sterling. Yields will reflect the credit rating of the borrower, but yields will be **higher** than for gilts.

2 USES AND APPLICATIONS OF FIXED INTEREST INVESTMENTS

2.1 The nature of fixed interest investments allows them to be used for a number of different applications, which we shall examine in turn.

Income-producing investment

2.2 The **fixed interest** produced by this type of investment makes it suitable for a number of different applications. As **part of an investment portfolio,** fixed interest investments can be used to produce a **guaranteed level of income.** This can be essential in some applications. Where a trust has been set up on an **'interest in possession'** basis, the trustees must ensure that they do not favour one class of beneficiary over the other. The individual with the interest in possession should receive an income and the remaindermen should get capital appreciation. The income produced by **equities** in the **form of dividends** is rarely high enough to achieve this alone. A portion of the trust can be invested in **fixed interest securities** to ensure this.

2.3 **Individuals who have retired** also need a secure income. This can be provided directly by a **portfolio of gilts** or indirectly via **an annuity.** Purchased life and compulsory purchase annuities both use long term gilts to underwrite the return.

2.4 Those approaching retirement can no longer afford to take risks. Moving their investments progressively into fixed interest investments as retirement nears is an effective strategy. It provides greater income returns than deposit investments and will, at least in most cases, keep pace with inflation.

2.5 For individuals with **Self-Invested Personal Pensions (SIPPs)** seeking to make pension fund withdrawals, guaranteeing the income without compromising the remaining capital can be an issue. Many have found a solution in the use of interest payments from **STRIPS,** a gilt derivative. A fixed capital outlay can be used to purchase a known income for a set period.

Question 3.5

How would the use of STRIPS provide income to an individual taking pension fund withdrawals?

Producing fixed capital sums

2.6 **Fixed interest investments** normally produce capital at **maturity** when they are redeemed. This can be used to meet a repeated need for capital sums such as with school fees. **Gilts** can be purchased with maturity dates that allow them to guarantee payment of school fees at a fixed date in the future. Medium-term gilts are best for this application, because the term is right and the relative lack of popularity of these against **longs** and **shorts**makes the returns attractive.

2.7 **STRIPS** could also be used for financial outgoings such as school fees. Fixed amounts of capital can be purchased for the required dates in the future at a discount.

Tax planning

2.8 With **gilts** and most fixed interest investments, the **return of capital** at redemption is exempt from **capital gains tax**. As such, individuals liable to the highest rates of income tax can choose stocks trading at below par (less than £100 per £100 of stock). Fixed interest investments with **running yields** below current interest rates will still have similar redemption yields to those with higher running yields. The difference is made up in **capital appreciation** over the time. For those higher rate taxpayers, this increase in capital is **exempt**, giving them a tax advantage. Organisations that are exempt from tax are happy to use fixed interest securities with the best yield irrespective of whether it is in the form of income or capital. With interest rates at low levels, as they are currently, few (if any) gilts are trading below par.

Question 3.6

Which of the following investments will give a better return for a higher rate taxpayer?

(a) A gilt with a nominal yield of 7% purchased for £100 at par with 5 years to maturity
(b) A gilt with a nominal yield of 3% purchased for £80 with 5 years to maturity

Risk reduction

2.9 As individuals near retirement their investments inside and outside of their pension become very important. In these circumstances, it is important to **insulate** them from **market fluctuations**. **Fixed interest securities** are a good vehicle for this and a gradual switch to them from five years or more before retirement can achieve this goal.

2.10 A further benefit of this exercise is that, in many cases, the intention will be to **buy an annuity**, either compulsory purchase via a pension or purchased life. In either case, the switch to **fixed interest investments** maintains the purchasing power of the money. If **interest rates fall** prior to retirement, then a fixed investment will effectively buy **less income**. **Fixed interest securities** will tend to increase their **capital values** to match the prevailing interest rates. This **larger capital sum** can buy more annuity and make up for any loss.

Speculation

2.11 As the **capital values of fixed interest investments** will **change** with movements in interest rates, they can be used as a **vehicle for speculation**. If an interest rate fall is anticipated, stocks can be purchased and sold for a profit after the announcement. If a rise is anticipated, **gilts** can be **'sold short'** (without holding them) and **repurchased** after the announcement, with the difference as tax free profit (capital gains are exempt from CGT). **Repos** can be a vehicle for speculation on interest rates. As a derivative of gilts, a small premium can give the speculator access to gains (or losses) on large amounts of stock.

Issue and redemption of fixed interest securities

2.12 Where **fixed interest securities** are issued directly to the investment market, they are called **'tap' stocks**. This can only be done where the **issue is relatively small**. Larger issues will be made by **auction** or **tender**.

Auction

2.13 With an **auction**, investors are invited to **bid for the stock**. Bids are put in for the amounts of stock required at the price the investor is prepared to pay. If bidders are successful, they will pay the price bid. Unsuccessful bids, for amounts of stock up to £500,000, can be allocated stock at an average price based on the range of successful bid prices.

Tender

2.14 As an alternative to an auction, a **tender** will state a **minimum price** and individuals can 'tender' a price above this for a specific amount of stock. Tenders will be accepted in descending order to the point at which the issue is not quite fully subscribed, when the issuers will usually **set a price**. All the successful applicants then pay the same set price. It is essential that the issuer **sets this price correctly** to ensure a **good secondary market** in the issue.

Redemption

2.15 Most **fixed interest investments** have a fixed **redemption date** but some do not and are redeemed when they are no longer commercially viable. As an example, an undated 10% stock is essentially a loan at 10% for the issuer, which is acceptable where prevailing interest rates are higher, but when they fall below this level it is no longer competitive. In this case, the bonds will usually be redeemed and the money borrowed elsewhere. In contrast, the 3½% War Loan actually has a redemption date of 1951 or after, and, as things stand, the 'or after' clause has been used and the stock has not been redeemed. It is unlikely to happen until interest rates fall below 3½% and the loan is no longer competitive.

The yield curve

2.16 Under normal circumstances, **fixed interest securities** with **long periods** to run to redemption will have **higher yields** than another with the same coupon but a shorter term to run. However, as there is a greater risk over the longer term that things will go wrong, eg inflation will rise, the economy will go into recession etc the effect tails off giving the normal yield curve.

The normal yield curve

2.17 Market analysts draw graphs to depict this.

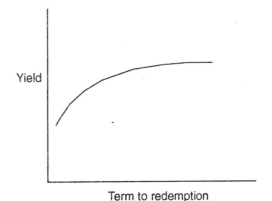

Figure 1: Normal yield curve

Question 3.7

Draw a yield curve for the same fixed interest security as in Figure 1 assuming investors were even more pessimistic about the future.

Exam focus point

It is essential that you can draw the yield curve and label the axes of the graph properly as it may be asked in the examination.

The flat yield curve

2.18 The **yield curve** is effectively a **barometer for the economic outlook**. If the market decides that the economy has a stable outlook without, for example, an increase in interest rates or inflation, the **yield curve can flatten out**. Where interest rates look to be reducing in the future, this may also be the case (see Figure 2).

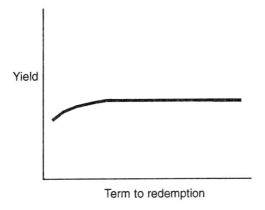

Figure 2: Flat yield curve

The inverted yield curve

2.19 When the markets look forward and see good news, such as **falling interest rates** and **falling inflation** combined with a **tight fiscal policy**, the yield curve may become inverted. This will only tend to happen for a relatively short period of time, because when future interest rates and inflation are predicted to be the same as today, the curve will return to more normal shape with a slight increase. In addition to this, the supply and demand effects of traders switching to shorter term instruments with higher yields pushes up prices and corrects the yield curve.

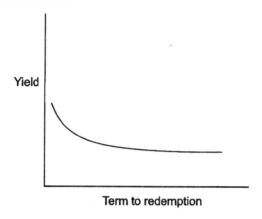

Figure 3: Inverse yield curve

Exam focus point

The examiner has reported that many candidates confuse the normal yield curve and the reverse yield curve.

2.20 The **yield curve** is actively used in the UK and US as a **market prediction tool**. In 1991, Campbell R Harvey came up with the **link** between the **inversions** of the yield curve and **recessions** in the US. He postulated that inverse yield curves had preceded the last five US recessions. It is generally agreed that the yield curve can **accurately forecast** the turning points of the **business cycle**.

3 FACTORS WHICH AFFECT FIXED INTEREST INVESTMENTS

3.1 **Fixed interest investments** (bonds) are subject to a number of factors that will affect the returns in terms of income or capital. These factors can either act on individual investments or on all fixed interest investments simultaneously. Those that act on individual investments are known as specific factors, those that act on all investments are known as market or systematic factors.

Specific factors

3.2 Individual investments will be affected by the following factors.

- The investment's **coupon**
- The investment's **term to maturity**
- **Options** on the investment
- The investor's **tax** status
- The issuer's **credit rating**

Coupon

3.3 The **size of the coupon** will have a number of different effects because of its relationship with **prevailing interest rates**. These factors are linked to the price of the investment through the following equation for an irredeemable bond.

$$\frac{\text{Coupon}}{\text{Prevailing interest rates}} \times £100 = \text{approximate price}$$

3.4   If prevailing interest rates were 7% and an investor wanted to buy an investment with a coupon (face value interest rate) of 10%, the price would be

$$\frac{10\%}{7\%} \times £100 = £142.86$$

Conversely for an investment with a coupon of 5% the price would be

$$\frac{5\%}{7\%} \times £100 = £71.43$$

These calculations ignore the **time to redemption,** which also **influences the price.** The level above or below par (£100) means that the investment appeals differently to different investors, because it has tax implications and these supply and demand effects will alter the price. Therefore, be aware that the above calculation is only approximate.

3.5   The coupon will also impact on the **volatility of the investment. Low coupon bonds** are **more volatile** than high coupon bonds because the return is dependent on the return of capital at maturity rather than the interest. As much of that return is determined later in the life of the investment, the prices will also be more sensitive to news.

Question 3.8

Calculate an approximate price for an undated gilt with a nominal yield of 12% when base rates are standing at 7%.

Term to maturity

3.6   As the **term to maturity** of a fixed interest investment increases, the applications for which it is used will change. Long term investments, particularly **gilts,** are popular for **underwriting annuities.** Short-term investments tend to be used by financial institutions to enable them to make use of cash sums not currently required. This increases the demand for these relative to those with medium-terms which in itself causes an effect as it makes the redemption yields on medium-term investments more attractive.

3.7   As we have seen, from the **yield curve** the term of the investment will also impact on the extent to which it reacts to the economic outlook.

3.8   The **longer the term,** the **more volatile** the investment will be. The reason for this is that the longer the term, the less the effect of differences of capital at redemption. The capital will not fluctuate, but the interest element will. This means that the prices will fluctuate more than an investment where the capital repayment makes up a sizeable proportion of the return, for example with a shorter-term investment.

Options

3.9   The **options** on a **fixed interest investment** will affect the investment return that it gives. If a fixed interest investment has an **option to convert** to a different type of investment, such as an ordinary share, at a fixed time in the future, then near the time to conversion it will take on more of the characteristics of the new investment.

Tax status of the investor

3.10   The **capital gains** on fixed interest investments are usually **exempt** from **CGT.** As such, a stock that yields the majority of its investment return as capital will be **more attractive** to

higher rate taxpayers and this factor may even alter demand for particular stocks in the marketplace. For individuals who are **non-taxpayers** (or are **tax exempt,** such as a pension fund or a charity) this will make little difference. These investors may choose a stock with a high yield if they require income, or may just look for the best redemption yield based on their tax status.

3.11 Since 1998, **gilt coupon payments** have been payable **gross**. This enabled stockholders to receive gross payment if they wished to do so, irrespective of which stocks they chose or who they were. Prior to this, some stocks paid their coupon gross and others net. This factor used to affect the demand for stocks, with those paying coupons gross being more in demand than those paying net.

Issuer's credit rating

3.12 With **fixed interest investments, the credit rating of the issuer** is the **most important factor** in determining the **investment return**. The reason for this is that investors will seek a **'risk premium'**, a higher rate of interest, depending on the risk of interest or capital not being repaid.

There are a number of **credit rating agencies** (such as Moodys and Standard and Poors) that will rate governments, companies and even individual issues of stock.

3.13 Moodys uses the following ratings.

Moodys rating	Standing as an investment
Aaa	Bonds which are judged to be of the highest quality
Aa	Bonds which are judged to be of high quality by all standards
A	Bonds which possess many favourable attributes and are to be considered as upper-medium-grade obligations
Baa	Bonds are considered as medium-grade obligations, they are neither highly protected nor poorly secured
Ba	Such bonds are judged to have speculative elements; their future cannot be well assured
B	Such bonds lack the characteristics of a desirable investment, assurance of interest and principal repayments over any long period of time may be small
Caa	Bonds of poor standing, they may be in default or there may be elements of danger with respect to principal or interest
C	The lowest class of bonds, issues with this rating have extremely poor prospects of ever attaining investment standing

3.14 Moody's applies numerical modifiers 1, 2 and 3 in each generic rating category from Aa to Caa. The modifier 1 indicates that the issuer is in the higher end of its letter rating category; the modifier 2 indicates a mid-range ranking; the modifier 3 indicates that the issuer is in the lower end of the letter ranking category.

3.15 These classifications have been tested statistically by Moodys in several **'loss by experience' surveys**. Over the period 1920-1997, bonds with **Aaa** ratings had a 0% chance of defaulting within one year and a 0.82% chance within ten years. In contrast, **B** rated bonds had a statistical chance of defaulting within one year of 6.8% and a 43.9% chance within ten years.

3.16 Stock issued by governments will be rated on the **stability of the government**. As such, **gilts** and **US Treasury bonds** have interest rates only marginally above prevailing interest rates. Moody's has published **'sovereign ceilings,** which are effectively the maximum credit rating for long-term fixed interest investments in a country. The ratings for the UK and US are both **Aaa**, the highest. Bonds issued by countries such as Russia or Malaysia will need to have a suitably **large risk premium** to be attractive enough to overcome fears of **default**. Russia has a rating of B and Malaysia Baa. The **credit ratings** are **reviewed** on a regular basis.

3.17 Some stocks are not issued by individual governments, but by **syndicates of countries**. These are normally **underwritten** by the governments of the countries underlying the syndicates and, typically, have a very good credit rating. These stocks are called '**supra-nationals**' and are issued by organisations such as the World Bank. Such organisations are rarely, if ever, allowed to fail. This in itself enhances the security.

Question 3.9

If an investor were to purchase a portfolio of B rated bonds (junk bonds), what yield over the base rate would represent a reasonable rate of return assuming default is running at 6.8% per annum?

3.18 A company can issue several **different classes** of **loan stock** and, as such, the order of repayment will reflect on the inherent risks and the return from the investment. On liquidation, it is likely that **debentures** will be repaid first, followed by **secured loan stock**, then **unsecured loan stock**. After this, **preference shares** will be repaid. The later the investment is in line for repayment, the higher the risk premium will be.

Market (systematic or systemic) factors

3.19 Certain factors will affect all fixed interest investments. These include:

- Government **monetary policy**
- Government **fiscal policy**
- **Comparative investment returns**

Government monetary policy

3.20 **Monetary policy** in most countries will be controlled by the direct or indirect manipulation of interest rates. In either case, **government fixed interest instruments** are used to effect these changes and the policy followed will always impact on fixed interest investments in one way or another.

3.21 **Monetary policy** in the UK is managed and implemented by the **Bank of England**. Changes in interest rates will affect **fixed interest investment** prices directly, as previously described.

Question 3.10

How would a tightening of monetary policy affect fixed interest security prices?

3.22 The effect of monetary policy in the economy will be either inflationary or deflationary. **Rising inflation** will tend to **reduce** the effective rates of return from fixed interest investments and reduce demand. **Falling inflation** will **increase** real rates of return and may be indicative of recession. Fixed interest investments will become more popular as real rates of return increase and as fears of a significant drop in the equities markets prompt a move to safer investments.

Fiscal policy

3.23 **Government fiscal policy** will also impact on fixed interest markets in two ways. It will act **directly** by its influence on the economy and, **indirectly**, by reflecting on the money available for investment and the relative taxation of investments.

3.24 **Lower taxes** can lead to **increased growth** and, hence, increased inflationary pressure. but higher taxes cause the opposite. However, taxes can be **manipulated** specifically to make investments more or less attractive. The **exemption** from **Capital Gains Tax** is a major benefit for the private investor and recent changes to the taxation of coupons improved the demand for **gilts**. However, the introduction of **personal equity plans (PEPs)** in the 1980s **reduced** the demand for **fixed interest stocks** from the private investor, as money was diverted into the new tax-exempt equity funds. The balance was redressed to a certain extent by the introduction of **corporate bond PEPs and ISAs**.

3.25 In the UK, **gilts** are also central to **fiscal policy**. The government will use **gilts** to finance any public sector deficit. This issue of stock will increase supply and may well effectively reduce demand, which will be reflected in **gilt prices** in the secondary markets. When public borrowing is reducing, the net effect of **redeeming gilts** without issuing new ones could be to contract the supply of quality stock in the market which could tend to increase prices.

Comparative investment returns

3.26 The attractiveness of fixed interest investments will always be relative to other forms of investment and is directly or indirectly influenced by monetaryand fiscal policy. In times of buoyant **economic growth**, the returns from fixed interest investments will appear **poor** with respect to **equities**. During times of **recession**, fixed interest is **a safe haven** for many investors because of its **low risk returns**.

4 METHODS OF ANALYSIS

4.1 In order to **compare** individual fixed interest investments **against** other types of investment, such as equities or cash investments, it is important to know how to **measure** the **investment returns**. In order to achieve this, a good understanding is required of pricing this type of instrument and the various methods of calculating yields.

Fixed interest security pricing

4.2 Stocks traded on the **Stock Exchange** are purchased by reference to their **nominal value** which is that on the loan certificate. The price of the stock may differ from this, but is usually quoted in terms of pounds per hundred pounds of nominal value. **Gilts** have historically been priced in pounds and thirty seconds of a pound but, since 1998, have been quoted in decimals.

4.3 As with other traded securities, complications can arise because of the **spread** between the **purchase price** and **sale price**. Single prices published in a newspaper, or on the Internet, would be a mid-market price.

Question 3.11

Would a buyer pay more or less than the quoted mid-market price?

4.4 The **timing** of the sale will have a further impact on the price. Stocks are effectively sold with their accrued dividend up to the **'ex-dividend' date**. Published prices described as 'clean' do not usually show the effect of the accrued interest up to the point of sale. Information providers that allow for the accrued interest in their prices are quoting 'dirty' prices, which are usually quoted to six decimal places.

4.5 The rules relating to the treatment of coupon payments in the special **'ex-dividend' period** on gilts were changed on 31 July 1998. Prior to the change, gilts sold **three weeks prior to payment** were sold without the dividend but the **ex-dividend** period has now been **abolished**.

Bond yields

4.6 The **value** of a **fixed interest security** relative to other types of investment will depend on the **investment return**. It is important that these returns can be expressed in a form that can be compared with other investments. The financial press typically quotes the **'running' yield** and the **'redemption' yield**.

Running yield

4.7 The **running yield** is effectively the **level of income** produced by the investment. An investor will receive a return based on the nominal yield and the purchase price of the bond. £100 of stock yielding a 6% coupon will produce income of £6 (usually in two six monthly instalments of £3). The income received in percentage terms will be dependent on the price paid for the investment. If an investor pays £90 for £100 of stock, the **yield** can be **calculated** by dividing the **coupon** or **nominal yield** by the **purchase price**. Multiply the figure by 100 to express the answer in percentage terms.

£6/£90 × 100% = 6.66% per annum

Question 3.12

Calculate the running yield on £100 of stock purchased for £115 with a coupon of 8%.

Redemption yield

4.8 The running yield measures of the income produced by a fixed interest investment. However, it does not take into account **changes in capital value** which, as discussed earlier, can make up a significant proportion of the return. In order to do this, we must calculate the **change of value in capital** into the return.

4.9 The **calculation of redemption yield** requires the use of an **internal rate of return calculation (IRR)**. This calculation involves an iterative process and as such is not possible to do with total accuracy except with a financial calculator. In the examination, an **approximation of the redemption yield** will be acceptable. The approximation involves calculating the effect of changes in capital averaged over the term to redemption. This figure is added to **running yield** to give a **close approximation** of the **redemption yield**.

4.10 The **redemption yield** is the **preferred measure of return** on fixed interest investments because the redemption yield:

- Takes account of all cash flows from the bond
- Reflects all capital gains or losses
- Makes adjustment for the time taken until each cash flow is received

- Allows comparisons between different bonds on a comparable basis

4.11 EXAMPLE: REDEMPTION YIELD

A gilt is purchased for £90 for £100 nominal value of stock, with five years to run. If the nominal yield is 6%, as in the example above, the running yield will be 6.66%.

At maturity, the repayment of capital will be £100, some £10 more than the purchase price. This equates to an additional return of £10/£90 over the five years = 11.11% or 2.22% per year. By adding this to the running yield of 6.66%, we get an approximate redemption yield of 8.88%.

4.12 SOLUTION

To calculate this accurately we would input the following into our financial calculator.

PV	FV	PMT	P/YR	N
–£90 (the initial cost of the bond, -ve to represent cash outflow)	£100 (future value)	£3 (½ yearly interest)	2 (payments per year)	10, there are 10 six-monthly payments

BEG/END should be set to END as the payments are in arrears.

If we then solve for I/YR, we should get a figure of 8.49638. This is fairly close to our approximation of 8.88%. The figure we have obtained using the financial calculator is the nominal yield. To calculate the effective yield we would have to calculate:

$$((1 + \text{Nominal } \%/(100 \times \text{P/YR}))^{\text{p/yr}} - 1) \times 100.$$

Alternatively, having obtained the nominal yield most financial calculators will have an **EFF%** button to achieve the same result = 8.68%.

Question 3.13

Calculate the redemption yield on £100 of stock purchased for £115 with a coupon of 8% with 5 years to run to redemption.

5 RISK AND RETURN

5.1 With fixed interest investments, as with all other types, the level of return will vary with the **level of risk** that the investor is prepared to take. Typically, fixed interest investments pay a **known amount of interest** for a **predetermined period**. The nominal or face value of the investment is then returned in full. Whether or not this happens in reality will be down to the issuer so it is very important to identify its credit rating.

5.2 As we have already stated, the **lower the risk** of a fixed interest investment, the closer the returns will be to prevailing interest rates. The **higher the risk** taken by the investor, the greater the return they will require (known as the risk premium). From the UK perspective, the only risk-free fixed interest investment will be **gilts** and Treasury Bills. Therefore, if we can establish the **average returns** from long gilts, then we can determine the minimum return on fixed interest investments. According to the Barclays Capital Gilt-Equity survey, the past average returns generated by gilts in real terms were 1.1 per cent over the period from 1899 to 2003. In comparison, equities produced a return of 5.1 per cent. More recently, over the last 20 years, real returns on gilts were 6.1 per cent, UK equities 8.0 per cent, and cash 4 per cent. This clearly shows the trade-off between risk and return.

Question 3.14

An investor has ten years until he intends to retire. Which would normally be more appropriate: investment in gilts or in equities?

5.3 Investors in fixed interest investments face **different types of risk** that can influence their returns, including **financial risk** and **credit risk**. Credit risk from a reduction in the creditworthiness of a bond issuer can be called a **non-systemic risk**.

Financial risk

5.4 Investing in fixed interest investments presents a number of risks.

(a) The risk that inflation will **reduce** the real return from the investment (**inflation risk**)

(b) The risk that interest rates will **move against** the investor and that they would have been able to get a better return elsewhere. (This is a **systemic risk**.)

(c) The risk that **sale of the investment** prior to the redemption date could result in an **actual loss** of capital

(d) Where the fixed interest investment is denominated in a different currency from that of the investor, there is a risk that **exchange rates** could move in the wrong direction to **reduce income** and **capital returns** (eg in sterling terms)

(e) If the government were to borrow heavily through new issues of gilts, the resultant increase in supply of bonds could put downward pressure on the prices of fixed interest securities: this is a **political risk**.

5.5 To avoid currency risk, an investor restrict investment to sterling denominated stock and, once purchased, hold it to redemption. For those looking to reduce the effects of inflation, **index-linked investments** can be purchased. These increase both the income and capital in line with the **RPI** and will provide an **additional interest payment** above this. This form of investment may or may not provide a better return than a normal fixed interest investment depending on the **level of inflation**. However, the difference in yields between normal fixed interest investments and similarly dated indexed linked investments is an excellent indicator of the market's view of inflation over the period to redemption.

Components of return

5.6 The choice of investment can have a real impact on the extent to which the above factors will influence the overall return. In order to minimise the changes in return, we are essentially seeking a security with low levels of volatility and the main measure of this with a fixed interest stock is called **duration.**

5.7 **Duration** is a measure of the average, cash-weighted term-to-maturity of a gilt or fixed interest security. There are two commonly used forms of the calculation, **Macaulay duration** and **modified duration**.

5.8 **Macaulay duration** is useful for constructing portfolios of bonds to fund a fixed or known liability (a process known as immunisation).

5.9 **Modified duration** is an extension of **Macaulay duration,** in that it is the ratio of the **Macaulay duration** to the inverse of the bond's yield. It is a useful measure of the sensitivity of a bond's prices (the present value of its cash flows) to interest rate movements.

Modified duration is often regarded as the best single measure of a portfolio of gilts or fixed interest securities' or an individual security's volatility (or exposure to market risk). One useful feature of **modified duration** is that it is a prospective measurement: it identifies a potential gain/loss in value before it occurs. As an example, if a security has a modified duration of 1.5, this indicates that if a 1% change in overall market interest rates were to occur, the value of a security will a change by 1.5%. **Modified duration** can be used with a variety of different securities and a figure of between one and three is considered to be low to moderate risk.

Credit risk

5.10   As discussed in the previous section, the **creditworthiness of the issuer** is a significant factor in the level of return provided by a fixed interest investment. The investor has to appreciate that the **risk premium** he is receiving from a slightly less secure issuer may ultimately result in a loss of interest or capital or both.

5.11   Taking this to the extreme is the **US junk bond market**. The popularity of this market is cyclical, but those seeking exceptional yields on their investments will buy fixed interest investments of 'below investment grade' when the risk premiums rise to high levels. The risk that several of the stocks in a portfolio will default are just as high and, in these circumstances, loss of capital and reduced interest on the portfolio as a whole will occur. It is important that investors in the fixed interest markets understand the implications of this risk and, in particular, the credit ratings given to investments by credit agencies. The definition of junk bonds mentioned above is a Standard and Poors rating of BBB or less.

Chapter roundup

- **Fixed interest investments** generate interest, usually at a fixed rate, until such time as the capital is repaid.

- Issuers of fixed interest securities include:

    ○ Governments - gilts, local authority bonds
    ○ International organisations - eurobonds, bulldogs
    ○ Banks and building societies - corporate bonds
    ○ Companies - corporate bonds

- **Gilts** are UK central government bonds, of short, medium, or long term (some are undated, so may never be redeemed). Coupons (interest) are paid gross. Gilts can be broken down into derivative instruments:

    ○ STRIPS (Separate interest income and capital repayment)
    ○ Repos (sale and repurchase)

- **Corporate bonds** are higher risk than gilts. They may be:

    ○ Debentures (loans secured on company assets with special terms and conditions)
    ○ Loan stock (often unsecured)
    ○ Demutualised building society perpetual subordinated shares
    ○ Preference shares (equity, not bonds)
    ○ Convertibles (fixed interest bonds which may be converted into equity)
    ○ Deep discount bonds (no interest - increased capital)

- **Eurobonds** are issued and underwritten internationally in a foreign currency.

- Fixed interest investments can be used:

    ○ To produce **income** (eg pensions)
    ○ To produce **fixed capital sums** (eg school fees)
    ○ To **improve tax planning**
    ○ To **reduce risk**
    ○ To **speculate** on capital market fluctuations

- Fixed interest securities can be issued by **direct issue to the market** (tap stocks), by **auction** or by **tender**.

- **Yields** are generally higher for securities with a short time left to run.

- Return of income or capital for fixed interest investments is affected by **specific factors** (coupon, term to maturity, options, tax status, credit rating) and by **market factors** (monetary policy, fiscal policy, comparative returns).

- Fixed interest securities are **priced** by reference to their nominal value. The investment return of a stock is quoted as its **running yield** (level of income) and its **redemption yield** (level of income plus change in value of capital).

- As with all investments, the level of risk affects the level of return. This risk comprises:

    ○ **Financial risk** (inflation, poor comparable returns, loss of capital on early redemption)
    ○ **Credit risk** (the higher the risk premium, the greater the chance of default by the issuer)

> **Quick quiz**
>
> 1 What is a eurobond?
> 2 What is a bulldog?
> 3 What is a gilt STRIP?
> 4 Typically which is the higher risk, loan stock or debentures?
> 5 What types of investment return does a preference share produce?
> 6 What fixed interest investment derivative can be used to speculate on interest rate moves?
> 7 What would be more preferable as an investment for a higher rate taxpayer, a gilt trading at above par, or one of a similar term trading at below par?
> 8 What might the gilt yield curve look like when inflation is expected to fall and remain low?
> 9 If an investor wanted to compare returns from a gilt with an equity, which yield figure would be most useful?
> 10 If an investor were totally risk averse, suggest a fixed interest investment that might be suitable for him.

The answers to the questions in the Quick Quiz can be found at the end of this Study Text. Before checking your own answers against them, you should look back at this chapter and use the information in it to correct your answers.

Answers to Chapter Questions

3.1 Long gilts are used to underwrite annuities, mainly compulsory purchase and purchased life.

3.2 Eleven, being ten interest payments (two per year) and the repayment of capital at maturity.

3.3 Repos give investors exposure to large quantities of gilts in exchange for the payment of a small premium.

3.4 Convertibles have the attributes of both. When there is a long time to run to redemption they behave more like fixed interest investments. As redemption nears, they take on more and more of the characteristics of the underlying equity.

3.5 A STRIP is a gilt derivative. Income and capital payments from gilts are separated into individual financial instruments. They are ideal for an individual seeking withdrawals from a pension as they can be used to provide a guaranteed income payment on a specified date. Each income payment can be purchased separately using capital from the pension fund.

3.6 (a) This would return 5 × £7 = £35 as income which would all be subject to income tax.

(b) This would return 5 × £3 = £15 as income which would be taxed and £20 as capital which would not be taxed.

Gilt (b) gives the better return for a higher rate taxpayer.

3.7 The greater the pessimism, the more pronounced the curve will be:

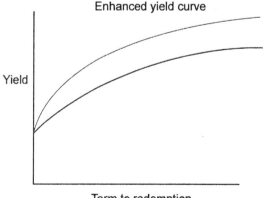

3.8 If base interest rates were 7% and an investor wanted to buy an investment with a coupon of 12%, the price would be

$$\frac{12\%}{7\%} \times £100 = £171.43$$

3.9 In order to achieve a yield in excess of the base rate, the yield would need to be 100/(100 – 6.8) –1 = 1.073 – 1 = 7.3% over the base rate to compensates the investor for loss of capital. Yields would need to be above this to allow for additional risk premium and make it acceptable to investors.

3.10 A tightening of monetary policy is deflationary and is usually accompanied by increasing interest rates. This will reduce capital values of fixed interest investments. Coupons will become less competitive relative to deposits.

3.11 A buyer would pay more than the mid-market price, a seller would receive less.

3.12 The running yield is £8/£115 × 100 = 6.96%

3.13 A gilt is purchased for £115 for £100 nominal value of stock, with five years to run. The nominal yield is 8%, therefore the running yield will be £8/£115 × 100 = 6.96%.

At maturity, the repayment of capital will be £100, some £15 less than the purchase price. This equates to a loss of £15/£115 over the five years = 13.04% or 2.61% per year. By subtracting this from the running yield of 6.96%, we get an approximate redemption yield of 4.35%.

Using a financial calculator:

PV	FV	PMT	P/YR	N
–£115 (the initial cost of the bond, –ve to represent cash outflow)	£100 (future value)	£4 (½ yearly interest)	2 (payments per year)	10, there are 10 six monthly payments

I/YR = 4.61%

Nominal★ EFF = 4.66%

★This is the effective rate

3.14 With ten years to run until retirement, the investor would be recommended to use both. He should increase the percentage of gilts to equity with each passing year, eg

Years to retirement	% of equities	% of gilts
10	90	10
9	80	20
8	70	30
7	60	40
6	50	50
5	40	60
4	30	70
3	20	80
2	10	90
1	0	100

PRACTICE QUESTION 3

Mr Smith has a number of gilts. State the level of risk and type of investment return he would expect to receive from this type of investment. Explain how you would compare the returns between different investments of this type. (9)

Chapter 4

EQUITY INVESTMENTS

Chapter topic list	Syllabus reference
1 Characteristics of equity investments	2.3
2 Methods of analysis	2.3
3 Company restructuring	2.3
4 Venture capital markets	2.3
5 New issues	2.3
6 Risk and return	2.3

Introduction

This chapter looks at **equity (share) investments** and examines the methods of assessing whether a particular share represents good value for the investor or not. We will go on to look at how companies can be restructured and the way that these issues affect their value. Later in the chapter, we will describe the ways in which listed and unlisted companies can raise money for expansion or development. Finally, we will examine the risks involved with these investments and the potential rewards.

1 CHARACTERISTICS OF EQUITY INVESTMENTS

The London stock market

1.1 The world's first joint-stock company - the Muscovy Company - was founded in London in 1553 and shares were traded in this, and other companies, via brokers in the Royal Exchange in London from that time. In 1760, the brokers were banned from the Royal Exchange for rowdy behaviour and a group of 150 brokers formed a club at Jonathan's coffee-house. Over time, this has grown into the **London Stock Exchange.**

1.2 The London Stock Exchange is the **fourth largest** in the world after New York, Nasdaq and Tokyo.

1.3 There are over 1,500 shares listed on the main domestic market in London and over 400 on the international market. A further 700 or so are listed on the Second-tier Alternative Investment Market. There are some **16 million private investors** in shares on the London Stock Exchange, which is quite unusual as these private investors make up a large proportion of the volume of trading. However, less than 20% of the market capitalisation is held by private investors, the rest being held by institutions.

Classification of equity investments

1.4 There are a number of different methods of **classifying equity investments,** covering various aspects.

- Market rating
- Size of company
- Sector
- Financial strength
- Cyclical influence

Market rating

1.5 Shares can be **categorised** by their **market rating.** Each stockbroker will rate the most popular companies' shares as a **buy, sell** or **hold** depending on its view of the future for that share. These ratings will **influence** the **demand** for the share, which will in turn influence **price movements.** Those recommended as a **buy** will typically increase in price, those as a **sell** will reduce. This also influences other factors such as the **price earnings (P/E)** ratio of the share. Highly rated shares will have higher P/E ratios than the sector average and the converse is true. When a stockbroker revises a company's rating up or down, the shares price can move dramatically.

Size of company

1.6 One of the most common categorisations of share is by size, or more precisely **market capitalisation.** Broadly, companies are split into those with large, medium and small market capitalisation (often called smaller companies) and the market uses a number of indices to do this.

1.7 The *Financial Times* publishes a series of indices, including the following.

FT 30	made up of shares in the 30 largest companies which together make up some 40% of the total UK market
FTSE-100	made up of the largest 100 companies by market capitalisation
FTSE-250	made up of the next 250 largest
FTSE-350	the FTSE 100 and the FTSE 250 combined
FTSE All-Share	the top 950 or so shares of 'larger' companies
FTSE Small Cap	an index made up of about 350 specific shares of 'smaller' companies
FTSE AIM indices	a series of indices relating to the Alternative Investment Market
FTSE Tech MARK All-Share Index	high growth medium and small cap technology stocks
FTSE Tech MARK 100	the top 100 technology shares under £4 billion by market capitalisation

1.8 There are also indices for European and international shares such as the FTSE/S&P Actuaries World series of indices and the FTSE Eurotop, which is a pan-European large cap index.

1.9 The relatively new phenomenon of the **index tracker funds** brings an interesting twist to modern markets. The fund managers purchase shares in the index being tracked and follow its movement. When a share is added to, or falls out of the index, this can influence the price of the share. This is because of the various tracker funds buying or selling the shares to enable them to track the index. For this reason many stockbrokers issue a **buy recommendation** on shares that are due for **future inclusion** in an index. Index tracker funds are examined in more detail in Chapter 9.

Question 4.1

How is the price of a share likely to move if it is dropped from an index and why?

Sector

1.10 The market is further broken down by the business of the **company issuing the shares**. This has a number of **advantages** for comparison purposes. Financial statistics can be compared for companies in the same line of business and the *Financial Times* publishes indices for **each industrial sector**. These represent a market average for the sector and can be used for comparison against individual shares.

1.11 **Index tracker funds** do not always reproduce the index exactly. Some use sampling and computer modelling to represent index movements. In these circumstances, representing the industrial breakdown of the index in the sampling or modelling is essential for accurate index tracking. It is not always possible for a unit trust to track the FTSE-100 index fully as some shares may have a market capitalisation of more than 15% and this is the maximum holding in any one share.

1.12 The main industry sectors used in the **FTSE Eurotop 300 Index**, and are:

- Resources
- Basic industries
- General industrials
- Cyclical consumer goods
- Non-cyclical consumer goods
- Cyclical services
- Non-cyclical services
- Utilities
- Financials
- Information technology

Each of these sectors is divided up further. For example, the 'financials' sector is broken down into the following further subdivisions:

- Banks
- Insurance
- Life assurance
- Investment companies
- Real estate
- Speciality and other finance

Question 4.2

What type of index could be used for a company that is active in several industrial sectors?

Financial strength

1.13 In the previous chapter we discussed how companies were **rated** for **creditworthiness** in order to ascertain the risk of investing in **fixed interest securities** issued by them. The same situation applies with **equities**. The higher the credit rating of the company issuing the shares, the greater the financial strength of the company itself. Some investors feel that they wish to **limit their exposure** to risk and only choose companies that are very unlikely to go into liquidation. The higher a company's credit rating, the less likely this is.

> **KEY TERM**
>
> The term 'blue chip' is often applied to the largest companies with the highest credit ratings, those normally considered of the highest financial standing.

Cyclical influence

1.14 Many shares are influenced by the **current phase** of the **economic cycle**. Some shares follow economic cycles, increasing with an upturn in the economy and falling with a downturn. These are called **cyclical shares**. Others move in the opposite direction and are called **counter-cyclicals**. Categorising shares in this manner can be very good for **portfolio management**, where one of the key objectives is to reduce risk. A portfolio made up of a combination of cyclical and counter-cyclical shares can **reduce the effect** of the economic cycle.

1.15 For both **cyclicals** and **counter-cyclicals**, the degree to which they follow the cycles will vary from share to share.

(a) Some will show slight movements, but may amplify the economic changes.

(b) Not all cyclical shares follow the economic cycle exactly, some will have a cycle that precedes it and others will lag behind.

(c) Investors seeking early information as to changes in the economic cycle will keenly observe shares that have historically led the economic cycle.

1.16 In most cases, **cyclical companies** are those which produce luxury items, such as cars, motorbikes, furniture and toys. The reason for this is that consumers delay purchasing expensive goods when the economy weakens, and buy when it strengthens. Many service industries such as restaurants, holiday companies, airlines and health farms are also cyclical and profits fall as consumers 'tighten their belts'.

1.17 **Counter-cyclical companies** tend to include products and services that are used when consumers do not wish to spend, such as DIY retailers, tool hire shops and discount stores.

1.18 Some companies are not influenced by economic cycles at all and mainly include companies producing **necessary items** and services such as food and utilities (water, electricity, gas, and telecommunications). These are all traditional refuges for investors in times of economic slowdown.

1.19 Large **diversified** companies looking to expand will often try to ensure that they have subsidiaries both in phase and out of phase with the economic cycle to ensure they remain profitable despite the economic cycle.

Question 4.3

Would you expect shares in breweries to be cyclical, counter-cyclical, or not affected by economic cycles? Why?

2 METHODS OF ANALYSIS

2.1 For individual investors and portfolio managers, shares chosen must have the **potential** to provide **good investment returns**. These may provide an increase in capital or an income stream, but they must be reliable. The only way to assess the extent to which a share will continue to provide returns is to look at the company accounts which provide us with a range of measures that can be compared to other similar shares, and enable us to determine the value of a share relative to others. These measures include:

- The reliability of income
- The potential for capital growth
- The financial stability of the company

Reliability of income

2.2 For investors requiring an **income** from their investments there are two key factors that need to be considered: the **level of income** required and the **potential for future increases**. In many cases, this will be a balancing act between level of income now and level of income in the future. A situation may even arise whereby a very high income now can reduce the prospects for future income. Information used to determine the prospects for income should be used carefully, preferably by comparison with other shares in the same sector to ensure a like for like basis.

Question 4.4

Why is it necessary to compare shares with others in the same sector in order to determine prospects for income or growth?

Levels of income

2.3 The term **equities** usually refers to **ordinary shares** in a company, rather than **preference shares**. The main differences between the two are that ordinary shares carry voting rights, whereas preference shares do not. The **dividends** paid out by each are also different as preference shares usually pay **larger dividends** at a fixed level. (The term 'preference' relates to the fact that, in terms of income and capital, preference shareholders will get their money before ordinary shareholders.)

2.4 **Dividends** payable by a company will usually be quoted in pence. The figure given is quoted net of a 10% tax credit.

2.5 The **dividend yield** quoted is net of the 10% tax credit.

Gross dividend yield = Net dividend yield × 100/90

Gross dividend values are used for Income Tax returns, so it is important to know this grossing up calculation.

2.6 EXAMPLE: DIVIDEND YIELD

Suppose that XYZ Company shares are trading at £3.25. The last net annual dividend was 20p, so to calculate the **net dividend yield** we use 20p (the net dividend figure) divided by the current share price. Therefore the net dividend yield is:

$$\frac{20p}{325p} \times 100\% = 6.15\%$$

In order to calculate the **gross dividend** yield, it is necessary to gross up the dividend first. Dividends are paid with a tax credit of 10%, so to gross up the dividend it must be divided by 100% minus the 10% tax paid.

$$\frac{20p}{(100-10\%)} = \frac{20p}{90\%} = 22.22p \text{ gross dividend}$$

To get the **gross dividend** yield, the gross **dividend** is divided by the **share price**. This figure should be multiplied by 100 to get it into percentage terms.

$$\frac{22.22p}{325p} \times 100\% = 6.84\%$$

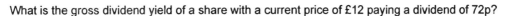

Question 4.5

What is the gross dividend yield of a share with a current price of £12 paying a dividend of 72p?

2.7 The **gross dividend yield** allows comparison with other types of investment. This is the figure usually published.

2.8 Care must be taken when comparing equity dividend yields to the yields on cash and fixed interest investments, because the dividend declared by a company may change year on year. **Dividend yields** are effectively a **'historical' measure** of yield as they only apply if the dividend issued in future is the same. One way around this is to look at the **prospective dividend yield**. To calculate this figure an estimate must be made as to the level of the future dividend which is then divided by the share price. Share recommendations and reports will often use prospective yields as they give a far more accurate impression of future returns.

2.9 Dividend yields illustrated on pages of financial information are only relevant for that day. The yield will be different for individuals who bought shares in the past, or who will be buying shares in the future, as the price they paid or will pay for the shares will not be the same.

Dividend reliability

2.10 The **reliability of dividend payment** is an important consideration. A company that pays dividends from reserves rather than income is not likely to be able to maintain them for any period of time. One of the **best measures** of dividend reliability is to look at the dividend in relation to income for the company. This can demonstrate the ability to continue payments at the current level or may even give indications as to possible increases or reductions in dividend payments in the future. The **ratio** of dividend payments to the income produced is called the **dividend cover**.

> **KEY TERM**
>
> **Dividend cover** determines how many times over the company could have paid the dividend based on current earnings. The figures for dividend cover are calculated 'per share', using the earnings of the company divided by the number of shares in issue and dividend payable. Dividend cover can be calculated gross or net. The latter is normally performed, and the earnings per share of the company are simply divided by the net dividend.

2.11 EXAMPLE: DIVIDEND COVER

Using the XYZ Company example again, the shares are currently trading at £3.25 and the last dividend was 20p. The income to the company in the previous year was £20 million and there are 15 million shares in issue. To calculate the dividend cover:

(a) Calculate the dividend = 20p (given here)

(b) Then calculate the earnings per share (EPS) = $\dfrac{\text{£20 million}}{\text{15 million}}$ = 133p per share

(c) Dividend cover = $\dfrac{\text{Earnings per share (EPS)}}{\text{Net dividend per share}}$ = $\dfrac{133p}{20p}$ = 6.65

(If you are given the price earnings ratio (P/E) it is possible to calculate the EPS figure by dividing the price by the P/E, eg assuming XYZ has a P/E figure of 2.44 then the EPS = 325p/2.44 = 133p)

2.12 The higher the dividend cover, the greater the certainty that the level of dividend payments will be maintained in the **future** and the greater the potential for **increases**. As was the case with dividend yield, figures may also be quoted based on prospective figures for earnings.

Question 4.6

Shares of NOP Limited are currently selling for £1.50. The last net dividend was 4p, and the current P/E figure is 10. Calculate the dividend cover.

Potential for capital growth

2.13 The **market rating** of a share will have a **major influence** on the price of the share. In effect, the market itself will evaluate the growth prospects for a share and participants in the market place will be prepared to pay a price that reflects that potential. This is most commonly represented by the **price to earnings ratio (P/E)**. In effect, the current price being paid does not reflect the current income provided by the company, it reflects the **potential for future income**. Consequently the greater the P/E ratio, the better the markets feel about the future prospects for the share.

Price earnings ratio (P/E)

> **KEY TERM**
>
> The **price earnings ratio** is the current share price divided by the last earnings per share figure. It is a historic ratio.

2.14 EXAMPLE: P/E RATIO

Using the figures for the XYZ Company, the price is 325p and the earnings per share (EPS) figure is 133p. The P/E ratio is 325p/133p = 2.44.

This is a low figure. Figures for P/E ratios of FTSE 100 shares in May 2005 ranged from 4.7 to 36.7.

2.15 Ideally, **P/E ratios** should be **calculated** on a **prospective basis**, using prospective earnings figures. P/E figures can **vary widely** with the market sector of the shares. As such, they should only be compared with other shares in the same sector to ensure comparison on a like for like basis.

2.16 Many market watchers carefully follow **P/E ratios**. There is historical precedent to suggest that when the ratios reach new highs, a market correction may well follow.

Question 4.7

At a particular time, the P/E for Barclays plc was 11.20. The P/E for HSBC plc was 16.05. Based on these figures, which of these two shares does the market rate more highly, and why?

Dividend growth

2.17 We can use dividends as the basis for determining whether a security itself represents good value for money based on the current and potential future dividend returns. **Gordon's Growth Model** is designed to do this.

2.18 The idea behind the model is that when analysing a security's performance, investors will draw conclusions about the risk and rate of return that they would find acceptable. For the purposes of this model, assumptions are made that the rate of return is dependant on the timing and amount of the dividend payments made using simple discounted cash flow principles. The model also allows for the rate at which the dividend rate increases, and this in itself provides a simplification of the assumptions required (as follows).

(a) The share will continue to pay dividends.

(b) The returns required by the market are greater than those provided by the dividends (ie the share price will also increase).

2.19 The simplified model is:

P =   d/r – g

Where: P is the price the share should be trading at

d is the expected dividend

r is the rate of return required by the market for shares with this risk rating

g is the rate of growth expected for the dividend

2.20 If we have a share with a dividend of 20p, with that dividend expected to grow at 10% (0.1) and the market requiring a return of 20% (0.2) for a share with this level of risk, we would expect the price to be:

20p/(0.2 – 0.1)= 200p

2.21 If this share were to be trading at 180p we would consider it undervalued. At 220p we would consider it overvalued.

2.22 Gordon's Growth Model can also be used in reverse, to calculate the expected returns from a security or a portfolio of securities based on security prices.

Financial stability of the company

2.23 The more **stable** the finances of a company are, the more reliable the investment returns from it are likely to be. There are four main statistics for analysing this.

- Net Asset Value (NAV)
- Company borrowing (sometimes called **gearing**)
- Company liquidity
- Cash flow

In many cases the information required for calculating figures can be found in the company accounts.

Net Asset Value (NAV)

2.24 The **Net Asset Value per share** is designed to look at the **underlying fundamental value** of a share. It looks at the worst case scenario, that of the company going into liquidation. The NAV gives an indication of what would be left to share amongst the shareholders after a forced sale of company assets. For most shares, the NAV will be **lower** than the **share value**, but shares can and sometimes do **trade** at a level **below** the NAV. This is particularly the case with shares in the investment trust sector.

2.25 Some investors take particular interest in shares trading at or below NAV in normal market conditions. When the asset value of a company is greater than the cost of buying it, it will become a potential **takeover target**.

2.26 To calculate the NAV, **the full value of all company assets, less liabilities, charges and provisions, is divided by the number of shares in issue.** However, some assets are not easily valued, such as trademarks and quality brand names, and in other companies the accounts may have purposely over or undervalued particular assets, making the NAV figure less relevant. The chapter on interpretation of company accounts examines these issues in more detail, but the calculation is:

$$\frac{\text{Current assets, less liabilities, charges and provisions}}{\text{Number of shares in issue}}$$

Company borrowing (gearing)

2.27 The **level of borrowing** of a company will have a serious impact on the way it can handle an economic downturn. The **greater the borrowing**, the **greater the interest payments** required. The higher interest rates rise, the more critical the level of borrowing becomes. During times of economic growth, high levels of borrowing can have a positive effect. The company effectively has more money to invest and the increased sales cover the interest payments. This is also known as having **increased gearing**. Either situation can effect the returns received by a potential investor.

2.28 The important issue with borrowing is the **amount of borrowing relative to the assets of the company.**

FORMULA TO LEARN

$$\text{Gearing ratio} = \frac{\text{Long and short term loans (less any deposits)}}{\text{Capital and reserves}}$$

2.29 A variation on the calculation, which is possibly more relevant to a shareholder, is the **level of debt relative to the equity held by shareholders** in the company:

$$\text{Shareholder gearing ratio} = \frac{\text{Long and short term loans (less any deposits)}}{\text{Equity held by ordinary shareholders}}$$

2.30 It is important to remember that in either case borrowing will include **fixed interest stocks** and **preference shares** issued by the company. For some applications, the figures are given in percentage terms (multiplied by 100).

Question 4.8

Company A has a gearing ratio of 10% and company B 20%. Which company is more likely to survive an economic downturn and why?

Company liquidity

KEY TERM

The **liquidity of a company** gives an indication as to whether the company can repay its short-term debts from its current reserves. It is effectively a measure of the company's solvency in the short-term. To calculate liquidity, current assets are divided by short-term creditors (those falling due within one year). Both figures can be obtained from the company accounts.

$$\frac{\text{Current assets}}{\text{Creditors falling due in a year}}$$

2.31 A **lack of liquidity** could indicate problems for a company in the event of an economic downturn. This could have a serious impact on the returns an investor might receive.

Cash flow

2.32 Without a steady stream of readily available cash, a company will go out of business. Companies need money to operate, so **insufficient cash flow** is a good reason for an investor to avoid a particular company. At the very least, **poor cash flow** can be an indication of **poor management**, which will ultimately reflect on investment returns.

2.33 It is very important to take care when **interpreting cash flow figures**. The level of cash flow required by a company will depend on the sector in which it operates. Cash flow figures should always be examined relative to the sector average or other peer shares within the sector.

FORMULAE TO LEARN

There are two possible calculations for **cash flow.**

$$\text{Profit-based cash flow} = \frac{\text{Profit before interest}}{\text{Interest payable}}$$

$$\text{Cash-based cash flow} = \frac{\text{Operational cash flow}}{\text{Interest paid}}$$

The figures for these calculations can be obtained from the company accounts.

3   COMPANY RESTRUCTURING

3.1 Investors and portfolio managers are required to take into account a range of issues relating to **how a company's ownership may be restructured**. Each will have a different impact on their holdings and may alter potential investment returns considerably.

Mergers and takeovers

3.2 Companies **merge** for a number of reasons: the businesses of the two companies may be complementary to each other, or the companies may be in the same business and wish to increase market share. A third alternative is that the company may wish to **diversify,** particularly if it primarily deals with a **cyclical industry**. Merging with a company with different cyclical influences can help to smooth profits throughout the cycle.

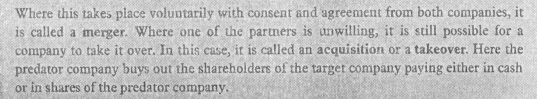

KEY TERM

Where this takes place voluntarily with consent and agreement from both companies, it is called a **merger**. Where one of the partners is unwilling, it is still possible for a company to take it over. In this case, it is called an **acquisition** or a **takeover**. Here the predator company buys out the shareholders of the target company paying either in cash or in shares of the predator company.

3.3   **Takeovers** are typically mounted by companies with **pro-active management** who will look to take over another company with less active management and so provide potential for growth. The **price to earnings ratio (P/E)** is often an indication of a suitable situation. As we said in the previous section, the P/E ratio gives an indication as to how highly the market rates the growth prospects of a company. Where there are two companies in the same business with different P/E ratios, the main difference in opinion is caused by the skills and ability of the management team.

3.4   A company with a **higher P/E ratio** may look to take over the one with the **lower P/E ratio**. The objective of this is for the merged company to take on the higher P/E with an increased overall value for the merged unit. However, although the P/E will often be higher than expected for a straight combination of the two companies, it may rise to that of the more pro-active company, given time.

3.5   For an **acquisition** to take place, more than 50% of the shareholders in the takeover target **must agree** to it. With a **merger**, 50% of shareholders in **both companies** must agree. To get this agreement, the shareholders will be looking to **benefit** in some way from the offer being made. This offer can be in the form of cash or shares (ordinary or preference) in the acquiring company.

Question 4.9

Is it possible for a company to take over another twice its size?

3.6   Whether shareholders in the target company will accept the offer or not will depend on the benefits offered to them.

(a)   In many cases, it will be a **premium** over and **above the market price** of the share and it is this factor that causes shares which are targets for acquisition to show substantial price rises.

(b)   The **form of the offer** may also have an influence as to whether the shareholders in the target company agree. If the company making the bid offers preference shares instead of ordinary shares, they are less likely to be successful. Preference shares are not popular with investors because, in order to buy other shares, they have to sell the preference shares first, giving rise to a capital gain and a potential tax charge. The situation is similar when a company offers cash but, in either case, an increased offer will usually work.

3.7 There is **no requirement** for the company bidding for an acquisition to **get consent** from its shareholders. Providing the company has access to sufficient cash to finance the deal, there will not normally be a problem, which leads to strange situations, such as smaller companies taking over larger ones. The source of finance for the takeover can come from any one of a number of sources, including raising the money themselves via rights issues and loan stock, borrowing from a third party, or even the release of un-issued shares to shareholders in the target company.

Panel On Take-overs And Mergers

3.8 In the UK, the body that **oversees** the process of merger and acquisition is the **Panel On Take-overs And Mergers (POTAM)**. POTAM has a series of set rules on the way this activity is conducted. It has set timetables for the process and a series of restrictions on the tactics employed. These issues tend not to be a problem for mergers, but are important for takeovers.

3.9 The **rules** overseen by POTAM are as follows.

(a) A bidder must **publicise** its intention to bid for a company once it owns **3%** of the target company. This is a Companies Act 1985 requirement.

(b) When a bidder has acquired **14.99%** of the target company, a period of one week must elapse before it acquires further shares.

(c) A further pause is enforced at **25%,** which allows the target company to consider the situation and communicate with its shareholders.

(d) When a bidder owns **30%** or more of the shares it must make an **offer for all of the remaining shares**.

(e) Once a formal bid has been announced the bidder has **60 days** from the day documents are posted to shareholders to secure the votes of more than 50% of the shareholders.

(f) The bid must detail the **full terms** of the offer including the cash or shares that are being offered.

(g) The voting process takes at least **three weeks,** as this is the minimum time that the bidder must allow the shareholders to consider their decision (within the 60 day period).

Decisions for the target company's shareholders

3.10 During the 60 days allowed for the bid, the target company will usually write to the shareholders. If the takeover is friendly, it may urge the shareholders to accept the offer. If not, it will usually set out why it feels that the shareholders should reject the offer. There could be a number of different reasons given for rejecting the offer.

(a) The offer is too small and **undervalues the company**.

(b) The management of the new company does not have the **interests of the company at heart**.

(c) The **independence** of the company is what gives it its appeal.

(d) That there would be a better fit with another bidder (a preferred alternative or '**white knight'**).

Question 4.10

If the management of the target company recommends a takeover, does that mean it will automatically take place?

3.11 Having been presented with the information from both sides, **each shareholder must decide whether to accept the bid or not**. There will be a number of factors to consider in making this decision.

(a) Does the **new management** have the ability to improve profits and growth in the combined company?

(b) Is the **value of the offer** appropriate with respect to the value of the company?

(c) Is the deal appropriate for the individual and what are the **capital gains tax** implications?

(d) Are stocks or shares, offered as part of the deal, ones that he would like to keep or will he need to sell them to **realise the value** and possibly incur a tax charge?

(e) Has the bid **increased share prices** to the level where it is worth selling (some bids collapse and the prices return to the pre-bid levels)?

(f) Is it worth rejecting the bid in the hope of a **better offer** from the same or even an alternative bidder?

Question 4.11

What are the problems with a bidding company offering preference shares as all or part of its offer?

3.12 Once all the factors have been weighed up and the decision has been made, the **shareholders** will either **vote in favour** of the bid or to **reject it**. If they vote in favour, then the acquisition will still not go ahead unless they are in the **majority of shareholders**. If a bid is rejected by the shareholders, it is still possible that an increased offer will be made by the bidding company, or an alternative one, which is then accepted.

Decisions for the bidding company's shareholders

3.13 It is important not to forget that there are two sides to the bid. **Investors and portfolio managers may be holding shares in the company making the bid**. In this case they will need to decide whether the bid is good news for the company - that the bid will improve the value of their shares and that they should hold - or whether it is bad news and they should sell. The considerations are similar to those for shareholders in the target company.

(a) Is the **cost** of the new company too high (aggressive bidding can drive up the prices) leading to a reduced share price for the bidding company?

(b) What are the **effects of raising the finance**? The further issue of shares or a rights issue can impact on key share valuation factors.

(c) Are the plans for the enlarged company **realistic**?

(d) Is the acquisition **necessary** - does it add something that was missing?

(e) Does the merged company provide the opportunity for **rationalisation of resources,** saving money or reducing costs?

(f)   Is the **management of the target company** important to the plans for the new company and, if so, will they stay?

Question 4.12

Do investors in a bidding company get a chance to vote on the deal?

Finance of mergers and acquisitions

3.14   When two companies **merge** by mutual consent, there is still a need to raise capital to 'buy' shareholders' approval in the target company. An **endorsement** from the management of the target company for the takeover will have **very little effect** if the shareholders do not feel that the deal is in their interest. Shareholders can, and do, vote against an agreed merger in the hope that another bidder with a bigger offer will emerge.

3.15   Both **mergers** and **acquisitions** require an **inducement** to get shareholders to agree. This may be in the form of cash, loan stock, preference shares or ordinary shares. The money to pay for this can be raised in a number of different ways. If the company has large reserves of cash, this can be used. The presence of large sums of cash in a business is often an indication that it is on the acquisition trail.

3.16   For those **without cash, a rights issue** can be used to raise cash from the existing shareholders. In order for this to work, they must be satisfied that the money is being raised for the right reasons, or they will not support it.

3.17   Another way to finance a merger or acquisition is to use shares that have been created but not issued and offer them as part of an 'open offer'. As an alternative, a company can issue new shares (ordinary or preference) or loan stocks subject to approval from existing shareholders.

3.18   Depending on the size of the acquisition, a bidding company may have to use **more than one** of the above methods to raise the required funds.

Analysis of mergers and acquisitions

3.19   In order to analyse fully the relative merits of mergers and acquisitions, a full investigation of the company accounts will be required. Fortunately, many stockbrokers will have already undertaken the appropriate research and rated the deal on the back of it. The analysis of most mergers and acquisitions will centre on the P/E figures before and after the deal.

3.20   EXAMPLE: TAKEOVER

ABC Company has made a bid for DEF Company.

	Shares in issue	Company earnings	Earnings per share (EPS)	Share price	P/E
ABC Company	15 million	£3,750,000	$\frac{£3,750,000}{15,000,000} = 25p$	£5.00	$\frac{500}{25} = 20$
DEF Company	16 million	£1,000,000	$\frac{£1,000,000}{16,000,000} = 6.25p$	£1.00	$\frac{100}{6.25} = 16$

ABC is offering one of its own unissued shares in exchange for 4 shares in DEF. Is the deal acceptable?

78

3.21 SOLUTION

After the merger there will be 15 million + (16 million/4) shares in issue = 19 million.

Earnings will now be £3,750,000 + £1,000,000 = £4,750,000

EPS will still be = £4,750,000/19 million = 25p

(a) If the P/E ratio remains the same at 20 then the price should remain the same at £5.00.

(b) It is highly unlikely, but if the P/E fell to the lower of the two (16) then the price of ABC will change to 25p × 16, or £4.

(c) The average P/E between the two is ((15/19 × 20) + (4/19 × 16)) = 19.16, giving a price of 25p × 19.16 or £4.79.

For the shareholders of DEF, if the P/E remains the same they will end up with 1 share at £5 for every 4 they owned at £1, a profit of 25% for them. If the P/E drops to 16, they will be no worse off and may well gain from future increases. If the P/E figures average out they will make a profit of $\dfrac{£4.79 - (4 \times £1.00)}{(4 \times £1.00)} \times 100\% = 19.75\%$

Shareholders of ABC are no worse off providing the P/E ratio after the merger remains at 20. If the P/E figures average out, their share price will drop to £4.79, a reduction of 4.2%. It is quite possible that the share would have an even lower rating immediately following the merger to reflect problems that may arise in bedding down the merger. This would result in a lower initial share price. However, this could rise with time and should eventually be offset by the fact that the merger should also provide future opportunity for growth. It is possible that the market will rate the merged company higher than ABC. In this case, both ABC and the ex-DEF shareholders will be better off.

Question 4.13

Why do the shares of bidding companies sometimes go down in value after a takeover?

Privatisations

> **KEY TERM**
>
> Privatisation is the conversion of state run companies to public limited companies in order to raise money, promote active management in the companies concerned and increase share ownership by private individuals. A further reason for privatisation was to remove the requirement for large subsidies to be paid to state-owned companies. The Conservative government in the 1980s actively used the policy of privatisation.

3.22 In many cases the companies concerned were **primed for privatisation** in advance by getting these, often loss-making, organisations to run at a profit. The money raised from share issues in these companies was used to write off debts for the companies and, in many cases, resulted in a good surplus for the government.

3.23 Individuals who purchased shares often saw **immediate profits** on their investments and the stag-ing of these new issues became a national pastime, with offers often being oversubscribed.   Supporters of privatisation suggest that even those who did not buy shares would benefit from greater efficiency from the firms, which through competition would reduce prices.

3.24 **Critics** of privatisation suggested that it **transferred assets** from all the people to just shareholders of the newly-formed company. There was further concern that the assets were sold off **too cheaply** (indicated by the rapidly increasing share prices) and that the only real beneficiaries were the shareholders. This argument resurfaces from time to time, as independent bodies continue to report on the costs and standards of service. In some cases (train services etc), the indications are that costs are increasing and standards are dropping.

3.25 This policy of privatisation has been pursued by UK administrations since 1979, and by recent governments in France, Japan (Nippon Telegraph and Telephone Corporation 1985, Japan Railways 1987, Japan Air Lines 1987), Italy, New Zealand and elsewhere. By 1988, **the practice had spread world-wide**, with communist countries such as China and Cuba selling housing to private tenants.

3.26 In the period 1980-93, the UK government paid **consultants** more than £258 million for advice on how to sell off nationalised industries and government services, and wrote off £15 billion of debt from 1979-95 in order to make state-owned companies more attractive prior to privatisation.

3.27 **Industries in the UK** privatised since 1979 include the following.

- British Telecom
- British Gas Corporation
- British National Oil Corporation
- British Airways
- British Airports Authority
- British Shipbuilders
- British Steel
- British Transport
- Powergen and National Power

- British Aerospace
- National Freight Company
- Enterprise Oil
- Jaguar
- Rover Group
- Water supply companies
- British Rail
- Docks Board

Demutualisations

> **KEY TERM**
>
> A **mutual organisation** is one that is owned by its members (customers) rather than shareholders. This includes building societies and some insurance providers.

3.28 One of the **key advantages** of mutual organisations is that they have **no shareholders** to satisfy and their major priority is to make money for members. The lack of requirement to distribute a proportion of their profits as dividends to shareholders is often cited as giving them a clear advantage. The extra money can be used to provide greater returns for accountholders (building societies) and policyholders (life assurance companies). In many cases, mutual building societies do **perform well** against their 'bank' competitors and the same is true of mutual insurance companies versus their proprietary competitors. However, there are also many proprietary companies amongst the top performers.

3.29 **Proprietary companies** would argue that, as they have to compete in an aggressive market place whilst keeping their shareholders happy by paying them dividends, it is **shareholder**

pressure that makes them **efficient,** improving the returns for their investors. Proprietary companies are also subject to different rules on issues such as liquidity and the ability to borrow, which can further improve efficiency.

3.30 One of the main reasons mutuals choose to demutualise is to **raise more capital** to allow them to grow more effectively. The demutualisation of Clerical Medical combined with its purchase by the Halifax (itself a demutualisation) injected some £800 million into the with-profits fund of the company. This money **increased the free asset ratio,** giving the company **more flexibility** in its choice of investments for the with-profits fund. It could now have a greater proportion of equities in its fund rather than property, bonds or cash.

3.31 For a company to **demutualise,** it normally requires the **consent** of 70% of its members where a postal ballot is used and, if there is a meeting, the meeting must give 60% support. Where the demutualisation is of a **friendly society,** the deed of incorporation regulating the society will **specify the percentage support** required for demutualisation. In order to secure this agreement, offers are made by the company to provide members with benefits in the form of cash, shares in the new company (ordinary or preference), or a combination of the two. Recent demutualisations have given benefits to the members ranging from a couple of hundred pounds to several thousand pounds.

3.32 When a company **demutualises** and becomes a **new company** in its own right, the company **changes its status** to a **limited company** and issues shares and any cash incentives to the members. Where the demutualisation is combined with a takeover by another company, such as with Clerical Medical and the Halifax, the incentive offered may be in the form of shares in the acquiring company. These could be ordinary or preference shares and may be accompanied with a cash payment. With the purchase of the Bristol and West Building Society by the Bank of Ireland, the incentive issued to members was a combination of preference shares in the Bristol and West and cash for long-standing members.

3.33 When **life companies** demutualise, the key asset of the company is the with-profits fund. One of the incentives to get members to agree to the process is to boost with-profits bonuses, and hence the value of with-profits policies, using the capital generated by the issue of shares. This can be combined with the issue of shares and/or capital.

Question 4.14

What form of incentive might be offered to encourage members of a mutual company to agree to a takeover by a proprietary company?

Management buy-outs (MBOs)

> **KEY TERM**
>
> A **management buy-out (MBO)** is a takeover of an existing company by its own management team. An MBO is an internal affair, unlike takeovers and mergers, and the management of the company raises sufficient capital to purchase the company from the current owners.

3.34 **Financing** such a venture is **difficult** because there tends to be very **little equity** and very **little security** for the lending, which often excludes conventional sources such as retail banks. As the borrowing has little security, it is very rare for one lending source to put up all the money. In most cases, the lending is shared by a number of different lenders.

Mezzanine finance

3.35 **Mezzanine finance** provides businesses with finance from several providers. Each different level of finance will have a different level of risk and, as the amounts of risk increase, the returns required by the lenders will be greater. Some will require a level of interest that increases with profit levels, others will require a share in the equity of the company. The ultimate sanction for lenders, to protect their money in such an arrangement, is a clause allowing them to take over the company if certain performance targets are not met.

Question 4.15

Would you expect a mezzanine finance deal to cost more or less than borrowing from conventional sources? Why is this?

4 VENTURE CAPITAL MARKETS

4.1 As discussed in Chapter 1, a good supply of capital is required to ensure good economic growth. However, there is a tendency for many lending sources to concentrate their efforts on lower risk lending. This will typically be secured by a fixed or floating charge over company assets. New business ventures tend not to have much in the way of assets to secure borrowing and it can be very difficult for them to get started. For these, the answer is **venture capital**, which may be sourced from wealthy individuals and companies with cash, or specialist Venture Capital Companies (VCCs). The principle of venture capital is that the lenders seek significantly higher returns than traditional lending which will often be in a different form to interest. The higher returns from the successful companies should offset the losses from those that do not survive and still provide a good profit.

Venture capital companies

4.2 **VCCs** are the **biggest lenders** in the venture capital markets. They are typically set up by large financial institutions as subsidiaries although they can be companies in their own right. Some are set up as investment trusts, others as finance companies. The large institutions are effectively investing a small part of their overall portfolio in this area to gain high returns. Providing it does not make up too large a portion of an overall investment portfolio, venture capital can provide **additional diversification**.

4.3 VCCs are set up with the business objective of providing finance for:

(a) **New** companies

(b) **Management buy outs (MBOs)**, where the management of a business buys the business from the owners

(c) **Management buy ins (MBIs)**, where an external management team buys a business from the owners

(d) **Expansion** of established companies

4.4 The **VCCs** providing the money will usually **negotiate** to **receive a share** of the company's equity and seek to **make a profit** by rapid growth in the value of its stake. Any money invested in a company is at risk. It may be lost if the company goes bankrupt, but the spectacular growth of the success stories will usually out-weigh the losses. VCCs operate at the conservative end of the risk finance market and will always endeavour to support a company that it is sure will survive. For this reason, they tend to favour MBOs, MBIs and expansion of existing companies as they represent a quantifiable risk. They also tend to deal mainly with larger companies and with investments of £1 million plus.

Business angels

> **KEY TERM**
>
> Business angels are private individuals who have money to invest (**risk capital**), and, typically, skills or experience to provide to a company just starting up. The sums of money involved could be £5,000-£100,000 or more. It is estimated that the number of active business angels in Europe is up to 1 million individuals and that the investment pool is up to around 20 billion Euro.

4.5 In return for their investment, business angels are looking for a **good return** on their money (growth rates of 20% plus per annum) and possibly a role in the new company, either acting as a consultant or a paid employee.

4.6 The relationship between the business and the business angel **benefits both parties**. The companies get their injection of capital and, often, the considerable business experience of the investor. This is of particular use where the business is based on an invention or innovation of one of the founders, which is not backed up by relevant business experience.

4.7 Business angels can work alone, or form themselves into **networks** and groups for the purpose of combining their marketing.

Question 4.16

An inventor is looking for finance to help her set up, market and produce her creation. Would a VCC or a business angel be more likely to offer her the money? Why is this and what form of return would the investor be looking for?

---

5 NEW ISSUES

5.1 A company will have **two main reasons** for issuing **new shares**:

- To **raise capital**, as is the case with a **new flotation**, a **rights issue** or an **open offer**
- To **adjust the share capital** or **share price** as in the case of **scrip issue** or a **share split**

5.2 In this section, we will examine each of these issues in turn.

New flotations

5.3 Companies issuing shares to the public via the stock market for the first time can do this in one of three ways.

- Via an **introduction**
- By a **placing**
- By an **offer for sale**

Introductions

5.4 With an introduction, a company will already have **existing shares** in issue, but they will be privately owned. For larger companies, there could be substantial numbers of shares already in issue. However, it will be **difficult** for these private investors to **buy** and **sell** the shares. An introduction to the stock exchange means that the shares can be actively traded in the market place. This course of action is particularly suitable for companies whose shares are already traded on a different stock exchange in the same or even another country.

5.5 Before allowing the share to be introduced to the stock exchange, extensive checks will be required to ensure that the company is **financially sound**. When a listed company goes into liquidation, it can have a severe impact on investor confidence, so it is in the interest of the stock exchange to take all appropriate steps to stop this from happening. If the stock exchange is happy with the financial situation of the company, the shares are introduced to the exchange and **trading can then commence**.

5.6 With effect from May 2000, the UK Listing Authority (UKLA) role was transferred from the London Stock Exchange to the FSA.

Question 4.17

PQR Company already has 1 million shares in issue. How would you expect the price of these shares to move following an introduction to the market? Give reasons for your answer.

Placings

5.7 A **placing** is a way of **issuing shares** in a private company that is seeking a stock exchange listing. The broker or issuing house will look for clients who are willing to buy large numbers of the new shares at a **fixed price**. The shares are offered to wealthy individuals and financial institutions rather than seeking applications from the public.

5.8 A placing can be used on its own, or in conjunction with an introduction. The advantage of this approach is that it requires no expensive marketing or advertising. The potential customers will be issued with a **prospectus** dealing with the issue. The fact that the shares are being offered to professional investors means that the prospectus only needs to contain the **details of the offer** rather than the 'glossy' information required to impress the public. A further advantage of this method of introducing shares to the market is that it is very quick.

5.9 Placings are **not suitable for all issues of shares** as the London Stock Exchange stipulates that, where an issue is greater than £30 million, a proportion of it must be issued to the public.

Offers for sale

5.10 An **offer for sale** is one of the most common ways of promoting a new issue. It effectively offers shares to a large number of private and institutional investors and is most suitable for very large issues, typically greater than £30 million. This method of offering shares ensures a **wide distribution** of shareholdings and ensures an **active and liquid market** in the shares when they have been issued. An offer for sale can be used on its own or in conjunction with a placing. There are three main ways to offer shares for sale.

- Fixed price offer

- Tender offer
- Subscription offer

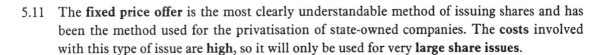

> **KEY TERMS**
>
> With **fixed price offers** shares are offered for sale at a set price which is easy to understand. This has an additional benefit in that it enables the issue to be underwritten.
>
> The process of **underwriting** is where one or more financial institutions agree to buy any shares unsold after the offer period. They will receive a set payment for this service, whether they buy all or none of the shares on offer. Without a fixed price, it would be far more difficult to establish an appropriate payment.

5.11 The **fixed price offer** is the most clearly understandable method of issuing shares and has been the method used for the privatisation of state-owned companies. The **costs** involved with this type of issue are **high,** so it will only be used for very **large share issues.**

5.12 The issue will be **priced to sell,** which has in the past lead to the offers being oversubscribed. This is enhanced by the fact that most shares will **move to a premium** on the first day of trading, attracting the 'stags' looking to make money quickly. In some cases the premiums have been so high that some investors, even public figures, have been tempted to break the law and subscribe more than once.

5.13 There is a **minimum requirement** for the offer to be **published** in at least two leading daily newspapers. In any event, the success of the issue will be dependent on how well it is taken up so the costs of publicising the issue through advertisements in newspapers and on television can be extensive.

5.14 A common feature of privatisations is that the basis of the allocation of shares has been known before share certificates have been issued. This has given rise to a **'grey' market,** an unofficial market trading in the shares before they are actually issued. Prices on the 'grey' market or from spread betting companies are quoted in the news and will normally indicate in advance the premium over the subscription price that investors are prepared to pay.

5.15 For some issues, it is significantly more difficult to establish an appropriate price and, in these cases, a **tender system** is used. The system effectively uses the prices tendered by potential investors to fix the price. In view of the complexity of the system, it will usually only be open to institutional and very large private investors.

KEY TERMS

Under a tender offer the issuer invites bids from investors, but indicates a suggested minimum price. Based on the prices tendered, the price will be fixed at a level where the shares will be oversubscribed. This ensures demand for the shares in the secondary markets, which in itself increases the liquidity of the issue. The result of fixing the price at this level is that successful subscribers will not receive the full number of shares they tendered for.

A subscription offer is a variation on the tender offer. It is used to float shares in a totally new business but the difference is that it allows the promoter to call the issue off if there is not sufficient interest in it. The main use for subscription offers is with the launch of new investment trusts. An investment trust is a company whose business is investing in the shares of other companies but it is important that the promoter of the issue should not lose money. As such the shares will be only partially underwritten by other financial institutions and they retain the right to cancel in case of insufficient subscribers.

Question 4.18

Which of the above methods of bringing shares to the market might be used for a very large privatisation? Give reasons for your answer.

Rights issues

KEY TERM

A rights issue is a method for an existing listed company to get additional capital from its current shareholders. New shares are created and offered to sale to current shareholders based on their current holdings. For each share owned, a rights issue offers the right to purchase further shares, for example on a 1 to 2 basis (1 new share for every 2 owned). They are used by a company to raise money for any reason, such as mergers and takeovers (discussed earlier in the chapter).

5.16 **Rights issues** are a UK phenomenon supported by the 'shareholder value model' of share ownership. Issues effectively **dilute the rights** of existing shareholders and can lead to a **reduction in current share values**. The UK approach is to offer the rights issue to current shareholders first to allow them to protect their investment if they want to.

5.17 The new shares issued will be priced at **below the current market value** of the share. This allows for any price movements between the time the rights issue is announced and the time it reaches the market. The objective is that the price should still be at a **discount to the market price** of the share. It is for that reason the UK favours the rights issues system. If the existing shareholders take up the offer, they will still own the same proportion of the company. If the new shares are issued at a lower price, they will get the benefit (which should average out with the value of their shares to leave them no worse off). If the new shares were issued at a lower price to new owners, it would give them an advantage. This is because the new shares will be the same as those already in issue, except at a discount.

Question 4.19

Dowelrod Engineering offers a one for four rights issue at £2.50. The current share price is £3.00. What is the likely share price after the issue?

5.18 Although the shares are offered to existing shareholders first, they are **not obliged** to buy them. The existing shareholders may sell their 'nil paid' rights to purchase the new shares to a **third party** (enabling them to recoup some of the discount) or, alternatively, may not act at all. If they do not act, their rights will usually be sold on the open market and they will **receive the benefit**. When the rights issue reaches the market, the price of the share will average out between the cost of the rights issue and the current value of the shares.

Shares	No. of shares	Price	Total value
Initial shares	1,000	£2.00	£2,000
New shares issued	500	£1.60	£800
After the rights issue	1,500	Average price £ 1.87	£2,800

A quick way of calculating this is as follows.

$$\frac{200p + 200p + 160p}{3} = 187p$$

5.19 Assuming the shareholder **takes up** the rights issue he will be no worse off than before. If he does not and **sells his rights,** he may be worse off. This will be the case if the rights sell for less than the drop in the share price.

For example, if he receives 15p for the right to each share, he will receive $500 \times 15p = £ 75$.

His new shares are now worth £1.87, total £1,870.

If we add the £75 back in, the new value of shares and cash is £1,945.

A price of 26p for the rights would be have been required to put him in the same position as before.

5.20 The above situation will only be the case if the market **averages out** the price exactly. In reality, this will not happen. The market may perceive that the issue is being made for the right reasons and will improve the prospects for the company. In this case, the new price will be higher than the average. The opposite can also be true.

Question 4.20

Instead of buying the shares in Dowelrod Engineering, the investor is offered 32p per share for his rights. Will he be better or worse off?

Open offer

5.21 An open offer is similar to a rights issue in that shares are offered to existing shareholders first. The main difference is that the rights to the offer cannot be 'sold on', so refusing the offer will dilute the current shareholders' value. This type of offer is used by Internet/ technology companies to raise money.

Scrip issues

5.22 The facility to make a **scrip issue** is particularly useful if a listed company builds up **large cash reserves** without any particular reason for using them. The issue of shares instead of dividends reduces the level of the reserves. The new shares can then be issued at no cost to the existing shareholders in proportion to their existing holdings, for example 1 for 2. A capitalisation issue is, in effect, a rights issue made **free of charge**, because the company has paid for it out of reserves.

5.23 This issue will **change the balance sheet**, reducing the reserves and increasing the issued share capital. There is no net gain or loss of money to the company, so the **Net Asset Value (NAV)** of the company remains the same. The value of the shares held by the individual shareholders remains the same, except that they now hold more shares.

5.24 **Restructuring** the company in this way will affect the measures of value applied to the shares. The **earnings per share (EPS)** figure will reduce in proportion to the number of shares issued because earnings will remain the same, but the number of shares will increase. The **price to earnings ratio** should stay the same. Although the change to the EPS will have an impact on the P/E ratio, the price of the share will drop, probably to the point where the P/E ratio is the same as it was before.

5.25 EXAMPLE: SCRIP ISSUE

Rodwell Engineering shares are currently priced at 40p and there are 1 million in issue. Rodwell announces a 1 for 4 capitalisation issue. The new price for Rodwell will be:

$$\frac{4 \times 40p + 0p \,(\text{the newly issued share})}{5} = 32p$$

5.26 The change in price can have a **positive effect**. Shares priced above certain levels can be described as 'heavy' or 'overpriced' and become less desirable, particularly from the point of view of the private investor. Companies in this position may restructure to bring the price down, possibly via a **capitalisation issue**. A share will tend to become more popular when it has a lower price, increasing demand and therefore the share's price, giving a better deal for the investor.

Question 4.21

Welldrow Engineering has a build-up of cash reserves that it wishes to give to back to its investors in the form of a one for five scrip issue. The share price is currently £5.00. What is the expected price after the scrip issue?

Share splits

> **KEY TERM**
>
> A **share split** is where a company replaces each share in issue with two or more shares. It can be used to achieve the same effect as a scrip (capitalisation) issue without the need to call on cash reserves.

5.27 After a share split, the nominal value of the share will be **reduced** in proportion to the new shares issued. All shares in the UK have a nominal value, as expressed in the full name for the share, eg Barclays plc Ordinary 25p shares. This value bears no relationship to the market price of the share (currently, 544p). The nominal value relates to the original equity in the company, and only has significance for accounting purposes.

5.28 The effect of a company performing a split on its shares is to reduce its share price in proportion to the new shares issued. As an example, if Barclays did a 2 for 1 split the shares would become Barclays Ord. 12½p shares. The market would initially value the shares at around £2.72, but this would change in trading, of course.

5.29 As mentioned with respect to scrip issues, the money price of a single shares may be too high and this may put off investors. In the UK, a figure of around £10 per share starts to have this effect although higher prices per share are more usual in the USA. A 2 for 1 split will bring the share price down to £5.

6 RISK AND RETURN

6.1 Of the three main direct investments - cash, fixed interest investments and equities - equities carry the **greatest risk** and correspondingly offer the **greatest potential for return**.

Income

6.2 The income produced by shares can **vary widely** depending on the type of share and country of issue but, either way, companies are not obliged to pay a dividend on their equities. However, very few shares that choose to pay regular dividends decline to pay them, even if this means dipping into reserves. The dividend income from a share effectively represents the profits of a company that it chooses not to reinvest. Because of this, and the fact that many do choose to reinvest profits, the actual level of income an individual can expect to receive from a portfolio is 2-4% on the capital invested. This can be increased if a portfolio is specifically chosen with the production of income in mind, but is seldom as high as the income available from other investments.

6.3 **Dividend income**, although being typically lower than that available elsewhere, can be attractive because it tends to **increase** with the share price. The **dividend yield** from a particular share will tend to remain the same, which means that as the share price rises so does the dividend. When buying a share, the investor is effectively **fixing the price**, with the result that in percentage terms relative to the original investment, the **income is increasing**. This can be very useful where the investor is living off the income, such as in retirement, as it will in most cases keep pace with and may even outstrip inflation. **Dividend income** is suitable for any application where the need for income increases, such as with school fees and nursing home fees, providing the investor is happy with the low initial yield.

Question 4.22

Dowelrod Engineering has traditionally kept its dividend yield at 3%. If an investor originally bought shares at £1.00, what rate of income return on the original investment will he be getting when the share price is £3.00?

Capital growth

6.4 **Equities** provide no guarantee of capital growth and there is an underlying **risk** of the total loss of capital invested. This is even the case where a company has significant assets. The reason for this is that the shareholder is the last in line for distribution of the value of assets if the company is wound up. This emphasises the value of the **Net Asset Value calculation (NAV)** as it gives an idea of the money that will be paid out if a company is wound up. However, it does assume that the figures have been calculated correctly. It has been known for a company to value its assets above that which is reasonably realisable. Other assets are intangibles such as quality brand names and the value of these is not easy to calculate. Effectively, the **maximum risk** for a shareholder is that he is liable to the extent of the **value of his shares**. He will not be required to pay further sums even if the debts of the company exceed the assets of the company.

6.5 Despite the risk, overall, **shares** have consistently **outperformed** cash or fixed interest investments, and have shown **substantial growth** even allowing for inflation. A number of studies regularly look at the comparative performance of gilts and equities. As a general rule these indicate that equities frequently outperform fixed interest investments.

The process of transformation

6.6 The **differences** in returns from the three direct investments can be used to illustrate the process of transformation that underlies the whole of the financial system. All three investments play their part and the differential in return between them is vital.

6.7 Many cash investors are looking for **instant access** to their money, or at least the ability to get at it within a clearly defined period of time. A bank or building society has many such investors. It can also be reasonably sure that they will not all want their money at once and can invest at least part of it into other direct investments. In this way, **short-term investments** are 'transformed' into those requiring a longer period of investment. In exchange for the longer term of investment, the **returns are greater** than the interest being paid out on the cash investments and the profits can be used to subsidise the running costs of the accounts and still provide a profit for the financial institution.

6.8 The Bank of England effectively underwrites the process by being the **lender of last resort** when a bank has a liquidity crisis.

The benefits of a balanced portfolio

6.9 There are clearly **risks with equity investment** and there is always the chance that individual shares can perform badly. However, a **reasonable sized portfolio**, spread over different business areas and geographical locations, can reduce the risk significantly. A skilled portfolio manager can gain the full returns associated with this class of investment and eliminate a large proportion of the risk by suitable share selection.

Chapter roundup

- Equity investments may be **classified** by:

  - Market rating (buy, sell or hold P/E)
  - Market capitalisation (small, medium, large - important for tracker funds)
  - Industry sector
  - Financial strength
  - How cyclical/counter-cyclical the share is

- The company behind the equity investment is **rated** for: reliability of income (dividend stream); potential for capital growth; financial stability (NAV, gearing, liquidity, cash flow).

- The **ownership** of a company may be restructured in a merger or takeover; this affects the price of both the bidder and the target company.

- **Privatisations** and **demutualisations** have stimulated the market and continue to do so.

- **Venture capital** is often vital for new business ventures which have few assets for security and little capital. This can be provided by VCCs or business angels.

- Companies **issue new shares**:

  - To raise capital (flotation by introduction, placing or offer for sale; rights issues)
  - To restructure capital (scrip issues, share splits).

- Equity investments are **riskier** than cash or fixed interest investment, but carry a higher average return in the form of income and/or capital growth in the long run.

> **Quick quiz**
>
> 1   In what way are the equity investors on the London Stock Exchange different to those of other stock exchanges around the world?
>
> 2   How can an investor tell how the market rates a particular share?
>
> 3   What would a share whose price moves in the opposite direction to the economic cycle be called?
>
> 4   What type of share is unlikely to be affected by economic cycles?
>
> 5   How might the income from a share with a dividend yield of 2% change in the future?
>
> 6   What is the main measure for the 'reliability' of a dividend?
>
> 7   What does the Net Asset Value of a share tell a potential investor?
>
> 8   What is financial gearing?
>
> 9   Why would it not be reasonable to compare cash flow figures from a bank with those of a retailer?
>
> 10   What are the main differences between a merger and an acquisition?
>
> 11   How many days does a bidding company have to take over a target company?
>
> 12   What are the main ways of financing a merger or acquisition?
>
> 13   What piece of financial information can be used to assess the markets feelings on a merger or acquisition?
>
> 14   Is privatisation a British phenomenon?
>
> 15   Who must agree to plans to demutualise a mutually owned company?
>
> 16   What is 'mezzanine' finance?
>
> 17   What is a 'business angel'?
>
> 18   What are the three main ways of issuing shares to the stock market for the first time?
>
> 19   What are the three main methods of offering shares for sale?
>
> 20   What are the main reasons for a company having a rights issue?
>
> 21   What sort of company might be interested in making a scrip issue?
>
> 22   How does a share 'split' differ from a rights issue?

The answers to the questions in the Quick Quiz can be found at the end of this Study Text. Before checking your own answers against them, you should look back at this chapter and use the information in it to correct your answers.

Answers to Chapter Questions

4.1   The price of a share dropped from an index is likely to fall. One of the reasons is that the funds that track that index will need to sell that share to replace it with the share that is replacing it.

4.2   For companies active in a number of different industrial sectors, it would be wise to look at the indices for all areas in which the company operates. The accounts of such companies are usually broken down by industrial sector so that such comparisons can be made.

4.3   One might expect breweries to be cyclical, as going to the pub is a 'luxury'. There is, however, evidence to suggest that they are neutral and some have even postulated that they are counter-cyclical. Although generally people tend to go out less during an economic downturn, the pub is a cheap night out. People also tend to drink more during an economic downturn!

4.4 Companies operating in different industrial sectors will operate in quite different ways. As an example, the financial services industry requires little in the way of expenditure on raw materials, because it is service based. Building firms on the other hand need to buy building plots and raw materials for houses. The accounts of firms operating in these areas will be quite different as will expectations on the income and capital growth from the shares.

4.5 The first thing to do is to gross up the dividend. With tax at 10% we do this by dividing the dividend by 100% – 10% (90%).

Gross dividend 72p/90% = 80p

Gross dividend yield in percentage terms = Gross dividend/Share price × 100 = 80p/1200p × 100 = 6.67%.

4.6 The dividend is 4p

To calculate the EPS we can divide the market price by the P/E figure = 150p/10 = 15p

The dividend cover = EPS/dividend = 15p/4p = 3.75

4.7 The market would appear to favour HSBC, as the P/E ratio is higher, at the time of the quoted figures. This means that buyers in the market place were prepared to pay 16.05 times the earnings per share for HSBC, but only 11.20 times for Barclays. The market may have been expecting better growth from HSBC and was therefore paying more for its shares on the basis of prospective earnings.

4.8 Company A. This is because its borrowing is only 10% of its assets, unlike B where it is 20%. In the event of an economic downturn, sales and profits will typically fall. This means there is less money available to pay interest on borrowing, so the more money that is borrowed the less likely it is a company will survive.

4.9 Yes, providing it can get more than 50% of the shareholders in the target company to vote in favour.

4.10 No, the majority of shareholders must still vote in favour of it.

4.11 Preference shares are considerably less popular than ordinary shares. Many shareholders will want to sell them and reinvest their money elsewhere and this action could lead to a CGT charge.

4.12 No, but they can always sell the bidding company's shares if they believe the deal is not good for the company.

4.13 There can be several reasons, but the actual cost of the offer made for the target company is significant and will impact on the accounts, and the ratios and figures derived from them. The other main reason is the investors' perception of the reasons behind the deal and whether they feel it puts the bidding company in a better position which may cause them to sell, reducing the price.

4.14 The offer can be in the form of cash or shares. The shares can be ordinary or preference shares. Demutualising life companies have an additional option, to declare an additional with profits bonus.

4.15 Lenders under a mezzanine finance deal are taking more risk than a conventional lender might, due to lack of collateral on which to secure the borrowing. With such a deal, the lenders that take the greatest risks will expect the greatest returns. The returns will probably not be in the form of straight interest, and at the highest risk levels the return is likely to be in the form of equity in the company.

4.16 It is unlikely that a VCC would offer her support as VCCs tend to favour large going concerns. Hers is also probably too small and would probably be too high risk. Business angels would be a more likely source of money, as they tend to deal with smaller and riskier ventures. In terms of an investment return, they would probably be looking to get jobs in the new company, to protect their investment, and would want equity in the company once it is established.

4.17 The price should rise. The increase in the liquidity of the shares will make them more attractive to investors who, after an introduction, would be in a position to buy and sell shares far more easily. This would normally increase the share price substantially.

4.18 Assuming there were a large number of shares to take to the market, an offer for sale would probably be used. The reason for this is that if it is a large issue, £30 million plus, then a proportion of the shares must be offered to the public. It is highly likely that the offer for sale will be on a fixed price basis. This is clearly understandable by the public.

4.19 $\dfrac{4 \times 300p + 250p}{5} = 290p$

4.20 For every four shares he has, the price will fall by 10p each, giving 40p. For each rights issue he sells, he will receive 32p. He will be 2p per share (8p/4) worse off.

4.21 $\dfrac{5 \times 500p + 0p \,(\text{the newly issued share})}{6} = 417p$

4.22 The dividend payable at £3.00, assuming a 3% yield, will be 9p. Based on an original purchase price of £1.00, the return is now 9%.

PRACTICE QUESTION 4

Mr Smith has a number of equity investments. State the level of risk and type of investment return he would expect to receive from them. Explain how you would compare the returns between different investments of this type.   (9)

Chapter 5

DERIVATIVES

Chapter topic list	Syllabus reference
1 Characteristics of derivatives	2.4
2 Options	2.4
3 Futures	2.4
4 Warrants	2.4
5 Covered warrants	2.4
6 Risk and return	2.4

Introduction

Derivatives can act both as investments and as a tool to alter the risk profile of an investment portfolio. In this chapter, we examine the main types of derivatives, the ways in which they are used, and the risks involved with the use of these investments, as well as the potential rewards.

1   CHARACTERISTICS OF DERIVATIVES

> **KEY TERM**
>
> **Derivatives** are financial instruments whose market value is derived from an underlying index, interest rate, or asset, including other securities. They can be used for investment in their own right, but in this role represent very high-risk investments. Derivatives were developed and are typically used for the management of risk as part of a portfolio and, as understanding of financial markets and risk management continues to improve, new derivatives are often created.

1.1   While many consider derivatives a **modern invention,** they have been in existence since the late 1600s, when Amsterdam traders used futures and options in the trading of Dutch East India Company shares.

Main types of derivative

1.2   There are two main types of derivative: **exchange-traded** or **over-the-counter (OTC).** Exchange-traded derivatives are more standardised and offer greater liquidity than OTC contracts, which are tailor-made to meet the needs of buyers and sellers. In this section, we will only be examining **'exchange traded'** derivatives.

1.3 There are many different types of **exchange-traded derivative** including:

- Options
- Futures
- Warrants
- Forward contracts
- Mortgage-backed derivatives (including STRIPs and REPOs)
- Structured notes
- Inverse floaters
- Caps, floors, and collars
- Swaps

In this chapter we will only be dealing with the three main types: **options, futures** and **warrants**.

Trading in derivatives

1.4 Derivatives are usually traded on **specialised exchanges**. In the UK, warrants are an exception. They are traded via the **London Stock Exchange** with other equities. Options and futures are traded through the **London International Financial Futures and Options Exchange (LIFFE)**.

1.5 Various countries have their **own exchanges**. Some will have two or more if futures and options are traded on different exchanges.

Country	Specialist exchange
Argentina	Rosario Futures Exchange (Mercado a Termino de Rosario) ROFEX
Australia	Sydney Futures Exchange SFE
Austria	Austrian Futures & Options Exchange (Osterreichische Termin Und Optionenborse) OTOB
Belgium	Belgian Futures & Options Exchange BELFOX
Canada	Toronto Futures Exchange TFE
China	China-Commodity Futures Exchange, Inc of Hainan CCFE
Europe*	EUREX
Finland	Finnish Options Exchange (Suomen Optioporssi Oy) FOEX
France	MONEP (Marche des Options Negociables de Paris) MONEP
France	MATIF (Marche a Terme International de France) MATIF
Germany	Deutsche Terminborse DTB
Hong Kong	Hong Kong Futures Exchange Ltd HKFE
Ireland	Irish Futures & Options Exchange IFOX
Italy	Italian Derivatives Market IDEM
Japan	Tokyo International Financial Futures Exchange TIFFE
Netherlands	Netherlands AEX-Options Exchange
New Zealand	New Zealand Futures & Options Exchange Ltd NZFOE
South Africa	South African Futures Exchange SAFEX

* **Note** EUREX is the combination of a number of different derivative markets including Amsterdam, Brussels, LIFFE, Lisbon and Paris. It aims to integrate all these markets into a single platform.

Country	Specialist exchange
Spain	Mercado Expanöl de Futuros Financieros MEFF
Sweden	The Swedish Futures and Options Market (OM Stockholm AB) OMS
Switzerland	Swiss Options & Financial Futures Exchange AG SOFFEX
UK	The London Securities and Derivatives Exchange OMLX
UK	London International Futures & Options Exchange LIFFE
USA	Chicago Board Options Exchange CBOE
USA	Chicago Board of Trade CBOT

2 OPTIONS

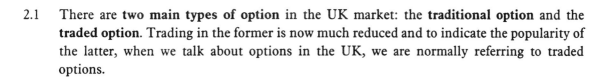

KEY TERMS

Options are standardised contracts giving the buyer the right, but not the obligation, to buy or sell an asset at a specified time at a pre-set (strike) price. They come in two varieties: calls and puts.

A **call** gives the right to buy 1,000 of a particular share or index at the strike price before a specified expiration date.

A **put** gives the right to sell 1,000 of a particular share or index at the strike price before the put expires.

2.1 There are **two main types of option** in the UK market: the **traditional option** and the **traded option**. Trading in the former is now much reduced and to indicate the popularity of the latter, when we talk about options in the UK, we are normally referring to traded options.

2.2 Outside the UK, there are **other differences in options**. UK options are similar to the American option, which can be exercised at any time up to expiry. In contrast, European options can only be exercised at the expiry date. There is an active market in the UK for European style options on the indices, where investors make use of the fact that they cannot be exercised prior to expiry.

Traditional options

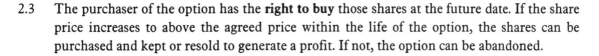

KEY TERM

With a **traditional option**, the holder of the share can sell the rights (an option) to the underlying shares, which can be taken up to a predetermined date in the future, for a premium over the current price.

2.3 The purchaser of the option has the **right to buy** those shares at the future date. If the share price increases to above the agreed price within the life of the option, the shares can be purchased and kept or resold to generate a profit. If not, the option can be abandoned.

2.4 Traditional options are **less popular** today, mainly due to the lack of liquidity in the market. Before the holder of the shares can sell his options, a buyer must be found. This is essentially a **primary market**, where the owners of shares sell options on their shares to those wishing to buy. If there are no buyers they cannot sell, or will at least have to wait until a buyer is found. Once the option has been sold, the holder of the stock has to wait until the purchaser of the option either exercises it or abandons it before they can do anything with the underlying shares. Traditional options are considerably **more inflexible** than their 'traded' cousins.

Traded options

KEY TERM

Traded options can be written as 'calls', the right to buy a fixed asset at a fixed price in the future, or 'puts', the right to sell a fixed asset at a fixed price in the future. In exchange for this right, the purchaser pays a 'premium' plus commission to the stockbroker. The main difference between these and traditional options is that they can be bought and sold at any time through an actively traded market place, which means there is a secondary market as well as a primary market. The purchaser of the option may exercise the option, sell it or let it expire.

2.5 Options are named by type, underlying asset, strike price and expiry date (usually the third Friday in the expiry month). If an investor buys the XYZ 1150 April Call at 20p, this means they have rights on the following basis.

XYZ	refers to the underlying share, XYZ ordinary shares.
1150	£11.50, the 'strike' price (the price at expiry) of the shares if exercised.
April	the date the option expires (on the third Friday in April) and must be exercised.
Call	this means the option gives the right to purchase shares.

The premium per share on the contract is 20p. Each contract is an agreement for 1,000 shares, so this will cost 20p × 1,000 = £200 per contract.

Question 5.1

The UVW 1200 July Call is currently trading at 103p. How much would it cost to buy three contracts?

Time value

2.6 Traded options are rarely exercised and not usually prior to expiry. The main reason for this is that each traded option has **time value** in it, so the longer the time to expiry, the higher the value of the option. If an investor were to exercise the option early, he would lose this time value. This can be seen by looking at a series of XYZ Call options with a strike price of £11.50, with different expiry dates.

XYZ 1150 April Call - premium 20p
XYZ 1150 July Call - premium 99p
XYZ 1150 October Call - premium 126.5p

Strike price

2.7 The other factor that affects the price of an option is the **'strike' price**, the price at which the option can be exercised. Looking at 2 XYZ Call options with different strike prices can demonstrate this. The share price at the time was £11.56. The 1150 option could be exercised for a 6p return, (known as the **intrinsic value**). The 1200 option has no intrinsic value. The rest of the value is **time value**, as shown below.

1.   XYZ 1150 April Call - premium 20p   <u>6p</u> **Intrinsic value**
                                            <u>14p</u> Time value
                                            <u>20p</u>

2.   XYZ 1200 April Call - premium 4p   All **time value**

2.8 There are specific terms to describe the **relative value** of the **current share price** and the **strike price**. Where the option is trading at above the strike price with a call, or below it with a **put,** they are described as being **in the money.**

2.9 If the option is currently standing at a loss (the share price is **below** the strike price with a **call,** or **above** with a **put**), this is described as being **out of the money.** Where the strike price and share price is the same the option is described as being **at the money.** The value of the option in each case is made up solely of time value.

2.10 Broadly speaking, the above terms give an indication of the potential **risk/reward ratio** of each. The **highest risk** options are typically **out of the money** The chances of them giving a return rely on significant movements in the share price. If this does not happen, they will **expire worthless.** To reflect the higher risk, the **premium** for the option will be **lower.** If the share price does move in the expected direction, the percentage **returns** on money invested can be **very high.**

Question 5.2

Which of the following options would probably be the lowest risk?

    UVW 1200 July Call @ 103p
    UVW 1250 July Call @ 77.5p

The current price of UVW is 1204p.

2.11 The further **'in the money'** an option is, the more chance there is of a **return at expiry.** To reflect this, the **premium** will be **higher.** However, the percentage returns made will be **smaller** than with an 'out of the money' option.

Expiry

2.12 If the investor holds the **option to expiry,** he has a **choice.** He can **receive the profit** on the option or he can **exercise the option.** With a **call option,** this will involve **paying the strike price** after which he will receive the shares. With a **put option,** he will deliver the shares in **return for the strike price** for them.

2.13 In practice, most options **expire worthless,** which is one of the reasons they are **high risk** as an investment in their own right.

Uses of options

2.14 Options can be used for any of the following purposes.

- As an **investment**
- To **hedge** against the price movements of assets within a portfolio
- To **anticipate cash flow**
- To provide **fast access to inaccessible markets**

Options as an investment

2.15 Options are a **versatile investment** as they can be traded or exercised as required. Many investors **buy** and **sell** them and **never exercise** them, but use them as an **investment** in their own right. Used in this way, options can provide **large returns** for a very **small investment**, but the **risk** to the invested capital is **very high**. Options provide all their return in the form of an **increase in capital**, they produce **no income payments**.

2.16 EXAMPLE: OPTIONS AS INVESTMENTS

If an investor thinks a share will rise in value, options could provide a very good return. As an example, if an investor thought XYZ Company shares, currently priced at £11.50, would be priced at £12.00 at the end of April, he may be able to buy the 1150 April Call at (say) 20p.

The cost of one contract would be £200 (20p x 1,000). This effectively gives him exposure to 1,000 XYZ shares, which would normally have cost £11,500. The most he can lose with the option is the £200 premium and he could gain a lot more. If the shares make it to £12.00 he will receive 50p for each share at the expiry of the option (50p × 1,000 = £500). For an investment of £200, he has received a return of £500, a return of 250% on the capital employed, compared with a 10.4% gain if he had held the shares directly.

2.17 The **profits made** are very much tied in with the **price on expiry**. Figure 1 shows the return per share depending on the share price of XYZ at expiry.

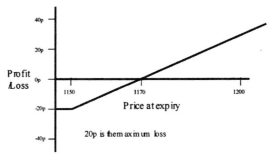

Figure 1 Call traded option price at expiry vs profit/loss per share

2.18 Options are similar to betting in risk terms, but they are very good for **speculating on short-term share price changes**. As an investment, the **dealing costs are low** relative to the value of underlying assets. They can be dealt with far more quickly than purchasing the underlying asset (especially when purchasing an index) and a **small increase** in the **value of the underlying asset** can yield a **large increase** for the investor.

2.19 If a **portfolio manager** thinks that a market may fall, but does not wish to miss out on any growth, it is possible to switch his investments into cash or fixed interest investments. A small proportion of the fund, eg 10%, can be used to buy options in the shares that the portfolio was originally invested in. If the markets fall, 90% of the money will be safe. If it rises, the options will gain in value and assuming they are appropriately geared will provide a similar return to having the whole of the portfolio invested.

Question 5.3

What is the maximum loss that could be made on the purchase of a UVW 1200 July Call contract at 103p?

Options for hedging

> **KEY TERM**
>
> If an investor feels there is a risk that share prices will move down but is not in a position to sell, for example due to a CGT liability arising, options can be used to reduce the risk. Reducing risks is called **hedging**.

2.20 EXAMPLE: OPTIONS AS HEDGES

If an investor holds 1,000 XYZ shares currently at £11.50 and he thinks they are going to go down, he can avoid selling by using a 'put' option. The XYZ 1150 April Put is selling at 14p, one contract would cost 1,000 × 14p = £140. This would give the right to sell shares at 1150 whatever happens to the price. If the price falls to 1100 by expiry, he will receive 50p per share. If this is settled as cash, he does not have to deliver the shares. If the price moves the other way, the maximum he can lose is the premium paid, 1,000 X 14p = £140.

If the value of his XYZ shares is now £11,000, he has lost £500 from the original value. The options will provide him with 1,000 × 50p = £500, but he paid a premium of £140. The net affect is that his shares are worth £11,000 and the profit on his options is £360 making a total of £11,360. This has given him a measure of protection against the fall.

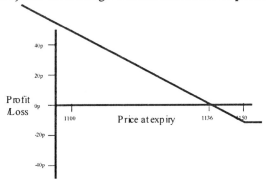

Figure 2 Put traded option price at expiry vs profit/loss per share

Question 5.4

What is the maximum loss that can be made on an XYZ 1200 April Put contract purchased at 44p?

Use of options to anticipate cash flow

2.21 This works in the same way as hedging. A manager, anticipating the arrival of a sum of money into the portfolio and who feels that the market could move significantly before it arrives, can buy options to get the benefit of any movement between now and **the time the money arrives** at minimal cost.

Writing options

2.22   So far, we have only considered the **purchase of options**, but as with all financial instruments, there must be **buyers and sellers**. **Selling options** is called '**writing**' and this process provides the seller with a very different form of investment.

2.23   For an **option buyer**, the **maximum loss** is the **amount of the premium**. The **maximum loss for a seller** is, theoretically, **unlimited**. When an option is sold, the seller receives the premium and will pay commission to his stockbroker. On writing options, there will also be a requirement for the payment of **margin**, which is a guarantee to the exchange clearing house that he will meet his commitment. (We will discuss this in more detail later.)

2.24   Writing options is a very **valuable alternative** for a **fund manager** to **produce additional income**. Statistically, 95% of options expire worthless, which means that in 95% of cases the writer receives the premium without having to do anything. When a '**call**' option is written, the maximum profit for the writer is the amount of the premium, but the maximum loss is unlimited, for example, with the XYZ 1150 April Call at 20p.

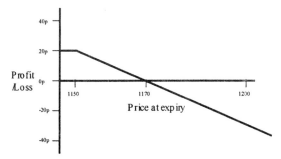

Figure 3 Call traded option writing price at expiry vs profit/loss per share

2.25   As the price increases above £11.50, the level of profit will fall. At £11.50 and above, at expiry the option may be exercised. If the price is up to £11.70, the fund manager can offset the premium received against any loss. Where the share price is above this level at expiry, the losses will increase and are technically unlimited. If the manager holds the shares, this is not a problem, because he can either deliver the shares, or sell them to cover the liability. If he does not own the shares, he is described as writing '**uncovered**' **options**.

Question 5.5

What is the maximum loss that could be made on the writing of a UVW 1200 July Call contract at 103p?

2.26   When a '**put**' option is written, the maximum profit for the writer is the level of the premium. The maximum loss is limited to the strike price of the share less the premium paid.

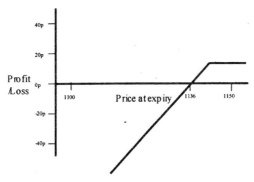

Figure 4 Put traded option writing price at expiry vs profit/loss per share

As the share price drops below the strike price, the option may be exercised. Down to £11.36 this is offset by the premium but, below this level, the fund manager will be expected to buy the shares at £11.50. This sets the maximum loss at £11.36 as they have received the 14p premium, and assumes the shares are worthless at expiry.

2.27 Where there are sufficient funds, and there is an intention to purchase the underlying shares, writing **'put'** options can be low risk.

Question 5.6

What is the maximum loss that can be made on writing an XYZ 1200 April Put contract at 44p?

3 FUTURES

KEY TERM

A 'future' is a contract to buy or sell a standard quantity and quality of an asset or security at a specified date and price. Originally, futures were based on physical assets such as cocoa or gold but a large number of contracts written today are based on financial assets, such as the value of an index or a gilt series. Futures are similar to forward contracts, but are standardised, traded on an exchange, and are valued (or 'marked to market'). The 'marking to market' provides both parties with a daily accounting of their financial obligations under the terms of the futures. The counterparty to a futures contract is the clearing corporation on the appropriate exchange. Futures are often settled in cash or cash equivalents, rather than requiring physical delivery of the underlying asset.

3.1 As a future is a **contract,** buyers and sellers must be matched exactly and it is the role of the **clearing house** to ensure this happens. As a contract, in theory, the goods on a commodity future must be delivered. In reality, however, 99% of futures transactions do not result in the delivery of the asset. The individual concerned will purchase an equal, but opposite, future cancelling out the transaction. Contracts can be bought or sold. The **buyer** is described as being **'long'** and will have to buy the goods if the contract goes full term. The **seller** is described as **'short'** and will have to supply the goods if the contract goes full term.

3.2 Where the **futures contract** is **not cancelled** out before expiry, it must be **settled for cash,** or **delivery of the physical asset.** The seller has to deliver to the buyer the appropriate quantity and quality of the physical asset and, in exchange, the buyer must pay the closing price of the futures contract on the date of expiry.

3.3 Where **futures contracts** relate to **non-physical assets** such as those based on bonds, interest rates and indices, they will be settled for a **cash payment** known as the **Exchange Delivery Settlement Price (EDSP)**.

Contract specification

3.4 Every contract will have an **individual specification**. This is issued by the exchange on which it is traded.

Exam focus point

The G70 examination has, in the past, asked specific questions on the FTSE 100 Index Future, which is traded on the London International Financial Futures and Options Exchange (LIFFE). Here is the specification.

FTSE 100 Index Future Specification

Unit of trading:	Valued at £10 per index point (eg value £50,000 at 5,000.0)
Delivery months:	March, June, September, December (nearest 3 available for trading)
Delivery day:	First business day after the Last Trading Day
Last Trading Day:	10.30 - Third Friday in delivery month
Quotation:	Index points
Minimum price movement:	0.5 (this is the 'tick')
Tick value:	£5.00
Trading hours:	08.00 - 17.30
Contract standard:	Cash settlement based on the Exchange Delivery Settlement Price.
Exchange Delivery Settlement Price (EDSP):	
	The EDSP is based on the average values of the FTSE 100 Index every 15 seconds inclusively between 10.10 and 10.30 (London time) on the last trading day. Of the 81 measured values, the highest 12 and lowest 12 will be discarded and the remaining 57 will be used to calculate the EDSP. Where necessary, the calculation will be rounded to the nearest half index point. In the event of the third Friday not being a business day, the last trading day shall normally be the last business day preceding the third Friday.

3.5 EXAMPLE: FUTURES CONTRACT SPECIFICATION

If a fund manager bought one FTSE 100 futures contract when the FTSE stood at 5,000 points, the value of this contract is (£10 × 5,000) or £50,000. The fund manager has effectively bought into the movement of £50,000 worth of shares. If the FTSE moves to 5,500, the contract is now worth (£10 × 5,500) or £55,000, so he has made £5,000. If the FTSE moves to 4,500, the contract is now worth (£10 × 4,500) or £45,000, and he has lost £5,000. In order to participate in this movement he will need to put down a **margin payment**.

Question 5.7

What is the value of a FTSE 100 contract when the market stands at 5,750?

Margin and counterparty risk

3.6 In order to ensure that participants in options contracts and the writers of option contracts can fulfil their obligations, they are required to **place money** (or suitable investments such as **gilts**) with their brokers who pass it on to the **clearing house**. This system of payments **minimises the risk** that the counterparty will not meet their side of the contract (**counterparty risk**). On the following working day after the contract has been purchased, the buyers and sellers are required to place an initial amount of money (known as **initial margin**) which will cover some or all of their liability as a result of price movements for the previous day. The **level** of this initial margin is **pre-set** and the level required **varies** between each type of contract, but as an example the margin on a FTSE 100 Index contract is £2,500. Any outstanding balance of margin will be repaid when the contract is cancelled or expires.

3.7 The **value of the contract** will **vary** on a daily basis and ongoing losses must be covered by further margin payments. This money is called '**variation margin**' and must be deposited by close of business on the following day. These transactions take place on a day-by-day basis with daily losses and gains credited to the trader's **variation margin account**. The effect of this is that, by the time the contract is closed out, almost the full amount of any profits or losses has already been credited.

3.8 When market volatility exceeds pre-determined levels, there may be a call for additional margin known as '**intra day margin**'.

3.9 If a trader **does not meet** any of the above **calls for margin** then the exchange will **close** all of his open positions immediately to stop further losses.

The clearing house system

3.10 The **clearing house** matches the buyers and sellers of futures and options. To do this, it must ensure that all transactions for purchases and sales correspond. It must also ensure that all contracts are honoured via the clearing members of the exchange and that the appropriate margin payments have been made to cover positions where one of the counterparties is at risk.

Uses of futures

3.11 Futures can play the same roles for managers of portfolios as **options**.

4 WARRANTS

> **KEY TERM**
>
> **Warrants** work in the same way as options, but will tend to be written over longer periods of time. They confer on the holder the right to buy shares at a future date at a fixed price. If on that date the price exceeds the fixed price on the warrants, the investor will exercise his rights and buy the shares. The shares can then be sold or kept if required.

4.1 A company may **issue warrants** and there is both a **primary** and a **secondary market** in them. Warrants are financial instruments in their own right and can be sold on. A warrant does **not produce income** and will only provide an investment return in the form of a **capital gain** (or loss) when sold or exercised. Warrants are highly geared investments and present a **very high risk**, but also a very great potential for reward.

4.2 Warrants can be issued in conjunction with any share, but one of the **key uses** of warrants in the UK is with **investment trusts**. **Investment trusts** are companies whose business is buying and selling the shares of other companies. As they are shares in their own right, they are subject to supply and demand in the market place. Where demand falls, so does the price. The **market capitalisation** of an investment trust can fall to **below its Net Asset Value (NAV)**.

4.3 Where the **discount to NAV** is very **high**, the investment trust may decide to act to **stimulate demand**. One option is to **split their trust** into a number of different financial instruments including warrants. As each of these financial instruments will appeal to different investors, the demand increases. Investment trusts also sometimes issue warrants as a 'sweetener' with a new issue of shares, to provide some compensation for the fact that the shares may trade at a discount to the net asset value.

4.4 **Warrants** can be **purchased** in the **same way as shares** through a stockbroker. Stockbrokers require investors who want to trade warrants to sign a **Warrants Risk Notice**. This explains that warrants can be a **very-risky investment** and, by signing it, the investor is accepting the consequences of investing in this high-risk instrument.

4.5 From the point of view of an investor in a company that has issued **warrants**, it is important to take into account the effects on individuals exercising them. This will result in an increase in the numbers of shares, with no increase in underlying capital. There is effectively a dilution of share capital.

5 COVERED WARRANTS

> **KEY TERM**
>
> **Covered warrants** are unlike ordinary warrants in that they are issued by financial institutions and are based on an underlying asset which may be a share or an index. Covered warrants give the holder the right but not the obligation to buy (call) or sell (put) the underlying asset at a specific (strike) price. Settlement can be in the form of the underlying asset or for cash (particularly for indices, as there is no specific underlying asset).

5.1 **Covered warrants** were introduced to the UK markets in 2002.

5.2 One attractive feature of assets purchased by exercising the right to buy is that they are free of stamp duty. Covered warrants are however fully subject to Capital Gains Tax.

5.3 Covered warrants allow investors to take a position in a range of shares and a number of stock market indices, for example the FTSE-100 Index, the Techmark Index or the Dow Jones Industrial Average. If an investor thinks that the **underlying asset** or **index** is going to **rise**, they can purchase a **call**, and if they think it will **fall**, they can purchase a **put**.

5.4 Covered warrants are **similar** to traded options in that they are purchased in call and put form, are based on an underlying asset or index, and have a strike price. In addition to this they may be **American style** (can be exercised at any time) or **European style** (can only be exercised at the end of the term). If the warrants are exercised early, the time value will be lost. Covered warrants are **dissimilar** to traded options in that they may have expiry dates which are years rather than months away. This allows a greater time for the investment to move in the required direction.

5.5 Example: Covered warrant issued by Société Générale Group

Underlying	Type	Spot	Strike	Expiry	Parity	Bid	Ask	Gearing	Change	EPIC code
FTSE 100	Call	4084	4500	20 Jun 03	1000	19.8	20.1	20.5x	+6.40% ↑	S502

5.6 Here are explanations of the information in the table.

FTSE-100	The underlying asset, in this case the FTSE 100 index
Call	The type of warrant – this one provides a right to buy
Spot	The current level/price of the underlying (FTSE 100)
Strike	The level at which the warrant can be exercised. In this case the spot (the current level of the FTSE-100) was 4084 and the strike was 4500. This option is 'out of the money' because the strike price is higher than the spot. If the FTSE-100 Index rises to 4600, the option will be 'in the money'.
Expiry	The date at which the warrant expired, 20 June 2003
Parity	The number of warrants you would need to buy to reflect one share in the underlying asset in full, also called the conversion ratio. (For an index, a 'share' in the index represents £1 per point. So, in this case, 1000 warrants must be bought to reflect a holding of £4,084 in the FTSE-100 Index.)
Bid	The selling price of the warrant
Ask	The buying price of the warrant
Gearing	The ratio of the rate at which the warrant will move relative to the underlying asset. If the FTSE-100 Index rises or falls by 1%, this warrant can be expected to rise or fall in value by approximately 20.5%
Change	Today's change in the value of the warrant
Epic	A code used by the Stock Exchange to identify a stock

5.7 Where the current (spot) price of the underlying is above the strike price of the warrant, there is some 'intrinsic' value but the total price will be greater than this intrinsic value. This additional element of the price reflects the time value. This is the additional value in view of the fact that the warrant has until its expiry date to increase or decrease in value and generate a profit. Where a covered warrant is out of the money, it has no intrinsic value and the premium is all time value.

5.8 Further examples

Underlying	Type	Spot	Strike	Expiry	Parity	Bid	Ask	Gearing	Change	EPIC code
Vodafone	Call	115	50	02 Jul 03	1	66.4	66.6	1.7x	-1.19% ↓	S001
Vodafone	Call	115	100	02 Jul 03	1	29.8	30.1	3.8x	-2.44% ↓	S002
Vodafone	Put	115	90	02 Jul 03	1	9.6	9.9	11.8x	-1.52% ↓	S003
Vodafone	Call	115	110	05 Nov 03	1	28.9	29.2	4.0x	-1.69% ↓	S004
Vodafone	Put	115	80	05 Nov 03	1	9.7	10.0	11.7x	+0.51% ↑	S005
Vodafone	Call	116	130	05 Nov 03	1	20.8	21.4	5.5x	-1.40% ↓	S006
Vodafone	Call	115	150	03 Mar 04	1	19.3	19.6	5.9x	-1.02% ↓	S007

5.9 (a) The warrant with EPIC code S001 has a spot of 115 and a strike of 50. This covered warrant is 65p 'in the money': it has 65p in intrinsic value. The bid price is 66.4p. Therefore there is 1.4p in time value.

   (b) S004 has a spot of 115 and a strike of 110. It has 5p in intrinsic value. It has a total value of 28.9p. Therefore the extra over the 5p is made up of time value (23.9p).

   (c) S007 is 'out of the money' as the spot is lower than the strike. The total value of 19.3p is made up of time value.

5.10 In terms of risk, the whole of the premium paid for the covered warrant (but no more) is at risk. Unlike spread betting, financial futures or writing options, there is no margin requirement and there is no risk of losing more money than has been invested.

5.11 Covered warrants represent a low cost method of investing in individual shares and are a convenient way of investing in an index. They can be used in a number of ways.

   (a) Simple investment – where an investor feels that a share or index will rise, they represent a low cost method of participating in the rise.

   (b) They can be used if an investor thinks a share or index will fall, by using the 'put' type of warrant.

   (c) They can be a risk management tool, allowing an investor or portfolio manager to increase the gearing of a portfolio, or to restrict losses:

      (i) If Vodafone is bought directly it would cost 115p and can fall in value by 115p

      (ii) If Vodafone is purchased via the covered warrant S004 (see above), it will cost 29.2p and can only fall by a maximum of 29.2p. However, the losses will be more steep than for the holding of the shares.

   (d) They can be used to liberate capital from a portfolio, for example as above. By replacing each Vodafone share and replacing it with a covered warrant, it is possible to liberate 85.8p per share.

5.12 Covered warrants are a potentially valuable tool for investors and portfolio managers. They can be used in **Self-invested Personal Pension (SIPP)** portfolios, providing a greater range of investment opportunities for these funds. Historically, SIPPs have not been easily able to benefit from highly geared investments, or to make money from a fall in the market.

6 RISK AND RETURN

6.1 Derivatives occupy a position at the **high end of the risk spectrum**. They do, however, provide the potential for **exceptionally high returns**. Because of this, many traders actually expect a large proportion of their deals to fail completely, or make no profit and the few that succeed will cover all of their losses.

6.2 Derivatives are subject to three main types of risk.

   • **Market risk**
   • **Liquidity risk**
   • **Credit risk**

Market risk

6.3 The **high degree of gearing** of most **derivatives** makes them **highly susceptible to market movements**. A small downward move in the stock market will result in a much larger downward movement for a derivative. If a share is purchased at the wrong time and the market moves against it, it may still be possible to sell for 90% of the purchase price. With a derivative, most of the value can be wiped out with a similar market movement.

6.4 EXAMPLE: MARKET RISK

The current price of XYZ shares is £11.30. Options for the XYZ 1150 April Calls are currently trading at 20p. If the share price falls by 10%, the shares will reduce to £10.17. If the price is £10.17 on expiry, the traded option will expire worthless, resulting in the total loss of the original investment.

Liquidity risk

6.5 **Exchange-traded derivatives** tend to be **reasonably liquid** and not much of a problem for a trader. However, **over the counter (OTC) derivatives** are highly customised instruments and there may be a substantial chance that they cannot be sold at a reasonable price within a reasonable time frame. To make matters worse, levels of liquidity may decrease further or disappear completely as markets turn down.

Credit risk

6.6 Exchange traded derivatives tend to use some form of clearing house system to **reduce the risks** of counterparties **defaulting**. There is an actual incentive for exchanges to eliminate counterparty risk altogether if they wish to encourage high turnover. Derivatives traded in the OTC market do not have the same protection. OTC instruments are subject to the risk that the issuing party may default.

Derivative returns

6.7 All **derivatives** will provide a measure of gearing in their return. Because of this, a particular investment may yield **returns** of many times the money used for the investment. This gearing will **vary** with the **type of derivative** and as to whether the derivative is being **sold** (written) or **purchased**.

6.8 EXAMPLE: DERIVATIVE RETURNS

The current price of XYZ shares is £11.30. Options for the XYZ 1150 April Calls are currently trading at 20p. If the share price rises by 10%, the shares will increase to £12.43. If the price is £12.43 on expiry, the traded option will return 93p (1243-1150). For a premium of 20p, this gives a profit of (93 – 20)/20 or 365%.

Use of derivatives by investment fund managers

6.9 **Fund managers** can use **derivatives** in a number of ways to help them to **simulate financial markets** and to **manage the risk on a portfolio.**

Simulation of financial markets

6.10 There are a number of situations where **fund managers** will wish to **simulate the movements** in financial markets. One of the main ones is where managers wish to **track a particular index** or market, but do not have sufficient funds to make it economically viable to buy all the shares of an index. They can still **reproduce index movements** in their funds by **buying options or futures** in the index. These methods are used with **tracker funds** and with various forms of **guaranteed equity bond**.

6.11 When dealing with markets such as those in the Far East, or other **emerging markets** such as those in 'new' Europe, it can be highly impractical actually to hold the shares. The reasons for the difficulty could include local laws, local taxation, the requirement to deal through nominees, or just the difficulty and expense of dealing in that market. **Index futures** provide a fast and effective way to buy into those economies from the UK without the **additional cost** of dealing in the shares themselves. As an additional benefit, by dealing from the UK, the only consideration is UK tax and not that applicable locally.

6.12 EXAMPLE: ANTICIPATING CASH FLOW

Where a fund is expecting a particular sum of money at a time when markets are expected to rise, this can be very frustrating for the fund managers. If they do not wish to miss out on future price movements, they could buy FTSE 100 index futures to simulate them having the shares. If the FTSE 100 currently stands at 5,500, the value of one contract will be £10 × 5,500 = £55,000. If the fund manager is anticipating a payment of £165,000, then we can establish the number of contracts required to replicate the price movement of this money by dividing the value required by the value per contract, £165,000/£55,000 = 3. The fund manager can buy 3 contracts to replicate the market movements on his anticipated money. There will be a requirement for initial margin. For the FTSE 100, a regularly traded contract, this is likely to be £2,500 per contract.

Question 5.8

How many FTSE 100 future contracts would need to be bought to simulate £1,000,000 of shares if the FTSE 100 was at 5,500?

Portfolio risk management using derivatives

6.13 One of the main reasons derivatives were created was as a **tool** to **manage risk on a portfolio**. A **portfolio manager** may wish to hedge against a number of risks to his portfolio including **currency risk** or **market risk**.

6.14 Some companies that manage **offshore funds** 'hedge' them and others do not. Some will offer both types of fund to give the investor a choice. **Hedging** effectively **removes the risk** of currency movements between the currency of the investment and the currency of the investor affecting the value of the investment. The purchase of appropriate **futures contracts** will mean that any **changes in the currency**, up or down, will be reflected by a **cash adjustment**. This effectively allows investors in the US to benefit from the growth in the UK without being affected by the strength of Sterling, which would act to reduce gains.

6.15 Where a **fund manager** in any market feels that prices are due to take a sudden **downturn**, it may not be possible to do anything about it. It may well be that the **liquidation of the portfolio** will have significant **Capital Gains Tax** implications. Even if this were not the case, the liquidation of a large fund would cause an excess of shares in the market, which could depress prices. On top of all this, if the market does not fall as expected, he will have to repurchase the shares, incurring further costs. To get around this he can use an **option or futures contract,** providing there is one appropriate to the shares he wishes to sell.

6.16 EXAMPLE: HEDGING WITH FUTURES

If a fund of £1 million were invested in FTSE 100 shares, the investor could buy FTSE 100 puts or sell FTSE 100 futures. If we assume the market stands at 5,500 we can examine the effect of the following. Using **futures**, with FTSE 100 at 5,500, each contract would have a value of £10 × 5,500 or £55,000. To hedge a £1 million portfolio, he would need to sell (1,000,000/55,000) 18.2 contracts. If we assume he sold 18 contracts for a value of (18 × £55,000) = £990,000, the margin requirement would be in the region of £45,000 (£2,500 per contract).

If the market moved down 500 points as expected, the contract is now worth (£50,000 × 18) = £900,000. If he cancelled his position, he would get back £90,000 on top of his margin and his profit would be £90,000, which would offset most of the downward movement of the portfolio.

If the market moves up 500 points, the contract is now worth (£60,000 × 18) = £1,080,000 and he would need to pay £90,000 less his initial margin to cancel the position. He would have lost £90,000, but this would have been offset by the rise in the value of the shares. If the market stays at the same level, he would be in the same position except for the commission on the futures.

Hedge funds

6.17 Although some managers use derivatives as part of a primarily asset based investment strategy, others do not. Any fund that is not primarily asset based tends to be called a **hedge fund**.

6.18 Traditionally, hedge funds were the preserve of institutional investors and wealthy individuals. The funds are primarily unregulated and are only marketed to professional investors. These funds can potentially provide very high returns, while subjecting the investor to a very high risk. Many are marketed on the basis that by using derivatives they can make money whether overall markets are rising, falling or static. Despite the well respected names getting involved in this market, many within the industry advise extreme caution. In 2005, there are concerns that some hedge funds could be in trouble, although the extent of any problem remains to be seen at the time of writing.

6.19 Unlike asset based funds, which tend to be linked to or benchmarked against various indices, hedge funds aim to deliver absolute returns. This can leave the fund manager considerable freedom to invest, and regular articles appear in the financial press regarding conventional fund managers leaving their current positions to set up their own hedge funds and hedge fund collections, sometimes called 'boutiques'. Managing this new type of fund gives managers the freedom to use a range of financial strategies such as borrowing against the assets in the fund (gearing), using derivatives, and taking short positions (selling shares in the hope that prices will fall, then buying them to equalise the position).

6.20 For the very wealthy investor seeking an element of very high risk investments, hedge funds could form a small part of a large overall portfolio. This should be accompanied with similar investment and risk warnings that might apply to a managed derivative portfolio. However, in addition to the high risk nature of the largely non-asset based underlying investments and because these funds are not very 'transparent' and can hide all manner of issues such as abnormally high gearing levels, hedge funds should not be recommended to an inexperienced investor.

Chapter roundup

- Derivatives may be **over the counter** (tailor-made) or **exchange-traded** (options, futures, warrants).

- An **option** is a right to buy or sell an asset at a specified time at a specified price, the strike price.

- **Options** come in two forms:
  - Traditional (primary market only, a buyer must be found when they are sold)
  - Traded (primary and secondary market)

- A **call** is the right to buy an asset at a fixed price in the future

- A **put** is the right to sell an asset at a fixed price in the future

- A **future** is a contract to buy or sell a standard quantity and quality of an asset at a specified date and price.

- **Options and futures** can be used: as investments; to hedge; to anticipate cash flow; to provide access to inaccessible markets.

- A **warrant** is a right to buy a share at some future date at a fixed price.

- Derivatives **are risky** investments, being subject to: market risk, liquidity risk and credit risk and the impact of gearing. **Returns** can be high.

- Fund managers use derivatives to **stimulate financial markets** and **manage portfolio risks**.

- **Hedge funds** could be of interest mainly to the wealthy or very experienced investor.

Quick quiz

1   What are the two main types of derivative?

2   What is the main difference between a traditional option and a traded option?

3   What is the 'strike' price of a traded option?

4   What are the two main choices for the holder of a put option at expiry, where the strike price is below the market price?

5   What is the maximum loss on the purchase of a call option?

6   What is the maximum loss on the sale of a call option?

7   What is the maximum loss on the sale of a put option?

8   What does the phrase 'marking to market' mean?

9   List the three main types of margin payment.

10   What form of investment return does a warrant provide?

11   What are the three main risks for investors in derivatives?

12   Why might a portfolio manager wish to simulate financial markets?

13   How could the manager of a FTSE 100 share based portfolio hedge against a possible fall in equity markets?

14   In the event of a market move in the opposite direction to that anticipated, which has the less risk, the purchase of a future or an option?

The answers to the questions in the Quick Quiz can be found at the end of this Study Text. Before checking your own answers against them, you should look back at this chapter and use the information in it to correct your answers.

Answers to Chapter Questions

5.1   Each contract is for 1,000 shares, so at 103p per share, a contract will cost £1,030. For three contracts the cost will be £3,090.

5.2   The UVW 1200 July Call @ 103p is the lower risk as it is 4p in the money (has 4p intrinsic value). The UVW 1250 July Call @ 77.5p is 46p out of the money and represents considerably higher risk.

5.3   The maximum loss will be the premium paid, which for one contract of 1,000 shares at 103p would be £1,030.

5.4   The maximum loss will be the premium paid, which for one contract of 1,000 shares at 44p would be £440.

5.5   It is theoretically unlimited, as the writer will have to pay the difference between the actual price and the strike price, whatever it is.

5.6   The maximum loss is £12.00 per share, if the value of the share is £0 at expiry, but the writer of the option will have received the premium of 44p, limiting the loss to £11.56 (£12.00 – 44p) per shares, giving a total loss on a contract (1,000 shares) of £11,560.

5.7   At 5,750, a FTSE 100 contract would be valued at £10 × 5,750 = £57,500.

5.8   If the FTSE 100 currently stands at 5,500, the value of one contract will be £10 × 5,500 = £55,000. To simulate the price movements of £1,000,000 worth of shares, the number of contracts required would be £1,000,000/£55,000 = 18.2, but it is only possible to deal in whole contracts.

PRACTICE QUESTION 5

Mr Jones is the manager of an investment portfolio for a pension scheme. The portfolio is invested in a range of FTSE 100 shares and has a current value of £750,000. He believes that over the next few weeks the market will turn down significantly from its current level of 6,500 and he would like to protect the capital value of the fund.

(a)   Explain how he could use FTSE 100 index futures to protect the value of the fund.   (6)

(b)   How many contracts will Mr Jones need to buy to protect the full value of the portfolio?

(6)

(c)   Approximately what will the initial margin requirement be?   (2)

(d)   Give two other derivative transactions that would allow Mr Jones to profit from a fall in the FTSE 100 index, with a brief explanation as to how.   (4)

Part C
Collective investments and investment trusts

Chapter 6

UNIT TRUSTS AND OEICS

Chapter topic list	Syllabus reference
1 Collective investments and the regulatory framework	3.1
2 Unit trusts	3.1
3 Open ended investment companies (OEICs)	3.1

Introduction

It is common for adults in the UK to have money in a collective investment of some kind, whether in a PEP, an ISA, an investment trust, a unit trust or a life assurance policy. Even those who have not taken specific action to invest money directly may be invested in collective investments indirectly via a company or personal pension scheme. In this chapter, we will compare the investment objectives, tax treatment, charges and pricing, and methods of dealing in available types of collective investment. (ISAs and PEPs are covered in more detail in a later Chapter of this Study Text.

1   COLLECTIVE INVESTMENTS AND THE REGULATORY FRAMEWORK

Why collective investments?

1.1   **Collective investments** could be seen as occupying the **middle ground** in the **risk spectrum** and can provide good levels of growth with an acceptable level of risk. It is this fact that makes them the popular choice for many pension and investment schemes.

1.2   One of the **main objectives** for **private investors** is to **protect their money against inflation**. As we have seen in previous chapters, this can be done by investing in **direct investments** such as **equities** and **fixed interest securities**. There can be **several problems** involved with the private investor doing this.

   (a)   Few investors have the **expertise** required to deal directly on their own and, although it is relatively easy to deal in the markets today by phone or computer, the **risks** can be very high for the novice. **Collective investments** get around this problem by using **experienced investment managers** to manage investments on **behalf of investors**.

   (b)   In order to create a **sufficiently diversified portfolio,** a relatively **large investment** in each asset is required. To keep costs to a reasonable level an investor would need to be dealing in investments of £1,500 or more and have 20 or more different holdings. The proliferation of telephone and internet dealing services is bringing the costs down but, despite this, in order to have a reasonable spread of investments, fairly **large amounts of capital** are needed. Where a portfolio is reliant on a **limited number of securities** it is not able to diversify widely, significantly increasing the specific risk in the portfolio.

BPP
PROFESSIONAL EDUCATION

Collective investment schemes get around this by **pooling the money** of many investors.

1.3 There are many **advantages** for a private investor to use **collective investments** rather than direct investments, as follows.

(a) The **investment decisions** are made by a **fund manager** with specialist knowledge and up-to-the-minute access to relevant information.

(b) They can allow **access** to **specialist marketplaces** in which the investors would not normally have the expertise or ability to deal, for example technology stocks or emerging markets.

(c) Investments from many investors within a scheme are **pooled** allowing the manager to purchase a **wide range of investments** to provide a **balanced portfolio** that would normally be beyond the reach of the individual investors because of the capital required.

(d) The **pooling of investments** allows the fund managers to purchase **securities in bulk** at a reduced cost.

(e) Investors can normally invest relatively **small amounts** in such schemes on a regular or one-off basis.

(f) Pooling allows investments to be **diversified** within a type (for example different equities), across different types (for example gilts, property and equities) and across different geographical areas.

(g) Pooling reduces the **investment risk** for the investor as the reliance on any individual security is reduced.

(h) **Administration** for the investment holder on such schemes is **much reduced** compared to holding the securities directly, as summaries, for example of the income tax position, are provided on a regular basis.

(i) **Collective investments** can provide access to **investments with tax advantages**, like PEPs, ISAs, pensions or offshore roll-up schemes.

(j) Collective investments provide for a range of **different investment objectives** between income only and capital growth only, or any combination of the two.

Open-ended and closed-ended funds

KEY TERMS

An **open-ended investment** is one where the total amount invested in the scheme can be increased.

With a **closed-ended investment**, this is not the case.

1.4   The two types have distinctly different attributes.

Open-ended investments	Closed-ended investments
• The purchase price closely reflects the underlying net asset value (NAV) of the investment	• The investments must be purchased from another investor, the price is subject to supply and demand and may not reflect the underlying value (NAV), high demand increases the price, low demand reduces the price
• New investors can bring in new money allowing the fund managers to invest in new opportunities	• Where the price is greater than the underlying value of the investment, it is described as being at a 'premium' to NAV, where it is below it is at a 'discount' to NAV
• When investors sell, assets must be sold to release cash to pay them possibly disrupting set policies and strategies	
• Unit trusts, OEICs and life assurance investments are open-ended, as are many offshore investment funds	• There is no new money coming in, fund managers must sell assets in order to buy more
	• When investors sell there is no need to sell assets as the total amount of money invested remains; the same set policies and strategies can be maintained
	• Investment trusts and some offshore funds are also closed

1.5   **Collective investments** can also be categorised by their **legal structure**. By far the most common structure for collective investments around the world is a **corporate structure**. These can be in closed or open-ended form. In the UK, **investment trusts** and **Open Ended Investment Companies (OEICs)** are companies whose purpose is investment. The difference between the two is that an investment trust is a closed-ended structure, while an OEIC is an open-ended structure. OEICs are alternatively called **Investment Companies with Variable Capital (ICVCs)**.

1.6   An **alternative** to a **corporate structure** is a legal structure such as a trust. An example of this in the UK is a unit trust. Outside the UK, collective investments exist in both open-ended and closed-ended structures.

Question 6.1

How will the price of a unit trust vary with changes in the value of the underlying trust? How would this differ from an investment trust and why?

FSA rules: the CIS Sourcebook

1.7   The first set of FSA regulations covering authorised unit trusts (AUTs) and OEICs/ICVCs is found in the FSA's **Collective Investment Schemes** Sourcebook coded '**CIS**' in the FSA Handbook. As already mentioned, '**ICVC**' (**Investment Company with Variable Capital**) is an alternative term that can be used to refer to an OEIC.

1.8   CIS currently runs in parallel with a new set of FSA rules contained in a new Collective Investment Schemes Sourcebook named '**COLL**'. Funds have until **13 February 2007** to switch to the new COLL rules. From that date, CIS will no longer apply for any scheme.

1.9   Below, we outline the **CIS** rules first, and then we look at **COLL**.

Types of authorised fund

1.10 For **CIS** purposes, there are the following **categories of authorised fund**:

- Securities schemes (funds for transferable securities, including equity funds and bond funds)
- Money market schemes
- Futures and options schemes
- Geared futures and options schemes
- Property schemes
- Warrant schemes
- Feeder funds
- Fund of funds schemes
- Umbrella schemes

1.11 Funds may be **UCITS schemes,** meaning that they conform to the European UCITS Directive and can be marketed throughout the European Economic Area (EEA).

Investment rules

1.12 Authorised fund managers of AUTs and ICVCs must ensure that, taking account of the investment objectives and policy of the authorised fund as stated in the most recently published prospectus of the authorised fund, the scheme property of the authorised fund aims to provide a **prudent spread of risk**.

1.13 The CIS Sourcebook sets out the securities in which funds may invest. These must be **freely transferable securities**. The trust deed of an AUT will state that the trust may invest in FSA-permitted securities and will identify any further narrower investment rules of the trust itself. Investment limits will be set out in the scheme particulars or fund prospectus.

1.14 At least 90% of a securities fund must be invested in **approved securities**: these are securities listed in an EEA state or in another recognised and regulated eligible market. The eligible markets used must be listed in the scheme particulars. **Unlisted (unapproved) securities,** which can make up 10% by value, may include units in other collective investment schemes constituting up to 5% of the value of the fund.

1.15 The following **concentration rules** are designed to ensure that authorised funds have a certain amount of spread or diversification.

- Not more than 10% of the total value of the fund may be held in the shares of a single company.

- The holdings exceeding 5% must not add to more than 40% of the fund in aggregate.

1.16 These rules mean that the most concentrated fund with the fewest holdings would have four holdings of 10% of the fund value each, with twelve further holdings of 5% each. Thus, a fund must have **at least 16 holdings** although in practice, funds typically have many more than this.

1.17 Funds may also **not hold more than 10% of the voting shares** of a particular company. A fund management company must not have more than 20% of the voting rights in a single company across all its funds.

1.18 A fund with more than 35% of its value in **government fixed interest securities** from a single issuer (eg, UK Government gilts) must invest in at least six different issues of stock. A single holding of a government fixed interest security must not exceed 30% of the fund value.

1.19 Equity funds and bond funds are allowed to use forward contracts or **derivatives** (futures, options or contracts for differences), to help reduce risk and costs or in the interests of efficient portfolio management that is 'economically appropriate'. A securities fund may hold a maximum of 5% of its value as **warrants** (securities giving an option to buy shares).

1.20 Funds are now available that specialise in derivatives, since legislation was introduced to permit futures and options funds, geared futures and options funds, option funds, property funds and warrant funds.

Cash and borrowings

1.21 Funds may hold cash only to provide **liquidity** and **cash flow**.

1.22 **Borrowings** by AUTs and ICVCs must be temporary and not persistent. Temporary borrowing is permitted against future cash flows but must not exceed, on any business day, 10% of the value of the scheme property. These types of funds cannot use borrowing as a means of **gearing** its portfolio in the way that an investment trust can.

FSA cancellation rules

1.23 To comply with **FSA cancellation rules,** firms selling unit trusts and OEICs must allow investors who have received advice 14 days in which to cancel their investment. The cancellation period does not apply for sales made at a distance rather than face-to-face.

1.24 Written notice of the right to cancel must be given:

- Before the agreement is concluded, and
- Within eight days after the agreement being concluded

1.25 The notice must be completed and returned by the customer within 14 days for the purchase to be cancelled. If those who are eligible choose to cancel their units and the market has fallen, they will receive the **offer price** on the date of cancellation. This could be less than their original investment. If the market has risen they will not benefit from the rise and will only be refunded their original investment.

1.26 If a firm does not give to a **retail customer** information about his cancellation rights, the contract remains cancellable and the retail customer will be not liable for any shortfall.

FSA rules: the COLL Sourcebook

1.27 As stated at the beginning of this section, the FSA has introduced a new Collective Investment Schemes Sourcebook (**COLL**) which will replace the previous Sourcebook for Collective Investment Schemes (**CIS**). COLL applies to ICVCs (ie, OEICs) and authorised unit trusts.

1.28 COLL provides a regime for product regulation, with the objective of protecting the consumer, and also implements requirements of the **UCITS Directive**. Until **13 February 2007** when the CIS rules ceases to apply, authorisation of collective investment schemes

BPP
PROFESSIONAL EDUCATION

under COLL remains optional and so the new COLL rules currently only affect some schemes.

1.29 COLL is designed as a two-tier approach, comprising:

(a) **Retail schemes**, which are promoted to the general public, and

(b) **Qualified investor schemes** (QIS), for institutions and expert private investors

1.30 **Retail schemes** are either **UCITS retail schemes** or **non-UCITS retail schemes**. However, there have been relatively few applications to set up non-UCITS retail schemes.

1.31 With **QIS**, fewer consumer protection rules apply than for retail schemes. QIS can invest in a very wide range of assets, with no significant limitation on the spread between buying and selling prices other than whatever is stated in the scheme documentation.

1.32 With regard to **gearing**, QIS are permitted to **borrow** up to 100% of the net asset value of the fund. QIS are also permitted to hold 'short' positions profiting from falls in prices and can charge performance fees. These possibilities make QIS very similar to **hedge funds**, which we discuss later in this Chapter.

1.33 A retail UCITS scheme is very similar to existing UCITS schemes, with the following limits (based on percentage of the scheme's value) applying:

- 20% limit on investment in other collective investment schemes
- 10% limit on investment in unapproved (unlisted) securities

1.34 Under COLL, there are the following new investment limits for non-UCITS retail schemes.

- 35% limit for investing in other collective investment schemes
- If a scheme does invest in a second scheme, that second scheme must not itself have more than 15% of its value invested in other collective investment schemes
- 20% limit on aggregate investment in unapproved securities and unregulated schemes

1.35 For **UCITS funds** replicating ('tracking') an index, the **concentration** limit is raised under COLL rules to permit a holding of 20% in a particular share, and up to 35%, but only for one share and only in exceptional market conditions. **Non-UCITS funds** under COLL have no concentration limits.

1.36 Under the new rules, both UCITS and non-UCITS retail schemes can invest in a variety of types of instrument, including **warrants and derivatives**, within their overall investment objectives, provided that they apply a risk management procedure.

1.37 A non-UCITS retail scheme can invest in an even wider range of assets, including gold or 100% investment in immovable property.

1.38 Non-UCITS schemes can also **borrow** up to 10% of the fund value on a **permanent** basis, while UCITS retail schemes are only permitted to borrow on a **temporary** basis.

1.39 Under the COLL rules, redemptions in non-UCITS retail schemes and QISs may be:

- Limited for up to six months in the case of property funds and in schemes offering a guaranteed return
- Deferred to the next valuation point if redemptions exceed 10% of the value of the fund, with proper disclosure to investors

1.40 COLL permits the **creation of units** on a **forward pricing basis** to take place up to **24 hours** after the relevant valuation point (previously, 2 hours).

1.41 In the past, the market capitalisation of some shares within an index has made it difficult for funds to track an index within the previous regulations. Under new rules, **index-tracking funds** are permitted to invest up to 20% of the fund value in particular share in order to replicate an index, or up to 35% in a single share in exceptional market conditions.

1.42 COLL also allows fund managers to charge **performance-based fees,** either at fixed fee rates or based on the value of the fund.

1.43 Overall, the new COLL arrangements are designed to allow flexibility in product design by scheme providers, coupled with the retention of consumer protection based on the needs of different classes of investor.

2 UNIT TRUSTS

2.1 **Unit trusts** are one of the most popular forms of collective investment in the UK. In March 2004 total investment together with OEICs stood at £246 billion. However, this type of investment is **specific to the UK** and few are sold outside the UK. It is partly for this reason that companies are increasingly turning to OEICs as an alternative to unit trusts by issuing new funds in this form, or by converting existing funds. This **corporate** form of **collective investment** is widely used in Europe and the US making them attractive to companies wishing to be active in world markets.

The structure of a unit trust

> **KEY TERM**
>
> A unit trust is an open-ended collective investment divided into units, each representing an identical fraction of the total underlying investment. The investment is set up under a trust deed and trust law determines the roles of the parties to the trust. Both the manager and trustee must be incorporated under law in a member state of the European Union, and must have an office in the UK. Authorised unit trusts must be approved by the FSA. The investor is effectively the beneficiary under the trust.

The trustees

2.2 **Trustees** of a unit trust must be FSA-regulated and **fully independent** of the trust manager. Trustees are required to have **capital** in excess of £4 million and, for this reason, will normally be a **large financial institution** such as a bank or insurance company. The role of the trustees is to protect the interests of the unit holders. They must:

(a) Establish and maintain a **register** of unit holders listing their names and addresses and details of the numbers and types of units held

(b) Ensure that the manager is **acting in accordance** with the trust deed

(c) Ensure the manager is **not in breach** of rules set out by their regulators

(d) **Hold the investments** underlying the unit trust including any cash and income from investments (all purchases will be in the name of the trustees)

    (e) **Replace the manager** if they believe that he is not acting in the investor's best interest, or if required to do so because of the manager not being able to continue (for example by insolvency)

    (f) Carry out the **proposals of a vote** by the majority of the unit holders (for example to remove the fund manager)

Investment objectives

2.3   The **trust deed** of each unit trust must clearly state its **investment objectives,** so that investors can determine the suitability of each trust. The limits and allowable investment areas for a unit trust fund, within the FSA framework of CIS or COLL as appropriate, are laid out in the **'trust deed'** together with the investment objectives.

The manager

2.4   The manager must also be **authorised** (normally through the FSA) and his role covers:

- **Marketing** the unit trust

- **Managing** the assets in accordance with the trust deed

- **Maintaining** a record of units for inspection by the trustees

- **Supplying** other information relating to the investments under the unit trust as requested

- **Informing** the FSA of any breaches of regulations while it is running the trust

2.5   Fund managers can perform these tasks themselves, or **subcontract** them to a third party.

Question 6.2

Who is ultimately responsible for the protection of the investor under a unit trust?

Buying units

2.6   Unit trust **units** can be purchased in a number of ways, via an intermediary, 'off the page' with a newspaper advert, over the phone or over the Internet. All of these methods will require **payment with the order,** or some form of **guarantee of payment.**

2.7   A **contract note** will be produced and sent to the investor as **evidence of the purchase.** It is important to keep this document **safe,** as not all unit trusts are required to send a certificate to back it up and, in this case, the contract note is the **evidence** that the transaction has taken place.

2.8   When a **unit trust investment** is made with financial advice, private investors are given 14 days to change their mind via a **cancellation notice.**

- If they choose to cancel, this does not guarantee they will get their money back.

- The cancellation will **terminate** the transaction without costs, but market movements could leave the investor with a loss.

- Cancellation notices do not apply to business investors, investors buying 'off the page', investors whose investments are being managed on a discretionary basis by an authorised person and those transacting business on an 'execution only' basis.

Selling units

2.9 Investors can **sell** their units through the same source that they purchased them, or can contact the fund managers direct, for example by telephone.

- A **contract note** will be produced the next day.

- Where a **certificate** was issued, the investor will need to 'renounce' the units by signing the **renunciation form** on the back.

- The renunciation form will ask for details as to the **number of units** the investor wishes to **sell**, if he is not disposing of the whole holding.

- Payments will be issued within five business days and will be sent together with a **balance certificate** for any remaining units held.

Question 6.3

If a unit trust that is not an index tracker chooses to hold the maximum amount of 10% in each of four different companies, what is the minimum number of companies that can be represented in the trust?

Categories of trust

2.10 Unit trust funds are categorised by the **Investment Management Association (IMA)**, as set out below.

UK sector definitions (IMA)

Funds principally targeting income - Immediate Income

UK Gilts
Funds which invest at least 90% of their assets in UK Government securities (Gilts)

UK Index Linked Gilts
Funds which invest at least 90% of their assets in UK Index Linked Government securities (Gilts)

UK Corporate Bond
Funds which invest at least 80% of their assets in Sterling-denominated (or hedged back to Sterling), Triple BBB minus or above bonds as measured by either Standard & Poor or equivalent – Moodys Baa or above. This excludes convertibles.

Global bonds
Funds which invest at least 80% of their assets in fixed interest stocks. All funds which contain more than 80% fixed interest investments are to be classified under this heading regardless of the fact that they may have more than 80% in a particular geographic sector, unless that geographic area is the UK, when the fund should be classified under the relevant UK heading.

UK Equity & Bond Income
Funds which invest at least 80% of their assets in the UK, between 20% and 80% in UK fixed interest securities and between 20% and 80% in UK equities. These funds aim to have a yield of 120% or over of the FT All Share Index.

Funds principally targeting income - Growing Income

UK Equity Income

Funds which invest at least 80% of their assets in UK equities and which aim to have a yield which is in excess of 110% of the yield of the FT All Share Index.

Funds principally targeting capital - Capital Growth/Total Return

UK zeros

Funds investing at least 80% of their assets in Sterling denominated (or hedged back to sterling), and at least 80% of their assets in zero dividend preference shares or equivalent instruments (ie not income producing). This excludes preference shares which produce an income.

UK All Companies

Funds which invest at least 80% of their assets in UK equities which have a primary objective of achieving capital growth.

UK Smaller Companies

Funds which invest at least 80% of their assets in UK equities of companies which form the bottom 10% by market capitalisation.

Japan

Funds which invest at least 80% of their assets in Japanese equities.

Japanese Smaller Companies

Funds which invest at least 80% of their assets in Japanese equities of companies which form the bottom 10% by market capitalisation.

Asia Pacific including Japan

Funds which invest at least 80% of their assets in Asia Pacific equities including a Japanese content. The Japanese content must make up less than 80% of assets.

Asia Pacific excluding Japan

Funds which invest at least 80% of their assets in Asia Pacific equities and exclude Japanese securities.

North America

Funds which invest at least 80% of their assets in North American equities.

North American Smaller Companies

Funds which invest a least 80% of their assets in North American equities of companies which form the bottom 10% by market capitalisation.

Europe including UK

Funds which invest at least 80% of their assets in European equities. They may include UK equities, but these must not exceed 80% of the fund's assets.

Europe excluding UK

Funds which invest at least 80% of their assets in European equities and exclude UK equities

European Smaller Companies

Funds which invest at least 80% of their assets in European equities of companies which form the bottom 10% by market capitalisation in the European market. They may include UK equities, but these must not exceed 80% or the fund's assets. ('Europe' includes all countries in the MSCI/FTSE pan European indices.)

Cautious Managed

Funds would offer investment in a range of assets, with the maximum equity exposure restricted to 60% of the Fund. There would be no specific requirement to hold a minimum % non-UK equity. Assets must be at least 50% in Sterling/Euro and equities are deemed to include convertibles.

Balanced Managed

Funds would offer investment in a range of assets, with the maximum equity exposure restricted to 85% of the Fund. At least 10% must be held in non-UK equities. Assets must be at least 50% in Sterling/Euro and equities are deemed to include convertibles.

Active Managed

Funds would offer investment in a range of assets, with the Manager being able to invest up to 100% in equities at their discretion. At least 10% must be held in non-UK equities. There is no minimum Sterling/Euro balance and equities are deemed to include convertibles. At any one time the asset allocation of these funds may hold a high proportion of non-equity assets such that the asset allocation would by default place the fund in either the Balanced or Cautious sector. These funds would remain in this sector on these occasions since it is the Manager's stated intention to retain the right to invest up to 100% in equities.

Global Growth

Funds which invest at least 80% of their assets in equities (but not more than 80% in UK assets) and which have the prime objective of achieving growth of capital.

Global Emerging Markets

Funds which invest 80% or more of their assets directly or indirectly in emerging markets as defined by the World Bank, without geographical restriction. Indirect investment e.g. China shares listed in Hong Kong, should not exceed 50% of the portfolio.

Funds principally targeting capital protection

Money Market

Funds which invest at least 95% of their assets in money market instruments (ie cash and near cash, such as bank deposits, certificates of deposit, very short term fixed interest securities or floating rate notes). These funds may be either 'money market funds' as defined by SIB, or 'securities funds' as long as they satisfy the criterion of concentrating on money market instruments.

Protected/Guaranteed Funds

Funds, other than money market funds which principally aim to provide a return of a set amount of capital back to the investor (either explicitly guaranteed or via an investment strategy highly likely to achieve this objective) plus some market upside.

Specialist Sectors

Specialist

Funds with a single country (other than the UK, Japan or the US) or a single sector theme.

Technology & Telecommunications

Funds which invest at least 80% of their assets in technology and telecommunications sectors as defined by major index providers.

Personal Pensions

Funds which are only available for use in a personal pension plan or FSAVC scheme. Present arrangements for unit trust personal pension schemes require providers to set up separate personal pension unit trust under an overall tax sheltered umbrella. These funds then in turn invest in the group's equivalent mainstream trusts. Pension funds are not to be confused with 'Exempt' funds which are flagged separately.

Note. IMA is a representative trade body. The categories above are not based on statute or FSA regulations.

Specialisation within categories

2.11 Within each category, there may be further **subdivisions**. This could include those trusts investing in 'blue chip' shares, cash (via the money markets), ethical shares, fixed interest stocks, indexed stocks, recovery situations and smaller companies, or those that seek to mirror the performance of a specific index, for example the FTSE or the S&P 500 Index.

Unit trust pricing

2.12 At any moment in time, **two prices** will be quoted for a **unit trust: a buying price** and a **selling price**. The **buying price** is the price that an investor will have to pay and the **selling**

price is the price he will receive on selling. The **buying** and **selling** prices can move within a range of prices, but the method of calculation for **maximum buying price** and **minimum selling price** is laid down by the FSA.

Dual/single pricing

2.13 Many industry commentators, including the FSA, believe that the **dual-pricing** system makes it difficult to compare charges on unit trusts. Investors **buy** from the fund manager at the **offer** price and **sell** units back at the **bid** price. Many within the industry also believe that this puts some investors off buying. Proposals from the FSA were in place to change this in the future but have since been shelved. The original plan was that **buying (offer) prices** and **selling (bid) prices** for unit trusts should **disappear** and be **replaced** with a **single mid price** for buying and selling units. The costs and charges involved in buying and selling would have to be quoted separately, but the legislation for this has never been finalised.

2.14 Many companies have **converted** their trusts into **open ended investment companies** (OEICs), which have always quoted a **single price**, rather than wait for new legislation.

Calculating the buying and selling prices of unit trusts

2.15 The methods of **calculation of maximum buying and selling prices** are within the syllabus for G70.

Full spread

2.16 The calculations for the **maximum buying and selling price** allow for the fact that if **new units** need to be created, then the **full cost** of the creation of the units can be charged as the **offer price**. Conversely if units are sold, the **maximum buying price** is based on the cost of **cancelling the units**. For most **unit trusts**, the difference between the **creation** and **cancellation** price will be in the range of 6-10% and is called the **full spread**. A typical **spread** actually experienced in the market will be in the range of 5-7%. The managers of the fund reserve the right to move the **spread** within the **full spread**.

Question 6.4

What is the maximum difference in price an investor could experience between buying and selling prices for units on two consecutive days?

Offer pricing

2.17 If the market is moving **upwards**, it is likely that investors will be **buying**. In these circumstances, managers can move the **spread** to the **top of the range**. This effectively means that the **offer price** being paid will be the **creation price** and **increases** the price for buyers. However, it also **increases** the price for **sellers of units** who will get a price of 5-7% **below the creation price** and considerably higher than normal. When this happens, prices are said to be on an 'offer' basis.

Bid pricing

2.18 If the market is moving **downwards**, it is likely that investors will be **selling**. In these circumstances, managers can move the **spread** to the **bottom of the range**. This effectively means that the **buying price** being paid will be the **cancellation price** and **reduces** the price for sellers. However, it also **reduces** the price for buyers of units who will get a price of 5-7% **above the cancellation price** and considerably lower than normal. When this happens, prices are said to be on a **'bid'** basis.

The manager's box

2.19 Trust managers can keep unit trusts **repurchased** from unit holders to enable them to supply units to purchasers without creating new units. This will **increase liquidity** in the investment and will help the manager avoid having to create and cancel shares every day. It also saves considerable money on the **acquisition** and **disposal costs** of the underlying assets, as units are **recycled** rather than being created and destroyed. The trust manager can use this to make large profits on the units sold **via the box**. In the right circumstances, the manager can effectively keep the **full spread**, representing a useful additional income stream that is not visible as a charge to the customer.

Question 6.5

What problems could a fund manager holding a large box experience, if investment markets drop significantly?

FSA formula for calculation of maximum offer price	FSA formula for calculation of minimum bid price (cancellation price)
Take the total cost of buying the underlying securities of the trust (at current market buying prices)	Take the total cost of selling the underlying securities of the trust (at current market selling prices)
Add stockbroker dealing commission and stamp duty	Deduct stockbroker dealing commission
Add in uninvested cash and accrued income since the last distribution	Add in uninvested cash and accrued income since the last distribution
Divide the total by the number of units in issue (to give **creation price**)	Divide the total by the number of units in issue
Add any initial charges	Deduct any exit charges applicable
Round to four significant figures	Round to four significant figures

---

Question 6.6

What is the key difference between the FSA formulae for calculating the maximum offer and minimum bid prices?

The valuation point

2.20 The **calculations** of **buying** and **selling price** will take place at the 'valuation point' – generally 12 noon.

2.21 Prices can be set on a **historic** or **future** basis. Where the price the investor pays is based on the **previous valuation point**, the pricing is described as **historic**. All units purchased up to the valuation point on the following day will be at the same, previous price. Where the investor pays a price based on the **next valuation point,** it is called **forward pricing.** All units purchased up to next valuation point will be at that price.

2.22 On a **historic pricing** basis, the manager creates units at the valuation point according to the amount of sales expected up to the next valuation point. If sales exceed expected levels, the manager must either move to forward pricing or risk loss of money for the fund if there is an unfavourable price movement.

2.23 On a **forward pricing** basis, the manager must create units at the valuation point sufficient to cover transactions since the last valuation point.

2.24 Under **CIS** rules, the manager must create units within **2 hours** of the valuation point. Under **COLL** (as already mentioned), he must do so within **24 hours** of the valuation point.

2.25 Each system has merits. With **historic pricing,** the investor knows the price he will pay for units, but the value of the underlying securities may not be reflected in the price paid. This is good if prices have moved up, but bad if they have moved down. Investors find future pricing confusing, as it is not possible to determine in advance the price they will pay, but the price will be **more reflective** of the **underlying value** of the securities. If the fund moves by more than 2% in value, the manager must quote on a forward basis.

Question 6.7

Where market prices have moved up significantly since the last valuation point which would be better for the investor, future or historic pricing? Why is this the case?

Charges

2.26 The **charges** on a unit trust must be explicit in the trust deed and documentation. They should give the current charges and the extent to which managers can change them.

2.27 Charges need to be made to cover the following **costs**

- Managing the fund
- Administration of the fund
- Marketing
- Regulation, registration and compliance
- General administration
- Direct marketing costs
- Commissions for intermediaries

2.28 These charges can be taken in one or more of three ways, via an **initial charge,** an **exit charge** or through **annual management charges.**

Initial charge

2.29 The **initial charge** will be **added** to the **spread** and will **increase** the **offer price.** Most managers will charge 3.0-6.5% on **equities** and less on **gilt** and **fixed interest funds** (1-4%) because of their lower dealing charges. Other funds with lower charges include **index tracker funds** and **cash/money market funds,** where the lower price reflects the lower burden of management. Where an initial charge is small or non-existent, there may be a further charge on exit.

Exit charges

2.30 As an alternative to initial charges, a trust may use **exit charges**. These charges are typically invoked where the investor sells the investment within a set period of time, eg five years.

2.31 The **exit charge** levied will normally be on a **sliding scale**, which varies from 5% if the investment is encashed in the first year and reduces by 1% for each subsequent year. After the fifth year, the exit charge will be zero, but the annual management charge will have been higher and the managers will have covered the cost of the initial charge. If the investment continues, they will still be getting their management charge at a higher rate.

2.32 The main advantage of **exit charges** over initial charges is that more of the investor's money is available to grow in the early years. This charging structure will also look more favourable on a charge-specific illustration.

Annual management charges

2.33 An **annual charge** of 0.5%–2.0% of the underlying fund is made to cover the ongoing cost of the investment management of the trust. The cost will vary with the level of management required on a fund. **Offshore funds** require more management and costs are likely to be **higher**. **Tracker funds** require less management and costs will be **lower**. Some funds such as **funds of funds (FOFs)** will have several tiers of management and will allow access to a wide range of investment managers via a single management company. In this case, each tier of management will need to recoup its costs and in these cases, annual management costs will be higher.

2.34 **Management charges** can be taken from income or capital, but historically has been taken from income. The main reason for this is that the charges could be offset against taxable income.

Question 6.8

How are annual management charges likely to be different for funds without initial charges?

Marketing issues

2.35 In order to be **marketed** to the public, a **unit trust** must be authorised by the FSA. This has a direct impact on the taxation of the fund, in that authorisation is a requirement for the trust to be treated as **exempt** from **CGT**. **Unauthorised unit trusts** are used for specific applications, where they are not marketed directly to the public, and are subject to corporation tax and CGT within the fund. Investors are liable to any additional income tax and CGT on disposal. There is a further form of '**exempt**' unauthorised unit trust which may be used as investments for pensions and registered charities. **Exempt unit trusts** are free of CGT on disposals within the fund and are subject to income tax rather than corporation tax.

UCITS certification

2.36 If the fund manager wishes to **market** the unit trust in **other member states of the EU**, he may apply for certification under **UCITS** (Undertakings for Collective Investment in Transferable Securities).

Taxation of unit trusts

2.37 Authorised unit trusts are **exempt from tax on gains** made within the fund, giving them an advantage, for instance, over life funds. Any income (other than dividend income from UK companies, which is not taxable) is taxed to corporation tax at **20%**. Foreign withholding tax on dividends will be offset against the tax charge, subject to double taxation treaties.

2.38 **Management expenses** can be offset against income from **non-UK equities**.

2.39 Unit trusts do not pay tax on gains from options or futures.

2.40 The tax treatment of distributions parallels the tax treatment of direct holdings of equities and interest.

2.41 If the trust holds more than 60% of its investments in **interest bearing securities**, the income is deemed to be interest and the distribution is made net of 20% tax, which can be reclaimed by non-taxpayers. 10% taxpayers can reclaim 10%, while basic rate taxpayers have no further liability. Higher rate taxpayers must pay 20% more in tax.

2.42 For equity unit trusts, the distribution is made with a 10% tax credit. The tax treatment for different types of taxpayer is then as for dividends from shares held directly. The tax credit cannot be reclaimed by non-taxpayers. The tax credit satisfies the tax liability for a basic or lower (10%) rate taxpayer, but higher rate taxpayers will be liable to an additional 22.5%. Non-taxpayers cannot reclaim the tax credit.

2.43 The individual is liable to **capital gains tax** on disposals of unit trust investments.

2.44 There is no stamp duty to pay on purchases of UK unit trusts.

Unauthorised unit trusts

2.45 In order to be **marketed** to the public, a **unit trust** must be authorised by the FSA. This has a direct impact on the taxation of the fund, in that authorisation is a requirement for the trust to be treated as **exempt** from **CGT**. **Unauthorised unit trusts** are used for specific applications such as **Enterprise Zone property** holdings, where they are not marketed directly to the public, and are subject to income tax and CGT within the fund. Investors are liable to any additional income tax and CGT on disposal. There is a further **exempt** type of **unauthorised unit trust** that may be used as investments for pensions and registered charities. **Exempt unit trusts** are free of CGT on disposals within the fund and are subject to income tax rather than corporation tax.

Question 6.9

For a higher rate taxpaying investor receiving a distribution of £450 from an equity fund, what proportion of the payment will be lost in tax, in total?

Equalisation payments

2.46 When an investor **buys** units in a **unit trust**, they are entitled to the income earned since the last distribution. However, **income** is **taxed differently** to **capital**. The accrued distribution has been paid for from capital and should be taxed differently. The **equalisation system** makes an allowance for this by treating the first distribution as part income and part capital (in the form of an equalisation payment).

2.47 The **return of capital (equalisation payment)** is not liable to income tax whereas the distribution is. The accrued distribution is averaged for all purchasers of unit trusts since the last distribution. This allows the same distribution to be paid to all unit holders, but those who purchased units since the last distribution will have it **split** into **income** and **equalisation** payments.

2.48 The **equalisation payment** is treated as a **discount** on the **purchase price** of the units. This discount **reduces** the **acquisition cost** and effectively **increases** any **capital gains** that could result on disposal, potentially giving rise to a higher CGT charge.

Share exchange

2.49 Most investment groups offer the facility to use **existing shares** to **fully or partly invest** into **unit trusts**. The fund manager can do this by **purchasing** the shares from the **investor** for inclusion into one or more of his own funds or sale if they are not required. In these circumstances they will normally buy the shares at the **purchase price** rather than the **sale price**, giving the investor a **better return**. Alternatively, they can purchase the shares from the investor and sell them via their own dealer, usually with **less commission** being charged.

2.50 There can be several **advantages for investors**.

(a) They can consolidate several smaller holdings of shares into a single investment.

(b) The cost of disposing of the investments could be less.

(c) The price gained could be better.

(d) The timings and amounts of the disposals could be co-ordinated to reduce capital gains tax. However, the liability to CGT is not reduced by the use of share exchange.

3 OPEN ENDED INVESTMENT COMPANIES (OEICS)

3.1 The **Open-Ended Investment Companies (Investment Companies with Variable Capital) Regulations 1996** provided for the incorporation in the UK of OEICs that fall within the scope of the European UCITS (Undertaking for Collective Investment in Transferable Securities) Directive. UCITS can invest only in **transferable securities** (eg listed securities, other collective investment schemes, certificates of deposit) and must be open ended.

3.2 With the implementation of FSMA 2000, the range of UK authorised OEICs was extended beyond transferable securities, to become similar to that of unit trusts. The range now included money market funds and property funds, for example. OEICs are alternatively termed **Investment Companies with Variable Capital (ICVCs)**. Authorisation as an ICVC defines regulations (ie the Treasury's ICVC Regulations) with which the fund must comply. The **Open Ended Investment Companies Regulations 2001** also apply.

KEY TERM

Open Ended Investment Companies are managed, pooled investment vehicles in the form of companies. They invest in securities with the objective of producing a profit for investors. In the international pooled investment markets, OEICs in several different forms are commonly used where in the UK we would use unit trusts.

Question 6.10

How is the price of an OEIC likely to move with changes in the value of the underlying fund?

3.3 **OEICs** have similarities with **unit trusts** in that they are both **open-ended collective investments**. However, with a unit trust, the units held entitle the owners to a share of the underlying trust assets. A share in an OEIC only entitles the holder to a share in the profits of the OEIC, but the value of the share will be determined by the value of the underlying investments.

3.4 **OEICs** also have similarities with investment trusts in that both have **corporate structures**. The objective of the company in each case is to make a profit for shareholders by investing in the shares of other companies. They differ in the fact that an investment trust is a **closed-ended investment** and an OEIC is open-ended. The open-ended nature of an OEIC means that it cannot trade at a discount to NAV.

Question 6.11

What is the main difference between an OEIC and a unit trust?

The structure of OEICs

3.5 The **fund manager** of an OEIC is called the **Authorised Corporate Director (ACD)**. The responsibilities of the **ACD** include the following.

- Day-to-day management of the fund
- Pricing of the fund
- Management of the investments
- Dealing in the underlying securities
- Preparation of accounts
- Compliance with OEIC regulatory requirements

3.6 In order to ensure that the **ACD** acts in the interests of **investor protection**, there is a further body known as the **Depository**. The responsibility of the **Depository** is similar to that of a trustee with a unit trust.

- Overseeing the management of the investment company
- Protecting the interests of the investor
- Valuation and pricing of OEIC shares
- Dealing in shares for the OEIC
- The payment of income distributions
- Generally overseeing the ACD

- Ensuring that the ACD is acting in accordance with his investment powers
- Ensuring the ACD is acting in accordance with his borrowing powers

OEIC investments

3.7 Rules governing permitted investments in OEICs were discussed in Section 1 of this Chapter.

3.8 As with **investment trusts,** OEICs may have several **different classes of share** in sub funds, each with their own separate client registers and asset pools, but within the framework of the main share structure. This will allow investors a great deal **more flexibility** than has ever been available to unit trust holders. These different structures can be priced differently and give access to different levels of risk and exposure to currency rate changes.

OEIC pricing

3.9 The shares in the OEIC express the entitlement of the shareholders to the underlying fund. Unlike any other company, the number of shares in issue can be **increased** or **reduced** to satisfy the demands of the investors. This removes one of the important factors relating to shares, that of supply and demand. In the stock market, there are a limited number of shares available in each company and an individual must sell the share before another can buy. The ability of an OEIC quickly to alter the shares in issue removes this constraint.

3.10 Although OEICs are **single priced instruments,** the **buying price reflects the value** of the underlying shares plus a notional allowance for the dealing costs of the investments and an initial charge on top. The **initial charge** will cover commission to intermediaries and other sales and management expenses. A further charge, known as a **dilution levy,** may be made with the agreement of the ACD. The **dilution levy** is paid in addition to the buying or selling prices and will have the effect of increasing the buying price or reducing the selling price. In effect, the **levy** covers the **extra costs** involved in the **creation** or **cancellation** of shares and mirrors the shift from **offer basis** to **bid basis** on a unit trust.

3.11 When the investor wishes to **sell** the **OEIC,** the **ACD** will **buy** it. The money value on sale will be based on the **single price** less a **deduction** for the **dealing charges.** The price may be further reduced by the **dilution levy.**

3.12 The **ACD** may choose to **run a box.** Shares sold back to the ACD will be **kept** and **reissued** to investors, reducing the need for creation and cancellation of shares.

Question 6.12

What are the main charges with an OEIC?

Buying and selling OEICs

3.13 Buyers will receive a **contract note** from the ACD on **purchase** or **sale.** Some time after **purchase** the buyer will also receive a **share certificate,** which may be in bearer form. **Bearer investments** are popular for some investors outside the UK, so an OEIC looking to actively trade in these markets may issue their certificates in this form. The certificate for bearer investments represents ownership of the shares so if the certificates are lost or stolen, ownership of the shares is also lost.

3.14 The **register of shareholders** must be **updated daily** and include all shareholdings of the ACD and those held in the box (if there is one) as well as those of the investors.

Taxation of OEICs

3.15 OEICs are **taxed** in a similar way to **unit trusts**. Interest, rent and foreign dividends not taxed at source will be subject to a 20% corporation tax charge. UK dividends will suffer no further tax other than the 10% deducted at source. The income accrued will be distributed with a 20% tax credit for a gilt fund or 10% if the funds is UK equity based. Capital gains within an OEIC are exempt from CGT.

3.16 **Distributions** (dividends) paid to investors in an OEIC are taxable in the same way as the distributions from unit trusts. They come with a **tax credit** of 20% or 10% that satisfies the **tax liability** for basic and lower rate taxpayers. **Higher rate taxpayers** are liable to an additional 20% or 22½%. **Non taxpayers** may **reclaim** the tax on interest distributions, but not equity distributions.

Advantages of OEICs over unit trusts

3.17 The main **benefit** to the UK investment industry of the adoption of **OEICs** over unit trusts is the fact that the **open-ended corporate fund structure** is the most **common** type of pooled fund both in Europe and the US, the two largest market places in the world. This gives the **fund managers** the ability to **market** their product across **the globe**. This is not possible with unit trusts as, for example, US citizens are not allowed to hold them directly.

3.18 The **multiple classes** of **share**, commonly used by OEICs, provide the investor with far more flexibility than is available to Unit Trusts.

3.19 Where an OEIC is based **offshore**, the distributions will **not be taxed** internally. This will provide a **benefit** to non-taxpaying investors, and a cashflow benefit to tax paying investors.

Advantages of OEICs for the investor

3.20 The introduction of OEICs was expected to lead to a **reduction in costs** and provide **total disclosure** and **transparency of charges**. At the same time, there is **no dilution** of **investor protection**.

3.21 The charges with **OEICs** may be lower than unit trusts, particularly when it comes to **cost of entry (setting up)** and **exit (surrendering the investment)** due to single pricing. However, care should be taken to ensure that the **dilution levy** is not used as a means to **reduce** the difference. Annual management costs depend on the **efficiency** of individual fund management companies, but are not set out as a separate charge as with unit trusts. It is still possible to **measure the costs** by looking at the 'total expense ratio' (TER) of the company. Figures for this are published in the press, allowing investors to make valid comparisons between investment managers.

Chapter roundup

- Collective investment can be **open-ended** (total amount invested in scheme can be increased or decreased - such as unit trusts, OEICs, life assurance) or **closed-ended** (investment trusts).

- Unit trusts are split into units, each of which represents an identical proportion of the underlying investments held. The investor is the beneficiary of the trust; trustees are responsible for the trust, the manager runs it day-to-day. There are generally **two prices** for a unit trust: a bid or buying price and an offer or selling price.

- **Charges** are made in three ways: the initial charge, the exit charge and the annual management charge.

Quick quiz

1 What is a closed-ended investment?

2 What are the two main legal structures for collective investments in the UK?

3 Which party to a unit trust is responsible for holding the trust assets?

4 What is the maximum an investor can lose if they invoke their cancellation notice on a unit trust?

5 What is the maximum proportion of a unit trust fund that can be invested in a single share?

6 What proportion of an investment trust must be invested in a specific geographical area in order for it to be categorised?

7 What is the 'manager's box' with a unit trust?

8 What happens when prices are fixed on a forward pricing basis?

9 List the three main charges that could apply to a unit trust.

10 What type of certificate is required for a UK unit trust to be marketed in other member states of the EU?

11 What are the two main parties to an OEIC called, and briefly, what is the role of each?

12 What is a 'dilution levy' on an OEIC?

13 What is the main benefit for the UK investment industry of the adoption of OEICs over unit trusts?

The answers to the questions in the Quick Quiz can be found at the end of this Study Text. Before checking your own answers against them, you should look back at this chapter and use the information in it to correct your answers.

Answers to Chapter Questions

6.1 Unit trust prices will mirror the underlying net asset value (NAV) of the fund, as it is an open-ended investment. This is not the case with an investment trust, a closed-ended investment, the price of which will generally follow the underlying fund value. The exact value is determined by supply and demand in the market.

6.2 The trustees.

6.3 The minimum number of holdings is 16, 4 companies at 10% of the fund each and 12 companies at 5% of the fund each.

6.4 In theory, it would be possible for the difference in prices to be the full spread, the difference between the creation price and cancellation price, together with any fluctuations in the underlying value of the fund.

6.5 The value of the units held in the box will fall. If the fall is greater than the full spread, they will make a loss. Even if buyers return to the market, they will make a loss on selling the units on and if they cancel the units, this would result in a financial loss for them as owners of the units.

6.6 The maximum offer price is based on the cost of creating units and the minimum bid price is based on the cost of cancellation.

6.7 Where prices have moved significantly since the last valuation point, the investor would be better off with historic pricing. The reason for this is that with historic pricing, the price paid by the investor will be that at the last valuation point and should be less than the current value.

6.8 Funds without initial charges will need to recoup their set-up and marketing costs somehow and will probably have a tapering exit charge. The annual management charge is likely to be higher than with a unit trust with initial charges, to recoup these costs, usually by the time the exit charge tapers to zero.

6.9 The dividend of £450 will be paid net of tax at 10%. The gross dividend is therefore £450/(100 – 10%) or £450/90% or £500. The taxpayer will also be liable to a further 22.5% of the £500 or £112.50. This makes a total tax charge of £112.50 plus the tax paid at source (£500 – £450) = £50, ie £162.50 or 32.5%.

6.10 As an OEIC is an open-ended investment, the price of shares will reflect the NAV of the company and move in line with the underlying investments.

6.11 They have different legal structures. An OEIC is set up with a corporate structure whereas a unit trust is set up in the form of a trust.

6.12 With an OEIC, the main charges on purchase will be the initial charge and possibly a dilution levy. On sale, there may also be a dilution levy. There should be no other charges as the annual cost of management is charged within the corporate structure of the instrument.

PRACTICE QUESTION 6

Fred Humbolt is a steelworker and has just inherited £30,000. Fred wishes to invest for growth and believes that there is a good chance that investment markets will rise. He wishes to invest in collective investments such as unit trusts or OEICs and is planning to remain invested for a period of at least five years. On reading an 'off the page' advert he came across the term 'historic pricing' and would like to know what it means.

(a) Briefly, outline the benefits of Fred using collective investments, rather than investing in shares. (6)

(b) Explain the term 'historic' pricing with reference to a unit trust. (2)

(c) What differences would there be in investor protection, if Fred bought his units 'off the page' rather than through an intermediary? (4)

(d) What are the responsibilities of a depository in the case of an OEIC? (6)

(e) Briefly, explain the tax treatment of an authorised unit trust. (4)

Chapter 7

INVESTMENT TRUSTS

Chapter topic list		Syllabus reference
1	The structure and management of investment trusts	3.2
2	Analysis and evaluation of investment trusts	3.2
3	Split capital structures	3.2
4	Charges on investment trusts	3.2
5	Other securities and classes of share	3.2
6	Investment objectives of investment trusts	3.2

Introduction

In this chapter, we look specifically at investment trusts. We will be examining their structure and the ways they can be used within a portfolio. We will go on to consider investment trusts with split capital structures and how they can be analysed and evaluated, together with all other forms of investment trust shares and derivatives. Finally, we will look at the ways in which they can be invested and the role of borrowing as part of the investment strategy.

1   THE STRUCTURE AND MANAGEMENT OF INVESTMENT TRUSTS

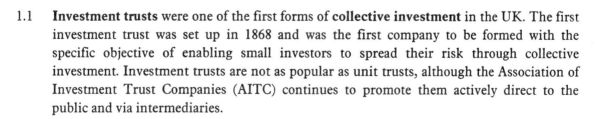

KEY TERM

An **investment trust** is a closed ended, collective investment with a corporate structure. It is a quoted company whose main assets are the shares in which it invests.

1.1   **Investment trusts** were one of the first forms of **collective investment** in the UK. The first investment trust was set up in 1868 and was the first company to be formed with the specific objective of enabling small investors to spread their risk through collective investment. Investment trusts are not as popular as unit trusts, although the Association of Investment Trust Companies (AITC) continues to promote them actively direct to the public and via intermediaries.

1.2   Investment trusts provide an **investment return** in the form of **dividends** and changes in the capital value of the shares.

1.3   The **price of shares** of an investment trust **rise** and **fall** according to **demand** for and **supply** of the shares of the investment trust, and not directly in line with the values of the company's assets, ie **the underlying investments.** In this way, investment trusts differ from unit trusts, whose unit prices are directly related to the market values of the underlying investments.

Association of Investment Trust Companies

1.4 The **AITC** is the **trade body** of **investment trusts** and was formed in 1932 to protect, promote and advance the interests of the individual investment trust companies. A number of investment trust companies are not members.

1.5 As part of its role in **promoting** investment trusts the **AITC** publishes **management information** on investment trusts broken down into sectors, providing more specific detail than the three categories normally published in the financial press.

Investment trust sectors

Country Specialists: Europe	Overseas Growth & Income
Country Specialists: Far East	Private Equity
Country Specialists: Other	UK Growth
Europe	UK Growth & Income
European Emerging Markets	UK High Income
European Smaller Companies	UK Smaller Companies
Far East – Excluding Japan	**Sector Specialists**
Far East – Including Japan	Alternative Energy
Global Emerging Markets	Biotechnology/Life Sciences
Global Growth	Endowment Policies
Global Growth & Income	Financials
Global High Income	Liquidity Funds
Global Smaller Companies	Mining and Natural Resources
Hedge Funds	Property
Japan	Restaurants, Pubs & Brewing
Japanese Smaller Companies	Smaller Cos Media Comms & IT
Latin America	Tea Plantations
North America	Tech, Media & Telecomm
North American Smaller Companies	Utilities
Overseas Growth	Zero Preference Shares

1.6 **Investment trusts** are listed as companies on the **London Stock Exchange**. From the investor's perspective, they are taxed like any other equity. They differ from **open ended investment companies (OEICs)** in that they are **closed-ended investments** and prices vary with the supply and demand of the market rather than the underlying value of the fund, as with an OEIC. This factor gives them a potential advantage. Because prices are **dependent on supply and demand**, the price of the shares can be **lower** than the **net asset value (NAV)** of the share. This allows investors seeking income to **buy** investment trusts at a **discount**, while the **income** produced by the portfolio is based on the market value of the underlying investments. Income yields are therefore enhanced.

1.7 The **conventional corporate structure** of an investment trust gives it a further advantage over unit trusts and OEICs because it can raise money to help it to achieve its objectives. The ability to **borrow** allows an investment trust to 'gear up' returns for the investor. However this gearing increases the volatility of returns.

Question 7.1

How might an investment trust with high gearing perform in a falling market?

The management of investment trusts

1.8 As a company, an investment trust has directors who are responsible for running the trust. The **objective** of a company is to **invest** the money of the shareholders, so decisions on **investment strategies** are very important. These decisions might be made by the directors themselves or may be delegated to a third party. Many investment trusts are run by fund management companies. In all decisions, the directors of the company should act for the **benefit** of the shareholders.

1.9 Decisions made by the management of the company are open to scrutiny by shareholders, who may act if they are **not satisfied** with the performance. One sanction for shareholders is to **sell** their holding, which could affect the share price. If the share price falls significantly, the company could become a takeover target for other trusts or even asset strippers.

1.10 Special resolutions, and those passed at the annual general meeting, will be subject to a vote by the shareholders. This will include **election of directors** and **appointment of professional advisers**. Some investment trusts also buy in other specialist services such as investment or registration services and the appointment of these will be subject to a shareholder vote.

2 ANALYSIS AND EVALUATION OF INVESTMENT TRUSTS

2.1 An investment trust share is similar to any other equity, except that the specific objective of the company is to invest money rather than to transact other forms of business. For most investment trusts, the main **performance statistics** analysed are:

- Share price
- Geographical spread
- Gearing
- Net asset value (NAV) performance
- Levels of discount/premium to NAV
- Dividend growth and gross yield

> **Exam focus point**
> All of these have been examined in Chapter 6 and will be examined in further detail later in this Study Text. It is particularly important that the premium/discount to NAV is clearly understood - we shall look at this below.

2.2 The nature of **split capital trusts** (as we shall see later) is quite different and this is reflected in the performance statistics used for analysis.

- Years/months to wind-up
- Redemption price
- Asset cover
- Dividend growth
- Classes of share and number of shares in issue
- Share price and NAV
- Gross redemption yields
- Hurdle rate
- Discount/premium

Analysis of NAV

2.3 The **net asset value** is the **net worth** of the company expressed in terms of the value of company assets per share, as discussed in Chapter 4. This value can be **greater** or **less** than the **share price**. Where it is greater than the share price, the investment trust is described as being at a '**discount**' to NAV, where it is lower, a '**premium**'. The level of premium or discount relates to the **demand for shares** and any factor that can influence demand will affect it. For example, if investment in the Far East becomes unpopular because of economic weakness, share prices will fall and the level of discount to NAV may increase.

Net asset value calculations

> ### KEY TERM
>
> The calculation of **net asset value** is one of the most important pieces of information for determining the value of an investment trust. It is essentially the **net worth** of an investment trust company's equity capital, usually expressed in pence per share and is calculated by totalling:
>
> (a) The value of the trust's listed investments at mid-market prices
> (b) The value of its unlisted investments at directors' valuation
> (c) Cash and other net current assets
>
> The company's liabilities are deducted from this figure, including any issued preference capital at their nominal value. The resulting figure is the **asset value** of the company. Dividing by the number of shares gives the **net asset value** per share.

2.4 The **net asset value** of a trust company with assets worth £9 million, with liabilities of £3 million and 12 million ordinary shares would be 50p per share, ie (£9 million – £3 million) divided by 12 million. However, this figure is an **undiluted figure**. It does not make any allowances for any warrants in issue (which we shall see in Section 5 of this chapter).

2.5 In order to allow for the effects of **warrant holders** taking up their subscription, the subscription price is added as an asset and the new shares created are added to the total number of shares. The calculation for **diluted NAV** is therefore:

$$\frac{\text{Net assets (assets less liabilities)} \; plus \; \text{warrant subscriptions}}{\text{Shares in issue} \; plus \; \text{new shares in respect of warrants}}$$

Where there are **convertibles** in issue, a diluted net asset value can be calculated in a similar way, as: Net assets *plus* Money subscribed by convertibles holders / Shares in issue *plus* New shares issued to convertibles holders.

Question 7.2

An investment trust has £12 million in assets and £2 million in liabilities. There are 10 million shares in issue together with 3 million warrants to purchase one share each, with a subscription price of 50p. Calculate the diluted and undiluted NAV figures.

Premium to NAV

2.6 Investment trusts can trade at a premium to NAV because, generally, the shares are in high demand. The demand can be due to a number of factors, but it is usually because investors believe in the management of the company and in their ability to make the **assets grow**. The level of **premium or discount** does not remain constant and can change. It is unusual however for an investment trust to remain at a premium for an extended period of time.

2.7 Where an **investment** trust is at a **premium,** the value of the underlying shares will be less than a similar trust at a discount. Consequently, any income produced is likely to be less, resulting in a lower yield.

Discount to NAV

2.8 Most investment trusts are priced at a **discount to NAV**. For investors seeking income, this is a good thing. If an investment trust has £1 million of assets and 900,000 shares in issue at a market price of 100p, an investor is effectively getting £1.11 worth of assets per share. If we assume a yield of 4%, then an investment trust investor will get 4.44p per share as a distribution (ignoring charges). An equivalent unit trust investor would only get 4p.

2.9 **Discounts** can also be good for investors if they are prepared to wait. If a discount narrows from 10% to 5%, then the **capital return** on the investment will also be 5% greater. This factor does also work the other way, where discounts can widen, reducing the investment return.

Question 7.3

How might the level of discount of an investment trust change if the fund managers were changed?

2.10 **Discounts** may be good news for investors, but the directors of investment trust companies have an incentive to eliminate them. Where there is a large discount, a company becomes a possible **takeover target**. Some investment trust companies rearrange the capital structure of the company to reduce the likelihood of a discount and to ensure that the investment trust shares are marketable. One common way of doing this is to issue warrants. Another is to split the capital of the company into several different classes of share which each produce a different form of investment return.

2.11 The following circumstances could cause the **discount** for an investment trust to **narrow**.

- Improved investor sentiment towards the general market.
- The reputation of the trust manager improves.
- The involvement of an arbitrageur or a takeover bidder.
- The period to wind-up of the trust is reduced.
- The introduction of a new ISA plan or other marketing initiative increases demand.
- The trust buys back its own shares, reducing supply.
- Fewer warrants are available.

3 SPLIT CAPITAL STRUCTURES

3.1 The income from a particular class of share will depend on the type of share it is. **Split capital investment trusts** allow investors and portfolio managers an opportunity to **tailor returns**. If a **low-risk** but **rising income** is required they can invest in **stepped preference shares,** and if a high risk, but increasing, income is required an **income share** might be more appropriate.

3.2   The **capital value** of all classes of share will vary up until the trust is wound up. At that stage, the amount of capital returned will depend on the class of share and the order of priority in which the trust is wound up.

3.3   **Splitting up** an investment trust imposes a measure of **gearing** on income and capital returns from the investment. An investment trust can be split into different classes of share:

Class of share	Income return	Capital return at redemption
Income ordinary	High/rising	Predetermined
Capital ordinary	None (with some minor exceptions)	Remaining surplus
Preference/stepped preference	Predetermined	Predetermined
Zero dividend preference	None	Predetermined

Source: AITC

Income shares

3.4   These pay regular dividends being surplus income on trust assets and have a predetermined maturity value, known as the redemption price (typically £1). The market price of these shares fluctuates above and below the redemption price, depending on dividend prospects and time to maturity. A variation on this type of share has no value on redemption: these are called annuity income shares.

Highly geared ordinary income shares (a variation on income shares)

3.5   Sometimes referred to as residual income and capital shares, these offer high income and an entitlement to assets remaining at maturity once payments have been made to the holders of zero-dividend preference shares.

Capital shares

3.6   These do not pay dividends, but holders receive all the capital left over when the preference and income shareholders have been paid their maturity values. The absence of guarantees means capital shares are inherently risky. When the trust matures, the capital shareholders are last in line for a division of the spoils; if there is nothing left, they could come away empty-handed. With this high level of risk comes the potential for impressive growth through **gearing**.

3.7   EXAMPLE: CAPITAL SHARES

FGH Investment Trust has 500,000 income shares (£1 at redemption) and 500,000 capital shares. It has an asset value of £500,000 with ten years to run to redemption. If the fund grows at an average 10%, the fund will be worth £1,296,871 at redemption. The income shares will be repaid at £1 each or £500,000. This leaves £796,871 for the capital share investors (£1.59 per share).

If the growth rate were 11%, the fund would be £1,419,710. This would give the capital shareholders (£1,419,710 – £500,000) = £919,710 (£1.84 per share). As we can see, small increases in the growth rate give large increases in capital returns.

Question 7.4

At what rate of growth would capital shareholders in FGH receive nothing at wind up?

Preference/stepped preference shares

3.8 These are preference shares that pay a fixed dividend. Normal preference shares pay the same dividend but stepped preference shares offer dividends that step up in value during the life of the trust. They both pay a predetermined redemption value when the trust is wound up. Again, commitments to pay fixed amounts make this category of share suitable for those with a low appetite for risk.

3.9 For example, a stepped preference share might pay a dividend at 5% in year 1, 5.25% in year 2, 5.5% in year 3 etc.

Zero dividend preference shares

3.10 **Zero dividend preference shares** generate no dividend income but they offer a fixed capital return or redemption value. The fact that they pay no income means they can be of particular interest for tax planning, especially if the annual capital gains tax allowance is used to shelter profits. For example, 'zeros' might be issued at £1, redeemable after 10 years at £2, paying no dividend in the meantime. As lower-risk investments that pay a set amount at a set time, they are appropriate for those needing capital at certain points, such as parents looking to pay school fees. Zeros rank first in the winding up of the trust together with other preference shares.

3.11 Although this is a relatively **low risk** investment it should not be considered in the same risk category as cash investments. This fact came very clearly to light in 2002 as fears were rising that some 'zeros' would not provide their expected return. The fact that no 'zero' had ever failed to pay out its predetermined return prior to that time made them very popular.

3.12 The popularity created great demand for zeros and investment houses issued many new ones. Regrettably the risk reduction on this type of investment is provided by the other types of split in the structure of the trust. To meet the demand, zeros were set up without the supporting structure of the other share classes simply by investing in other zeros and by using high levels of borrowing to gear up returns. This 'incestuous' circle of investment and high levels of borrowing has ultimately caused the problem with this share class. Zeros that are based on a 'sound' split capital structure and with minimum levels of borrowing remain a good low risk investment.

Other capital structures

3.13 Other **split capital structures** are possible. **Income and residual capital shares** (also known as ordinary income shares, or highly geared ordinary shares) offer a high and rising income plus all the surplus assets of the trust at the winding-up date after other prior-ranking classes of shares have been repaid. They have no predetermined redemption value and are last in the order of priority.

3.14 If issued by a trust in **combination** with a **zero dividend preference share**, they are entitled to all the income generated by the trust. If issued by a trust with a **stepped preference share**, they receive all excess revenue after the predetermined dividend payment to the other class of share has been made.

3.15 Income and residual capital shares are **highly geared** and offer the potential for **high dividends** and **capital returns,** although it does make them a relatively **high-risk investment.**

Analysis of split capital shares

3.16 When analysing split capital shares, the other classes of share available and the number of each in issue will have a **significant impact** on the returns.

3.17 The **main statistics** used to analyse current and potential future performance on split capital investment trusts include:

- Asset cover
- Hurdle rate
- Gross redemption yield (GRY)
- Gross yield

3.18 The relevant statistics will depend on which factors influence the price of the class of share. They can be used in the following way.

Class of share	Influences on price	Relevant statistics
Zero	Interest rates Proportion of underlying investment in other zeros	Asset cover Hurdle rate Gross redemption yield
Stepped preference	Interest rates	Asset cover Hurdle rate Gross yield of share Gross redemption yield
Income	Interest rates Dividend growth prospects Portfolio yield of trust	Asset cover Hurdle rate Gross redemption yield Gross yield of share
Income and residual capital	Dividend growth prospects Portfolio yield of trust Structure of trust Capital growth prospects	Hurdle rate Gross redemption yield Gross yield of share Level of gearing
Capital	Portfolio yield of trust Capital growth prospects Structure of trust	Hurdle rate Gross redemption yield Level of gearing

Source: AITC

Asset cover

KEY TERM

Asset cover compares the value of the investment trust assets with its liability for repayment of each class of share. It is used primarily with zeros, stepped preference and income shares.

3.19 If the **asset cover** is 1 or more, it means that there are already sufficient assets to repay that class of share at the predetermined price. However, as there is a priority order for repayment this may not be the case for other classes. The higher the asset cover, the greater

146
PROFESSIONAL EDUCATION

the chance of repaying that class of share on a winding up. If a share has an asset cover of less than 1, it indicates that in the event of a wind-up at that moment in time, the share class is not covered and the capital is therefore at risk. It can be used for capital shares, based on an assumed payment on wind-up, eg 50p.

Hurdle rate

> **KEY TERM**
>
> The **hurdle rate** measures the level of growth on the NAV on a compound basis required to repay each individual share class at the predetermined price. (For capital shares, a price is assumed, for example 50p.)

3.20 A high hurdle rate indicates that significant growth is required between the time the statistic was calculated and the winding up date. A negative figure indicates that the market could fall and the shares would still be repaid in full.

Question 7.5

If a class of investment trust has an asset cover of greater than 1, what do we know about the hurdle rate?

Gross redemption yield

> **KEY TERM**
>
> The **gross redemption yield** (GRY) is the total annual return from both income and capital. The figure can be used to compare returns between different classes of share and different types of investment.

3.21 Certain classes of share will provide a **variable return** on winding up (eg capitals, income, income and residual capital shares, warrants) and, as such, it is not possible to calculate an exact figure for GRY. In order to provide a basis of comparison, notional rates of growth are applied and the GRY is calculated assuming the capital return based on those rates of growth.

> **Exam focus point**
>
> In the examination, you may be asked to comment on an analysis, or even to compare the analyses of two or more different shares or share classes. It is important that you can do this.

BPP
PROFESSIONAL EDUCATION

Gearing with split capital investment trusts

> ### KEY TERM
>
> 'Gearing' typically refers to borrowing but, in a split capital trust, it also relates to the effect of the share structure of the company on the relative share price. Gearing, in all forms, exposes the investor to higher levels of risk. The higher the gearing, the greater the risk and the higher the potential reward.

3.22 With a **split capital trust**, it is the priority order that dictates the level of **gearing**. Effectively, the lower the priority for repayment, the higher the gearing. The level of gearing in each case will depend on the classes of share and the entitlement that each has.

3.23 **Split capital trusts** vary widely. While some may issue the same classes of share, these may be in different ratios or quantities, with different lengths of life. They may also have different investment policies, affecting the performance of the underlying assets of the company in different ways. The use of different classes of share from a **split capital investment trust**, alone or in combination with others, enables an investor to get the gearing they want on their investment.

Winding up split capital investment trusts

3.24 At the predetermined date, shareholders will be asked to agree to **wind up** the trust according to the procedure laid down in its Articles of Association. This will enable them to receive the predetermined or underlying value of their investment. They may also be given the option of **continuing** the life of the trust or of **rolling** their investment over into a new trust.

3.25 If the trust is **wound up**, the different classes of share are **repaid**, after **repayment** of any loans or debentures, out of the **assets** and according to their entitlement after expenses have been deducted. They are repaid in **order of priority**.

3.26 Although **split capital trusts** have a limited life (which may be extended if the shareholders vote in favour), investors are not obliged to hold their shares until the final winding-up date. They can be sold at the prevailing market price **at any time** during the life of the trust although the price will be dependent on market conditions at the time.

Priority order on winding up an investment trust

3.27 The different classes of share in a **split capital trust** are ranked in order of **priority**. Where the company has debt such as **debentures** or **loan stock**, these are ranked first before the shareholders to be repaid in winding-up. If the company has **warrants**, these are always ranked last and are paid after all other classes of share. Between these two, each share class then follows in a particular order, both with regard to dividends, paid from the income earned by the trust during its life, and to capital, paid from the assets of the trust at the winding-up date. For every variation on a split capital investment trust there is a predetermined sequence in which the various classes of share are repaid.

3.28 Different combinations of share classes may be issued and the following table lists the main examples of split capital trusts currently in existence, with the different shares in order of priority.

Combination of shares issued	Income and capital shares	Zeros, stepped preference, income and capital shares	Zeros, stepped preference shares, income and residual capital shares	Packaged units
Highest priority	Income	Zero*	Zero*	
		(Stepped) Preference*	(Stepped) Preference*	Packaged unit
		Income		
Lowest priority	Capital	Capital	Income and residual capital	n/a

* These are interchangeable. A few split capital trusts rank the stepped preference share before the zeros, but this is rare. In the exam, assume that zeros have priority.

4 CHARGES ON INVESTMENT TRUSTS

4.1 Investment trust shares are traded on the **Stock Exchange** like any other equity. Buying them may involve **commission** for the stockbroker, but this is unlikely to be greater than 1% of the value of the investment. **Stamp duty** of 0.5% is also payable on purchases.

4.2 Where **investment trusts** are purchased through the various savings and investment schemes run by the investment trust companies, the charges are unlikely to be any higher. This represents good value for money for **regular monthly investment**.

4.3 **Annual management charge**s are allowed for within the costs of running the company and are not normally visible. They may however, be determined from the company accounts from the various **expense ratios**.

4.4 **IFAs** are becoming increasingly aware of this versatile investment vehicle. Many have avoided promoting them in the past due to the lack of any reward on their part. Two things have happened to change this. The first is the wider acceptance in the market place of fees and the second is that investment trust schemes for distribution via IFAs are beginning to have built-in initial and management charges. The **initial charges** are tending to be in the region of 3% and **management charges** 1%. The problems with zeros and the FSA investigation into the sales of zeros together with high levels of customer complaints has deterred many IFAs from promoting this type of investment.

5 OTHER SECURITIES AND CLASSES OF SHARE

5.1 In addition to conventional unit trusts and splits, there are a number of additional securities and classes of share available within the framework of an investment trust. These include **warrants, C shares, S shares** and **packaged units**.

Warrants

> ### KEY TERM
>
> **Warrants** are highly geared, high-risk investments that confer the right of the holder to purchase a fixed number of shares at a fixed price on a fixed date or dates. The warrants are a security rather than a separate class of share and are transferable (ie, can be sold on). Warrants have no right to income: they only produce capital growth, and this is dependent on the price of the underlying share reaching the strike price at the expiry date when the warrants can be exercised. Where it does not, the warrants expire worthless.

5.2 EXAMPLE: INVESTMENT TRUST WARRANTS

A warrant gives the right to purchase a fixed number of shares on 30 April 2005 at £1.00. On that date, the share price was 93p. It would have been possible for the warrant holder to exercise their rights, but they would lose money as they are paying £1.00 for a share that they could buy in the market for £0.93. They should allow the warrant to expire worthless. If the price were £1.05, they could exercise the warrants, giving a profit of 5p each, less transaction costs.

5.3 As mentioned earlier in this Study Text, warrants are used on the **issue of new investment trust shares**. When new investment trusts are issued, there will be no discount to NAV available to investors subscribing to the issue. This can be unattractive, as most investors know that soon after starting trading the price will fall to a discount. In order to encourage investors to buy, warrants are issued as well. The warrants should have a value, even where the trusts are trading below the strike price. Over time, the price should be expected to rise and the warrant may become valuable, and so may be of interest to speculative investors. The sale price of the warrant helps to compensate the investment trust holder for a possible fall in the price of the ordinary shares once they become traded in the market.

Question 7.6

What choices are available to the holder of a warrant with six months to its exercise date?

C shares

> ### KEY TERM
>
> 'C shares' are shares floated after the original issue of ordinary shares, usually to **raise additional capital**.

5.4 **C shares** are quoted separately from the ordinary shares until the capital raised through their issue is fully or substantially invested in the investment trust. At this time, they are converted into the ordinary shares at a set ratio based on their **net asset value**. They are used to allow a trust to increase the number of shares and the funds under management without diluting the value of the existing shares.

5.5 The issue of **C shares** provides an alternative to using a **rights issue** to raise capital.

S shares

5.6 'S shares' are used to issue new shares on the market without going to the expense of launching a new investment trust company. They form a separate investment to the original share issue and the price of **S shares** will always be quoted separately. They are similar to 'C' shares except that they are never integrated into the main investment trust.

Packaged units

5.7 The investment trust managers of some **split capital trusts** have arranged for a combination of their shares to be traded together in what is known as a **'packaged unit'** (not to be confused with units issued by unit trusts). Such units usually comprise shares in the ratio at which those shares were originally issued. **Packaged units** have all the characteristics of an ordinary share issued by a conventional investment trust, although in some cases the component classes of share can be separated out and traded as separate securities if required. In many cases, the discount to NAV will be much reduced due to the increased demand created by the split capital structure.

5.8 **Packaged units** provide a benefit for the investment trust managers who are effectively getting the best of both worlds. The splitting of the units helps to reduce the discount on the shares and the recombination of them allows them to offer investors access to an investment with more 'conventional' characteristics.

6 INVESTMENT OBJECTIVES OF INVESTMENT TRUSTS

6.1 Ordinary investment trust shares provide a potentially increasing income and capital growth for their investors. As discussed previously, the tendency of **investment trusts** to trade at a **discount** can even give an increased level of income in comparison to an equivalent unit trust. However, the many different classes of investment trust share can be useful in a number of different investment situations.

6.2 **Income shares** provide a relatively low risk, with high and increasing income. Care should be taken to consider the most appropriate type of income share, as the level of **capital entitlement** will vary with each. The **gross redemption yield measure** will allow comparison with other investment trusts or other forms of investment such as **equities**, **fixed interest** or **cash deposits**. They may be useful in retirement planning as part of an income withdrawal plan. Some ISA providers are beginning to appreciate the characteristics of this class of investment and are launching funds based on them.

6.3 **Capital shares** provide highly volatile capital growth without income. This can be a potential advantage for individuals paying high rates of income tax who have not used up their CGT allowance. The shares can be used on their own as a **high risk investment** or could be mixed in a **portfolio** with **zeros**, giving potentially **higher capital returns** in a portfolio with reduced risk.

6.4 **Zeros** based on an appropriate split capital structure can be a relatively low risk investment and can provide fixed capital sums at a specific time in the future, eg funding school or university fees, or paying for a wedding or holiday. They can also play an important part in **portfolio planning** by altering its risk profiles. They may also be used as a tax-planning tool for higher rate taxpayers with unused CGT allowances.

6.5 **Stepped preference shares** are also relatively **low risk** investments, which provide steadily increasing income with a **known capital return**. They could help in retirement planning as part of an income withdrawal plan. They can also be used as part of a **portfolio** to provide increasing income, freeing other investments to produce longer-term capital gains.

Question 7.7

What type of investment trust would suit an investor seeking low risk investment and regular income?

6.6 **Income and residual capital shares** provide a high and rising income, but with **aggressive capital growth**. The risk may be minimised if used as part of a **planned portfolio**, perhaps mixed with other types of **income share** and **zeros**.

Investment powers of investment trust managers

6.7 An **investment trust** is a quoted company governed by the Companies Act and Stock Exchange regulations. The board of directors sets the investment policy of the company and will either make the investments themselves or appoint an **investment manager** to take control. The investment objective could be to focus on income or growth with UK or international shares, or alternatively could be to invest in a specialist investment (eg venture and development capital) or geographical area.

6.8 **Investment trusts** are subject to approval by HMCR (HM Revenue & Customs). This approval exempts them from corporation tax on capital gains within the company. The effect of this is to bring the taxation of investment trusts into line with **unit trusts**. Investors are liable for **income tax** on **dividends** in the same way as they would be with shares in any other company and may be liable for **capital gains tax** on **disposal**. In order to be approved, investment managers are restricted to investing in the shares of other companies. The shares may be in listed or unlisted companies.

6.9 One of the benefits of an **investment trust** over a **unit trust** is that, being a quoted company, it has the power to borrow. This allows the managers to **gear up** the performance of the trust.

The role of gearing in investment trusts

6.10 **Gearing** in investment trusts is caused by two main factors:

(a) The presence of **different classes of share**, which provides gearing for lower ranked share classes

(b) The ability of investment managers to **borrow money**. The money is channelled into investments

6.11 Two main factors come into play when investment managers **borrow**:

- An increase in the value of the assets purchased with the borrowed money
- Interest becomes payable on the loan

Where the growth exceeds the interest, which is likely in a **rising market**, the extra profits benefit the shareholders as a possible increase in **dividend and/or NAV**. Where this is not the case, which is likely in a falling market, the investors effectively lose. Overall, **gearing** increases the **volatility of the share** and the more highly geared a share is, the greater the movements will be with respect to the market.

6.12 The calculation for gearing is:

$$\frac{\text{Loans (less deposits)}}{\text{Capital and reserves}}$$

6.13 The loans may be in the form of **long or short-term bank lending**, or any issued classes of **loan stock** (including preference shares, which are classed as a loan).

6.14 EXAMPLE: GEARING I

UBC Investment Trust has capital and reserves of £10 million and loans of £2 million. The gearing of this company is £2 million/£10 million or 0.2. Gearing will usually be expressed in percentage terms, eg 20%.

If UBC uses the borrowing to increase its holdings in shares and markets move up, the net asset value of the company is increased by the growth on the borrowing less the interest.

Question 7.8

If UBC (see above) pays interest on its loan at a rate of 8% over a year and the value of the underlying investments increases by 20% over the same period, by what percentage will the NAV increase?

6.15 The greater the level of borrowing by a company, the greater the level of gearing in percentage terms. The **disadvantage** comes when investment markets go down. In these cases, the **gearing** amplifies the downward movement.

6.16 EXAMPLE: GEARING II

Assume that for UBC the underlying assets lose value by 20%.

(a) The value of the shares invested will be £12 million in total (assets plus borrowing).

(b) The assets will decrease by 20% or £2.4 million, plus the interest payable of 8% × £2 million = £160,000.

(c) The total NAV after the fall will be £12 million less £2.4 million, less £160,000 = £9.44 million, less the borrowing of £2 million.

(d) This gives a decrease in value from £10 million to £7.44 million, ie a 25.6% decrease.

Chapter roundup

- An **investment trust** is a company which invests in shares. Investors hold shares in the investment trust.

- When analysing the value of an investment trust's shares it is normal to look at: share price; geographical spread; gearing; NAV performance; levels of discount/premium to NAV; dividend growth and gross yield.

- **Split capital investment trusts** offer a range of types of share for the investor in income shares, capital shares, stepped preference shares and zero dividend shares.

- Analysing split capital trusts requires the calculation of asset cover, hurdle rate and gross redemption yield.

Quick quiz

1   What are the two main differences between an investment trust and a unit trust?

2   Who is responsible for the investment decisions within an investment trust?

3   What is the key factor in determining whether an investment trust is trading at a premium or discount?

4   If an investment trust were trading at a premium, how would the dividend yield compare with that of a similarly invested unit trust?

5   Which class of split capital investment trust shares could be used to provide a fixed increase in capital?

6   What is an income and residual capital share and in what form does it produce its investment return?

7   Which is more likely to repay the full amount at wind-up, a share with a hurdle rate of 5%, or one of 10%?

8   Which class of share in a split capital investment trust will be the most highly geared?

9   How does the diluted NAV calculation differ from the undiluted one?

10   Why are warrants issued with newly launched investment trusts?

11   What is a packaged unit?

12   What is the key difference in the investment powers of an investment trust manager and a unit trust manager?

The answers to the questions in the Quick Quiz can be found at the end of this Study Text. Before checking your own answers against them, you should look back at this chapter and use the information in it to correct your answers.

Answers to Chapter Questions

7.1   A highly geared investment trust will lose value more rapidly than the market.

7.2   The undiluted NAV = (£12m – £2m)/10m = £1

The diluted NAV = (£12m – £2m + £1.5m)/(10m + 3m) = 88p

7.3   It would depend on market perception of the new managers. This will reflect on the demand for the shares and the level of demand influences the level of discount.

7.4   If the fund produced exactly £500,000, the capital shareholders would not be paid. This would happen if there was no growth on the fund. If the fund assets lost value, capital shareholders would get nothing and the income shareholders would get back less than £1 per share.

7.5   If a class of investment trust share has an asset cover of more than 1, then the assets are already covered for repayment. If this is the case, the assets do not need to grow between now and redemption to cover them, so the hurdle rate will be negative.

7.6   The holder of a warrant with six months to the exercise date can continue to hold it until that time, or he may sell it on the open market at any time up to the exercise date.

7.7   A stepped preference share is a low risk type of investment trust that provides a fixed level of regular income and in some cases increase in capital. It is important to check the asset cover (which should be more than one) and the hurdle rate (which should be very low), as this indicates the likelihood of the return of capital on wind-up.

7.8   The value of the investments will be £12 million in total (the assets plus the borrowing). The assets will increase by 20% or £2.4 million, less the interest payable of 8% × £2 million

= £160,000. The total NAV will be £14.24 million, less the borrowing of £2 million, an increase in value of £12.24 million/£10 million = 22.4%.

PRACTICE QUESTION 7

Mary has £50,000 invested in each of two investment trusts. According to recent information sent to her, the statistical information on each is as follows.

	NBC Trust Zero dividend shares	CBN Trust Zero dividend shares
Share price	£1.00	£1.50
Net Asset Value	£0.90	£1.30
Price on wind up	£1.00	£5.00
Asset cover	2	0.2
Gross redemption yield	7.5%	11%
Hurdle rate	–5%	20%
Term to wind-up	5 years	5 years

She would like to ask you some questions about her investments.

(a)   Which of the above investments has the lower risk and why?   (2)

(b)   Which could produce the better return? Explain your answer.   (2)

(c)   List the main classes of share found in split capital investment trusts.   (4)

(d)   For each type of share listed, describe the form in which the investment return is produced.   (8)

(e)   What statistical factors can indicate the potential returns from a capital share?   (4)

Chapter 8

LIFE ASSURANCE BASED INVESTMENTS

Chapter topic list	Syllabus reference
1 Investment objectives of unit-linked funds	3.3
2 With-profit policies	3.3
3 Guaranteed bond products	3.3
4 Unit-linked pricing	3.3
5 Life assurance company taxation	3.3
6 Derivative based life assurance bonds	3.3
7 Broker funds and multi-manager schemes	3.3

Introduction

In this chapter, we will be looking at life assurance policies as investment products. The investment element was originally developed as a method of distributing underwriting profits to 'with-profit' policyholders and has remained popular over the last two hundred years. Over that time, the medium has extended and is currently used for lump sum savings, regular investment and annuity business.

1 INVESTMENT OBJECTIVES OF UNIT-LINKED FUNDS

1.1 In the past, **with profits** has been the traditional method by which life offices, many of them mutual organisattions, distributed their profits. In the 1970s, a new form of life assurance linked investment was developed called **unit-linking**. This combined a very flexible investment format with life assurance and has proved very popular. Today, **unit-linked policies** represent a large proportion of the total business sold.

1.2 Through their unit-linked funds, **insurance companies** aim to cater for the **full range** of investment objectives that an investor may have. The units are effectively **open-ended investments,** where the value of the unit is directly related to the underlying assets of the fund. The range of funds is very wide, with the unit prices occupying nearly two pages of the *Financial Times*.

Income and capital

1.3 Life assurance based investment vehicles could be employed to satisfy the requirement for **income** (distribution funds) **or capital growth.**

1.4 However **life and pension funds do not normally produce an income stream.** All the income arising from the underlying investments of the pooled funds will be reinvested, producing an increase in the value of the units. Investors may take **'income'** by encashing the appropriate number of units on a regular basis. However, care must be taken as this is not pure income: it is a combination of income and capital, which could give rise to **erosion of capital.** As with all investments, the production of income will have **tax consequences** and this will largely be dependent on the type of investment vehicle in which the units are invested, eg pension, unit linked bond.

Question 8.1

How do the prices of insurance 'units' vary with the value of the underlying fund?

Risk

1.5 The range of funds provided by companies will normally cater for a range of risk levels from **no risk** to **high risk.**

No risk

1.6 The **lowest risk funds** available to investors are **cash funds** and **building society funds.**

(a) **Cash funds** will tend to be invested in various types of deposit, including bank deposits, money market deposits and various types of short-term loan note.

(b) **Building society funds** will be invested in a range of building society accounts, or sometimes just a single one.

1.7 These types of fund tend to be used as a shelter when markets are turning downwards, or where an individual is nearing retirement or maturity and wishes to preserve the capital value of their fund. The nature of most UK **unit-linked arrangements** is that switching can be done without tax implications. This demonstrates one of the **advantages** of unit-linked investment - the ability to change investment strategy without incurring a tax liability - something that is not possible with equities, unit trusts or investment trusts.

1.8 While a 'no risk' label is often applied to cash funds, they are subject to provisions which allow for compensation subject to a maximum of 90% of the value of the units, in the event of the financial collapse of the issuing office.

Low risk

1.9 A range of **lower risk funds** is also available. These can potentially provide a higher return and will be invested in areas such as **gilts** or **fixed interest investments.** They cannot be classed as **'no risk'** because the **value of the** underlying instruments may fall or rise. **Fixed interest funds** also have the potential for **'credit risk',** particularly where fund managers are taking risks to secure higher returns.

1.10 Some companies offer a **low risk managed** or balanced **fund.** Such funds invest in a range of investments including **equities, fixed interest investments, property** and **deposits.** Where the mix favours a cautious approach, a description of **low risk** is fair. Such funds have resistance to downward movements in markets, as only a **small proportion** of the fund will be in **equities** and those chosen will be the **most secure** available. These funds can be used by those who are cautious by nature and those nearing retirement who may choose gradually to switch a larger and larger portion of their pension investment out of equities into gilts, for example.

1.11 **With-profit funds** are a separate case. They are traditionally described as **low risk,** although the underlying investments are more likely to be of moderate risk in nature. The reduction in risk is achieved by a system of withholding the full growth of the investment in good years to allow for a reserve to 'smooth' future returns over bad years. With-profit funds cannot be described as 'no-risk' and most companies will reserve the right to apply a **Market Value Reduction (MVR),** reducing investment returns in exceptionally poor market conditions, or premature surrender.

Moderate risk

1.12 **Moderate risk funds** would include managed funds with an appropriate mix of underlying investments, for example some of the UK funds where the equity element is mainly in 'blue chip shares'. The objective of this type of fund is to provide growth over the medium to long-term. This level of investment term should be discussed with the clients, as these funds will move with the **stock markets.** As such, they are unsuitable for individuals looking for an investment return within five years. This type of fund is used for all forms of **long-term investment** including pensions, although a gradual switch out of these funds towards retirement would be advised. Some life companies are offering various protection schemes on their pension funds. These funds allow for 'moderate' growth, but will be underpinned by some form of derivative to allow investors access to their money without loss within specified periods.

High risk

1.13 Most companies will offer at least one **higher risk fund.** Sometimes this will be in the guise of an 'actively managed' or 'adventurous' managed fund. More often, the risk will arise as a result of the nature of the underlying investment, eg smaller companies or Far East equities.

Question 8.2

What unit-linked funds might be most appropriate for an individual who was not prepared to take any risk with their investment?

Risk rating

1.14 Until recently, the **risk rating** of a managed fund has been somewhat uncertain. The category of managed funds has in the past been sufficiently wide as to cover funds with 5% invested in equities to those with 95% in equities. Clearly these funds will react quite differently to movements in the markets and the situation has caused considerable confusion for investors. To avoid this, the **Association of British Insurers Investment Classification Group** splits managed funds into the following categories.

(a) **Defensive managed,** with investment in equities limited to 35% of the fund

(b) **Cautious managed,** with investment in equities limited to 60% of the fund

(c) **Balanced managed,** with investment in equities limited to a maximum of 85% of the fund

(d) **Stockmarket managed,** able to invest up to 100% in equities at the manager's discretion

1.15 The **balanced managed category** was originally proposed at 80% equities. However, pressure from the industry managed to get the figure increased. The main argument was that the average proportion of equities in managed funds was 84%. The effect of the 80% limit would be to decimate the managed fund market, as many investors would not be prepared to invest in the 'stockmarket' managed category.

Geographical spread

1.16 For many investors, the ability to **invest globally** is an essential part of the investment strategy for reducing risk. An international spread will often weather the effects of a local problem. **Unit-linked investments** offer the opportunity to pick individual regions, such as Europe or Japan. As an alternative, many companies offer an international fund, which is essentially a managed balance of equities from all geographical areas.

2 WITH-PROFIT POLICIES

2.1 This type of policy was one of the earliest forms of pooled investment. They originally came about as a vehicle for distributing underwriting profits on life assurance policies, but as the surpluses became larger, they became an investment vehicle in their own right. With this type of investment, all the usual factors relating to **pooled investment** apply, for example, access to professional fund managers, spread of investment over asset type and geographical areas and economies of scale. However, they also have a further factor for **reducing risk**. Part of the income and growth of the underlying assets is applied to reserves. As already indicated, the reserve is used to provide funds in future years when returns are not as good to provide 'smooth' returns.

2.2 There are essentially two main types of 'with-profit' investment: **conventional** and **unit-linked**.

Conventional with-profits policies

2.3 **Conventional with-profits policies** are structured in a very different way from the unitised version, using a series of different types of bonus. This factor was contributory in the later move towards a simpler, more flexible unitised structure that uses units that increase in value (or number) with time.

2.4 The conventional with-profit policy is the original and traditional form of the life assurance policy. Although they may form part of an individual investor's **portfolio**, they are less likely to form part of a professional fund manager's portfolio.

> **KEY TERM**
>
> A conventional **with-profit policy** is set up for a **fixed term** and the return is in the form of an increase in capital value between purchase and maturity. This increase in value is based upon the sum assured of the policy and the bonuses added during the life of the policy.

2.5 The **sum assured** of the policy will vary from company to company, but will be based on the premium and term of the policy. This offers a **guarantee** in that, providing the investment is held to maturity, the sum assured is the minimum that will be payable. Together with bonuses added, it also represents the money that will be paid out on the death of the policyholder.

2.6 Once set, this **original sum assured remains the same**, but bonuses are added on top. These **bonuses** come in several different forms.

Bonus	When payable
Reversionary/ Normal bonuses	Paid **annually** in arrears: once added, they cannot be removed.
Special bonuses	These are declared under **extraordinary circumstances** (eg on demutualisation or takeover), or to reflect an unexpected exceptional increase in funds.
Interim bonuses	These are paid where **death** occurs between reversionary bonus payments and are proportional to the unpaid bonus.
Terminal bonuses	These are paid at the **end of the term (or on death)** and reflect the growth of the underlying assets over the term of the policy, over and above those previously distributed.

2.7 If these investments are encashed **before maturity**, the **encashment value** will be calculated by the life company actuary. The value is likely to be significantly less than the accumulated value of the sum assured and bonuses. The amount returned may even be less than the original investment.

2.8 The performance of a **with-profit investment** will depend on:

(a) The performance of the **underlying investments**, for example equities, fixed interest securities, cash and property

(b) Whether the company is **mutual or proprietary**: proprietary companies must distribute some profits to shareholders

(c) Profits from **other areas of the business** (particularly for a mutual company)

(d) The strength of the **company** (the level of reserves, measured by the free asset ratio) affects the company's ability to continue bonus payments when investment performance is low

(e) The **reserves**, which also impact on the ability of the company to increase the proportion of equities in the fund as life companies are required to have certain minimum levels of liquidity

2.9 The **bonus structure** of these investments provides smooth growth for the policyholder, which can be useful for risk averse investors planning for future events. A problem can be that when stockmarkets are racing ahead, investors expect excellent performance, while with this type of investment, the surpluses made when times are good are used to offset the bad times. The bonus structure also **reduces the flexibility** and **increases the complexity** of these policies relative to other types of investment.

2.10 The lack of flexibility with conventional insurance policies, combined with poor surrender values, has given rise to a **secondary market** in these policies. The policyholder may be able to obtain a higher sum than the surrender value by selling or auctioning the policy. Investment returns on these **traded endowment policies (TEPs)** if held to maturity can be attractive to some investors. Some investment trusts and unit trusts have been set up specifically with TEPs as their underlying investment.

2.11 The occurrence of **demutualisations** has also caused interest in with-profits policies. Policyholders of plans with mutual companies effectively have **ownership** of the company. In the event of a demutualisation they may receive an increase in bonus (usually by payment of special bonus), a payout, or shares in the new company.

Question 8.3

What level of risk might be attached to investing in an investment trust company with the objective of buying TEPs and holding them to maturity?

Unit-linked with-profits investment

2.12 The underlying investment principle of **unit-linked (or unitised) with-profits investments** is broadly the same as that of conventional policies. The surplus returns from good years are held in reserve to pay bonuses in bad years. However, with a unitised contract, **policyholders would not normally be treated as the owners of the company** and as such would not share in the underwriting profits on the life assurance business. They would also not normally receive any form of payment in the event of a demutualisation or take-over.

2.13 Rather than having bonuses, the investment is divided into **units**. Growth on these units can be achieved in one of two ways.

  (a) The **price** of the units can increase (known as variable units).
  (b) The **number** of units can increase (known as fixed price units).

2.14 In each case, the **rate of increase** is declared annually in advance (as opposed to being declared in arrears as with conventional with-profits). **Unitised with-profits** works like a bank account, with interest added on a daily basis, for example, if the interest rate declared was 3.0% then at the end of the year the investment would have increased in value by 3.0%, with a little bit being added each day.

2.15 The unitised with-profits investment provides a **fixed return**, although the assets underlying the fund will fluctuate in value. This may mean that the underlying growth of the assets within the **with-profits fund** can be higher or lower than the guaranteed rate of return applied. There are two mechanisms for adjusting this.

  (a) Where the underlying value of the assets is **greater** than the growth on the with-profit fund, a terminal bonus may be declared as a percentage of the fund, which will make up part of the difference. This mechanism is not designed to make up all of the difference, as some money will be kept to provide a surplus for future years.

  (b) Where the value of the assets is lower than the value of the with-profit units, a **Market Value Reduction** may be applied.

2.16 Care must be taken in reading the 'small print' on these policies as most units are guaranteed **not** to decrease in value, but this does not necessarily mean that there is no **possibility of loss of capital**. A penalty will be deducted from the encashment value of the units if the **MVAF** is applied. However, the existence of the market value adjuster does not mean that it will be used. Its use may cause loss of customer confidence in the product. Having a **market value adjustment** means that a unitised with-profits product cannot be classed as a 'no-risk' investment. It must be described as a 'low-risk' investment.

2.17 UK unit-linked life assurance products fall into two main categories: those for **regular savings,** and those for **lump sum investment.**

Regular savings in unit-linked with-profit policies

2.18 **Life assurance funds** form the investment element of a number of different types of life assurance product. In these contracts, regular investments buy units in the fund or funds chosen by the policyholder. The cost of the life assurance provided by the policy is **deducted** by the cancellation of sufficient units on a monthly basis to provide the sum assured.

2.19 Typically, the contracts mentioned above are primarily **'life assurance' contracts** and the investment element is purely incidental. Nonetheless, some **'savings' contracts** make use of the tax treatment of life assurance policies and apply it to savings. These policies are normally called **Maximum Investment Plans (MIPS).** They provide the minimum possible life cover (75% of the value of the premiums paid over the term), that qualifies them to be taxed as a **life assurance policy.** In many cases these will be qualifying policies so there will not normally be any further tax liability on maturity or encashment providing the policy has run the shorter of 75% of the term or 10 years.

2.20 The use of **regular savings** on unit-linked products allows investors to take advantage of **'pound cost averaging'.** This effectively provides higher returns on regular investment than a single investment. The **volatility** of the **investment fund** is also a factor, with the more volatile funds showing this effect to a greater extent.

2.21 The **unit-linked funds** underlying the investment can be **changed** at the request of the investor. A **switch** will change the units already purchased to other available units, whereas a **redirection** changes the funds in which future contributions will be invested. To make a complete change from one fund to another, **switching and redirection** is combined. For example, with a switch from the European fund to the Managed fund, the switch exchanges existing European units for Managed fund units while the redirection ensures that future contributions buy Managed fund units. One of the advantages of **life assurance** based investments is that these switches can take place at **minimal cost** (redirection is usually free and some companies offer one or two free switches per year while others offer all switches free), without disturbing the tax status of the plan. A switch between unit or investment trusts would incur charges and constitute a chargeable event for capital gains tax purposes.

Question 8.4

How does the cost of changing investment strategy with life assurance based investments compare with unit trusts?

Lump sum investments in unit-linked with-profit policies

2.22 Life assurance investments can be an appropriate investment vehicle for a **lump sum.** Such policies are usually termed unit-linked investment bonds.

(a) The **pooling of assets** combined with professional investment management helps to **reduce risk** but can still provide returns linked to stockmarkets over the longer term.

(b) The ability to **switch** life assurance funds allows major changes in investment strategy with the minimum of effort and with **no tax consequences.**

(c) From the investor's point of view the administration and paperwork is **simplified.**

2.23 Investment of **lump sums** into insurance policies does also have its critics, who point out that the costs are higher, most of this going into commissions for the adviser, and that this form of investment is less versatile and less tax-effective than other forms of investment. These policies have a place in **investment portfolios** for many investors, but advisers need a thorough understanding of the taxation of this type of investment to avoid paying **unnecessary tax** and, of course, commission can be rebated to enhance allocation rates.

2.24 **Unit-linked investment bonds** can provide a full range of **risk profiles** for the investor, from the cautious **with-profit funds,** to the most adventurous of **overseas equities.** This form of investment can also meet the investor's requirement for **income** or **capital.**

2.25 If an **'income'** is required, this can be provided by the **encashment of units** on a regular basis. Technically speaking the regular payments are not income: they are regular **disposals of capital.**

2.26 Where a **regular income** is required, a variation on the **unit-linked bond,** called a **distribution bond,** can be used.

Distribution bond

2.27 The objective of a **distribution bond** is to provide a competitive and rising income while allowing steady **capital appreciation** in real terms over the longer period.

2.28 In order to produce income, a **distribution bond** will invest in a mixture of **gilts, fixed interest securities, convertibles** and **high yielding equities.** The difference between a distribution bond and an ordinary bond is that a distribution bond has a separate fund into which the income from the main fund is placed. This is quite different to the production of income with an ordinary **unit-linked bond,** where income is reinvested within the fund and there is no way of separating the two.

Question 8.5

Is it possible for capital to be eroded with a distribution bond?

2.29 The income is placed into the separate fund, typically called an **'income'** fund and can be distributed on a regular basis, eg quarterly or half yearly. The advantage of this is that it allows investors to **encash units** representing just the income rather than both income and capital.

2.30 All **encashments,** whether from the **'income'** units or the **main fund,** are deemed by the **Inland Revenue** as return of capital and are taxed in accordance with the normal rules relating to non-qualifying life insurance funds.

2.31 In addition to the income arising from the **'income units',** withdrawals can normally be made from the main units of the investment, just like a normal **unit-linked bond.** This can provide additional income **flexibility** for the holder.

Question 8.6

Would you expect the unit price of units in a distribution bond to increase in value faster or slower than a similar fund not linked to a distribution bond?

---

3   GUARANTEED BOND PRODUCTS

3.1   For some investors there will be a requirement for **no risk investments**. Life assurance companies have two products that may appeal to this type of investor – the **guaranteed income bond** and **guaranteed growth bond**. Both are still life assurance bonds and are taxed accordingly, ie income produced is treated as capital.

> ### KEY TERMS
>
> **Guaranteed income bonds** provide a fixed 'income' over an agreed term. At the end of the term, the original investment is returned.
>
> With a **guaranteed growth bond**, the **capital value** of the bond **increases** at a pre-agreed rate over the term. Encashments prior to maturity will be subject to penalty charges and may return less than the original capital invested.

3.2   Technically, life assurance bonds are **safer** than bank or building society investment in that the **Financial Services Compensation Scheme** will return 90% of the value of the investment in the event of a company failing, **without a limit**. Bank and building society compensation is limited to £31,700, as mentioned earlier.

Single premium endowment policy

3.3   Although this product is not a '**bond**', it is very similar in a number of ways. As a non-qualifying life assurance product, it is taxed in the same way. The underlying investment is a **with-profits endowment** and provides its capital growth in the form of **reversionary bonuses** added on an annual basis and a **terminal bonus** on encashment, in much the same way as a regular premium endowment policy. If held to maturity, it will guarantee to pay a minimum of the sum assured plus bonuses accrued to date.

Offshore bond products

3.4   As an addition to their UK product range, some life companies also issue **life assurance products** through **offshore subsidiaries**. This allows investors to take advantage of some of the tax differences in territories such as the Isle of Man, Eire, Jersey and Guernsey. Some territories apply low tax rates for overseas investors while domestic investors cannot benefit from these tax breaks.

3.5   There can be problems with this strategy, as some '**tax havens**' do not have taxation agreements with other countries. Withholding tax (tax deducted) on income received may not be recoverable by the offshore fund.

3.6   As an example, the **Isle of Man** is a popular domicile for offshore life assurance offices. The Isle of Man does not have taxation agreements with any other countries, so typically the tax deducted at source on dividends cannot be reclaimed.

3.7   This does not have to be a problem as the dividend yield in many markets is low. Japan has yields of less than 0.5% and even the UK, historically a country for high dividend yields, produces average yields in the region of 2 – 6% on the FTSE.

3.8   Some companies will be based in areas such as Eire, which as part of the EU does have a number of taxation agreements although in many cases it may not be cost-efficient to reclaim the tax. One approach is to invest in **equities** with **low yields**. The effect on the fund should not be too significant as only the dividend would be taxed. The tax on a fund that is 75% invested in equities with a rate of tax on dividends of 25% and a yield of 2% would be 0.375% ($0.75 \times 0.25 \times 0.02 = 0.00375$).

Question 8.7

What would the tax penalty be on a bond fund totally invested in equities, with a yield of 0.5% per annum and a tax rate on dividends of 20%?

3.9 Many companies with these **offshore subsidiaries** offer a greater range of funds through their offshore company than they do with their UK companies. This in itself can prove an attraction for individuals looking for **highly specialist funds**.

3.10 One area of specialisation for offshore life assurance funds is to have those funds denominated in other currencies eg dollars or euros. This effectively gives exposure to the currency as well as the underlying fund assets. When used with deposit account based funds, the risk is primarily in the movements in currency value relative to sterling rather than the return which is usually a relatively well known quantity. Using this principle with equities effectively increases the risk as the return is dependant on the asset values and relative currency values. It is possible to make significant losses if the assets and the currency move in the wrong direction and, even if the asset value goes up, the currency value could fall, leaving a net loss (or *vice versa*). On the other hand, if both increase there is the potential for greater overall returns. It is unusual for an individual without specialist knowledge to wish to take this level of risk, but these funds can be useful for individuals who live in another country and are simply working in the UK, linking the value of their investment to their home currency.

3.11 Despite the potential loss of withholding tax, there are also tax advantages of investing offshore. **Offshore bonds** are taxed on encashment. The growth of the investment is allowed to **roll-up gross** and **no tax** is charged until the policy is encashed. This means that additional growth is gained on the untaxed income, which is compounded until that final encashment. This can result in better gains for the life funds. However, these tend to be cancelled out by the charges, first because it is more costly to deal in overseas markets and, secondly, because the life company cannot offset its costs against taxable income.

Personalised bonds

3.12 A further variation on the bond, often distributed through the offshore subsidiaries of life assurance companies, is the **personalised bond**. These are bonds where the investor can choose exactly which securities make up his investment, shares, fixed interest investments, offshore funds or even life assurance funds.

3.13 Formerly, the **Inland Revenue** (now HMRC) reserved the right to tax these on a 'look through' basis, meaning that where the individual underlying investments could be identified, they would be taxed according to their type. They argued this on the basis that a **highly personalised bond** was merely a tax efficient wrapper for a **shrewd investor**. This was challenged in the courts in the **Willoughby case**. The court came down in favour of **Willoughby** stating that a **highly personalised bond** is still a **life assurance bond** and should be taxed accordingly.

3.14 The loss of this case by the Revenue gave rise to changes in legislation and a new batch of legislation to **increase the tax liability** on this investment. For bonds where the benefits are, or may be, closely linked to a **portfolio of assets** that is personal to the policyholder, an additional tax charge arises on deemed gains equal to 15% per annum of the sum of the premiums paid and the total of deemed gains from previous years. A **deemed gain** can also arise on **termination,** and all of this is chargeable in addition to chargeable gains assessed in the normal way. This effectively kills off the **highly personalised bond.**

3.15 The post-Willoughby regime ceased in April 2000. Investors could switch into other products at that time and if they gave up their rights to choose their own investments and moved into pooled funds, they avoided the new tax.

4 UNIT-LINKED PRICING

4.1 **Unit-linked funds** are **open-ended investments** and, as such, reflect the value of the fund underlying the units. Like unit trusts, there is a **buying price** (the offer price) and a **selling price** (the bid price). The difference between the two will typically be 5%, although some companies now have single priced funds.

4.2 Where the **underlying assets** are property or other assets that are difficult to sell, insurance companies reserve the right to delay the transaction by a set period, for example six months in the case of property.

Unit-linked charges

4.3 **Charges** are levied on UK and offshore unit-linked life assurance policies in a number of ways. These could include one or more of the following.

 (a) **Establishment charge,** a fee payable in percentage terms from all money paid into the policy, can be in the region of 1 – 3%.

 (b) **Policy fees,** mainly with regular premium contracts

 (c) **Zero allocation periods,** a method of covering the charges early in the life of the policy

 (d) **Reduced initial allocation,** as above, but usually spread over a longer period of time

 (e) **Reduced allocation** throughout the policy with regular premium contracts

 (f) **Capital units** (special units with very high charges), are not as common as they once were. These units, bought with early premiums (the first 6-24 months premiums), are subject to high regular charges, eg 3% or 6% per annum

4.4 The difference of the **bid offer spread** (normally 5%) is built into the charging structure.

4.5 **Management charges** are also quoted on most of the policy information. It can be in the region of 0.75% to 2.0% depending on the type of fund and whether the company issuing the life policy manages the fund. The charges on **with-profit funds** tend to be **lower** (they are larger funds with less requirement for management) and companies with **wide ranging fund links** tend to be **higher** (eg the management of specialist funds is more costly). In either case, the **annual management charge** will be deducted on a regular basis, and usually from within the fund itself. This reduces the need for the company to make a separate, visible reduction in units.

Question 8.8

Which has the higher charges, an investment trust or a life assurance bond?

---

5 LIFE ASSURANCE COMPANY TAXATION

5.1 For UK life assurance products:

- Dividends are taxed at 10%.

- Income from **deposits**, **gilts** and **fixed interest securities** are taxed at 20%.

- **Unfranked income** and other income such as rents are taxed at the life assurance companies' rate of corporation tax of 20%.

- **Capital gains** are also chargeable to corporation tax of 20% (but do still benefit from indexation).

5.2 The tax deducted within the **life assurance funds** removes any further tax liability for lower or basic rate taxpayers. Higher rate taxpayers are liable for a further 20%. Non-taxpayers may not reclaim the tax paid.

5.3 There is no liability on the investor to **capital gains tax** on this type of investment. **All of the tax levied is income tax**.

5.4 With **offshore** life assurance funds, no tax is deducted within the fund. As such, UK resident policyholders are liable for **income tax** in full on the amount of the chargeable event.

5.5 Holders of both UK and offshore policies will be eligible for **top slicing relief** if the chargeable gain from a non-qualifying life assurance policy takes them from the basic rate tax band to a higher one.

Exam focus point

Full details on the taxation of life assurance policyholders are covered in G10 *Taxation and Trusts*, which is assumed knowledge for the G70 examination.

Question 8.9

Would a unit trust or a UK life assurance bond be a better investment for a non-taxpayer and why?

---

6 DERIVATIVE BASED LIFE ASSURANCE BONDS

6.1 Many investors are simply not prepared to take risks with their investments and hence the **guaranteed income and growth bond market** is active and competitive. However, issuing this type of investment is only effective for life companies in the right tax position, who wish effectively to 'buy-in' money. For other companies these products are just not practical, or the rates they could offer would be uncompetitive. The demand for **risk free investments** has lead to the introduction of bonds with underlying guarantees in the form of **derivatives**.

6.2 The principle of this type of investment is that the investor will get his money back as an absolute minimum when the bond matures, typically in five years time. In addition, he may also get further growth, based on the movements of **predetermined stock market indices.** Pre-set levels of movements in the indices will give rise to set levels of return. Effectively, the products get the benefit of being 'risk free' and giving levels of return equivalent to stock market returns. However, care must be taken in the description of this type of investment, as it will only provide the guaranteed minimum return at the **end** of the term. Any attempt to access the money in the meantime will result in penalties and possibly loss of capital.

6.3 The concept of an investment that **guarantees** to return the original investment and yet has the potential to lock into stockmarket returns is a good one to market, even if there is considerable complexity underlying it.

6.4 For potential investors, it is important for them to understand that although they will get their money back as an **absolute minimum** they will have **lost money** in real terms if this minimum is all they receive. Although inflation is currently at moderately low levels, inflation of 3% per year will mount up over five years reducing purchasing power by almost 14%.

6.5 **Some funds do not offer all of the original capital back as part of the guarantee,** so care must be taken when interpreting the small print.

Guarantees and stock market links

6.6 In order to achieve the **combined effect** of a **guaranteed return** and a **return linked to stockmarkets,** life companies combine various investments within the framework of the life assurance bond. Typically, a proportion of the invested money goes into **low risk guaranteed growth investments** and the rest goes into a **derivative** based on the stockmarket indices of one or more different countries.

6.7 The **low risk** investment ensures that the investors will get the guaranteed portion of their money back. The role of this part of the investment is to take the money that remains invested after the **bid offer spread** (5% or so) and the cost of the **derivative** (10-15%) - some 80-85% of the original investment - and grow this back to the **full (or guaranteed) value** over the five year term.

6.8 There will also be a **high-risk** portion of the investment to buy in to one or more **stock indices.** These derivatives are unlike the **exchange-traded derivatives** discussed in Chapter 5. They are tailor-made **over-the-counter (OTC) derivatives,** especially set up to meet the needs of buyers and sellers. The investments themselves are very **illiquid** and cannot be traded. Each purchase of the derivative will be quite specific and will cover a set amount of investment, eg £10 million.

6.9 The fact that the underlying derivative is only available in set tranches means that bonds that use them are also only available on a **limited basis.** Each issue of bond will have a set size of issue and once this is gone, the company will not be in a position to sell more unless it **renegotiates** for an extension of the original or a new derivative to underlie the issue. The **prices** of the derivative will also **change rapidly,** so often life companies will set an investment up with a **time limit** and invite investments from **IFAs** as intermediaries, and directly from the public. Changes in the **cost** of the derivative during this period will be met by the life company. When the money is in, they buy the **high** and **low-risk** investments and the term of the bond begins. If the **take-up** of the bond issue is not high, they can reserve the right to cancel it before they buy the derivatives. In this case the investment money will be returned to the investors.

Types of derivative based investment bond

6.10 There are broadly **three main types of derivative based bonds** which each represent a different mix of the underlying investments.

- Guaranteed equity bonds
- Middle income bonds
- High income bonds

6.11 **Guaranteed equity bonds** will produce all of their investment return in the form of **capital growth**. The level of return will be based on one or more indices, often in combination, eg the FTSE 100, DAX 30 or Nikkei 225. The investment will usually guarantee to return, at least, the value of the original investment, so will appeal to investors who look for **stock market performance**, with the long stop of getting their original investment back.

6.12 **Middle income bonds** will also grow, based on the movement in one or more indices. They provide an income in the region of 4-8% of the original investment per year. The income will be **guaranteed**, and the higher the income, the lower the expected additional capital returns will be. This type of investment will usually guarantee to return a **minimum** of the original investment value, less the income paid out during the term of the policy. The typical expectation for a **middle income bond** is to pay the guaranteed income and provide a small amount of growth in addition to returning the original investment, although there are no guarantees to this. This type of investment will appeal to individuals who need a guaranteed income, but are looking for the potential of growth on top and with the ultimate fall-back position of getting their money back.

6.13 **High income bonds** can produce guaranteed income levels of 8-12%. Again the total returns will be based on the movements in one or more indices. The **guaranteed** minimum return will typically be the value of the original investment less the income paid out over the term. The typical expectation for this type of investment is to get a **return** of the original investment at the end of the term (in addition to the income paid out), but again this is **not guaranteed**. Growth on top of this may be a possibility for some bonds, but it is unrealistic to expect much. This type of investment will appeal to those needing a large guaranteed income. The additional risks taken with this type of investment can lead to a return of the original capital as well as the income, where similar income levels with other investments would almost certainly deplete the capital.

Tax issues

6.14 Problems with the underlying structures of this type of investment can cause additional unexpected tax charges in addition to the tax levied on chargeable events.

7 BROKER FUNDS AND MULTI-MANAGER SCHEMES

> **KEY TERM**
>
> **Broker funds** are effectively life funds that have been 'customised' by the intermediary. The broker bond funds themselves are made up of other funds run by the life company, but mixed by an intermediary. The intermediary will change the makeup of the broker funds to suit a predetermined objective. The funds can be accessed via unit-linked life assurance bonds purchased via the relevant intermediary.

Advantages of broker funds

7.1 A possible advantage of this type of investment is that **active management** can occur without any intervention from the investor. For **unit-linked** life assurance investors, the choice of funds often only happens once, when they buy the investment. Relatively few investors or advisors get involved with **switching funds** to make the best of market movements.

7.2 With **broker funds**, an investment professional will monitor markets continuously and will make changes as a result. This could yield **better results** than sticking with the same fund or investors themselves making the decisions, as they will not normally have the time or the facilities to watch all markets and act accordingly.

7.3 **Broker fund managers** can change the mixture of underlying assets, so if **equity markets** are forecast to be moving **down** the money can be switched to cash or fixed interest investments. If equity markets are moving **up**, the proportion of equity investment can be increased to capitalise on it. With **overseas equities**, certain geographical regions do better and worse over time. **Broker funds** can allow the intermediary to **switch** from those areas doing badly to those doing well to maximise the return on the investment. However, in practice, timing the market in this way can be difficult to achieve.

Disadvantages of broker funds

7.4 **Broker funds** are often criticised for their **charges**. The investor is effectively subject to two levels of charges, one from the life company and the other from the intermediary making the investment decisions. On top of the life company charges, a further 0.5-3% management charge can be added for asset allocation decisions taken by the intermediary. In view of this a greater return is required to put investors in the same position.

7.5 In exchange for this **extra charge**, most investors would expect to see returns that are better than the life company's own funds, by at least as much as the extra charge. In some cases, however, the performance is worse than the life company's own managed fund(s) and represents poor value for money.

Question 8.10

What is the best benchmark that can be used to assess the performance of a broker bond manager?

Multi-fund manager schemes

7.6 While **broker managed funds** are in decline, **multi-fund manager schemes** are on the rise. These schemes give clients access to the investment management expertise of a number of investment houses within the framework of a single unit-linked life assurance investment. The schemes often allow switches at low cost between funds, giving access to hundreds of different fund/sector/management options.

Multi-manager schemes

7.7 **Multi-manager schemes** or **funds of funds** are similar to broker managed schemes in that the investor chooses an investment objective and invests in a fund which has that objective. The role of the manager is to achieve the appropriate goal by investing in the collective funds of a wide range of investment houses. Frank Russell is one of the best known.

Manager of manager funds

7.8   A further variation on the managed fund principle is the **manager of manager fund**. This is similar to a multi-manager arrangement except that instead of choosing funds run by other fund managers as part of their collective fund, they pass sums of money to other managers directly to manage for them. These other managers are given strict investment objectives and can be replaced if they do not achieve them. These schemes still represent a two-tier management system and are therefore costly.

Chapter roundup

- **Life assurance offices** offer a wide range of funds to satisfy the objectives of most investors.

- **With profit funds** smooth out the variability of the underlying investments.

- High returns on the underlying assets will be held back to provide returns for periods when returns are below average. As a consequence with profits funds may be considered low to medium risk.

- Conventional with profit funds offer several types of bonus including reversionary/normal, special, interim and terminal. Income may be generated from with profits funds only by encashment.

- Most life assurance investments are now issued in **unit linked form**. These are open ended investments where the value of the unit is directly related to the net asset value of the fund.

- Unit linked funds are very flexible, allowing switches between funds with different asset classes. Income may be generated by encashing units or by purchasing a **distribution bond** which has separate income units.

- Charges on unit linked investments may take the form of policy fees, zero or reduced allocation periods and capital units.

- **Guaranteed income** and **growth** bonds offer investors low risk investment products.

- Life assurance investment taxation is complex. The fund suffers tax on both income and capital gains. Holders can withdraw up to 5% of the initial investment on a tax deferred basis per annum (cumulative). Chargeable events (encashment, withdrawal greater than 5%) result in an assessment to tax. Lower and basic rate taxpayers are deemed to have met their liabilities. Higher rate taxpayers may be subject to a further 20% tax charge on gains. Non taxpayers may not reclaim tax suffered.

- Offshore life assurance policies may suffer withholding tax.

- For UK taxpayers, the gains from offshore bonds can roll up gross, saving tax for lower rate taxpayers and potentially increasing returns for higher rate taxpayers.

- The benefits of gross roll-up are often diminished by higher charges.

- The employment of derivatives has facilitated the growth of guaranteed and stock market linked bonds.

- Broker funds are insurance based investments where asset allocation decisions are made by IFAs.

- The additional charges on broker bonds can outweigh the benefits.

- **Multi-fund manager arrangements** can offer a wide range of investment funds managed by a variety of different investment houses. These funds can be mixed and combined to cater for a wide range of investment strategies.

- Multi-manager schemes give access to funds that can invest in the best of all other managed funds. The fund selection is made by a full time investment professional.

Quick quiz

1   How do unit-linked life assurance based investments address the need for income?

2   Why are with-profit funds not classified as 'no-risk'?

3   What category would a managed fund with 90% of its assets invested in equities fall into?

4   What are the main factors that will influence the performance of a with-profit investment?

5   Why is it that, if unitised with-profit fund prices can only increase in value, investors will not necessarily get back all of their original capital with a unitised with-profit investment?

6   Which type of investment will benefit most from pound cost averaging, a regular or single premium investment?

7   Why does a unit-linked investment bond, not produce 'real' income?

8   In what way is a single premium endowment like an investment bond?

9   What factors reduce the effect of 'gross roll-up' for an offshore investment bond?

10 Which type of life assurance based investment does the case of Willoughby v. Inland Revenue refer to?

11 How are increases in capital value taxed with a life assurance bond?

12 What happens if a life company issues a derivative based guaranteed equity bond and there is little interest from investors?

13 What would typically be the guaranteed minimum return from a high-income bond?

14 Why are the charges on a broker bond higher than an ordinary life assurance bond?

The answers to the questions in the Quick Quiz can be found at the end of this Study Text. Before checking your own answers against them, you should look back at this chapter and use the information in it to correct your answers.

Answers to Chapter Questions

8.1 Insurance units are open-ended investments. They should change directly in response to changes in the value of assets underlying the fund.

8.2 A cash fund or a building society fund.

8.3 TEPs themselves are a fairly low risk investment. However, there is the risk of a discount on the investment trust widening. Good performance is also reliant on the ability of the fund managers to pick good policies to buy.

8.4 With a life assurance investment, switching or redirection can achieve a change of strategy, both at little or no cost and with no tax consequences. Changing strategy with a unit trust will usually involve the investor with a bid-offer spread on the new units and the potential for a CGT liability.

8.5 Where the income and capital are separated, it is possible just to take the income and leave the capital untouched, unlike the situation with a normal unit-linked investment bond, although the value of this capital can reduce.

8.6 With a normal unit-linked fund income in the form of interest, rents and dividends is re-invested and increases the fund price. With a distribution bond, the income is placed in separate units, so the value of the main units will not increase as quickly.

8.7 The tax penalty would be 0.1% per annum (100% × 20% × 0.5%).

8.8 The charges on an investment trust would be lower as there is no specific bid-offer spread and the differences between the buying and selling prices tend to be quite small. There will also be no explicit fund management charge with an investment trust. The costs of investment management can be found in the accounts, but they are likely to be significantly less than an equivalent life assurance bond.

8.9 A unit trust would be better as there is no taxation within the fund except dividend credits at 10% which may not be reclaimed. With a UK life assurance bond, income and gains are taxed within the fund and are not reclaimable.

8.10 The life assurance company's own managed fund would be the best benchmark for comparison.

PRACTICE QUESTION 8

(a) Explain the main advantages and disadvantages of investing in a life assurance managed fund rather than constructing an individual portfolio of shares. (12)

(b) How can the use of a Multi manager Scheme improve the situation? (4)

(c) Briefly explain the role of derivatives in a guaranteed equity bond. (4)

Chapter 9

INDEX TRACKER FUNDS

Chapter topic list	Syllabus reference
1 Index tracker funds	3.4
2 Tracking the index	3.4
3 Tracker funds for portfolio planning	3.4
4 Selection of tracker funds	3.4

Introduction

Index tracker funds have been popular in the USA for some time, but it is only comparatively recently that they have become widespread in the UK. Sales of tracker funds in the UK grew rapidly in the late 1990s. Sales in 1997 alone were £1 billion (three times more than in 1996). In the UK, there were over 50 of these funds available from 29 different management groups and the numbers have increased significantly since then.

1   INDEX TRACKER FUNDS

Investment objective

> **KEY TERM**
>
> The investment objective of an **index tracker fund** is to produce investment returns based on movements in a specific index.

1.1   There can be a number of reasons for choosing **index-tracking investments**. For individuals with relatively small investments, investing in the index gives them **access** to many shares allowing the **non-systematic** risk to be reduced. With direct investment, the number of shares an individual can invest in is dependent on the amount they have to invest. The costs of investment will restrict them to relatively small numbers of different equities.

1.2   **Stock market indices** are, in most cases, an excellent representation of the investment activity in a country or geographical region. For a **world-wide portfolio,** the problems of managing to reproduce the movements of markets in individual countries would be highly impractical for all but the largest fund. Investing in a fund tracking a world-wide index provides a solution, particularly as they now exist in various forms for most indices world-wide.

1.3 An additional factor for **international investors** is that some markets are not easily accessible. In some markets, **liquidity** is a problem and the **pricing** of shares can be **variable,** so investing in a fund that tracks that index is a solution. The expense of dealing in local markets combined with local taxes can make them impractical but index funds can get around this, as most investors will find a fund available in their own country, reducing dealing costs and simplifying the tax situation.

Question 9.1

What type of investor would be best suited to tracker fund investment?

1.4 For many investors, the impartial nature of **index based investment** is a benefit. Fund managers may pursue active investment strategies in an attempt to beat a specified index and, historically, many fail. According to HSBC Asset Management, only 17.9 per cent of active funds in the UK equity sector outperformed the **all share index** in ten years to 1999. In the struggle to beat the index, decisions are made and risks are taken but, at the end of the day, this will be no guarantee of **success**. A fund that reproduces the relevant index has a good chance of success without the requirement for an active management strategy. In addition, tracker funds have lower management charges, little research and decision-making activities, an expense for most funds.

Types of tracker fund

1.5 In the UK, **tracker funds** are available in the form of unit trusts, investment trusts, OEICs, offshore funds, pension funds and life assurance and investments based in the UK and offshore. The most popular **tracker funds** in the UK tend to be **unit trusts** or OEICs, but essentially there is no problem in any type of pooled fund setting itself up to track an index.

1.6 There is also a type of security tradeable on the stock market called an **exchange-traded fund** (ETF). ETFs reproduce the FTSE 100 and various sectors of the UK market including telecoms and finance indices in a single share. ETFs, now common in the USA, are tradeable in real time like any other equity. ETFs are set up by **Barclays Global Investment** and some other providers to invest in the underlying investments of each index.

Advantages of using tracker funds

1.7 One of the key advantages of using a **tracker fund** is the fact that performance is **consistent** and has been considerably better than many actively managed funds. Few actively managed fund managers beat the appropriate index on a regular basis.

1.8 The **risks are lower**. Many fund managers in an attempt to beat the index will take greater risks to achieve the same result. From the portfolio theory perspective, this is inefficient.

1.9 The investment management of tracker funds is considerably less onerous than with actively managed funds resulting in **lower management charges**.

1.10 The use of an **index tracker fund** can eliminate **specific risk** (non-systematic risk). However, they are still subject to **market risk** (systematic risk).

Question 9.2

How would the downturn of a particular industrial sector affect the returns from an index tracker fund?

Limitations in using tracker funds

1.11 The main limitation with the use of tracker funds is the **lack of flexibility** over the investment objective. The only objective available with a tracker fund is to **track the index**. The returns are geared to **capital returns** rather than dividends or interest, so there can be problems for investors seeking income. These problems can be overcome where the tracker fund forms part of a structured portfolio.

1.12 **Tracker funds** must track the index **down** as well as **up** and the stockmarket weakness from the last half of 1998 onwards demonstrated this quite clearly. **Actively managed funds** have total flexibility to pursue a **defensive strategy** when markets are weak. **Tracker funds** do not have this ability. In addition to this, new cash flows into actively managed funds can be used to 'bargain hunt' after a serious drop. However, despite having the ability to buck the trend in a falling market, in the stockmarket falls (for example, during the period 1998 to 2002) few actively managed funds resisted the downturn any better than the tracker funds. In practice, it is very difficult for an active fund manager to predict stock market trends. Even so, when **markets** are **performing poorly**, some actively managed funds do perform better than tracker funds. Investors, and the advisers that operate on their behalf, may be able to pick the more successful funds.

1.13 Not all **index funds** manage to track accurately and generate a tracking error. This error should be random but, in any one quarter, it could be 1%. When charges are taken into account as well, investment returns may be lower than actively managed funds.

1.14 For each index tracked by a fund, there can be limitations. The **FTSE 100 Index**, being the index of top companies in the UK weighted by market capitalisation, is considerably exposed to overseas market conditions because the companies that make up the index have many interests abroad. The price of the FTSE 100 Index of shares is dependant on a few companies so movements in the prices of these companies can have a big influence on the index, an issue that is considerably less apparent with an index such as the **FTSE All Share Index**. On the other hand, the **FTSE All Share Index** has so many constituents it will be costly to replicate, as shares will be purchased in smaller quantities. There is also the possibility that **tracking errors** will occur if the index is not accurately replicated. The share spreads for these smaller shares will be considerably larger (up to 10%) than for the FTSE 100 constituents and this will **reduce the returns** and **reduce the performance**, as the index assumes all purchases and sales at mid-market price.

Question 9.3

Which tracker fund would be affected more by a drop in UK equities, one tracking the FTSE100 or one tracking the FTSE all share index? Explain why.

2 TRACKING THE INDEX

2.1 There are three main approaches to tracking an index, which may be used individually or in combination with each other.

- Full replication
- Optimisation
- Stratified sampling

Full replication

2.2 The fund manager actively **replicates the index** by buying all of the stocks in the index, in proportion to their weighting. This is the most accurate method for tracking the index.

Stratified sampling

2.3 In this method of tracking, **equities** are purchased that are representative of the market sectors that make up the index. One or more **'representative' shares** are purchased in the weightings of the appropriate market category. This method can give a very good approximation of the movement of the index at considerably less cost than full replication. There will be some tracking errors, as no single share, or combination of shares, can exactly represent the movement of all the individual shares in a specific category. As the requirement of this form of tracking uses less shares, it can give savings in cost.

Optimisation

2.4 It is possible to **simulate** the movements of an index using complex mathematical (statistical) models. **Optimisation** can be done manually, but more typically will be modelled on a computer. The model indicates the amount and timing of appropriate equity purchase that will provide fund values in line with the index. This method of **simulating the index** saves money by dealing in smaller numbers of shares, as with stratified sampling. However considerable management expertise can be required to operate the model effectively and the statistical data employed is historic, and therefore may not reflect current risk return characteristics.

Question 9.4

Which method of tracking requires the least investment management expertise to operate?

3 TRACKER FUNDS FOR PORTFOLIO PLANNING

3.1 Despite the limitations of **tracker funds**, they can be very useful as **part of a portfolio**. The use of these funds in conjunction with other investments can overcome the **limitations** relating to investment objectives. If an income is required, other assets in the portfolio can produce this.

3.2 Tracker funds can **reduce non-systematic risk** arising from the equity portion of a **portfolio**. In terms of portfolio theory, **tracker funds** (providing they track accurately) are very close to the efficient frontier in that they provide close to the maximum return for the given level of risk.

3.3 Tracker funds are not totally 'efficient' as charges are levied on the fund, which **reduces the returns**. However, the efficient frontier cannot normally be achieved in a managed portfolio, because of dealing charges. The use of tracker funds removes most of the costs involved.

3.4 The use of tracker funds for **indices** from all over the world can provide **geographical spread,** with **efficient investments,** without concern for local trading conditions and taxation. However, care must be taken over the currency in which **the fund is denominated** as this can add additional risk.

3.5 With a tracker fund, it is possible to quickly invest large sums of money in wide-ranging geographical areas. They also provide the ability to **change strategy** and **redistribute** the money elsewhere equally quickly. **Changing strategy** in an actively managed portfolio is something that would be quite difficult to achieve by investing in pooled funds, let alone the underlying equities themselves.

3.6 Tracker funds based on **weighted indices** are automatically allocated by market capitalisation and industrial sector, driven by the composition of the index.

3.7 Tracker funds can, and do, form an **effective investment** for use in the **self managed portfolios** of private investors. However, their use is less widespread in professionally managed portfolios. It could be difficult to justify portfolio management charges when the choice of shares underlying the investment is out of the hands of the investment manager.

Question 9.5

What problems might arise if using tracker funds based offshore to invest in specific geographical areas?

4 SELECTION OF TRACKER FUNDS

4.1 As with all types of investment, care must be taken when selecting tracker funds. Logically, an investor would be looking for the **best performing tracker,** but it is essential to take into account movements in the market during the performance measurement period. A tracker that over- performs the index in a **bull market** may well under perform it in a **bear market.** Consistent over-performance would be nice, but would effectively stop it being a tracker fund.

4.2 In order to fully assess the performance of a tracker fund, a **fund history** is required, preferably one that covers highs and lows in the underlying index. Where this is achieved, the tracking accuracy (ie low tracking error) would be a good indication of a good fund.

4.3 The **fund charges** on tracker funds will vary from company to company. Providing the fund tracks accurately, the fund with the lowest charges should give the greatest investment returns.

4.4 The more money a fund has the closer it can get to **full replication,** which gives the most accurate tracking. **Larger funds** will mean that the quantities of shares bought and sold will be larger, providing economies of scale. Assuming the savings are passed on to the investor this should reduce costs. The cost of managing a tracker fund should be similar whether it has £100,000 or £1 million invested, but the more investors there are the more these costs can be spread. If these savings are passed on, charges can be reduced further.

Chapter roundup

- **Index trackers** aim to reproduce the movements in a specific **equity** or **bond index**. They are **passive funds**.

- Trackers are characterised by **low costs** and outperformance of the majority of active funds.

- However passive funds will underperform the best active funds and cannot pursue defensive strategies.

- Tracking may be achieved by **full replication**, **optimisation** or **stratified sampling**.

- Tracker funds are effective in **reducing non-systematic** risk and facilitate asset allocation between different international equity and bond markets.

- Choice of fund is determined by tracking error, and charges.

Quick quiz

1 How can tracker funds help investors seeking investment with a wide geographical spread?

2 Why are the charges on an index tracker fund typically less than an equivalent non-tracker fund?

3 Which is the most accurate method of replicating an index within a tracker fund?

4 What type of risk is removed by the use of tracker funds and how is this achieved?

5 What are the key criteria used for selecting the individual tracker funds from different companies?

The answers to the questions in the Quick Quiz can be found at the end of this Study Text. Before checking your own answers against them, you should look back at this chapter and use the information in it to correct your answers.

Answers to Chapter Questions

9.1 An investor who is not risk averse, and seeks high levels of capital growth over the medium to long-term.

9.2 The downturn of a single industrial sector may have little or no effect on an index tracking fund. As some sectors turn down, others improve and it is the balance of this happening that will impact on returns.

9.3 The FTSE All-Share Index would probably be affected more, for a number of reasons.

(a) The FTSE All-Share Index is made up of all the shares in the UK and, although it includes the multinational companies, they will make up a smaller proportion than the majority of companies whose interests are mainly based in the UK.

(b) The FTSE 100 has a large number of multinational companies so will be less affected by a UK turn down.

(c) In the event of a turn down in the UK many investors shelter in the quality stocks, particularly utilities, which are mostly based in the FTSE 100.

(d) When UK markets turn down, investor confidence in the smaller companies of the FTSE all share will fall faster than with the larger companies.

9.4 Full replication of the index is simply a question of buying the underlying shares in the index in the proportions in which they are represented in the index. This requires little or no investment management skill.

9.5 Where funds are not based in the UK, it is possible that although the fund is priced in Sterling, the underlying investment is made in a different currency. This could potentially give rise to currency risk.

PRACTICE QUESTION 9

(a) List the advantages of a tracker fund over a similarly invested actively managed fund. (4)

(b) List the advantages of a tracker fund over investing in individual shares. (5)

(c) Explain how and why the fund performance of two tracker funds might be different. (7)

Part D
Other investments

Chapter 10

OTHER INVESTMENTS

Chapter topic list	Syllabus reference
1 Unlisted securities	4.1
2 Tax incentive schemes	4.2
3 Physical assets and commodities	4.3
4 Property	4.4

Introduction

There are a range of investments outside the more conventional cash, fixed interest and equity investments and the pooled funds that are based on them. This chapter looks at their structure and special features and examines the methods of investment and the risks and returns of investing in each.

1 UNLISTED SECURITIES

1.1 In addition to the 3,000 or so **listed shares** in the UK, there are considerable numbers of other unlisted ones. These shares do not qualify for a full listing on the main market shares, but are none the less very important to the British economy.

1.2 **Unlisted shares** are not as easy to buy and sell as their listed counterparts but, in recognition of their importance, the government has tried to encourage ownership of these shares in the last few years, by the use of tax incentives.

1.3 In most cases, shares are **unlisted** because they do not qualify for the stringent qualifications to obtain a listing (including a minimum market capitalisation of £700,000 and a trading record of three years). For some companies, the requirement to provide detailed information about the company and the way that it is run, is too high a price to pay for a listing and there are a number of large companies who choose to remain unlisted.

1.4 Although they are not listed on the main market, it is still possible for private investors to buy them through the **Alternative Investment Market (AIM)**, **OFEX** (an independent market in unlisted shares) or, indirectly, via **Venture Capital Trusts**, the pooled investment for this type of share. Some shares are not available by this route and can only be bought directly from other shareholders of the business or 'over-the-counter' through a stockbroker.

Question 10.1

What problems might arise if an investor wanted to buy shares from an existing shareholder, but not via any form of exchange?

Risks and rewards of investment in unlisted shares

1.5 The smaller a company is, the greater the capacity for growth it has. It is small enough to **change strategy** quickly and to **follow trends** in the market place, taking opportunities where it can find them. Companies can double or triple in value in a very short period of time, potentially providing **large rewards** for the shareholders. However, a share is only worth what someone else will pay for it and matching buyers and sellers for unlisted shares is not always easy. The **potential for growth** in these companies is huge, but so is the **potential for failure** of the business and the **total loss** of **investment capital**. These investments give **high potential rewards** matched with equally **high risks**.

1.6 The **risks for investors** in unlisted companies fall into two main categories: the **risk of the business** and the **risk of the investment**. **Business risk** relates to the risk of the company failing, or performing poorly. **Investment risk** relates to the ability of the investor to realise the value of the investment and benefit from the gains.

Business risks

1.7 Unlisted shares are subject to the same risks that affect listed companies and a few others as well.

   (a) **A lack of diversification**, as most unlisted companies operate in a very restricted market with a limited number of products and a limited client base

   (b) Dependant on the health of the UK economy, as few will have interests outside the UK and will be **severely affected** by the **local economy**

   (c) **A lack of financial resources**, with many directors having already put up their homes as securities on loans, most unlisted companies will have a limited ability to increase borrowing or increase cash available in the event of a crisis

   (d) **Total dependence** on a small number of key individuals, such as inventors, designers or software specialists whose loss to a competitor, injury or death would cause severe problems

   (e) **Limited expertise** to deal with the legal financial or marketing aspects of a business and limited funds to purchase these services from a third party

Investment risks

1.8 These **investment risks** are specific to the use of **unlisted investments** and relate to additional costs and problems involved in realising returns from this type of share.

   (a) **Higher dealing costs** as a result of the lack of an active market in the shares

   (b) **Larger share spreads** which can be 10% or more in many cases

   (c) **Problems with market liquidity** with fewer shares in issue: matching buyers and sellers can be very difficult

(d) **Valuation of business or shares**, as it can be very difficult to ascertain the value of an unlisted company because there are far fewer requirements to publish financial information than with listed shares

(e) **High price volatility** caused by all of the above factors

(f) The **ultimate value** of the shares may be determined by other factors such as control of the company, for example a non-controlling shareholding can be worth considerably less than a controlling one and the controlling shareholder and the emergence of a controlling shareholder can severely reduce the value of other shares

---

Question 10.2

What are the main effects for an investor of increased price spreads and increased charges?

Suitability of unlisted shares for private investors

1.9 Investing in **unlisted shares** presents the investor with exceptionally **high risks**. These risks can be reduced if an individual has specific **experience in the market sector** they are seeking to invest in. The **inside knowledge** will help them understand the business influences on the success of the company, allowing them to put any financial constraints into perspective. However, even these individuals may have a **problem** when it comes to **realising the investment**. Even if the value of a company has doubled in the time that an investor has held the share, the price that someone else is prepared to pay for the shares may not have.

1.10 **Investment** in unlisted shares is only suitable for very **experienced investors** with knowledge of the business in which the company operates, unless there is an **investment professional** acting on their behalf. Even then, the risks are high. A slightly lower risk method of investing is via tax-exempt pooled investments specialising in this type of investment, such as **venture capital trusts**. This reduces the risks by providing an extra layer of professional investment management and the tax savings increase the effect of any gains.

Tax incentives for unlisted shares

1.11 Despite the opportunities for phenomenal investment returns, the **risks** of unlisted shares are still **too high** for most investors. In a bid to ensure that financial support for these companies is available, the government has introduced a number of tax efficient schemes for investing in this type of asset, such as **EIS** or **VCT** schemes.

1.12 **Direct investment** in unlisted shares also attracts **tax advantages** on **income** and **capital gains**. Investment companies and individuals investing in **'qualifying shares'** in unquoted trading companies can set losses on a disposal of the shares against their income for tax purposes. For shares issued on or after 6 April 1998, the definition of trading companies that can qualify will be brought into line with those under **EIS** and **VCT** schemes. Capital gains on these investments benefit from 'business' rate of 'taper relief', which can reduce tax levels to 25% of their original level in two years of ownership.

2 TAX INCENTIVE SCHEMES

2.1 There is a considerable level of additional risk for investors in unlisted shares, but this capital is needed as the lifeblood of small companies. In order to offset these risks and encourage investment in small companies, the government has introduced schemes with tax incentives to encourage investment in small businesses. These are outlined below.

Venture Capital Trusts (VCTs)

2.2 **Venture Capital Trusts (VCTs)** were introduced in 1993 as a way for new and unquoted companies to obtain funding from investors.

> ### KEY TERM
>
> **Venture Capital Trusts** are investment trusts that invest in unlisted, rather than listed companies. The additional risks involved mean that few investors would touch them if it were not for the tax breaks.

2.3 The VCT **tax incentives** were introduced to help investors overcome this risk, so schemes that manage to avoid it are not within the spirit of the investment. Gordon Brown's first Budget recognised this and tightened up the rules on VCTs to **exclude** schemes that are low risk, those offering guarantees or being property backed.

VCT tax incentives

2.4 The **tax incentives** provided on a VCT are subject to the investor holding the investment for three years otherwise the tax benefits will be taken away.

2.5 Investors in VCTs get tax rebates of 40% (2004/5 and 2005/6 tax years) on their investment on the maximum of £200,000 per tax year. The relief is given in the form of a 'tax reducer', which is effectively a tax reduction of 40% of the amount invested from their tax bill. The investor does not need to be a higher rate taxpayer to get the rebate at 40%. Dividends paid by VCTs (up to an annual £200,000 limit investment limit) are exempt from further taxation.

2.6 **Capital gains** made on VCTs are **exempt** from capital gains tax, providing contributions do not exceed £200,000 per tax year, whether or not the investment has been held for three years.

2.7 **Reinvestment relief** – introduced in April 1995 – allowed investors to reinvest the proceeds from other gains that would be liable to CGT and defer them until the disposal of the VCT. This relief ceased to be available in 2004.

Question 10.3

What income tax benefit would a non-taxpayer get from a £20,000 investment into a VCT?

Restrictions on VCTs

2.8 For a VCT to qualify for the **tax advantages,** it must conform to a number of conditions.

(a) The unquoted companies in which a VCT may invest are **limited** to those with a market capitalisation of £15 million or less (prior to the investment by the VCT).

(b) A VCT may **not invest more** than £1 million in total in each year in any one unquoted trading company.

(c) The **VCT's portfolio** must be at least 70% invested in **new shares** and **loan stocks** of unquoted companies: they have three years to get to this level. In addition to this, 30% of the value of the VCT portfolio must also be invested in new ordinary shares of qualifying companies.

(d) No more than 15% of the fund can be invested in any individual company.

(e) At least 10% of the investment in each company must be in ordinary shares without preferential rights.

(f) The **balance** of the investments can be in other shares or loan stock with a minimum 5-year term. As a result of this, it is possible, within the framework of these rules, for a VCT to be set up with 30% of its investments in loan stocks or shares in blue chip quoted companies. This would **reduce** the **overall risk** of the investment and a number of VCTs are set up on this basis.

(g) Certain property-backed activities are **excluded** for VCTs, including farming and market gardening, forestry and timber production, property development and operating or managing hotels, guesthouses and nursing or residential care homes.

Investment in VCTs

2.9 VCTs are available to investors aged 18 or over. There is typically a **minimum investment** of £1,000 and a **maximum** of £200,000 for all investments in all schemes in each tax year. Investors should be in a position to invest for a minimum of three years in order to qualify for all of the tax advantages. Additional rules were introduced in the 2000 Budget to ensure that investors are not disadvantaged if the company is restructured or goes into receivership during the minimum investment period. The 2002 Budget also introduced rules allowing mergers and acquisitions/takeovers without affecting the tax status.

2.10 Although the underlying investment is in shares, which would not have significant charges, there will be costs involved in **packaging** and **marketing** the VCT framework for the underlying investment. Shares in **Venture Capital Trusts** are issued periodically in the form of **limited offers** by various financial institutions. Typically, there will be an initial fee in the range of 2% to 7% for investment.

2.11 Investors need to be aware that they are exposing themselves to considerable risks with VCTs, including all of those that apply to investing in unlisted companies discussed previously. The **risks** are reduced slightly because the VCT is a pooled investment with a spread of companies and professional investment managers, but they are still considerable. The **tax incentives** go some way to improving the situation and some of the underlying companies could perform exceptionally well.

2.12 These investments are only suitable for the private investor as part of a **larger portfolio**. Care should be taken to invest only in schemes sponsored by established financial institutions, as there is little in the way of investor protection.

Question 10.4

Do VCTs represent a higher or lower risk than direct investment in unlisted equities? Give reasons for your answer.

Exam focus point

Changes to legislation such as that with Venture Capital Trusts is often listed, particularly where questions have been identified as having been poorly answered in the past.

Enterprise Investment Schemes (EIS)

2.13 The **Enterprise Investment Scheme (EIS)** was introduced in the 1994 Finance Act to **replace** the previous Business Expansion Scheme (BES). EIS schemes are similar in a number of respects to VCTs.

KEY TERM

EIS schemes invest in individual companies whereas VCTs spread investments and the risk across several companies. There are also differences in the investment limits and the way that dividends are treated.

2.14 By having less diverse investments, the **risks** with **EIS schemes** are **greater** than with VCTs. It is generally considered that, in the case of the EIS, the tax incentives do not outweigh the risks which results in the product being considerably less popular.

EIS tax incentives

2.15 The **tax incentives** provided on an **EIS** are subject to the investor holding the investment for three years. Where this is not the case, the tax benefits will be taken away. Additional rules were introduced in the 2000 budget to ensure that investors are not disadvantaged if the company is restructured or goes into receivership during the minimum investment period.

2.16 Investors in EIS schemes get **tax relief** of 20% on their investment up to a maximum of £200,000 per tax year (2005/06). The relief is given in the form of a **'tax reducer'**, in the same way as a VCT. They can have income tax relief for the previous tax year where an investment is up to £25,000 in shares issued in the first half of the following tax year. With EIS schemes reinvestment relief remains available. The relief allows the proceeds of other investment to be reinvested into an EIS without having to pay tax on the gain.

2.17 The **Enterprise Investment Scheme** and capital gains tax reinvestment reliefs were rationalised in April 1998 to create a unified scheme. Shares sold after three years are **exempt** from **capital gains tax** if a gain is made, but any gains deferred have to have tax paid on them at the prevailing rates when the investment ends. Unlimited deferral of capital gains tax is possible, for individuals who reinvest in eligible shares. Losses can be set against either income tax or capital gains tax (eg the deferred gain) unless the Enterprise Investment Scheme relief is withdrawn. Investors can defer substantial chargeable gains by investing in qualifying companies, whether or not they are able to qualify for income tax relief under the scheme.

Restrictions on EIS

2.18   Only companies with **gross assets of less than** £15 million before an investment, and **no more than** £16 million after it, can participate in the scheme.

2.19   An EIS investor may not invest in a company in which they already own more than 30% of the shares, directly or indirectly. However, in a move to encourage **'business angels'**, the investor can subsequently become a **director of the company** and receive a reasonable remuneration provided that, at the time of his investment, he was not connected with, or employed by, the company.

2.20   To qualify as an **EIS investment,** an unlisted company must have carried on a qualifying trade for at least three years. As with VCTs, certain companies are deemed to represent a lower level of risk and, in a move to stop them from benefiting from the tax advantages under an EIS, they will not qualify. Some property-backed activities will be excluded; farming and market gardening, forestry and timber production, property development and operating or managing hotels, guesthouses, nursing or residential care homes; and some financial activities are also excluded; include providing finance, leasing, legal and accountancy services.

Investment in EIS

2.21   Investors must be aged 18 or over and not **'connected'** with the businesses invested in by the fund. Typically, a **minimum investment** will be £2,000 per company. Investors should be in a position to invest for a minimum of three years to avoid tax charges and the potential of capital loss in the short-term. This represents a very **high-risk investment.** Typically, most investors will invest in ten or more companies to get a reasonable **spread of risk.** On this basis, a reasonable EIS portfolio would be £20,000 while the maximum EIS investment is £200,000.

2.22   EIS shares tend to be a **limited issue,** but information can normally be found in magazines and newspapers, or may be available from stockbrokers or an independent financial adviser. An initial fee in the range of 2% to 7% is charged to cover **launch costs.**

2.23   **EIS investments** are very **high risk** and the lack of underlying diversification means that companies can and will fail. For the investor, the **tax incentives** and the **spectacular performance** of some EIS companies may **outweigh this risk.** Spreading the investment over a number of different companies, rather than restricting investment to one or two, can reduce the risks.

2.24   These investments can be suitable for the **private investor** as part of a **larger portfolio,** but care should be taken only to invest in a scheme sponsored by an established financial body, as there is limited investor protection.

Question 10.5

For an investor with £10,000 to invest, which would generally be lower risk, an EIS or a VCT? Give a reason for your answer.

BPP
PROFESSIONAL EDUCATION

Enterprise Zone buildings

2.25 Since the 1980s, the Government has encouraged business development in certain designated areas or **Enterprise Zones**, such as London's Docklands, using tax concessions.

2.26 There is potential for **significant gains** but there is also **significant risk** and, in practice, many of the schemes based on enterprise zones have failed to meet investor expectations.

2.27 In addition to the **tax incentives**, planning restrictions in the zone are relaxed, which makes development significantly easier. Businesses in the zones will be offered **'no business rates'** deals (also called a **'rates holiday'**).

2.28 For the investor, an **income** is produced in the form of **rent** once the commercial property is let out. Interest on money borrowed to build the property can be offset against this.

KEY TERM

It is possible to invest in enterprise zone buildings directly or via an unregulated collective investment scheme specialising in this type of investment called an **Enterprise Zone Trust**.

Enterprise zone building - tax incentives

2.29 Investment in commercial properties generally attracts an **industrial buildings allowance (IBA)** on expenditure for industrial buildings, factories and hotels. The allowance is given on 4% per annum of the cost of building, but not on the cost of the land.

2.30 In an **enterprise zone**, the buildings that attract the allowance are widened to include shops and offices and the level of the allowance is increased to 100%. Any **tax relief** not taken straight away is given in annual instalments of 25% of the full cost.

2.31 The **HMRC** (the new name for the Inland Revenue) defines the life of a building as 25 years. Buildings that have benefited from the 100% IBA will be required to pay back some of the benefit via a balancing payment if the building is sold on within the 25 year period.

2.32 **Partial disposal**, such as the sale of a lease, will not attract a tax charge if it takes place more than seven years after purchase. The investor will continue to hold the freehold.

Restrictions on enterprise zone buildings

2.33 **Enterprise zone buildings** must be **commercial** to qualify for the **tax incentives**, although a far wider range of commercial property is allowed than with the **IBA**. There are no minimum or maximum investment levels to qualify for the **tax incentives** and individuals may offset the IBA against all forms of income at the full rate of tax paid.

Investment in enterprise zone buildings

2.34 It takes a very **large investment** to purchase buildings in an enterprise zone directly, so many investors purchase via an **Enterprise Zone Trust**. Direct investment would only be available to the largest of private investors.

2.35 **Investments via a trust** can be made with some schemes for £10,000 or less and there is a benefit when spreading the risk across a number of different schemes. If a direct investment goes wrong, it can wipe out the investors. For the investors in a trust a loss will be a problem but, as most trusts are spread across a number of developments, at least some of the capital would remain. A professional will **manage investments** via a trust which can increase returns by adding expertise to the selection and purchase of properties and renting them out for the best price.

2.36 **Investing via an EZT** can also bring disadvantages as the costs will be higher to cover literature, marketing and compliance costs together with additional management expenses. In addition to this, there will be less control over the method and timing of the disposal of the property which could, potentially, lead to a tax charge for the investor.

2.37 Both the **direct investor** and those investing **via a trust** will potentially lose out when properties are **sold**. Although the original buildings benefited for 100% (IBA), any subsequent purchaser will only get 4%. This will reduce the price that a purchaser might be prepared to pay, potentially causing a **reduction** in the **value of the investment** for the investor.

2.38 This type of investment is a very **high-risk long-term investment** whether it is done directly or via an **EZT**. It is only suitable as a small part of a **larger portfolio**.

Question 10.6

What is the minimum term of investment in an enterprise zone building?

---

3 PHYSICAL ASSETS AND COMMODITIES

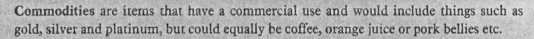

KEY TERMS

Physical assets can include cars, paintings, jewellery, stamps and coins.

Commodities are items that have a commercial use and would include things such as gold, silver and platinum, but could equally be coffee, orange juice or pork bellies etc.

3.1 Physical assets tend to produce any **investment return** in the form of a **gain in capital value** rather than producing an income. They will be purchased at one price and sold at another, hopefully for a profit. Very few investments of this type are capable of producing an income, but some do. Vintage cars can be hired out (for weddings or to appear in films), which may produce a net income but, in many cases, simply mitigates the cost of keeping and maintaining the asset.

Physical assets

3.2 Various physical assets are **collectible** and the desire by collectors to continually expand their acquisitions puts **upward pressure** on the prices of 'collectible' items. An increase in price turns something from a purchase to an **investment**, and the ability to increase value by buying and selling continues to drive prices higher.

3.3 The UK has a variety of collectors of all sorts of items from antique furniture or vintage cars, to teddy bears, thimbles or lawnmowers. In many cases, these are hobbies rather than investments, but nonetheless, when things get a value, dealers and professional investors will become interested.

3.4 This type of investment has a number of unique features that need to be understood by investors if they are to increase in value.

3.5 Many physical assets are described as '**pride in possession**' objects, as they confer additional benefits to their investment value. Works of art can be used to put on the wall and admired, vintage cars can be given the occasional run out, and coin and stamp collections can also provide a lot of pleasure.

Storage and maintenance of physical assets

3.6 **Physical assets** often require the **input of money** to enable them to **maintain their value**. Many of them will require specialist attention or restoration. Fine art can devalue quickly if not kept in the right conditions and restored appropriately as required.

3.7 Most **physical assets** require proper **storage** and/or **security** which then gives rise to further expense, such as secure display cabinets, secure premises and a good insurance policy.

Trading in physical assets

3.8 Buying and selling **physical assets** will usually involve additional expense as many are sold and acquired through auction or a third party introduction. This can add 10-15% to the price of an item, and VAT is also added if the items are purchased via a shop or registered trader

3.9 There will often be **liquidity problems** with this type of asset as buyers and sellers must be matched exactly in order for a transaction to take place. This will give a widely differing value for physical assets.

3.10 Physical assets are quite unlike financial instruments as an investment. Where a share is sold, it has a known value and there is a definite market to buy and sell them. Conditions are set up so that it is not normally possible to sell counterfeit goods. However, the price and quality of physical assets will **vary** considerably and people may be tempted to pass damaged and repaired goods as if in perfect condition, or sell things that are not what they seem, such as a good **counterfeit**. It is a relatively simple matter for individuals to **artificially** push up prices at auctions by **false bidding**. Trading in physical assets requires skill, understanding and experience and even the professionals have been caught out at some time or other.

3.11 The markets in most of the valuable collectable assets are monitored via the prices being achieved at auction and subject to statistical analysis. This allows professional investors the ability to examine **market movements** and **valuations** with a view to helping them pay and set better prices. **Art Sales Index Ltd** is the main company monitoring sales of fine art, monitoring 420 different auction houses to collect their statistics. They regularly publish turnover statistics from the auction houses of the main centres for fine art, New York, London and Paris. Fine art investment is a serious business and statistics from UK auction houses alone indicate an annual turnover of over £500 million, and a world annual turnover of some £2 billion. Indices are available also for vintage cars, coins and stamps.

Question 10.7

What additional costs might an investor face with an investment in fine art?

Taxation of physical assets

3.12 Many **physical assets** fall into the category of chattels or personal possessions. Where these have a value of up to £6,000, they will not be liable to **capital gains tax**. The process for the calculation of **capital gains** on **chattels** that exceed £6,000 is complex, but is covered in the G10 *Taxation and Trusts* syllabus. Although this is assumed knowledge it is extremely unlikely that this will be examined as part of this exam.

3.13 Other assets, whether or not for personal use, are subject to capital gains tax when sold for a profit. Special rules apply for wasting or depreciating assets such as boats, whose value is deemed to decrease from the time of purchase. Many wasting assets are **exempt from CGT**, which might seem like an advantage but in reality, as in the boat example above, stops investors from offsetting known losses on those assets against gains on other assets.

3.14 Cars for **personal use** are **exempt** and may be bought and sold with any profits being **free of CGT**. Problems may arise when cars are purchased and sold several times (eg more than 12) during the year as the **Inland Revenue** may consider that the individual is a trader for taxation purposes.

Investing in physical assets

3.15 Many individuals have **small collections** of stamps or coins, or the odd antique that has been passed down through the family, and this does not usually present a problem. However, in order to deal or trade in these assets in any volume, a **significant amount of expertise** will be required. When this is combined with the storage and security issues and the costs involved in buying and selling, it tends to make them largely unsuitable for many investors.

Commodities

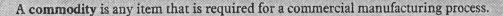

KEY TERM

A **commodity** is any item that is required for a commercial manufacturing process.

3.16 The levels of **supply and demand** for **commodities** influence the **price**. Some individuals feel that they can anticipate changes in these and can profit from them by **buying and selling commodities**. Prices can change dramatically and large amounts of money can be made or lost. However, this form of investment is highly speculative and prices can move either way. **Commodities** such as coffee can be **wiped out** by freak weather conditions, or the market can be unexpectedly **flooded** with a commodity that was expected to be in short supply.

Storage and maintenance of commodities

3.17 Many **commodities** are traded in exceptionally **large volumes**. In these cases, safe appropriate storage for the commodity can be an expensive issue. They may also need to be 'delivered' to the purchaser, all of which requires the input of money. Private investors will rarely, if ever, be in a position to deal with commodities themselves for these reasons. Dealing in **commodities via derivatives** avoids these problems.

Trading in commodities

3.18 **Commodities** can be sold directly, traded through markets and exchanges, or simply sold by auction. In some cases, the purchaser is required to verify the quality of the goods and high levels of expertise are required for this.

3.19 A far more popular way of investing in commodities is via the **futures market,** as issues such as storage, transportation, or the quality of the underlying goods become irrelevant. In many cases, these will simply be paper transactions, as positions can be opened or closed without there being any underlying commodity. The nature of the **future** as a financial instrument makes it highly unsuitable for all but the most experienced investor.

Taxation of commodities

3.20 The way a transaction is treated for **tax purposes** will depend on whether it is a personal or business transaction. Commodities with a limited life, such as tea or coffee, could be treated as a wasting asset and these could also be taxed differently, depending on the circumstances. A private individual regularly dealing in these areas could be considered a trader and subject to income tax.

Commodities as an investment

3.21 These are **high-risk** and **volatile investments** that require a great deal of expertise to buy and sell. There is enormous potential for things to go wrong and a great deal of additional cost involved if dealing in the commodity itself. They would not be suitable for a private investor.

Question 10.8

What factors influence the value of commodities in the market place?

Commodities - futures and options

3.22 The cost of **trading** in actual commodities can be very high and would normally be outside the scope of all private investors. However, some do invest indirectly via **futures** or **options on futures**. This is an exceptionally **high-risk form of investment** which requires significant amounts of expertise and skill. The instruments are **highly volatile** and **highly geared**, and depending on the nature of the position taken, the **potential for loss** can be **unlimited**.

3.23 Even armed with knowledge and expertise, **serious losses** can result. Investors can be caught out by the calls for extra margin, sudden movements in the wrong direction, poor strategy and poor advice. In view of this, and the exceptionally high risks involved, this type of investment is not at all suitable for the private investor.

3.24 **Portfolios of derivatives** managed by investment professionals can be a way of reducing the risk, whilst maintaining most of the potential for gains. However, the money allowed for this form of investment activity should be limited to a **small proportion** of a **large portfolio.**

Question 10.9

Which investment carries the greater risk, direct investment in commodities or investment in commodity derivatives?

Types of transaction in commodity futures and options

3.25 Broadly speaking, the main types of transaction were described in chapter 5, but the main variations will be summarised here. The initial choice will be between **commodity futures and options written on those futures**.

3.26 With **options**, the greatest possible loss is the premium paid for the option. It is quite common for traders to buy options and sell them to close their positions without owning the underlying asset. The **potential returns** for investors are **highly geared**, with the possibility of profits in excess of 100%. These are the most common transactions for private investors.

3.27 Every financial instrument must have a **buyer** and a **seller**, including options. For option contracts to be available for purchase, there must be a **seller**, or a **writer**, of the option. Writers of options relating to commodities face all the risks outlined in Chapter 5, and the additional risk that the commodity they own could be worthless.

3.28 **Buyers of futures** are effectively liable to the extent of the price of the asset at the time it is purchased. They will receive a return in line with the full movement of price of the underlying asset. To achieve this, they must put down initial margin of a proportion of the value of the contract and meet any calls for additional margin as it is made. This provides a good measure of **gearing** for the investor. There are risks involved, but a number of private individuals do invest in this type of transaction. It is also the more common transaction for **portfolio managers** of **private portfolios**.

3.29 As discussed in Chapter 5, one of the main reasons for selling futures is to 'hedge' against price movements. This is mostly the province of larger companies. The main risks with selling futures is that there is **no upper limit** on the price of the commodity.

3.30 If the seller of the future does not own the underlying assets, he will have to buy them (or pay the equivalent cash value, less the price at which the deal was struck). This makes this transaction **very high-risk** if uncovered.

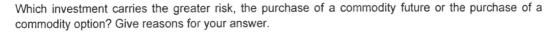

Question 10.10

Which investment carries the greater risk, the purchase of a commodity future or the purchase of a commodity option? Give reasons for your answer.

Physical assets and commodity investments as an alternative to equities

3.31 The bulk of UK investment is invested in **fixed interest investments, equities** and **cash**. Investment in **physical assets** and **commodities** is transacted in significant quantities but will only be a fraction of that invested in equities.

3.32 Both **portfolio managers** and **investors** benefit from the absolute **liquidity** in the market of **listed shares** and the widely available detailed research into the individual companies.

With the exception of cash investments, no investment medium is easier to access. Investments can be made directly or indirectly via **pooled funds** and **managed portfolios**. Investments can be purchased 'off the page', over the Internet, from banks and building societies, high street share shops, or even a stockbroker.

3.33 **Physical assets** can show spectacular **gains** or **losses**. The classic car market has had a number of rises and falls in the last 20 years. Many that bought when the market was at its peak in the late 1980s will still have cars worth substantially less than they paid for them. In the meantime, storage, maintenance and restoration will have all been a drain on financial resources.

3.34 **Collectibles** typically do not have a liquid market. Buyers and sellers can be matched in auction houses, but often the prices achieved will be dependent on those attending. **Physical assets** could have widely different values depending on where and when they are sold.

3.35 For each type of physical asset, there will usually be some source of intelligence on the market but information goes out-of-date very quickly and it can be difficult to keep up with changes. Investors in physical assets need to have a great deal of knowledge in order to avoid problems with purchasing poor quality items and, in many cases, there is little investor protection. *Caveat emptor* (let the buyer beware) is an important principle with this type of investment. Money can be lost quite easily and the ability to make it is largely a question of knowing the market exceptionally well. This form of investment can provide excellent returns, often better than equities, but with risks that can be a lot higher.

3.36 **Physical assets** do provide one form of return that can not be matched by equities, the ability to use or appreciate the investment, such as driving a vintage car or looking at a work of art.

3.37 **Commodities** do generally have **liquid markets**, and there is considerable market intelligence to support the decisions of investors. The use of **futures** and **options on futures** can insulate the investor from the physical side of the market eliminating the need for storage, security and transportation. However, the **price of commodities** is very **volatile**. Like shares, a wide range of local and global economic factors can influence them.

3.38 Few investors invest directly in **commodities.** Most invest via **options** and **futures**. Those that do will be large companies or very wealthy individuals because the underlying volatility of commodities means that the rewards and the risks are considerably higher than those of equities.

3.39 The market in UK futures and commodity options on **LIFFE (the London International Financial Futures and Options Exchange)** is currently limited to five underlying assets.

- Cocoa
- Robusta coffee
- White sugar
- Feed wheat
- Rapeseed
- Milling wheat
- Corn
- Potato

For a wider range, the American exchanges such as the **Chicago Board of Trade (CBOT)** can be used.

3.40 **Commodity futures** and **options prices** are subject to high **volatility** and the financial instruments are subject to a high degree of gearing.

3.41 The **main investors** for these assets will be **companies**, but there is a small core of **private investors** prepared to put their money in **managed portfolios** or **directly into the market**. These individuals are prepared to take considerably higher risks than an equity investor but, in return, expect exceptionally high returns on the transactions that pay off. This type of investment requires considerable investment experience and access to good market intelligence. The advent of the Internet and satellite communication means that even private individuals have access to this information and can trade very successfully.

Question 10.11

How does the level of intelligence in the market vary between physical assets, commodities and equities?

---

4 PROPERTY

> **KEY TERM**
>
> **Property** investment (in land and buildings) provides return in the form of an increase in capital value and can, if all or part is rented out, provide an income stream.

4.1 The **property sector** is **divided** into **residential** and **industrial** and **office** (the latter two known as **commercial**), with distinctly different investment characteristics. Each will be influenced by different factors, such as rent and capital values and they also tend to be taxed differently.

4.2 One of the main characteristics of investing in property is the **high initial cost**. In many cases, it will be necessary for the investor to borrow money in order to cover the initial cost. Where this is the case, the cost of the borrowing becomes a significant factor in the level of investment return.

4.3 It is possible for individuals to invest in property without the need for a large initial outlay or borrowing. **Investment in properties** can be made indirectly via the **shares** of companies involved in properties or, even more indirectly, via **pooled funds** some of which hold actual property but others specialise in the shares of property companies. Some managed funds include a small percentage of property in their **portfolio** as part of the **asset allocation**. Investing in the shares of property companies allows investors to share in the profits of building residential properties as well as the returns from renting.

Residential investment

4.4 For most individuals, **residential property** represents the biggest investment they will make. With average prices paid for a house in the UK of £163,615 in April 2005 (*Source:* Halifax plc) and rising monthly, the house is the most valuable asset that most people are ever likely to own. Increases in the value of residential property allow many the opportunity for a reasonably sized cash lump sum on retirement, as a larger property can be sold and replaced with a smaller property at lower cost. Typically, out-of-town properties are cheaper because of the lack of local employment and increased travelling costs of getting to work.

Main residence

4.5 Investment can be in the form of ownership of a **main residence** or other residential properties to be **rented** out. The definition of an investment is an **asset that provides a return** and a main residence falls within this definition. The **investment return** is in the form of an **increase in capital value** and it can also provide income in the form of rent from one, or more, rooms rented out. There can even be tax incentives for this approach when renting a room out under the **'rent a room' scheme**.

4.6 **Capital gains** on an individual's main residence are exempt, which represents a benefit potentially worth many thousands of pounds. **Rental income** up to the single person's annual allowance under the **'rent a room' scheme** is also **exempt** from **income tax**.

4.7 **Prices** of residential property do fluctuate (there have been two separate downturns in the last ten years), but if it is for private residence, and if the residents are likely to remain in the property for some time, this is less of a problem.

4.8 Problems can arise where an individual is **unable to meet mortgage payments** as a result of **rising interest rates**. Property is quite **illiquid** and disposal is not usually an option. Where this is accompanied with **negative equity** (the house value being less than the original loan taken out) the situation is worse. As payments are missed, interest mounts up and the debt can spiral out of control.

Residential property for letting

4.9 For as long as humans have lived in sheltered dwellings, **renting** property has taken place. As an **alternative** to **equity investment**, there are some advantages. Residential property tends to increase steadily whether the equity markets are up or down and rents are paid irrespective of the underlying earnings of the individuals renting. Even those who cannot afford to rent from their own resources can be subsidised by social security payments. Expenses involved in renting are normally deductible for tax purposes.

4.10 Unlike equity investments, there can be significant **running costs** with renting out residential property.

- Acquisition costs
- Maintenance of the property
- Advertising and marketing costs
- Management and agency fees (if used)
- Loan repayments
- Buildings insurance
- Unpaid rent
- Court costs to gain evictions and to get payment of unpaid rents
- Council Tax

4.11 **Rental return** on a property will vary depending on its location. Factors that will influence rent are the local public amenities, the distance to the middle of town, the local levels of crime and poverty, the level of traffic and the presence of open space. When tenants change, the property owner may face a **void period** with no rent receivable, while new tenants are found.

4.12 The **level of income** received from property investment is also dependent on the proportion of time the property is actually let out. Finding tenants is an essential part of the property owners' role. This can either be done by advertising them or via a third party such as an agent. A third option is to use a management company, whose job is to rent out the property, collect rents and arrange for maintenance. Although this is usually the most effective way of renting a property, the **management company** will usually want 10% or more of the rental income as a commission.

Question 10.12

What problems might arise if a property is not let out for a large proportion of the time?

4.13 Renting certain types of accommodation can be more profitable than others but there can be risks as well. **Student lets** can bring in money as the accommodation is basic, usually in a poor area and has a high level of occupation, but there are also considerable risks of damage and non-payment. Whatever the basis of the student let, location is vital. For example, there must be an educational institution nearby. A good source of local employment, such as an airport, can also be influential for successful letting. Maintaining a good relationship with the local employer or university can be beneficial, as they will often help you to promote your accommodation on notice boards at prime locations within the site.

4.14 **Residential property investment** is popular with private individuals and companies. A number of large institutions will also be involved such as universities, who will own properties in the town to rent to students. Financial institutions may also take a stake or own large tranches of residential property.

4.15 The requirement for rented accommodation and housing generally continues to increase. Competition for building sites is increasing and there is currently a debate over the proportion of **green belt** that is being used. Legislation is due to be passed imposing **minimum limits** in each area for developers to redevelop formerly developed 'brown belt' sites.

4.16 In the late 1970s and 1980s, legislation favoured the tenant. Owners had problems getting them out and getting payment and redress in the event of damage with the result that many owners were put off letting. This led to there being many empty houses at the same time as a housing crisis. The government of the day shifted the balance in favour of the property owner, improving their ability to get out reluctant tenants and allowing rent to be paid directly to the landlord by the government in the case of tenants on social security. The proliferation of **assured shorthold leases** has tempted many property owners back into the renting market. Future legislation favouring one or other party could improve or reduce the prospects for investment returns from residential investment property.

4.17 The **income produced** from the **rents** is treated as Schedule A income for the individual or company. In each case, expenses incurred can be offset. **Capital gains** on the property will normally be subject to **capital gains tax** for an individual and **corporation tax** for a company.

Furnished holiday accommodation

4.18 There is a specific type of let for **furnished holiday accommodation**, which is subject to the following rules.

(a) The property must be **furnished**

(b) It must be let on a **commercial** basis

(c) It must be available for letting for no less than **140 days** per year

(d) It must be actually let for **70 days** per year (averaged over all properties held)

(e) It must not normally be in the **same occupation** for more than 31 days in a seven month period (including the 70 days)

4.19 The tax advantages of this type of let include the following.

(a) **Relief for losses** (including the facility to offset these against other income), normal schedule A losses do not apply

(b) **Capital allowances** are available on furniture (the renewal and wear and tear basis do not apply)

(c) The income qualifies as **net relevant earnings** when calculating how much can be paid into a personal pension

(d) Capital gains tax **rollover relief, retirement relief, relief for gifts of business assets** and **relief for loans to traders also apply**

4.20 A further advantage of this type of arrangement is that the owners could use the holiday accommodation for themselves part of the time.

Commercial property

4.21 The price of **commercial properties** is considerably **more volatile** than residential because of the influences of a wide range of factors. These include local government subsidies, tax breaks, communication networks (roads, rail etc), the local and regional economy and even trends and fashion.

4.22 These issues do not just affect factories and other large commercial buildings, they are just as likely to affect a shop on a High Street. Something as simple as the introduction of double yellow lines or a one way system can put potential customers off, or divert them away, and the commercial value of the property can be **significantly diminished.**

4.23 Commercial property is broken down into four categories, each of which are further subdivided.

(a) **Office:** tends to be subdivided by the additional facilities they offer such as parking, air conditioning, lifts and raised floors

(b) **Retail:** shop (A1), office with shop frontage (A2) and hot food/takeaway (A3)

(c) **Industrial:** light industrial (B1), general industrial (B2) and warehouse/storage (B8)

(d) **Other:** such as leisure, pub, petrol station, garage and car park

4.24 As with **residential property** it is possible to **invest directly** by buying the property itself, via shares in property companies, or indirectly via pooled funds investing in the shares of property companies such as **unit trusts** or **Enterprise Zone Trusts**. The cost of purchasing directly is likely to be considerable, putting it out of reach for many private investors who are more likely to invest directly.

4.25 **Pension funds** are **large investors** in **commercial property**. It is not only the very large pension schemes that are involved, smaller **SSAS** and **SIPP schemes** are also significant owners of commercial property. Commercial property is also a common investment for **with-profit funds** because of excellent returns in the form of rent and the increases in capital value. In many cases, they funded the original development, providing even more scope for increases in capital value. An examination of many shopping centres will often reveal a plaque stating the name of the financial institution or company involved in the development.

4.26 The ownership of property can be via a **freehold** or **leasehold**, which will have an impact on investment returns.

Question 10.13

Why might the trustees of a small pension (SSAS or SIPP) scheme be interested in investing in commercial property?

Commercial property as an investment

4.27 The owner of the **freehold** will **lease** the property out to the **leaseholder** in return for **rent**. The agreement between the leaseholder and the owner of the freehold is significant. It details factors such as the term of the lease, the levels of rent, arrangements for rent reviews and whether or not the leaseholder has responsibility for maintenance of the building. These are all factors that will affect the **investment return** for the owners of the freehold and the **value of the lease** to the leaseholder.

4.28 A number of other factors dictate the **value** of the **freehold** or **leasehold** in addition to the terms, for example, the supply and demand of commercial property in the area can have a significant impact. Where there is ample commercial property in an area prices will be depressed.

4.29 For the businesses looking to rent the properties, **access to their customers** will be of vital importance, and the presence of good communications will increase the value of a property. For retail property, a supply of customers walking by would be ideal. For a haulier, the presence of a good motorway network would be important.

4.30 Current trends and fashions will have an impact. The current fashion for **out-of-town shopping centres** has hit the value of city centre retail properties and increased the price of development land out of town.

4.31 The presence of **government subsidies** will often attract business to the area, pushing up demand for commercial premises. Building in **enterprise zones** has significant advantages for the original developer. The **lower taxation** and **relaxed planning regulations** will reduce their costs and have the potential to increase the level of investment return on property built there.

4.32 **High local taxes** (the uniform business rate) can be a deterrent for business and may impact on the rents available for properties in that area.

Question 10.14

How does building in an enterprise zone influence the income and capital returns from commercial investment property?

4.33 Compared to equities, commercial properties are somewhat **illiquid investments**. Some commercial properties remain unsold for years and there can be additional problems where an industrial building was built for a specific purpose. In many cases, the property will only be useful for someone in the same business. Even **pooled investments,** which are usually quite liquid, often have special rules relating to funds with significant commercial property investment. It is usual for such funds to be able to invoke a six-month delay on the sale of units under certain circumstances. This is to protect them in the event of a large number of units being sold at the same time, which might necessitate the sale of some of the underlying assets.

4.34 **Commercial property investment** can provide **significant returns,** much of it in the form of a **good income stream.** Many shares will provide their investment return in the form of an increase in capital and a limited income stream. However, both are subject to the potential for volatility in investment returns.

4.35 For direct investors, the **pricing** of commercial property is often an issue, as even independent valuations can differ wildly. The investment into all forms of property is significantly different from that of equities, in which there are many similar transactions and much market intelligence.

4.36 Establishing the **value of commercial property** as an investment requires considerable specialist knowledge. A good understanding of the local area is vital to allow the investor to understand the supply and demand issues in that area. An investor will need to understand the types of business that could possibly operate from the property and marketing the property to appropriate potential tenants requires specialist skills. Knowledge of the **capital values of property** and the local levels of rent are also prerequisites. For these reasons, few private individuals would be in a position to invest directly in commercial property based on their own knowledge, although investors might seek specialist professional advice. For those wanting commercial property in their portfolio, **pooled investment** relies on the skills of the **fund manager** to deal with most of the issues.

Indirect investment in property

Property company shares

4.37 If a client wants an exposure to property but does not have sufficient capital to purchase a property, he may buy shares in **companies that own or develop properties.** A company that holds properties over the medium or long term is likely to have a steady income from rents paid. A development company makes much of its return from profits on sale, and so earnings may fluctuate from time to time.

4.38 A property company can diversify by holding many properties, and the shareholder gains the benefit of that diversification in lower risk as compared with owning one or two properties. For information on the performance of property shares, the investor can refer to the property sub-index of the FT-SE Actuaries indices. The prices of property shares tend to be more volatile than the actual property values. The price of the shares will move with supply and demand, and may diverge from **underlying asset values. Gearing** (borrowing) by the company can increase the share price volatility. The share price can be affected by **systematic** factors affecting the stock market as a whole, as well as factors specific to the company or the property sector.

4.39 Compared with direct investment in property, a significant advantage of this means of investing in property is **liquidity**. The investor can realise his investment in a listed property company easily through a stockbroker, since there are market makers who must quote prices for all listed stocks.

Property funds

4.40 Originally, **unit trusts** were prohibited from directly investing in property and could only invest indirectly via property shares. This has now changed and unit trust and Open Ended Investment Company (**OEIC**) managers can invest directly into commercial property. At the launch of such a fund, the manager must be confident that he will attract sufficient funds to make adequate property purchases to establish a well spread portfolio.

4.41 There are however restrictions on the proportion of the fund that can be invested in leases with less than 60 years to run, or in unoccupied property. There are also restrictions on holding mortgaged property, which limit gearing. No more than 15% in value of the fund assets can be invested in a single property. Additionally, there are unit trusts and OEICs that invest in **property company shares**.

4.42 As with unit trusts and OEICs generally, the investment will be redeemed at net asset value. However, if many investors choose to sell at one time, the unit trust or OEIC may need to invoke its right to postpone encashment of units/shares until property can be sold. This possible restriction in **accessibility** makes property funds potentially less liquid. As for all unit trusts, OEICs and investment trusts, there is no capital gains tax within the fund, but investors are subject to capital gains tax on gains when they sell the units or shares.

4.43 There are also **Enterprise Zone Trusts**, which we looked at earlier.

Property investment trusts

4.44 **Property investment trusts** are pooled investments but are only permitted to invest in shares and securities of property companies, not in property directly. They are permitted to borrow, which increases the risk for the investor, as well as the possible return. The share price of the trust will fluctuate with supply and demand for the shares of the trust, and may be at a discount or a premium to the net asset value.

Real Estate Investment Trusts (REITs)

4.45 Real Estate Investment Trusts (REITs) are '**tax-transparent' property investment vehicles** which were first formed in the USA, where the name 'REITs' originated. Other countries, including Japan, the Netherlands and France, now have their own versions of **REITs**. The UK is expected to follow, with **UK-REITs** being proposed. The exact form of UK-REITs is not yet known, and there will not be legislation until **2006** at the earliest.

4.46 **Tax-transparent property investment vehicles**, such as REITs, distribute nearly all of their taxable income to investors. Provided they do this, the vehicles are granted exemption from capital gains tax and from corporate taxes. Investors pay tax on the dividends and capital growth at their own marginal tax rates, thus avoiding the double taxation that affects investors in UK property companies currently.

4.47 It is anticipated that existing UK **property companies** may choose to **convert** to become REITs. When France introduced similar funds in 2003, converting companies had to pay an 'exit tax' amounting to half of their capital gains tax liability over four years. It is expected that the UK Treasury is likely to put a similar provision in place, when REITs are introduced.

4.48 The UK Treasury hopes that introducing a UK version of REITs might bring **offshore property investment vehicles** back onshore, thus allowing them to be better regulated. However, since offshore vehicles do not pay UK tax, they might not be attracted back onshore, particularly if they have to pay a tax to convert to the new type of company.

Insurance company property funds

4.49 **Life insurance companies** have funds that invest specifically in commercial property. An investor can choose regular premium or single premium investment plans (which may be termed '**life assurance property bonds**'). The value of units is directly linked to the net asset values of the properties held. The fund is not permitted to borrow.

4.50 Although these funds are more liquid than direct investments in property, the fund retains a rarely invoked right to postpone encashment of units if necessary. This could be necessary if many investors wish to encash units at a particular time, necessitating the sale of properties – a process than could take some time.

4.51 Income and capital gains are subject to tax within the fund at 20%. This cannot be reclaimed by non-taxpayers and higher rate tax payers will pay additional tax.

Offshore property funds

4.52 Many UK investment managers now operate **offshore property trusts,** for example in Guernsey. These trusts are **closed-ended,** meaning that, as with conventional investment trusts, new shares are not created or cancelled when investors buy or sell. These stocks are relatively high-yielding and have proved attractive to many retail and institutional investors over recent years, when many investors have sought to reduce their exposure to equities.

4.53 Because the trusts are registered offshore and are not subject to UK tax, they can pay out dividends that are close to the underlying yield on UK commercial property, with the tax liability depending upon the tax status of the investor. Until the introduction of a REIT/PIF structure in the UK, these funds stand as very similar to the proposed PIF. Many trade at a premium to the net asset value of the underlying investments. Onshore (ie, UK) property companies have, in contrast, often traded at a discount to NAV, partly because of the unfavourable tax structure.

4.54 **Advantages of pooled property investments**

- The investor is 'buying' expert property management.

- The investor can buy into a large well spread fund. This can be spread according to type, eg office, warehousing, retail and geographically, with reduced risk because of this diversification.

- Although there is some illiquidity in the pooled finds, particularly in the property fund and the Enterprise Zone schemes, liquidity is greater than with direct investment.

- A relatively small amount of money can be invested in a pooled fund. A substantial sum would need to be committed to the purchase of even a modest commercial property.

Disadvantages of pooled property investments

- The investor does not have direct control over the properties.
- It may be difficult to realise capital quickly particularly from a property bond or Enterprise Zone scheme.
- The Enterprise Zone schemes are illiquid and high risk.

Chapter roundup

- Various alternative opportunities exist for investors with high risk, tax minimisation objectives.

- **Unlisted securities** offer potential for high growth but have high business risk and are illiquid.

- The taxation of returns on unlisted securities is minimised when they are held within **Venture Capital Trusts (VCTs)** and **Enterprise Investment Schemes (EISs)**.

- VCTs are investment trusts, investing primarily (70%) in unlisted securities. Tax incentives include 40% tax relief on investment, CGT relief on gains, exemption from income tax on dividends. These reliefs are granted on the first £200,000 invested where the investment is retained for three years.

- EISs tend to invest in a single companies and are more risky than VCTs. The tax reliefs are similar to those for a VCT except that it is possible to use re-investment relief to defer tax on rolled over gains.

- Investment in tax efficient **enterprise zone property** which attracts 100% writing down allowances is normally by means of appropriate trust, an EZT.

- Investment in **physical assets** is normally for the expert investor.

- Such assets will not generate income and are often illiquid. If liquidity is required commodity derivatives offer an alternative.

- **Property** generates income and capital gain. It is regarded as an inflation hedge, in the long run. There are various methods of investing in property indirectly, through funds.

- **Commercial property** may be segmented into office, retail and industrial classifications. It is an area requiring specialist knowledge.

Quick quiz

1   What are the main methods of buying unlisted shares?

2   What are the main business risks for an unlisted company?

3   Briefly, what tax advantages are available for investment in unlisted shares directly and indirectly via collective investment schemes.

4   What is the maximum investment for an individual into a VCT in any tax year?

5   What is the maximum proportion of a VCT fund that can be invested in quoted investments?

6   Can a business angel with a shareholding in a company via an EIS become a director of the company and still benefit from tax advantages?

7   What is the pooled investment relating to enterprise zone buildings called?

8   What problems arise on the subsequent sale of an Enterprise Zone building?

9   What costs might an investor need to consider if investing in physical assets rather than financial instruments?

10   Why is that trading in physical assets is considerably more expensive than trading in financial assets?

11   What problems might an investor experience if investing directly in commodities rather than via derivatives?

12   Which would typically be lower risk, commodity futures, or commodity options?

13   What is the maximum potential liability for the purchaser of a commodity future?

14   Why are commodity derivatives so volatile?

15   How does the cost of borrowing influence the returns on property as an investment?

16   What is the main problem with any form of property investment?

17   What additional advantage can a holiday let provide for the owners of the investment over and above the investment return?

18   How does the volatility of commercial property values compare to residential?

19   What are the main details covered by the lease agreement?

20   How liquid are pooled investments where the underlying investment is commercial property?

The answers to the questions in the Quick Quiz can be found at the end of this Study Text. Before checking your own answers against them, you should look back at this chapter and use the information in it to correct your answers.

Answers to Chapter Questions

10.1   The main issue will be establishing a fair price. The holder of the shares can effectively ask what they want for the shares, as the investor has a very limited choice. With shares purchased via an exchange, the large number of transactions can provide a fair estimate of the share value and there will be more than one person to buy the shares from, which will promote competition amongst the sellers.

10.2   Shares with wide spreads and high charges need to perform better to produce the same overall level of investment return.

10.3   A non-taxpayer would receive no income tax benefit from VCT investment. Tax reducers reduce the income tax liability only to the extent that an individual has a liability.

10.4 VCTs present less risk than direct investment in unlisted equities as the investor's funds are pooled and spread over a wide range of equities. A professional fund manager effectively makes the buying and selling decisions, reducing the risk further.

10.5 A VCT is generally lower risk than an EIS as it is a pooled fund and the underlying investment is spread over a number of different shares. It is possible to spread the risk with an EIS by buying shares in more than one company, but the minimum per company is typically £2,000. For an investment of £10,000, this would only allow an investment in five companies, which provides considerably less spread than with a VCT.

10.6 There is no minimum term, the only consideration is the amount of money the investor can recover and the tax penalties there may be on it. Where a building is held for 25 years there will be no requirement for a balancing payment. Where a partial interest, such as a lease, is sold on after more than seven years there will be no requirement to pay a balancing payment since the investor will still own the freehold of the property.

10.7 Investors in fine art will need to consider the additional costs of storage, security, insurance, and possibly, restoration at some time in the future which will all reduce the final investment return. In addition to this, there may well be considerable costs in auction fees for buying and selling.

10.8 The supply and demand of the asset is the main factor influencing the prices of commodities.

10.9 Commodity derivatives represent the greatest risks as these instruments 'gear up' the market movements of the underlying commodities.

10.10 With the purchase of a commodity future, the investor is fully exposed to movements in the price of the underlying commodity, whether up or down. With an option, the investor is gaining exposure to the upside in return for paying a premium. The maximum downside is the loss of the premium, so the option carries the least risk.

10.11 The level of market intelligence available usually varies with the level of trade in each investment. Equities are traded in the greatest volume of the three and there is a great deal of market intelligence in newspapers, magazines, specialist journals, on the television, on the Internet etc. Commodities are next in terms of volumes of trade and there is significant intelligence in newspapers, specialist journals and on the Internet. For physical assets, there is limited market intelligence because volumes of trade are considerably smaller, but also because there is such a wide range of assets to invest in. The best sources would tend to be specialist magazines and the Internet.

10.12 When a property is not let, most of the charges and costs continue to mount up. When this is accompanied by a lack of income, the investment returns can turn to losses. Other problems can be an increased risk of criminal damage to the property, which potentially reduces the capital value as well as the income.

10.13 The trustees of the scheme will be the owners of the company. Investing in commercial property via the pension scheme allows them to get the benefit of commercial property investment within the tax-free environment of the pension. The investment return to the pension scheme is the rental income (typically from the company that rents the property from the pension scheme at a commercial rent). The pension scheme benefits from the rent paid to it tax-free and the gains on the property are also tax-free. The investment proceeds are used to pay for pensions in retirement. In some cases the company can rent the property themselves from the fund providing them with business premises.

10.14 Investing in property in an Enterprise Zone should increase the income produced as a result of the tax concession and relaxed planning regulations. Capital returns are likely to be reduced as the subsequent purchasers will not get those tax concessions and will not be willing to pay as much for the property.

PRACTICE QUESTION 10

Martin Reynolds has been collecting antique fob watches for six months. He has also recently inherited £50,000 that he would like to invest for long term capital growth. He is rather keen to invest the money into his new hobby but, being prudent, decided to seek your advice as to whether this would be the right course of action. Martin is a higher rate taxpayer and he has brought an advertisement for the XYZ VCT, on which he would like your advice. He feels this will give him better opportunities to save tax than any other investment vehicle, as he has no further leeway to increase his pension contributions.

(a)   What are your initial thoughts as to the suitability of investment in antique fob watches for Mr Reynolds?   (2)

(b)   What expenses might Mr Reynolds incur if he continues to invest in antique fob watches?
                                                                                              (6)

(c)   What problems might Mr Reynolds encounter if he needed to sell his collection?   (6)

(d)   How suitable would the VCT be for Mr Reynolds?   (2)

(e)   Briefly describe the tax advantages of a VCT.   (5)

(f)   Mr Reynolds also tells you he is considering moving into a new house and renting his old house out to students as his bank is prepared to lend him the money under a buy to let scheme. What facts relating to the house should he consider before going ahead?   (7)

Part E
Interpretation of accounts

Chapter 11

INTERPRETATION OF ACCOUNTS

Chapter topic list	Syllabus reference
1 Accounts and accounting principles	5.1
2 Using accounts in investment decisions	5.2
3 Accounting ratios	5.2
4 Investor ratios	5.2

Introduction

When making direct investments in a company, for example as part of an investment portfolio, it is vitally important to understand how healthy the company is from a financial standpoint.

Much of this information can be provided by the **company's accounts** (which are included in its financial statements). The company's ability to repay the various forms of loan stock depends on financial strength and there are many agencies that assess this for companies and publish their results. To assess the growth potential for a share is considerably more subjective. Information is there in the accounts, but the methods of assessing it vary widely. In this chapter we examine the **elements** of a **company's accounts** and the principles and practices used in their construction. We then examine what conclusions it is possible to draw from the data.

1 ACCOUNTS AND ACCOUNTING PRINCIPLES

1.1 The **Companies Acts** make it a legal requirement for a company to provide a 'true and fair' set of accounts and determine some aspects of the content of company accounts. The Accounting Standards Board sets out accounting standards which companies must follow in order to comply with **Generally Accepted Accounting Principles (GAAP)**. Starting with accounting periods beginning on or after 1 January 2005, **listed companies** must prepare its financial statements in accordance with **International Financial Reporting Standards (IFRS)**. AIM companies are proposed to switch to IFRS in 2006.

1.2 The **annual financial statements** for a **listed company** generally contain the following sections, which can then be used to gain information about a company from the investment perspective.

- A Chairman's statement
- A directors' report
- A profit and loss account or income statement
- A statement of total recognised gains and losses
- A balance sheet
- A cash flow statement
- An auditors' report
- Notes to the accounts

BPP
PROFESSIONAL EDUCATION

The Chairman's statement

1.3   The **Chairman's statement** is required by the London Stock Exchange listing rules for quoted companies. The statement will tend to show the company from the best possible perspective and will contain information relating to the following.

(a)   The company's **future business strategy**

(b)   Any future business **plans**

(c)   The **performance** of the company relative to its market and current economic factors

(d)   Performance prospects for the **forthcoming year**

(e)   The performance of **different divisions** of the company

(f)   Any items of **particular relevance** occurring during the year, eg mergers, acquisitions, share buy-backs

Question 11.1

List the information that would normally be contained in the chairman's statement.

1.4   The chairman's statement is clearly **subjective,** but the contents can give an indication of the future potential of the company, and can explain any poor performance in the previous year and the measures taken to avoid it in future.

The directors' report

KEY TERM

The **directors' report** contains mainly statutory information relating to the running of the company, which will also be recorded elsewhere in the accounts.

1.5   From the **investment perspective,** it will give a review of business, the operating and financial review, if not provided elsewhere, and the amount of the **proposed dividend,** together with any **transfer from reserves** to cover it. This section can also provide information relating to major changes in **value of assets** and any differences between the **book value** and **market value** of significant assets. Clearly each of these factors could have a serious impact on the return from an investment in both income and capital terms and should be of interest to the investor.

The profit and loss account

KEY TERM

The **profit and loss account** is a historical document based on the **previous accounting period**. It shows whether a company is managing to sell its goods or services for more than the cost of producing/providing them over the period covered.

1.6 The international term for the profit and loss account is the **income statement**. Profit and loss account figures need **careful interpretation** as a profitable company can still run out of money, for example, if it is investing heavily in capital goods such as land or buildings while lacking the cash to pay for it. In addition to this, the profit and loss account only takes into account the level of profit, not when the goods are paid for (or even if they have been paid for), so it should not be read on its own. A profitable company can quickly reverse its fortunes if the cash flow is not positive.

1.7 What the profit and loss account does look at is the costs of materials, wages and overheads, each of which can have an impact on the value of a company. An increase in the cost of materials can quickly **reduce** a company's **profitability**, whereas a restructuring of the workforce may yield results in the form of reduced wages and overhead costs.

1.8 The profit and loss account also looks at the costs of **selling, administration and distribution** of products and services because any potential future changes in these costs could affect profitability.

The statement of total recognised gains and losses

> **KEY TERM**
>
> The **statement of total recognised gains and losses** is a relatively new requirement for company accounts. The information provided would have previously appeared in notes, but has been summarised here to allow the non-professional reader to gain some insight into the company's profitability.

1.9 This statement takes into account figures in the **profit and loss account** and the **balance sheet**, to give an indication of the profitability of the company irrespective of whether it has actually been realised. The document effectively cuts through valuation and currency adjustments to give a **real indication** of profitability. This is useful information for a potential investor.

The balance sheet

> **KEY TERM**
>
> The **balance sheet** indicates what a company's assets and liabilities are at the end of accounting year, subject to various assumptions provided in the notes.

1.10 The balance sheet is of importance to **prospective investors** and will **impact** on **share prices** for a number of reasons. The overall size of a company can affect its **creditworthiness** from the perspective of potential for borrowing and the cost of borrowing. A company that poses a lower risk for repayment of a loan will be charged lower interest rates. The size of the company also reduces the investor's risk of losing money, although this is not an absolute guarantee. However the balance sheet is drawn up under the historical cost convention and will not reflect the market value of the firm, even if certain assets have been recently revalued, such as land and buildings.

FRS17

1.11 Relatively recent changes to the make up of the balance sheet are causing particular concern at the moment. **FRS 17** details the requirements for companies to account for shortfalls in the position of final salary pension schemes in the balance sheet. Due to the poor performance of equities in recent years, many are running at a substantial deficit.

1.12 FRS 17 sets out the accounting treatment for retirement benefits and medical care during retirement.

1.13 **Requirements of FRS 17**

(a) Pension scheme assets are measured using market values

(b) Pension scheme liabilities are measured using a projected unit method and discounted at the AA corporate bond rate

(c) The pension scheme surplus (to the extent it can be recovered) or deficit is recognised in full on the balance sheet

(d) The movement in the scheme surplus/deficit is analysed into:

  (i) The current service cost and any past service costs: these are recognised in operating profit

  (ii) The interest cost and expected return on assets: these are recognised as other finance costs

  (iii) Actuarial gains and losses: these are recognised in the statement of total recognised gains and losses.

1.14 FRS 17 is fully effective for accounting periods beginning on or after 1 January 2005.

The cash flow statement

KEY TERM

The **cash flow statement** is a summary of cash movements in and out of the company.

1.15 From the company perspective, the **supply of cash is vital**. Without it there will be problems in continuing in business, as suppliers will not get paid, employees cannot be paid and the marketing, selling and distribution costs cannot be met. Even companies with a **healthy balance sheet** can have **problems** when the cash flow is not positive.

1.16 From the investor's perspective, **cash flow** is very important. With a reasonable level of cash flow the company can expand; without it, it may contract. Either of these situations will impact on share prices.

The auditor's report

1.17 The **auditor's** report must indicate to whom the report is addressed and which financial statements have been audited. The auditors will express their **opinion** on the accounts and the extent to which they can be seen as representative of the financial situation of the company.

KEY TERM

The **auditor's report** is a signed and dated statement giving the auditors' opinion on whether the accounts represent a true and fair picture of the company's financial position and that the company's accounts have been prepared in accordance with statutory requirements and with the appropriate accounting standards.

1.18 The **auditor's opinion** may differ from the impression given by that of the company accounts and any such opinions must be reported. The report may contain a statement of fundamental uncertainty which the auditors are required to draw attention to within the accounts, as they may be important in ascertaining the true picture. A good example of this may be **legal action** outstanding against the company, which may **impact** on the **company's financial position**.

1.19 Where there is **insufficient information** for the auditors to draw a **conclusion**, or they disagree with the approach taken in the accounts, they are required to draw attention to the source of the problem.

1.20 The auditors may include a '**disclaimer of opinion**', where they have been unable to uncover sufficient evidence to support the position presented by the financial statements. In this case there will be a specific statement that they were unable to form the opinion as to whether the accounts are 'true and fair'.

1.21 In the event that the auditors believe that the company accounts are seriously misleading, they may include a statement of '**adverse opinion**' stating they feel the accounts are not '**true and fair**'.

1.22 Whenever the auditors are in **disagreement** over any aspect of the company accounts, there could be a serious **impact** on the **share price** of the company. The **company accounts** represent the only opportunity that most professional and private investors get to **examine** the **internal financial workings** of a company and any doubt could cause them to invest elsewhere.

Question 11.2

What does it mean when the auditors make a statement of 'adverse opinion' in their report?

The notes to the accounts

1.23 People who regularly examine company accounts have a tendency to look at this section first. It describes the **accounting policies** used and the **method** by which all the numbers in the accounts have been calculated. Careful examination can occasionally reveal factors that may easily be missed by looking at the accounts themselves.

2 USING ACCOUNTS IN INVESTMENT DECISIONS

The role of accounts and annual reports in investment decisions

2.1 The main concern of the **investor** is the return he will receive on his investment. This will take the form of **income** from the **dividends** distributed by the company and the **increase** in share value that can be realised on sale. For many of the most popular shares, the reports, accounts and even the daily activities of the company are scrutinised in detail by the investment houses. The result of all this investigation is published in a variety of investment reports and all of the FTSE 100 Index shares will be covered in this way. Outside the FTSE 100, the level of scrutiny reduces and with some 3,000 equities available in the market place, it would take a long time to cover them all.

2.2 Many investors believe that careful analysis of the company's figures gives them an opportunity to spot value that has not yet been noticed by others, so they buy in and wait for others to reach the same conclusion and also buy, thus increasing the share price. It also works the other way: close scrutiny of the figures can give clues as to future weakness in a company, such as an inability to manage cash flow effectively. Such factors can pass relatively unnoticed until the company starts to have problems, at which time it can hit the share price. An appreciation of this can result in the prudent investor having sold up and moved on before the problems come to light.

2.3 There can be several limitations to this approach, as follows.

(a) The investor is reliant on the information provided and despite regulations governing the form and content of accounts, a measure of 'creativity' can often be used to disguise problems for some time (as in the case of Enron, for example).

(b) The accounts and report look at past performance rather than future prospects, with the exception of the Chairman's report, which will look at the future trading environment.

(c) The accounts will normally be prepared on an historic cost basis, so that the values shown for assets and liabilities may differ from their actual value now.

(d) The accounts cannot predict the future trading environment, which can be affected on a number of different levels, including global conditions, local conditions and sector conditions which can all severely impact on profitability and, hence, share price and dividend levels.

(e) The accounts do not and cannot allow for unpredictable factors such as future legislation, litigation from disgruntled customers, takeovers, mergers, employment problems, raw material cost variations caused by, for example, the weather, or changes in fashion.

(f) In times of extreme market conditions, investor sentiment can move prices significantly with little or no reference to fundamental value, future potential profits or to anything else.

2.4 Despite all of this, an examination of the company accounts can provide information on relative value, which is the value of a particular share relative to others in the same and in other sectors. Good control of cash flow can help a company to grow faster than the others in its sector when market conditions are buoyant, hopefully giving large increases in the share prices. In the event of a downturn, such a company has a greater resistance to going out of business and its share price will remain strong relative to others, even if not in absolute terms.

Question 11.3

Identify briefly the limitations to using data provided by the company accounts in making investment decisions.

Variation in data between types of company

2.5 When considering the **data** provided by the company accounts, we should consider the **sector** the company is in. The particular **sector** which is involved has a **significant impact** on the range of 'normal' values that can be applied to any statistics or ratios derived from the accounts.

2.6 Each industry will have different figures relating to costs, eg financing, production, sales and marketing and distribution. These will, in turn, be derived from the fact that every industry is different. In order to compare the accounts of companies from **different industries** using **financial ratios**, we need to know the 'normal' range of figures for that sector. Companies such as Dun & Bradstreet and Robert Morris Associates can provide such information.

Question 11.4

What are the four main areas of costs in a company's finances that can vary from industry to industry?

Financing

2.7 **Different industries** will require **different levels** of **cash flow**, and hence their requirements for borrowing will differ.

2.8 Some industries, such as banks and insurance companies, may produce **surplus cash flow**. For them there will be a requirement to invest **surplus capital**. Their profitability will depend on these **investment returns**. Other industries will require huge amounts of credit, as the cost of producing their goods or services is very high and they must maintain stocks and sell on credit. For them, the cost of borrowing will be an important issue, along with the ability to borrow further funds quickly. An example of this might be manufacturing companies, where raw materials need to be purchased, or retail companies where cash flow is required to purchase stock. In either case the level and cost of **credit** they receive from their suppliers will have a significant impact on the company accounts. However, we must note that many retailers retain the advantage of making their sales on a cash basis.

Production

2.9 The length of time and costs of **producing** goods or services will impact on the accounts significantly. A company that manufactures aircraft, for example, will be expected to meet all the costs of construction, including raw materials and employees' time, before they can sell it. Another example of this might be the construction industry, where it takes a fixed period to build a house, an office or a bridge. Often the work will not be paid for until completion and, in the meantime, this will have an **impact** on the **cash flows**.

2.10 As a contrast, with a **service industry** the 'product' is generally 'produced' at the time of its sale, for example, office cleaning services. The services are provided and paid for almost immediately, unless credit terms have been agreed, and again these differences will affect the company's financial position as shown in the accounts

Sales and marketing

2.11 Some products 'sell themselves', such as utilities, gas, electricity and water. Even in these days of increased competition in the **utilities market,** they are still very much goods and services that people need. Tobacco on the other hand is a very different product, one in which branding and market name is everything. Consequently, the **marketing and advertising budgets** for tobacco companies can make up a large proportion of their costs. With such **high costs**, the success or failure of such campaigns can make a significant impact on the company's profitability.

Distribution

2.12 For service industries, the cost of **distribution** can vary enormously. Banks and building societies, for example, have for many years relied on branch networks to distribute their services. More recently, branch networks have become less significant, with cash machines, supermarkets and the internet being alternatives. A bank with a large branch network may be paying huge amounts to own or to lease properties. These assets and costs will be reflected in the company accounts, but may not necessarily be a good thing if other banks can distribute their services more cheaply in other ways. In contrast, other service industries will have little or no costs of distribution.

2.13 Where goods are **manufactured** and **sold on site**, distribution costs can be **low**. On the other hand, for other industries the distribution can be most of the cost of the product, a good example of this being aggregates, which cost a relatively small amount to extract but a relatively large amount to transport.

Multinational and diverse companies

2.14 The **profits** of multinational and diverse companies can be made in a number of different areas, making it difficult to compare such a company with others. As a result of this, there is a requirement under the **Companies Act** for all such companies to separate out accounting information for each geographical area it transacts business in and, within that, each class of business. This makes it easier to compare each part of the business with companies transacting the appropriate class of business.

2.15 Analysis of such companies for investment purposes can be a very complex affair. It may be possible to compare like-for-like in each subsection of the business, but the **investment return** will relate to the **overall performance** of the business. In many cases, it is effectively a case of measuring the whole as the sum of the parts.

Question 11.5

What are the main problems associated with comparing the financial information from diverse or multinational companies with other companies?

3 ACCOUNTING RATIOS

3.1 The **company accounts** provide an overall picture of a company. However, investors often wish to make more detailed and more specific comparisons which can be done by looking at a number of **financial ratios**. These should be used carefully as, like all the figures found in the company accounts, they will not be able to give us an absolute measure. They can, however, be used to give relative measures between companies in the same sector, or even between different sectors.

3.2 These ratios are often grouped into the following categories.

- **Solvency** ratios
- **Profitability** ratios

- **Cash management** ratios
- **Investor** ratios

3.3 In order to examine these ratios in more detail, a set of sample accounts for **ABC Ltd** has been provided in the Appendix to this chapter. The information provided is:

- A profit and loss account
- A balance sheet
- A cash flow statement

Solvency ratios

3.4 A business is **solvent** when its assets exceed its liabilities and it can pay its debts when they are due. However, to get a better picture of solvency, we can look at it over three different time periods.

- The long and medium term
- The short term
- Immediately

Long and medium term solvency

3.5 The main measures of long and medium-term solvency are:

- Financial gearing
- Interest cover

KEY TERM

The **gearing ratio** or **financial gearing** ratio or 'financial leverage' ratio looks at the long-term loans of the company, including loan stock and preference shares, as a ratio of the company's capital and reserves (net assets).

$$\text{Gearing} = \frac{\text{Long - term loans}}{\text{Capital and reserves}} \times 100\%$$

3.6 **Financial gearing** can be measured as long-term borrowing divided by capital and reserves.

$$\text{Gearing} = \frac{\text{Long - term loans}}{\text{Capital and reserves}} \times 100\%$$

3.7 Using the 31 December 2004 balance sheet of ABC Ltd from the **Appendix to this Chapter** gives us a figure (remembering to include preference shares of £100,000) of:

$$\frac{£105,000 + £100,000\star}{£636,000} \times 100\% = 32\%$$

$\star$ Borrowings due after 1 year + preference shares

3.8 Once again it is important to remember that this absolute figure must be compared to the average gearing of the industry the company operates in. However, it would seem to be a reasonable level of gearing. When assessing the potential borrowing powers of a company, long and short term loans will be taken into account. Broadly, the higher the financial gearing, the lower the borrowing capacity.

Exam focus point
The examiners report in April 2002 stated that many candidates have trouble calculating gearing.

Question 11.6

How might a potential investor calculate the gearing of a company from the company accounts?

KEY TERM

Interest cover looks at the company's ability to service its debt, since it shows how many times a company's interest liability could be paid out of its profits.

$$\text{Interest cover} = \frac{\text{Profit before interest and tax}}{\text{Interest payable (gross)}}$$

3.9 Using the 2004 profit and loss account figures for ABC Ltd from the Appendix, the **interest cover** is:

$$\frac{210,000}{39,000\,*} = 5.38 \text{ times}$$

* Interest payable plus preference dividends (£25,000 and £14,000)

An alternative to this is the 'cash based' calculation for interest cover:

$$\text{Interest cover} = \frac{\text{Operational cash flow}}{\text{Interest paid}}$$

Using the cash flow statement figures for ABC Ltd from the Appendix:

$$\frac{254,000}{39,000} = 6.51 \text{ (sometimes expressed as a \%, ie 651\%)}$$

3.10 From the investor's perspective, interest cover can indicate if a company currently or in the future may become **unable to service the level of debt it has.**

Short-term solvency

3.11 **Short-term solvency** can be measured by the **current ratio,** which relates to the company's ability to service its short-term borrowing. To do this it is necessary to look at the relationship between current liabilities (from the balance sheet)

KEY TERM

$$\text{Current ratio} = \frac{\text{Current assets}}{\text{Current liabilities}}$$

3.12 For ABC Ltd at the end of 2004:

$$\frac{256,000}{237,000} = 108\%$$

Whether this is a good figure or not will be very dependent on the type of business concerned. A manufacturing company would expect to have a current ratio in excess of 100%, whereas a supermarket would expect to have a ratio of less than 100%.

Immediate solvency

> **KEY TERM**
>
> The **quick ratio** is called a number of different things, including the **liquidity ratio** and the **acid test ratio**. From the investor's perspective, it will give insight into the company's ability to resist a sudden down turn. It excludes stocks which might be difficult to sell quickly at book prices.
>
> $$\text{Quick ratio} = \frac{\text{Current assets } less \text{ stocks}}{\text{Current liabilities}}$$

3.13 Using the 31 December 2004 balance sheet for ABC Ltd from the Appendix, this gives us a figure for the **quick ratio** of:

$$\frac{158,000}{237,000} = 0.67 \text{ (sometimes expressed as a \%, ie 66.7\%)}$$

> **KEY TERM**
>
> The Altman 'Z' score
>
> This is a solvency ratio made up of eight other ratios.

3.14 The **Altman 'Z' score** is another solvency ratio, although rather more complex than the ones we have seen so far.

3.15 The ratio is made up of eight other ratios and you will not be expected to list them in the examination. The additional complexity makes it considerably more accurate. A score of 3 or more is good, whereas a score of less that 1.8 indicates a high possibility of financial embarrassment.

3.16 The 'Z' score has been accurate in predicting financial collapse up to five years in advance and over one year is considered to be 70% accurate.

Profitability ratios

3.17 Each **business** is different and will provide a different **level of return** depending on the **relative risk** of the business. A small grocery business may turn in small regular profits. Venture capital companies are very high risk and may turn in large profits, or spectacular losses. The prospects of such companies can be hard to measure, as it is not a like-for-like comparison.

3.18 A ratio commonly used to measure profitability of a company is the **return on capital employed (ROCE)**. The figure excludes interest to remove the influences of different capital structures on the business; this allows us to measure companies on a like-for-like basis.

3.19 The figure for profit can be found on the **profit and loss account** and the figure used to represent capital employed is 'total assets less current liabilities' found on the balance sheet. There is some variability over the figures used for the capital employed, but the most commonly used this would be total assets less current liabilities, found on the balance sheet. From the Appendix, for ABC Ltd this would give us a figure of:

$$\frac{210,000}{769,000} = 27.3\%$$

3.20 The ROCE gives us a measure of the **percentage return on net assets** that has been achieved. The ROCE is often broken down into a hierarchy of lower order ratios, each of which can independently impact on profitability. The next layer down of the hierarchy includes two ratios, which together make up the ROCE. These are profit margin and asset turnover.

3.21 In order to improve profits, a company can start by improving **profit margin** or **asset turnover**. In turn these break down into further lower order ratios. This gives a method of improving profits by tackling the individual drivers of profit. Improvement of any of these lower order ratios will improve profits.

Operating leverage and 'break even' profitability

3.22 **Operating leverage** or **operational gearing** measures the ratio of a company's fixed costs to its total costs. A company's fixed costs are the costs that do not vary with the number of units produced. The level of fixed costs will vary between industries: for example, a utility company such as a telephone network provider may incur high fixed costs in building the network, while the variable costs per minute of calls provided may be very small. There is no standard benchmark for operating leverage, but if fixed costs are more than 80% of total costs, then operating leverage can generally be considered high.

3.23 Operating leverage is relevant to a company's **break even point.** To break even, a company's revenue must cover its total costs: its fixed costs plus its variable costs.

(a) A company with relatively low fixed costs can be profitable over a wide range of output, provided its prices are set high enough above its variable costs. Such a company has low operational leverage.

(b) A company with high fixed costs but relatively low variable costs can suffer large losses when demand for products is low, because its fixed costs are still incurred and are not covered by revenue. Such a company may earn high profits when demand is strong: because variable costs are low, once fixed costs are covered, a high proportion of revenue goes straight to the 'bottom line' and adds to profits.

Cash management ratios

3.24 The cash flow of a company is closely linked to its **solvency.** While cash flows at reasonable levels to keep creditors paid, a company can survive. When there is insufficient cash, a company will have serious problems, which could include not being able to purchase raw materials for production, marketing or distribution of its goods. In these circumstances, a company can rapidly become insolvent. The main methods of measuring cash management are to look at:

- Operational cash flow
- Interest cover
- Cash available for investment
- Working capital ratios

Question 11.7

What are the main methods of measuring cash management?

Operational cash flow

3.25 Many companies now produce an **'operating and financial review'** as part of the accounts. This is a report that provides additional information about the cash flow in a company. There is not a requirement to produce one, but it is part of a **voluntary code of practice** for companies where there is a legitimate public interest in their **financial statements.**

3.26 The report contains details of the **main factors** that underlie the business. It explains the way these factors have **varied** in the past and the way in which they are expected to vary in the future. It also provides a discussion on the **operating results,** listing the **main risks and uncertainties** that may affect the business in the future.

3.27 An analysis of cash flow can provide vital information to the investor, such as **how vulnerable the company is if cash receipts were to fall.** Using our data for ABC Ltd in the Appendix to this Chapter, the cash flow from operating activities is £254,000. This would appear to be a healthy cash position for a company of this size, but this is not always the case. For many companies reduction in receipts would soon start to put pressure on the business. Serious problems would start to emerge if the cash flow from operating activities were not able to cover outgoing payments for interest on loans and dividend payments, which would impact on investor returns for income and capital.

Interest cover

3.28 We looked at **interest cover** earlier and found that, for ABC Ltd, it was 5.38 times. This is a fairly healthy figure and demonstrates that the company would easily be able to cope with an increase in interest rates. For other companies this may not be the case. A reducing level of cover can indicate that the gearing level of the company is too high.

Cash available for investment

3.29 The level of cash produced internally can give a clear indication as to the extent to which a company could consider **capital expenditure** or **acquisitions** without the need to raise finance. The cash available is the total of:
- Operational cash flow
- Returns on investment and the servicing of finance
- Cash flow from taxation
- Dividends paid

3.30 All of these figures can be obtained from the cash flow statement.

	£'000
Operational cash flow	254
Returns on investment and the servicing of finance	(23)
Cash flow from taxation	(47)
Dividends paid	(55)
	129

3.31 The cash available for investment in this case is quite modest, but would allow the company to **consider some capital expenditure**. For other companies, larger figures might indicate a company on the acquisition trail.

Question 11.8

What figures from a company's accounts can be used to calculate the cash available for investment?

Working capital ratios

3.32 These **ratios** provide an insight into the **quality of the management** of a company. Potential investors will want to know that the company is being managed properly if they are to realise the **full potential** of their investment. For instance, **working capital ratios** provide information as to how well stock is being converted into sales, and whether the stock is being managed properly and creating profit for the company. They can also look at the company's debt situation and whether it is being managed well.

3.33 The following **four working capital ratios** are used on a regular basis.
- Stock turnover
- Stock days
- Debtor days
- Creditor days

Stock turnover

3.34 There are two methods of calculating stock turnover, either based on **sales** or on the **cost of sales**.

224

KEY TERM	Sales based	Cost of sales based
Stock turnover	$\dfrac{\text{Turnover}}{\text{Stock}}$	$\dfrac{\text{Cost of sales}}{\text{Stock}}$

3.35 Using our sample data for ABC Ltd, take the stock figure from the balance sheet and the turnover and cost of sales from the profit and loss account.

Sales based	*Cost of sales based*
$\dfrac{1{,}500{,}000}{98{,}000} = 15.31$	$\dfrac{780{,}000}{98{,}000} = 7.96$

3.36 These figures show the average number of times the stock purchased is turned over during the year. **Low stock turnover** can, depending on the type of company, indicate room for improvement in the management of stock, since having assets tied up in stock that is moving slowly will cost money. If the management can improve stock control, profits can be increased.

Stock days

3.37 Another way of looking at the same figures is to look at the number of days it takes to turn over the stock, by taking the reciprocal of the stock turnover. If this is multiplied by 365, it tells us the number of days it takes to turnover the stock.

KEY TERM	Sales based	Cost of sales based
Stock days	$\dfrac{\text{Stock}}{\text{Turnover}} \times 365$	$\dfrac{\text{Stock}}{\text{Cost of sales}} \times 365$

3.38 Using the data for ABC Ltd this gives the following figures.

Sales based	*Cost of sales based*
$\dfrac{98{,}000}{1{,}500{,}000} \times 365 = 24$ days	$\dfrac{98{,}000}{780{,}000} \times 365 = 46$ days

Debtor days

3.39 The ratio for **debtor days** gives information as to the number of days credit being given by the company to its debtors.

- The figure will vary with the type of business, but a peer comparison should show how the management of this company is performing relative to others.

- Comparisons of this statistic on a year-by-year basis can demonstrate whether the debtor situation is improving or getting worse. To compare like with like, turnover is used in this calculation, as the value of trade debtors is based largely on the price of sales.

> ## KEY TERM
>
> **Sales based**
>
> $$\text{Debtor days} = \frac{\text{Trade debtors}}{\text{Turnover}} \times 365$$

3.40 Using the data for ABC Ltd, take the turnover and cost of sales from the profit and loss account and the trade debtors from the balance sheet (debtors).

$$\frac{138,000}{1,500,000} \times 365 = 33.6 \text{ days}$$

3.41 According to this statistic the company is giving 33.6 days credit, on average. Clearly, **depending on the type of business,** this could be good or bad. For a retailer it could seem bad, but for a builder it could appear quite good. This figure can indicate how well the company could cope with a downturn. In this case there would be little leeway for reducing the credit terms if there was cash flow pressure on the company.

Creditor days

3.42 Another important statistic from the investor's point of view is the average period of credit being received by the company from its suppliers. The figure can usefully be compared with other companies in the same peer group. If the company is already receiving **long-term credit,** it is unlikely that it will be able to extend its credit further. On the other hand, a company with low creditors days could extend these to provide capital for expansion if required or improve cashflow. Cost of sales is used so that values are comparable, as with debtors days.

> ## KEY TERM
>
> **Cost of sales based**
>
> $$\text{Creditor days} = \frac{\text{Trade creditors}}{\text{Cost of sales}} \times 365$$

3.43 Using the data from the appendix, take the cost of sales from the profit and loss account and the trade creditors (long and short-term borrowings) from the balance sheet.

$$\frac{370,000 *}{780,000} \times 365 = 173.1 \text{ days}$$

*£133,000 + £237,000

3.44 These figures seem to imply that ABC Co. Ltd is getting **excellent credit terms.** There is a little leeway to extend their credit terms in the event of a cash flow squeeze.

Question 11.9

How can we calculate creditor days, based on cost of sales?

4   INVESTOR RATIOS

4.1   All of the ratios we have looked at so far provide information, in different ways, about the **financial health** of the company.

4.2   As discussed previously, ultimately **investors** are interested in their **investment return** in the form of **capital appreciation** and dividends. There are a number of ratios that look directly at the returns a company is producing, which allows it to be compared with others in its peer group.

4.3   There are **many ratios investors can use**. In this section, we examine the following.

- Earnings per share
- Dividends per share
- Dividend cover
- Dividend yield
- The price/earnings ratio
- Return on equity
- Net asset value per share
- Market to book ratio

Earnings per share

4.4   **Earnings per share (EPS)** represents the income to the business per share. Steady growth in EPS is what most investors are looking for. By examining this figure with other companies in a peer group it is possible to see the relative position of the company.

> **KEY TERM**
>
> $$EPS = \frac{\text{Profit after tax attributable to ordinary shareholders}}{\text{Number of shares in issue}}$$

> **Exam focus point**
> This ratio is examined in more detail in Chapter 4 on equity investments.

Dividend cover

4.5   The dividend cover shows how many times over the **dividend** could be paid out of available profit. The greater the **dividend cover,** the greater the certainty of **dividend payments**. Companies with **lower levels** of **dividend cover** may have to **reduce dividends** if **profits decline**. This figure is particularly important for investors seeking income.

> **KEY TERM**
>
> $$\text{Dividend cover} = \frac{\text{The profit attributable to ordinary shareholders}}{\text{Dividends paid}}$$

4.6 The figure for profit attributable to ordinary shareholders is derived from profit after tax and extraordinary items and preference shares dividends. Using the figures for ABC Co Ltd:

Profit after taxation	£125,000
Preference dividends	(£14,000)
Total	£111,000

4.7 Using our example data, taking data from the profit and loss account, this would give a figure of:

$$\frac{111,000}{55,000} = 2.36$$

4.8 Getting this **ratio** right is a **balancing act** for many companies. The payment of a **reasonable dividend** is important to many investors, but maintaining the level of that dividend is also important. If the company pays out too much to support the dividend in a bad profit year then it cannot retain the profits to fund future growth and profits may fall further.

Question 11.10

What problem might arise when a company keeps its dividend payments artificially high?

Dividend yield

4.9 **The dividend yield** shows to the investor the level of income they can expect to receive from their investment. The figure is **independent** of any **capital growth** and should not be considered as indicating the rate of return on the share. A **share** could produce a **steady dividend yield** but have a **reducing capital value**. The figures are calculated on **current share prices,** not necessarily those that the investor purchased at, and are potentially misleading for existing holdings. This ratio is also considered in more detail in Chapter 4.

KEY TERM

$$\text{Dividend yield} = \frac{\text{Dividend per share}}{\text{Today's market price for the share}}$$

The price/earnings ratio (P/E)

4.10 **The P/E ratio** is very important from the investor's perspective and is often quoted in investment-based comment on a company. Overall, the levels of **P/E** can also be a signal for an impending correction in market prices. When **P/E ratios** reach all time high levels, it is an indication that the share prices being paid are very high compared to the level of profits that companies are generating. This realisation usually precedes a general stock market correction, as it did in 1987 and 1998.

KEY TERM

$$\text{P/E ratio} = \frac{\text{Today's market price for the share}}{\text{Earnings per share}}$$

Question 11.11

How is the P/E ratio of a share calculated?

Return on equity

4.11 This figure is very similar to the return on capital employed figure, except that it looks at the return from the perspective of the **investor**. Rather than looking at the **market value** of the company, it looks at the **return** for the **investor** on **equity** in the company (the **shareholders' funds**).

> **KEY TERM**
>
> $$\text{Return on equity} = \frac{\text{The profit attributable to ordinary shareholders}}{\text{Capital and reserves}}$$

4.12 As with **dividend cover**, the **profit** attributable to ordinary shareholders is effectively the profit after taxation and extraordinary items, and preference share dividends (£111,000 from the profit and loss account). The capital and reserves is the total on the balance sheet.

4.13 Based on the example data in the profit and loss account and the balance sheet this would give a figure of:

$$\frac{£111,000}{£636,000} = 17.45\%$$

4.14 Using this figure, the shareholder or potential investor can see that the company is making an overall 17.45% return on its equity capital. As with all financial ratios, it would **be unwise to look at this figure in isolation**. Comparisons should be made with others in the same peer group and with previous years in the same company.

Net asset value per share

4.15 The **net asset value (NAV) per share** is the return that a shareholder would receive per share if the company was broken up and all the assets sold. It represents a **base figure** for share value. It can demonstrate opportunities where a share has been seriously undervalued by the market, but care needs to be taken. Again, it is useful for comparison of different shares, but certain sectors will have a lower NAV than others. Many **investment trusts** will trade a **discount to net asset value**, which means that the **asset value** for the company is **higher** than the **share price**. This situation is far more unusual in other sectors with the exception of when there is a severe **bear market**.

BPP PROFESSIONAL EDUCATION

KEY TERM

$$NAV = \frac{\text{Capital and reserves}}{\text{Number of shares in issue}} \text{ (per share)}$$

4.16 It is important to bear in mind that the **capital and reserves figure** must be read in conjunction with the notes to the accounts. It may well be that assets could be valued higher or lower than you would expect from a quick glance at the accounts.

Market to book ratio

4.17 This is a ratio derived from the **NAV** figure. It looks at the share price relative to the NAV and examines whether the shares are at discount or a premium relative to the NAV.

KEY TERM

$$\text{Market to book ratio} = \frac{\text{Today's market price for the share}}{\text{Net asset value per share}}$$

4.18 The lower the ratio is the lower the theoretical risk to the investor. A company with a **high market value** and a **low NAV** will not return the full value of the investor's money in the event of the company going into liquidation. Care should also be taken with companies having a low ratio. There will normally be a reason why such a company has been undervalued. If the reason for the low NAV is a general market downturn, such companies might represent good value and a good choice to take advantage of a forthcoming recovery.

Chapter roundup

- This chapter has looked at **company accounts** and examined some of the information that can be derived from them.

- **No one piece of information should be taken in isolation**. It is only by looking at the whole of the company accounts that it is possible to get the full picture. Individual figures can sometimes be 'massaged' by 'creative accounting' and investors may be well advised to take account of the notes to the accounts.

- Ratios should be used to **compare** companies or even one sector to another, rather than looking at them as absolute values. It is also important to look at how the figures have **changed over the years** in order to give information as to whether they are improving or worsening.

- From the **examination perspective**, the calculation of each of the ratios shown in this chapter is within the syllabus. Typically, an extract from a set of company accounts in the question will provide you with the data needed to answer it. There could also be questions on what each figure may mean from the investment perspective and whether a higher or a lower figure in each case represents strength or weakness.

Quick quiz

1   What is the formula for calculating financial leverage or 'gearing'?

2   What is the most common measure of company profitability?

3   What does the level of 'working capital' tell us about a company?

4   What does the 'cash available for investment' say about a company?

5   List the main ratios an investor might look at to determine whether to invest in a company.

6   How can an examination of a company's accounts affect investment decisions?

The answers to the questions in the Quick Quiz can be found at the end of this Study Text. Before checking your own answers against them, you should look back at this chapter and use the information in it to correct your answers.

Answers to Chapter Questions

11.1   (a)   The company's future business strategy

(b)   Any future business plans

(c)   The performance of the company relative to its market and current economic factors

(d)   Performance prospects for the forthcoming year

(e)   The performance of different divisions of the company

(f)   Any items of particular relevance occurring during the year, eg mergers, acquisitions, share buy-backs

11.2   A statement of 'adverse opinion' means that the auditors believe that the company accounts are seriously misleading and are not a 'true and fair' representation of the company's financial position.

11.3   (a)   The investor is reliant on the information provided and a measure of 'creativity' may be used to disguise problems for some time.

(b)   The accounts look at the past, with the exception of the chairman's report.

(c)   The accounts are prepared on a historic cost basis.

(d)   The accounts cannot predict the future trading environment which can be affected by global conditions, local conditions and sector conditions.

(e)   The accounts do not and cannot allow for unpredictable factors such as future legislation, litigation, takeovers, mergers, employment problems and raw material cost variations caused by, for example, the weather, or changes in fashion.

(f)   In extreme market conditions, investor sentiment can move prices significantly with little or no reference to fundamental value or future potential profits.

11.4   The costs that vary from industry to industry relate to:

•   Finance
•   Production
•   Sales and marketing
•   Distribution

11.5 Diverse and multinational companies transact business in different geographical regions and across different financial sectors. As such, their financial data must be broken down and analysed for each area individually.

11.6 To calculate the gearing of a company:

$$\frac{\text{Long - term loans (including preference shares)}}{\text{Capital and reserves}} \times 100\%$$

11.7 When measuring cash management you look at:

- Operational cash flow
- Interest cover
- Cash available for investment
- Working capital ratios

11.8 The figures used to calculate the company's cash available for investment are:

- Operational cash flow
- Returns on investment and the servicing of finance
- Cash flow from taxation
- Dividends paid

11.9 To calculate creditor days:

$$\frac{\text{Trade creditors}}{\text{Cost of sales}} \times 365$$

11.10 The payment of the extra dividend reduces the capital available for investment by the business.

11.11 To calculate the P/E ratio of a share:

$$\frac{\text{Today's market price for the share}}{\text{Earnings per share}}$$

PRACTICE QUESTION 11

(a) What does dividend cover measure? (2)

(b) Using the following details for ABC Ltd , calculate the dividend cover on the company.

Share price:	195p
Yield:	2%
P/E:	15

(6)

(c) What limitations might there be in using the information solely from a set of company accounts to determine whether to invest in a particular share? (6)

APPENDIX TO CHAPTER 11

ABC Ltd
Profit and loss account for the year ending 31 December

	2004	2003
	£'000	£'000
Turnover	1,500	1,290
Operating costs	1,300	1,120
Operating profit (profit before interest and tax)	10	7
Continuing operations	200	170
Profit before interest and taxation	210	177
Interest payable	(25)	(21)
Profit on ordinary activities before taxation	185	156
Tax on profit on ordinary activities	(60)	(47)
Profit on ordinary activities after taxation	125	109
Preference dividends	(14)	(14)
Profit for the financial year	111	95
Dividends to ordinary shareholders	(55)	(47)
Profit retained for the financial year	56	48

Additional notes:

Operating costs comprise:

	2004	2003
Cost of sales	780	616
Distribution costs	325	336
Administration expenses	130	120
Other sales overheads	65	48
Total	1300	1120

ABC Ltd
Balance sheets as at 31 December

	2004	2003
	£'000	£'000
Fixed assets		
Intangible assets	320	310
Tangible assets	430	390
	750	700
Current assets		
Stock	98	96
Debtors	138	125
Cash at bank and in hand	20	17
	256	238
Current liabilities		
Creditors: amounts due within one year		
Borrowings	(97)	(99)
Other	(140)	(129)
	(237)	(228)
Net current assets/(liabilities)	19	10
Total assets less current liabilities	769	710
Creditors due after 1 year		
Borrowings	(105)	(112)
Other	(3)	(3)
Provision for liabilities and charges	(25)	(15)
	(133)	(130)
Total	636	580

	2004 £'000	2003 £'000
Capital and reserves		
Issued share capital	200	200
Share premium account	252	252
Profit and loss account	184	128
	636	580

Note: there are £100,000 of preference shares in issue.

ABC Ltd
Cash flow statement for the year ending 31 December

	2004 £'000	2003 £'000
Net cash inflow from operating activities	153	134
Returns on investment and servicing of finance		
Interest paid	(25)	(21)
Interest received	16	15
Dividends paid on preference shares	(14)	(12)
Total	(23)	(25)
Taxation	(47)	(42)
Capital expenditure		
Payments to acquire tangible fixed assets	(16)	(14)
Receipts from sales of tangible fixed assets	2	2
Payments to acquire intangible fixed assets	(6)	-
Receipts from sales of intangible fixed assets	2	-
Total	(18)	(12)
Acquisition and disposals		
Business acquisitions	(12)	(11)
Expenditure on post acquisition re-structuring	(1)	(1)
Proceeds from business disposals	1	-
Total	(12)	(12)
Equity dividends paid	(55)	(47)
Cash inflow/(outflow) before use of liquid resources and financing	2	1
Management of liquid resources		
Net change in deposits	2	2
Net change in cash investments	1	1
Total	3	3
Financing		
Issues of ordinary shares	-	-
Redemption of preference shares	-	-
Proceeds of new borrowing	50	58
Repayment of borrowings	(15)	(14)
Net inflow/(outflow) from financing	25	44
Increase/(decrease) in cash	39	48
Operational cash flow	254	257
Operational expenditure	183	157

Part F

Investment portfolio management

Chapter 12

DEALING IN INVESTMENT MARKETS

Chapter topic list	Syllabus reference
1 Equity markets	6.1
2 Fixed interest markets	6.1
3 Dealing in investment markets	6.1
4 The London Stock Exchange	6.1
5 Other markets	6.1
6 Commission and other dealing costs	6.1
7 Registration and settlement procedures	6.1
8 Comparison of UK and other international markets	6.2

Introduction

In this chapter, we will examine the mechanics of dealing in UK equity markets, the roles of market makers and agency brokers, and the dealing costs, registration and settlement procedures. Later in the chapter we will look at procedures for dealing in UK markets and compare them with other international markets.

1 EQUITY MARKETS

> **KEY TERM**
>
> The **London Stock Exchange** (LSE), established in 1773, is the main market in the UK for dealing in equities and fixed interest investments as well as being the fourth largest in the world.

1.1   In the UK, the majority of equities are dealt with on the **London Stock Exchange**. UK companies will be listed in the **'main' market**.

1.2   The **Alternative Investment Market** is a less tightly regulated 'second tier' market operated by the LSE.

KEY TERM

The **Alternative Investment Market** was set up in June 1995 to provide a market for the issuing and sale of securities for companies that did not qualify for a full listing on the main market. For these companies, the AIM can be used primarily as a source of capital, but also as the first step towards a full listing when the company is able to meet the relevant rules.

1.3 These markets are both **primary** (ie, providing a means for companies to riase finance through new issues) and **secondary** (for trading in shares already issued).

1.4 In addition to the LSE, the UK has two other trading facilities for equities, **Virt-x** and **OFEX**.

KEY TERMS

Virt-x was created by the merger of Tradepoint and the SWX Swiss Exchange. It is a UK **recognised investment exchange (RIE)** and a European **ISD** regulated market supervised by the Financial Services Authority. The London-based exchange was created especially for **equity trading** by **fund managers, institutions, market makers** and **broker-dealers**. The exchange deals only in shares listed on the **main market** and Swiss 'blue chip' shares.

OFEX is a trading facility originally set up by J P Jenkins Limited as the principal market maker and deals in companies too small for a full listing. Other market makers are also now participating in OFEX. OFEX is both a primary and secondary market.

Question 12.1

Which is the main stock exchange in the UK for 'smaller companies'?

2 FIXED INTEREST MARKETS

2.1 The main market for **fixed interest securities** in the UK is the **London Stock Exchange**. In addition to the **main market** (of listed companies) and the **AIM**, the LSE also has markets dealing in **gilts, sterling bonds** and **eurobonds**.

2.2 **OFEX** also acts as a primary and secondary market in fixed interest securities.

3 DEALING IN INVESTMENT MARKETS

3.1 The main function of **investment markets** is to provide **capital** for business and the rewards for this can be considerable. The markets in all countries facilitate the movement of hundreds of millions of pounds every day and one particular market can deal with one or more different types of security. For example, the **London Stock Exchange** operates four markets for **equities**, three for **fixed interest investments**, and one for **warrants**.

3.2 There are two main systems for markets to operate on, **'order driven'** or **'quote driven'**. With an **order driven** market, the respective stockbrokers on the market floor match the **buy** and **sell** orders. It is usual these days for matches to be made by a **computer system**.

   (a) With an **order driven market**, all stockbroking firms are broker/dealers able to act as agency brokers representing clients in the market, or as principals buying and selling shares on their own account.

   (b) With a **quote driven system**, there is an **intermediary** between the buyers and sellers called a **'market maker'**. The **market maker** quotes a two-way price, eg XYZ Ltd 335 – 355p. The **lower price** is the **selling price** and the **higher**, the **buying price**. The difference between the two is called the **spread**, which is the **profit** kept by the market makers. The stockbrokers of buyers and sellers also deal with the market maker.

Question 12.2

Which type of counterparty is required for the quote driven system of dealing, but not for the order driven system?

4 THE LONDON STOCK EXCHANGE

4.1 The **London Stock Exchange** (LSE) has **two main roles**, that of a **primary market**, and that of a **secondary market**. The LSE is responsible for vetting applicants to the markets, and the share trading of companies already listed. Overall **regulation** of these markets is the responsibility of the FSA.

The LSE as a primary market

4.2 The LSE provides new issues through all of its markets with the exception of the gilts market. This includes the **main market**, the **Alternative Investment Market (AIM)**, and the markets dealing in international equities, emerging markets, fixed interest securities, eurobonds, traditional options and warrants.

Listings and issues on the main market

4.3 The **main market** comprising **listed companies** is the UK's **largest equity market** and it raises large amounts of capital for UK and international businesses. In order to get a listing, a company must satisfy the Stock Exchange that it meets the appropriate qualification requirements.

4.4 Before admitting a company, the exchange will look closely to ensure it is **financially stable**. Failure of listed companies can cause serious problems in the market and seriously undermine **investor confidence**. The Exchange will look to the company to provide data and documentation relating to:

- Trading history
- Financial records
- Management
- Business prospects
- Details of the securities to be listed
- The terms of any additional funds being raised via the issue

4.5 The information will be collated and included in a document known as the company's **'listing particulars'**. This document will provide investors with sufficient information to make an informed investment decision. It will also form part of the **marketing information provided** to potential investors and should include three years' audited accounts (ending not more than six months before the date of listing), although there are exceptions for certain companies, for example scientific research-based companies.

4.6 In order to be considered for listing, there must also be continuity of management within the company concerned during the period covered by the required accounts and the directors must have experience and expertise that is adequate to enable them to manage the business in a professional manner

4.7 International companies seeking a **listing** may already be listed on their own domestic market, but can seek a listing in London as well to promote their shares. Others may simply seek a listing in London because it is one of the main financial centres.

4.8 In order to get a listing, a company must appoint a **sponsor** approved by the exchange to handle its application. This can be a member firm, a bank, broker, firm of solicitors, accountants or other financial advisers. The application is made to the UK Listing Authority (UKLA) and the London Stock Exchange (LSE) simultaneously.

4.9 As already indicated, the LSE is supervised by the Financial Services Authority. The current UKLA rules stating the requirements for admission are detailed in what has been known as the **Yellow Book** although the FSA rules have been published in a purple folder. Some of the main rules are that the company:

(a) Must have a **three-year trading record** (some scientific research-based companies are exempted from this rule)

(b) Must have an equity **market value** of more than £700,000

(c) Must have at least **25%** of the company's shares in **public hands**

(d) Must issue a **prospectus** that complies with the LSE listing rules

4.10 Companies must also agree to:

(a) Make any **price sensitive announcements** via the LSE
(b) Make announcements of **dividend payments** via the LSE
(c) Prepare and issue **full year accounts within six months** of the end of the financial year end
(d) Issue **half year results** within **four months** of the end of the financial year end
(e) Provide certain **additional information** in the accounts

---

Question 12.3

Is it possible for a share to be listed on both the London and New York Stock Exchanges?

Listings and issues on the AIM market

4.11 The conditions for a security to get a listing on the **AIM** are considerably less onerous than those under the full listing, although the AIM is still **fully regulated** by the LSE. The main differences in listing requirements between the AIM and the official list are as follows.

(a) Companies do not need to meet the UKLA requirements.

(b) Companies are not required to be any specific size and are not required to have a full three years trading records.

(c) There are no ownership restrictions, ie it is allowable to have **less** than 25% of the issued securities being publicly owned.

(d) The prospectus provided by companies listed on the AIM must contain an investment warning to the effect that the AIM is geared towards smaller or emerging companies and that the rules are less demanding than those for a full listing.

4.12 **Admission** to the **AIM** is subject to having a **nominated adviser**. The nominated adviser has a duty to guide the directors to ensure they abide by the rules relating to an AIM listing. The adviser is also responsible for the process of obtaining the listing and will be required to advise the directors of their requirement to make the appropriate risk warning statements to existing and prospective investors.

4.13 The shares must be **listed** on the **Stock Exchange Automated Trading Service (SEATS plus)** if they are to be made available for purchase. Presence on the system can only be achieved **via a broker** and there will be a responsibility for the broker to maintain the page and keep it up to date. Because of this, a company will need a **nominated broker** who is prepared to take on this responsibility for them. A nominated broker is a requirement of an AIM listing.

Question 12.4

What are the key differences in requirements for the market value of shares issued for a listing on the main market and the AIM?

Emerging markets

4.14 The exchange has been involved in new listings from **emerging markets,** including listings for former members of the Soviet Union, China and Asia.

Fixed interest markets

4.15 The exchange's **fixed interest markets** are typically very active, although the number of new issues in recent years has been relatively low.

Eurobond markets

4.16 The **LSE** is a substantial force in the **Eurobond** markets. The instruments are normally bought and traded by a limited number of specialist institutional investors so the marketing of new issues is quite critical and requires specialist knowledge. International syndicates of banks underwrite the instruments.

The LSE as a secondary market

4.17 The **London Stock Exchange** provides a **secondary market** for securities on all of its markets. It must limit the dealing of shares to those where there is a 'proper market' and ensure that each company issuing shares provides adequate information so that the current value of each investment can be calculated. In doing this, the exchange provides protection for its investors. The LSE is required by the FSA to conduct an orderly market and to oversee and enforce compliance with its rules and to record all the transactions on the market.

The main market

4.18 Prior to October 1997, the **main market** was based on a competitive, quote-driven system with transactions operating through **market makers**. From then on, for larger capitalisation stocks, **brokers** could deal through the traditional system or alternatively they could deal through the new automated order book system, the **Stock Exchange Trading Service (SETS)**.

4.19 **SETS** is computerised and fully automated. The brokers of buyers and sellers input orders and the computer matches bid and offer prices automatically and conducts the deal on the screen. All deals are shown on the screen, making trading transparent. SETS is a very fast and efficient way of trading, bringing the London market in line with the increasingly high volume and competitive market.

4.20 The **order book system** applied initially to the UK's largest companies that make up the **FTSE 100 Index**. If a company subsequently moves out of the index, it will continue to remain within **SETS**. Shares in companies with a smaller capitalisation continue to be sold via a **quote-driven system**, with market makers quoting their best '**buy**' and '**sell**' prices.

4.21 The order book system can process four types of order.

Type	Details
Limit	The size of transaction and the price required are detailed and the transaction can be immediately executed if it matches an opposite order(s) (in whole or in part) on the system. If there is no match, the order remains on the order book until a suitable match comes along within the expiry date, or they are deleted.
Fill or kill	These are only executed immediately in full or rejected. It is possible with this type of order to specify a limit price.
Execute and eliminate	This order is transacted immediately with a specified price limit. It is similar to an 'at best' order but with a specified minimum price.
At best	The system immediately matches the order to the best price available on the system at that time.

Question 12.5

If an investor wishes to sell his shares quickly, but with a minimum price, what type of order would his stockbroker enter on the SETS system?

4.22 When the system was first set up, there were fears that many brokers would still deal through the **old system** because the average volume of eligible transactions taking place via the order book was only 31%. This has since increased considerably.

4.23 The **speed** and **transparency** of the **new system** has encouraged new trends in trading on the exchange. Traders are now dealing in automatic **'basket'** or **'portfolio'** trades and **index arbitrage deals** against the futures market. Such deals involve a trader buying or selling a range of shares quickly in a single transaction.

4.24 Trading for **non-SETS** securities continues to be transacted via **market makers**, on a competing quote system.

4.25 The **market makers** use a computerised system called the **Stock Exchange Automated Quotations (SEAQ)** service to display, to the rest of the market, **bid** and **offer** prices for their registered stocks. The prices are subject to a **transaction size**, known as the **Normal Market Size (NMS)** up to which the prices will be honoured. These prices are described as **'firm'**. Prices above **NMS** are described as **'indicative'**, the actual price can be negotiated with the market maker.

4.26 Normal market size will be different for each security. The figure is based on 2.5% of the security's average **daily customer turnover** in the preceding year and is intended to represent the size of a normal institutional bargain.

4.27 The **SEAQ** system can be accessed through a number of different screen-based information services and includes the following.

(a) The market makers' quotes to the marketplace (via the **price dissemination service**)

(b) The trade ticker, which displays all trades reported to **SEAQ**

(c) The market makers' bid and offer prices and **NMS** (this information is used to create the **'yellow strip'** that effectively displays the best bid and offer price for every SEAQ security, and the identities of up to four market makers quoting this price)

4.28 The **market makers** will have shares registered to them that are also registered to several other market makers and the larger the capitalisation of the share issue, the more there will be. In these cases, the quotes provided **compete** in the market, and the market makers who quote the lowest prices attract the business. They can make their prices more competitive by reducing the spread.

> ### KEY TERMS
>
> A **market maker** is essentially a member firm of the exchange that is obliged to offer to buy and sell securities in which it is registered throughout the mandatory quote period. They get their income by buying and selling stocks at a profit via the share spread.
>
> **Inter-Dealer Brokers (IDBs)** allow market makers to deal between each other anonymously.
>
> **Stock Borrowing and Lending Intermediaries (SBLIs)** arrange for market makers to borrow stocks from the large institutional investors to cover short-term needs.

4.29 Registered market makers must maintain quotes for their prices for a **specific period** (08.00-16.30, Monday to Friday), known as the **mandatory quote period**.

Question 12.6

What is the likely effect of market makers reducing their spreads?

The AIM market

4.30 **AIM** securities are traded on the **Stock Exchange Automated Trading Service (SEATS) plus** system. The system provides a combination of the principles of **SEAQ** and **SETS**. The system can show competing quotes from market makers, or firm orders.

4.31 At any time, the system will show:

- A **market maker quote**, if there is one (there could be two or more for AIM securities)
- Up-to-date **firm orders** issued by members
- **Information** on the companies traded on the system
- The **past trading activity** for each stock
- The name of the **corporate broker** (or nominated adviser for AIM securities)

Question 12.7

Is share trading on the Alternative Investment Market order driven or quote driven?

5 OTHER MARKETS

International and emerging markets

5.1 The **international equity market** operates through a similar competing market maker system as **non-SETS shares**. The market makers display their prices on a section of the **SEAQ** system called **SEAQ International**.

5.2 Emerging markets are also quoted on the **SEAQ International** system. The quotes are broken down into five different sections, Africa, Europe, Far East, India and Latin America. Each security must have at least **two market makers**, one of which must be nominated as the point of contact between the company issuing the security and the LSE.

5.3 **Eurobonds** and **depository receipts** are also traded via the same system. **Depository receipts** are certificates that represent ownership of a given number of a company's shares. They can be listed and traded independently from the underlying shares.

Gilt markets

5.4 The **LSE** has a secondary market only in **gilts**. The market operates via a competing market maker system.

5.5 There is a traditional link between the **Bank of England** and the **London Stock Exchange** via the **government broker**. The government broker is a member of the LSE board and supervises the Bank's dealing room within the exchange. There are a number of firms registered as **gilt-edged market makers (GEMMS)** operating in the dealing room and both brokers and institutional dealers have to compare the prices from the market makers to establish the best price available for a given gilt.

Fixed interest markets

5.6 The **fixed interest securities market** in the exchange is also based on the competing market maker system. Prices are published on the **SEAQ** system.

Virt-x

> ### KEY TERM
>
> **Virt-x** is an electronic, order-driven Stock Exchange for equity trading created especially for fund managers, institutions, market makers and broker-dealers. It aims to promote liquidity in the UK equity market and provide an alternative for these institutions. Access to the system can be gained using a normal personal computer.

5.7 **Virt-x** (formerly Tradepoint) is a UK **recognised investment exchange** and an **EU ISD-regulated market**, supervised by the **FSA**. The exchange can permit stock broking companies within the European Economic Area, Hong Kong and the United States to become a member. The exchange deals in most UK equities and Swiss 'Blue Chip' shares.

5.8 **Buy** and **sell** orders are posted **anonymously** in the order book and are automatically matched in price/time priority. All orders and the transactions that have been executed are published on the **virt-x ticker** (a constant readout of information on a computer system). The provision of this information provides an ideal situation for any stock market, total transparency of all transactions pre and post-trade.

5.9 All matched transactions are cleared via the **London Clearing House**, which acts as the central counterparty. The exchange is open from 7.30 to 17.30 (longer than the LSE).

Question 12.8

What is the primary function of the Virt-x stock exchange?

OFEX

5.10 Although often described as an exchange, **OFEX** is actually a **dealing facility** for deals transacted '**off exchange**'. It is operated by a **London Stock Exchange** member firm (**J P Jenkins Limited**), which, in turn together with other member firms, is regulated by the **Financial Services Authority (FSA)**.

(a) The exchange deals in the shares of smaller companies, some of which go on to an **AIM** listing. Investments provide little in the way of **investor protection** and all equities must carry the same **risk warnings** as with **AIM shares**.

(b) The liquidity levels of this market are considerably less than the others covered in this chapter, adding to the risks in investing in the shares traded on the exchange.

(c) **OFEX** is an unregulated dealing facility, in which J P Jenkins Limited is principal **market maker,** but many of the transactions are directly matched via the computer system. J P Jenkins Limited used to be the only market maker for OFEX, but other market makers are also now joining the market.

(d) OFEX itself acquired an AIM listing on 30 April 2003.

5.11 **OFEX** prices and information can be obtained from large information networks such as **ADP, Bloomberg, Topic (ICV-Topic 3), Reuters.**

6 COMMISSION AND OTHER DEALING COSTS

6.1 For every **share transaction** that takes place there will be a number of **costs** involved.

(a) The largest of these will be the commission to cover the expenses of the stockbroker and there will also be stamp duty of 0.5% on all purchases of shares (not fixed interest securities).

(b) In addition to these other costs, there will be a **Panel for Takeovers and Mergers levy** of £1 for all transactions over £10,000.

(c) Finally, stockbrokers may also add an **FSA charge** to go towards their costs of compliance, but many will only levy this on larger deals.

Commission

6.2 **Stockbrokers** make their money and cover the majority of their costs by making a small **charge** on every **transaction**. Traditionally, the charge levied was proportional to the work they had to do and many brokers offered different charges depending on the service being offered.

6.3 There were three main services on offer.

(a) **Discretionary portfolio management,** where a customer gave the broker a financial limit and he bought and sold shares for them at his discretion. This was the most expensive service.

(b) **Advisory service,** where the customer chose what to buy and sell on the advice of the broker.

(c) **Execution only service,** where the customer instructed the broker in which shares to buy and sell. This was the cheapest service.

6.4 Things have changed significantly over the last 10-15 years. The UK operates in a similar way to the US model of share ownership, where everybody can participate as they wish. This has caused the proliferation of **execution only services** via a number of delivery channels and the other two services have become far less popular and tend only to be used as part of a **planned portfolio structure.**

6.5 With the explosion of different routes for **buying and selling shares,** the **commission structures** have become equally **varied.** Some stockbrokers will have a structured percentage cost based on transaction size with a minimum commission figure, which varies from company to company. The figures range from £25 to £7.50. The £7.50 minimum figure favours investors making small transactions, such as privatisation issues, where transaction will be no more than £10,000 or so. However, as the transaction sizes get larger, this option may have a larger percentage basis, eg 1.25% on all transactions above this. The brokers offering a £25 minimum may charge 1%.

Size of transaction	Percentage cost	Minimum charge	Commission payable
£1,000	1%	£25	£25
£1,000	1.25%	£7.50	£12.50
£2,000	1%	£25	£25
£2,000	1.25%	£7.50	£25
£4,000	1%	£25	£40
£4,000	1.25%	£7.50	£50

6.6 Many brokers, particularly those with touch tone telephone or internet dealing services, will charge a **set fee** for any size of transaction for their high turnover customers, eg £7.50. There is a lot of sense in this, as from their perspective, there is no more work in a transaction of £100,000 as £1,000.

6.7 To reflect the point that all transactions cost the same regardless of size, some brokers use the percentage method but offer **reductions for larger transactions**. Reducing the cost in percentage terms for larger transactions will improve the situation, but is not quite as cost effective as the fixed fee basis. This method will tend to be used with the more labour intensive telephone service, for example:

- £15 minimum
- 1.5% on the first £2,000
- 1.25% on the next £5,000
- 0.80% on the next £10,000
- 0.25% on the remainder

Question 12.9

Based on the above commission structure, by how much would an investor better off accepting a flat £25 fee on a transaction of £4,000?

6.8 Typically, the commission will be **lower** for **gilts** and **fixed interest securities** and for the size of transaction, but **higher** on **traditional** and **traded options**.

7 REGISTRATION AND SETTLEMENT PROCEDURES

7.1 There are two main forms of **share ownership**, **registered ownership** and **bearer ownership**. In the UK, the majority of share ownership will be on some form of registered basis, but overseas the bearer system is more prevalent.

> ### KEY TERM
>
> With **bearer shares,** the holder of the certificate, (the bearer) has ownership of the underlying assets, so a transfer of ownership simply means passing over the share certificate. The method of transfer is simple and effective but, because of this, security precautions are advised. If bearer shares are stolen, the thief becomes the new owner and, without any form of registration system, the theft is difficult to prove. This form of security is well liked by criminals due to the untraceable nature of the investment.

7.2 The **CREST** system of registration in the UK has largely removed the need for share certificates, as a **computerised stock account** with **CREST** denotes ownership of the shares. This has considerable benefit as certificates cannot be lost or stolen.

Registered ownership

7.3 **Registered shares** can be held in the name of the actual owner (beneficial owner) or in the name of a 'nominee', the owner for administration purposes. Increasingly, the cut-price share dealing services maintain the shares purchased in a nominee account to reduce administration costs and allow them to reduce their brokerage charges. The simplified administration is also a **benefit** for **portfolio management.** As an example, all equity based PEPs and ISAs are run via nominee accounts.

7.4 **Nominee ownership** between individuals has the effect of forming a 'bare trust' and can be used for holding shares for those not able to deal with them personally, for example the mentally disabled or minors.

7.5 To ensure that **share holdings** held by brokers are **properly protected, FSA regulations** require them to set up a separate nominee company to hold the shares of the investors and keep them separate from those owned by the firm. They can maintain the shares of all investors in the same nominee account on a 'pooled' basis, or in a **designated account** for each investor. With the former, **CREST registration** provides each transaction with a uniquely identifiable code number.

7.6 Brokers offering **cut price execution only** services offer a very limited service. In most cases, the transactions will be held in a **pooled nominee account,** which reduces costs, but also means that all correspondence goes to the broker. This could include company accounts, invitations to the AGM or voting forms for board resolutions. In many cases, investors subscribing to these cut rate services sign a form to accept that only the important correspondence will be forwarded to reduce administration. In these circumstances, they also **waive their rights** to shareholders' perks.

Question 12.10

List the two main forms of share ownership.

Settlement procedures

7.7 Once a transaction for buying or selling a security has taken place, every stockmarket needs a mechanism for **transferring the money** from the buyer to the seller and the **ownership of the security** from the seller to the buyer (known as a **delivery versus payment** or **DVP system**). In some stock markets, this will be achieved as a **paper transaction**, where the existing share certificate is recalled, the stock register amended and a new certificate issued. This is a labour intensive and time-consuming task. Most markets have switched to some form of **computer based system** which saves the registrars of the companies traded in the markets considerable time because they can download information on the transfers of shares between investors on a daily basis.

7.8 On the **LSE**, a computerised settlement system called **Talisman** was in operation until 1997. Although the system was computerised for registration, nearly all transactions were based on the issue of share certificates. The current settlement system, **CREST**, came into operation in mid-1996, gradually taking over from the Talisman system. The **CREST system** is voluntary and investors can if they choose to opt out of the CREST system and receive **share certificates** instead.

7.9 The stages involved in a CREST transaction for a client holding a share certificate are as follows.

    (a) Client completes a CREST transfer form.
    (b) Client returns signed form to broker along with the share certificate.
    (c) Broker sends completed form and share certificate to CREST.
    (d) CREST sends transfer form and share certificate to the company share registrar.

7.10 The introduction of **computerised systems** for **settlement** means that most markets operate on a **rolling settlement** basis, rather than the more historical account basis where all deals were settled at the end of a trading period (two weeks in the UK).

7.11 **Rolling settlement** means that settlement will take place a specific number of working days after the transaction takes place. For UK and Irish equities and corporate bonds there is a three day **rolling settlement period**, described as T + 3. The 3 represents the number of working days after the transaction the settlement takes place. One of the main reasons for getting the **CREST system** into place was to improve the normal settlement periods on the **LSE** to three days, in line with other major markets.

7.12 As part of the settlement system, the HMRC collects **stamp duty**. This has to be done manually for **non-CREST transactions**. For **CREST transactions**, they can simply access the system to collect stamp duty payments. **CREST settlements** will show the term **Stamp Duty Reserve Tax (SDRT)** against the stamp duty payments.

Question 12.11

What is the mechanism for transferring money from the buyer of the shares to the sellers and the shares from the seller to the buyer?

The CREST settlement system

7.13 All brokers in the United Kingdom and Ireland now use **CREST**, directly or indirectly, for settling their equity trades, together with the great majority of custodians and investing institutions. The **CREST system** is run by a company called CRESTCo Limited and is owned by its customers in the financial community, a consortium of securities firms. The **CREST settlement system** was **extended** during 1999 to cover gilt and fixed interest markets.

7.14 **CREST accounts** operate like bank accounts and can be accessed by the user firms with the appropriate software and systems. There are two classes of membership accounts on CREST. **Members** of CREST system have their own accounts and they can operate the system on behalf of other sponsored members. These **sponsored members** include private individuals and corporate investors and trustees. **Members** have access to the **CREST system** via their own computer systems, but sponsored members can access details of their CREST account using software which can be run on a PC and downloaded from the CRESTCO Ltd web site.

7.15 The **CREST settlement system** uses two different types of account, one for the share being transferred, called the **stock account**, and one for the cash, called the **cash memorandum account**. When a transaction takes place, the stockbrokers of buyers and sellers (both will be members of CREST) input their part of the transaction. These are checked by the computer system to ensure that they match. No further action is taken until the settlement day.

7.16 On **settlement day**, the system will check to see that the stockbroker of the buyer has sufficient credit in their cash memorandum account and that the stockbroker of the seller has the right number of the appropriate shares in their stock account. Providing these match, the shares are moved from the seller's to the buyer's stockbroker's account and they are notified of the transaction. The buyer's stockbroker is notified of the liability to pay the settlement costs and they will then request their bank to make the payment at the end of the business day.

Question 12.12

What are the two types of account used in the CREST settlement system?

7.17 The **contract note** records a share purchase or sale, and will include the following details.

- Bargain date and time
- Client name
- Number, type and price of shares bought/consideration and type
- Full name of share
- Amount of commission
- Settlement date
- Transaction charge and Stamp Duty
- Broker's details

8 COMPARISON OF UK AND OTHER INTERNATIONAL MARKETS

8.1 We have looked at the way the LSE works, but the method of operation of other **international markets** for both their main and secondary exchange (like our AIM) varies considerably.

8.2 For **comparison purposes** we will look at the other major international markets in terms of:

- Size

- Dealing methods
- Specialist market participants
- Settlement
- Share ownership

Size of market

8.3 The **London Stock Exchange** is the leading securities market in Europe, with the German Frankfurt and the Paris Bourse competing heavily for business.

8.4 **Competition** for business in the **European economic area** is fierce and this is driving the constant **modernisation** of the London exchange. This has given rise to the creation of EURONEXT. EURONEXT was created by the merger of the stock exchanges of Amsterdam (Amsterdam Exchanges), Brussels (Brussels Exchanges) and Paris (Paris Bourse) on 22 September 2000. It is a fully integrated cross-border single currency stock, derivatives and commodities market.

8.5 EURONEXT was the first exchange to offer full integrated trading, clearing and settlement on a European basis. It is a unified order-driven trading platform based on the French system NSC. The central counterparty and netting and clearing house for all trades is CLEARNET, which together with EUROCLEAR is the settlement and custody platform.

8.6 The **New York Stock Exchange (NYSE)** is the world's **largest equities market**, with a total market capitalisation of more than $12.6 trillion. The US is also home of the **NASDAQ**, specialising in hi-tech stocks. **NASDAQ Europe** closed in 2003. Prior to the Asian crisis, the **Tokyo Stock Exchange (TSE)** was the second largest exchange in the world. It is a two-tiered market (like that of the UK).

Question 12.13

Which country has the largest stockmarket in the EU?

Dealing methods

8.7 New York, Tokyo, Germany and France are all **computerised order driven markets**. London is order driven for the **FTSE-100** (and other) **shares** via the **SETS** system which makes up a very large proportion of the market volume. Some transactions on the **AIM** market are order driven.

8.8 **Non-SETS shares,** and some transactions on the AIM markets, are transacted on a quotation based system using **market makers. NASDAQ** also operates on this basis.

8.9 Whether a market is **order** or **quote** driven, they all use some form of **computer system**. Some exchanges, such as the **LSE**, use more than one system.

Country	Location of main market	Name of market	Computer system
France, Belgium and Amsterdam	Europe	EURO-NEXT	EURONEXT is a fully computerised single currency (euro) stockmarket. It is a floorless order driven system with a fully integrated trading, clearing and settlement system based on the French NSC system. The central counterparty and netting and clearing house for all trades is CLEARNET, which together with EUROCLEAR is the settlement and custody platform.
Germany	Frankfurt	Deutsche Börse	Trading takes place on the floor of the Frankfurt exchange, both directly and via Xetra, the electronic trading system of Deutsche Börse. The name stands for Exchange electronic trading and was put into operation on 28 November 1997.
Japan	Tokyo	TSE	Trades are transacted via a computer system called CORES, the Computer-assisted Order Routing and Execution System. Members of the stock exchange are located and trade on the floor of the exchange.
UK	London	LSE	London uses three different computer systems, SETS for FTSE-100 shares, SEAQ for Non-FTSE-100 and international shares, and SEATs plus for the AIM.
US		NASDAQ	The NASDAQ stock market is a major national and international floorless stock market. It enables securities firms to compete freely via a screen-based trading environment.
US	New York	NYSE	The system is fully computerised, but still uses a trading floor. Brokers match trades with each other via a computer system called 'SuperDot'. The SuperDot system succeeded the DOT system, one of the first computerised trading systems, in 1984 and although significantly upgraded since is still in full use. The average order through SuperDot is transmitted, executed and reported back to the originating firm in 22 seconds.

8.10 The future of **stockmarket computer systems** is to fully automate the trading and settlement systems into one. The French **Supercac system** has achieved a high degree of integration with the settlement system, but the Swiss, with their exchange **SWX,** now merged with Tradepoint to form Virt-x, has the world's first electronic platform which ensures both fully automated trading and integrated settlement of all stock market transactions. The trading system is fully integrated from the investor making their request to purchase, to the acknowledgement of the receipt of the order confirmation of the transaction and the change of ownership of the securities.

Specialist market participants

8.11 Different **stock markets** have **evolved** in slightly different ways. Many markets have specialists or counterparties that take an active part in the trading process. The systems are far more prevalent with the quote driven system, where the market makers are effectively the intermediaries for the trades.

8.12 In the **LSE**, the **non-SETS** trading is done via a series of **market makers** that specialise in a number of shares. Most shares will have two or more market makers acting on their behalf.

8.13 The **NYSE** also uses specialists whose role is to act as both **market maker** and a **regulator** in one particular stock. Each specialist will have a position on the floor of the exchange and the dealing in that stock must take place at the specialist's post. Most specialists have responsibility for about twelve stocks.

8.14 The **Tokyo Stock Exchange (TSE)** used to have two types of member, **regular** and **saitori**. Effectively, the **regular** members were the equivalent of **stockbrokers** in the UK market, and the **saitori** members were a form of **market maker**. The two tier system was dropped in 2001 when the last saitori member withdrew.

8.15 **NASDAQ** is a **floorless exchange,** but uses market makers who are each responsible for a number of shares. The market makers operate via the computer system where they make a market in their registered shares.

8.16 The **Deutsche Börse** does not use market specialists. Brokers are effectively matched automatically via the computer system. However, the domestic banks own the majority of the broking houses and dominate the market place.

Question 12.14

Which UK shares can be traded without the intervention of a market maker?

Settlement

8.17 Most modern markets have a normal **settlement period** of T + 3, including New York, NASDAQ, Tokyo and London. Germany uses a normal settlement of T + 2 and can achieve immediate settlement T + 0 for some transactions. Most of the systems of the above markets are capable of faster settlement on some transactions and even CREST has the facility to provide settlement from T + 25, to T + 0, if required.

8.18 Just as with **trading systems,** the **settlement systems** for all markets are **computerised.** In many cases, unlike in the UK, investors in other countries cannot hold shares in their own name so the shares are held in a depository system, with the name of the individual as a nominee.

New York Stock Exchange (NYSE)

8.19 The NYSE settles transactions via the **National Securities Clearing Corporation**. Shares purchased on the exchange in the NYSE can be held personally, via a nominee, or through a depository, called the Depository Trust Corporation (DTC).

Tokyo Stock Exchange (TSE)

8.20 Settlements of funds and securities for transactions between member securities firms on the **Tokyo Stock Exchange** are also dealt with by the TSE itself. For settlements of domestic shares, the TSE opens a settlement account at **Japan Securities Depository Centre** (JASDEC, the central securities depository of Japan) to use the Central Depository and book entry transfer system of JASDEC.

8.21 The **TSE** administers **settlements** and **payments** of transactions and entrusts **Japan Securities Clearing Corporation** (JSCC, a wholly owned subsidiary of TSE) with practical aspects of securities settlement.

The London Stock Exchange (LSE)

8.22 **Shares** can be owned **personally** or via **nominees** on the LSE.

NASDAQ

8.23 Shares purchased via **NASDAQ** can be held personally, via a nominee, or through the **DTCC** (Depository Trust and Clearing Corporation), the main US depository.

The Frankfurt Stock Exchange (Deutsche Börse)

8.24 **Shares** purchased on the Frankfurt exchange must be held in **central depository banks** known as Kassenvereine, which are co-ordinated by a company called Deutsche KassenverVerein (DKV).

Question 12.15

Which stockmarket(s) have a normal rolling settlement period of T + 5?

Chapter roundup

- The equity markets in the UK consist of the London Stock Exchange (LSE) which incorporates the full market and the Alternative Investment Market (AIM) and Virt-x. OFEX is a trading facility.

- The LSE is the main market for dealing in gilts and corporate bonds.

- Markets have two main functions: primary, issuance of new capital; and secondary, trading of instruments.

- Listing rules exist to ensure only companies satisfying minimum levels of confidence, related to business activities and propriety of management, obtain a place in the market.

- Dealing on the LSE is via SETS or SEAQ.

- Costs incurred include stamp duty (but not on gilts), PTM levy and commission.

- Settlement is performed by CREST. Equities normally settle in T+3, gilts in T+1.

- The major overseas markets are in the US (NYSE and NASDAQ), Japan (TSE), Germany (DB) and EURONEXT.

Quick quiz

1 What facilities are there for buying shares in the UK, other than the facilities offered by the London Stock Exchange?

2 List the secondary markets in the UK for fixed interest securities.

3 Explain the main difference between a quote driven and an order driven market.

4 What is the role of the 'nominated adviser' for a company seeking a listing on the AIM?

5 Why does a company seeking an AIM listing need a stockbroker to sponsor it?

6 Which shares can be dealt in via the new SETS automated trading system?

7 What is significant about the price, as quoted on the SEAQ system, for share transactions larger then the Normal Market Size (NMS)?

8 What is the role of a GEMM in the London Stock Exchange?

9 How are transactions made on the Virt-x stock exchange published?

10 What are the three main types of service for buying and selling shares offered by stockbrokers?

11 What protection does the holder of a bearer have in the event of the certificate being stolen or destroyed?

12 What is the normal rolling settlement period for the London Stock Exchange?

13 What are the two types of account used by CREST to transfer money and shares between buyers and sellers?

14 Which is the world's largest stock exchange?

15 List three order driven stockmarkets.

16 How does the ownership of shares purchased via the EURONEXT stock exchange differ from those purchased via the LSE?

17 What is the name of the central depository for shares purchased via the EURONEXT stock exchange?

The answers to the questions in the Quick Quiz can be found at the end of this Study Text. Before checking your own answers against them, you should look back at this chapter and use the information in it to correct your answers.

Answers to Chapter Questions

12.1 The AIM is the main exchange for smaller company shares.

12.2 Market makers are involved in the quote driven, but not the order driven, system.

12.3 It is possible but, because of the cost, only the largest of companies will do it.

12.4 For a listing on the main market, a minimum value of £700,000 in shares must be made available to the public, whereas no such limit exists for an AIM listing.

12.5 They could use an 'execute and eliminate' order. Alternatively, a limit order could be used.

12.6 If a market maker reduces their spread, they are likely to attract more business, as the competing quote system means that traders will trade through them. However, market makers make their money via the spread, so a reduced spread means reduced profits.

12.7 Transactions on AIM can take place on an order driven or quote driven basis.

12.8 The Virt-x stock exchange is primarily a market for fund managers, institutions, market makers and broker-dealers. It allows anonymous traders.

12.9 Using the given commission structure on a £4,000 transaction, an investor would be charged 1.5% on the first £2,000 = £30, and 1.25% on the next £2,000 = £25, or £55 in total, which is £30 more than a flat £25 fee.

12.10 Shares can be registered in the name of the owner or via a nominee, who holds the shares on the behalf of the investor, or, alternatively, can be owned in bearer form where the certificate itself denotes ownership.

12.11 It is called the delivery versus payment (DVP) system.

12.12 The stock account for the shares and the cash memorandum account for the money.

12.13 The UK.

12.14 FTSE-100 and other shares traded via the SETS system are traded as directly matched orders.

12.15 None, since the UK stockmarket moved to T + 3 in 2001.

PRACTICE QUESTION 12

Mr Garland wants to buy some shares in a company that he feels has excellent prospects for the future.

(a)   List the costs that Mr Garland may incur in buying these shares and give an idea of the amount of each.   (8)

(b)   It turns out that the shares Mr Garland wishes to purchase are listed on the AIM. List any additional costs that may arise as a result of this.   (3)

(c)   Having purchased the shares on Monday 1 October, the investor receives a contract note that tells him that settlement is on a T + 3 basis and that he should have sufficient money in his portfolio account to cover the cost. When is the latest date by which the money has to be physically in his portfolio account?   (2)

(d)   List the different stockmarkets or trading facilities that operate in the UK for the purchase of equities.   (3)

(e)   List a market in the UK and overseas that operates on an order driven basis, then do the same for markets that operate on a quote driven basis.   (4)

(f)   Describe briefly what happens on settlement day for shares settled via the CREST system.
                                                                                                               (6)

Chapter 13

PORTFOLIO DESIGN

Chapter topics list	Syllabus reference
1 Portfolio design	7.1
2 Modern portfolio theory	7.1
3 Capital asset pricing model	7.1
4 Arbitrage pricing theory	7.1
5 Asset allocation and the role of the investment manager and adviser	7.2
6 Portfolio optimisation	7.2
7 Equity research methodology	5.2
8 Research information sources	5.2

Introduction

This chapter looks at the concepts and theory of portfolio design, including the methods for identifying and managing the main types of risk. We will take a closer look at the principles behind the capital asset pricing model and perform some calculations to demonstrate it in action. We will also be looking very briefly at the Arbitrage Pricing model. Later in the chapter, we will be examining all aspects of asset allocation for investment managers and advisers, including the different approaches to managing portfolios, such as optimisation and correlation matrices. Finally, we will learn how to evaluate the different classes of asset and the way in which they can be used in a portfolio to fulfil the customer's objectives.

1 PORTFOLIO DESIGN

1.1 The **design** of a **portfolio,** both in terms of **allocation of assets** and choice of **underlying investments,** is vital to achieving the objectives of the customer. One of the key problems to overcome is the **minimisation of risk** and the **maximisation of returns.** Considerable ongoing research has taken place into methods of measuring and controlling these factors and because of this, research into portfolios and models to base them on continues.

2 MODERN PORTFOLIO THEORY

2.1 In 1952, an article appeared in the Journal of Finance, called 'Portfolio Selection', written by Harry Markowitz. This was the start of the **modern portfolio theory (MPT)**. The ideas and concepts have been researched, improved and added to, resulting in the broad theory of portfolio selection we have today. In 1990, Harry Markowitz, Merton Miller and William Sharpe received a Nobel Prize for their work in this field.

KEY TERM

Modern portfolio theory looks at the way in which **risk averse investors** operating in a free market construct portfolios to **maximise** expected returns for any given market risk, and lays out an 'efficient frontier' between these two variables. The theory also examines and quantifies the benefits of a **diversified portfolio**.

2.2 The theory looks at methods of **construction of portfolios** with a range of different levels of market risk, increased or decreased by the use of **risk free assets**.

2.3 In a more general context, **MPT** provides a model for understanding the interactions between **systematic risk** and **reward**. In this capacity, it has had a significant impact on the way institutions construct their portfolios and the mathematics is used extensively for **financial risk management**.

2.4 In order to provide further insight into **MPT** it is important to understand the measurement of the two **key variables**, **expected returns** and **risk** (or **volatility**).

Expected return

KEY TERM

'**Expected return**' is the level of return anticipated from a portfolio or an individual investment. In most cases, it will be based on historic information, which starts to introduce weaknesses into MPT as '**past performance is no indication of future performance**'. It will, in most cases, be the best **approximation** for future performance. The expected return based on past performance is calculated statistically.

2.5 The expected returns are calculated on **past performance over a defined holding period**.

2.6 **EXAMPLE: EXPECTED RETURNS**

As an example, shares in MNO plc. have produced the following returns for the past 5 years.

Year 1	10%
Year 2	7%
Year 3	14%
Year 4	9%
Year 5	12%

There are a number of ways to ascertain the expected return in year 6. It might be possible to anticipate future results by the company and estimate a figure that may, or may not, be accurate. As an alternative, analysis of past performance may give a reasonable figure. A good place to start might be the average return, eg (10 + 7 + 14 + 9 + 12)/5 = 10.4%.

2.7 It is possible statistically to calculate a number of different averages. The **average** given above is technically described as the '**mean**'. Other statistical averages could include the '**median**' and '**mode**'. The **median** would be the return where, half the time, the share performed better, and the other half, worse. The **mode** is the most frequent investment return but, in this case, no return was repeated. Neither of these statistical measures would be valid with such a small sample. The situation might be different with a one month holding period, or more years of data.

Question 13.1

The shares of company PQR Co. Ltd have performed as follows over the last eight years:

Year 1 -	15%	Year 5 -	12%
Year 2 -	10%	Year 6 -	14%
Year 3 -	8%	Year 7 -	13%
Year 4 -	14%	Year 8 -	12%

Calculate the expected return for year 9.

Risk, or volatility

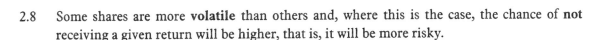

> **KEY TERM**
>
> The **risk** of an investment is the chance that it will not produce an average/expected return or will produce a loss. In the case of our example, the only thing we can immediately determine is that, based on past performance, there is a one in five chance that the return in year 6 will be 7, 9, 10, 12 or 14%. Although the investment has an average return of 10.4%, it is more risky than an investment which is **guaranteed** to generate 10.4%.

2.8 Some shares are more **volatile** than others and, where this is the case, the chance of **not** receiving a given return will be higher, that is, it will be more risky.

2.9 In order to use this concept to develop theories relating to **portfolios**, it is important that this 'volatility' can be calculated.

2.10 The main measure of **volatility** is **standard deviation**, which can be calculated using past returns data for the investment. It measures the degree to which values in a probability distribution vary from the expected return or value. As with all calculations based on statistics, the larger the pool of data, the more accurate the results. It is possible to calculate the standard deviation of our example data (MNO plc), although there is not sufficient data for it to be statistically significant. The Greek letter σ is used to denote standard deviation.

2.11 EXAMPLE: RISK/VOLATILITY

With our sample data, the standard deviation is 2.4. Statistically, if the data follows the normal distribution pattern, there will be a 68% chance that the return will be within one standard deviation of the mean, in this case 10.4%. Therefore, there is a 68% chance that the return will be between 8% and 12.8%. Taking this a step further, there is a 95% chance that the return will be within 2 standard deviations or between 5.6% and 15.2%. There is a 99% chance it will be within three standard deviations etc.

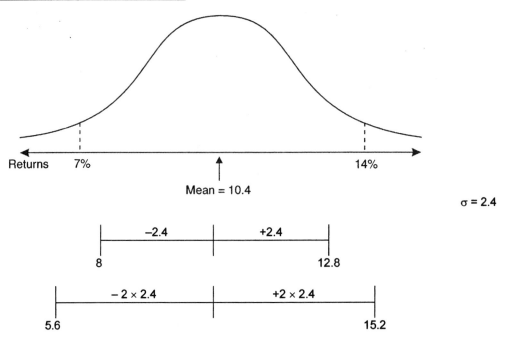

Returns 7%   14%

Mean = 10.4

$\sigma = 2.4$

| | −2.4 | +2.4 | |
| 8 | | | 12.8 |

| | − 2 × 2.4 | +2 × 2.4 | |
| 5.6 | | | 15.2 |

The higher the standard deviation, the greater the spread of returns, and therefore the riskier the investment.

2.12 FURTHER EXAMPLE: RISK/VOLATILITY

The calculation of standard deviation can be done on most scientific or business calculators. For the Hewlett Packard 10B, first clear the statistical register by pressing CLΣ, then each piece of data is entered followed by E+, eg 10 E+ 7E+ etc., press σx to get the standard deviation (2.41661). The figure can be calculated manually by the following route.

(a) Take the difference from the mean (10.4).
(b) Square the difference.
(c) Multiply the difference squared by the probability in this case 20%.
(d) Add together.
(e) Take the square root.

Return %	Difference from mean (10.4)	Difference squared	Difference squared multiplied by the probability (20%)
10	−0.4	0.16	0.032
7	−3.4	11.56	2.312
14	+3.6	12.96	2.592
9	−1.4	1.96	0.392
12	+1.6	2.56	0.512
		Total	5.840

The standard deviation will be the square root of 5.840 = 2.41661.

2.13 The **smaller** the standard deviation of the performance return of an asset is, the more **predictable** and **less volatile** it will be. This figure, as a proportion of the **mean**, is a measure of volatility in its own right.

2.14 The standard **deviation** of the **returns** gives a measure for volatility or risk but, later in the chapter, another figure for risk will be discussed, the **Beta** (ß). The ß of an equity, or any other security, is the volatility of the security as a ratio of the volatility of the market.

Question 13.2

Calculate the standard deviation for the returns from the shares of company PQR Co. Ltd.

Year 1 -	15%	Year 5 -	12%
Year 2 -	10%	Year 6 -	14%
Year 3 -	8%	Year 7 -	13%
Year 4 -	14%	Year 8 -	12%

Efficient frontier

2.15 An **efficient portfolio** is one that gives the highest level of expected return for a fixed level of volatility, or the lowest volatility for a fixed level of expected return. It sits on the border between achievable return/risk and unachievable levels. For example, an expected return of 5% is achievable, if the manager is prepared to accept volatility levels of 10%, but not if they will only accept 1%. The **efficient frontier** from the graph would indicate that the lowest achievable volatility for a 4% return is zero. This is the risk free return based on this graph. If one was prepared to accept 5% volatility, the expected return would be 10%.

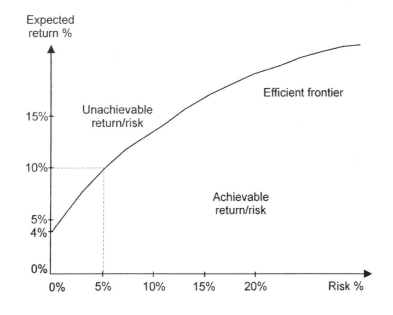

Question 13.3

Looking at the above graph, estimate the efficient frontier for volatility for an investor seeking a return of 15%.

Covariance and correlation of asset values

2.16 All **asset values** will **vary** according to a number of **market factors**. In some cases, they will move in the same direction. For example, if interest rates fall, the share prices of UK exporters will tend to increase because the interest rate change will affect the pound, which will make UK goods cheaper. However, the shares will move to a greater or lesser extent depending on the company's exposure to the factor. Companies that export a lot may move more than those that do not. It may also be that all shares will increase to a certain extent, but this will be for different reasons. The **shares of importers** will be **negatively correlated** for this factor and may go down. The extent of these relationships can be calculated using the statistical concepts of **covariance** and **correlation**.

2.17 There are many thousands of **different factors** that all **work together**. These factors alter the judgement of individuals buying and selling assets, which ultimately reflects in the price of the asset. As an example of two factors working together, reduced interest rates combined with an excess of production of computer chips in the Far East will both work together on the price of exporters of computer chips. The net effect may be for it to move up or down. Other factors could be:

- The chairman resigns
- The workforce go on strike
- A rival factory closes down
- The overall stock market moves up

2.18 All of these factors result in the price **movements** of **assets**. To **reduce this risk**, it is important to understand what these factors are and measure them, and appreciate how they correlate. **The Capital Asset Pricing Model** and **Arbitrage Pricing Theory** use correlations and covariances to model price movements.

2.19 The correlation coefficient measures the nature of the relationship between two variables. The correlation coefficient of any relationships ranges between -1 and 1.

2.20 For example, we would expect costs to rise when output rises, hence we would expect a positive correlation. Similarly we would expect quantity demanded to fall when the price of a good rises, hence we would expect negative correlation. These relationships are illustrated below.

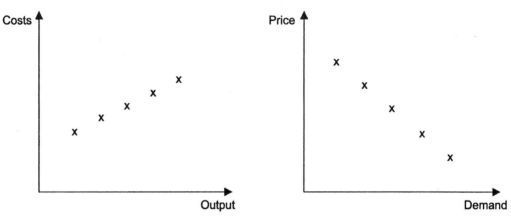

Note that the correlation coefficient is telling us something about the nature of the relationship; it is not telling us what the gradient of the graph is.

It is possible to calculate the correlation between two assets, x and y, using the following calculation.

$$\rho xy = \frac{\text{cov} XY}{\sigma X \sigma Y}$$

ρxy = correlation between X and Y

$\text{cov} YY$ = covariance between X and Y

σX = standard deviation of X

σY = standard deviation of Y

2.21 The covariance is defined to be the average of the cross products of two random variables.

$$\text{COV}_{xy} = \frac{\sum_{t=1}^{n}(X_t - X)(Y_t - Y)}{n - 1}$$

X_t = The actual value of the X series
Y_t = The actual value of the Y series
n = The number of values
X = The mean of all the X_t values
Y = The mean of all the Y_t values

The two main types of investment risk: systematic risk and unsystematic risk

2.22 For any individual investment there are an infinite number of factors that can affect returns, hence it is inefficient to identify the relationship between all of these risk factors and returns. Portfolio theory allows one to simplify the analysis of risk and return by categorising all risk factors as either **unsystematic** or **systematic risk**.

> ### KEY TERM
>
> **Unsystematic risk** or specific risk is the risk of price movements caused by all of the idiosyncratic factors that affect the asset. This could include, the performance of the company, the level of borrowing, market sentiment for the directors and so on. All of these risk factors will act on a particular asset and influence the price.

2.23 **Unsystematic risk** can be reduced within a portfolio by purchasing a **diverse selection of assets**. The basis for this is that not all assets will be affected by changes in specific risk factors so, in a neutral market, a widely **diversified portfolio** will also remain **neutral** as the increases in prices of certain assets cancels out the reduction in prices of other assets.

2.24 By choosing a **widely diversified portfolio,** the positive and negative correlation to factors cancel each other out. Using our importers and exporters as an example, as interest rates, and hence the value of the pound rise, importers do well, exporters do poorly and vice versa. In our **diverse portfolio,** there should be both importers and exporters, which should cancel each other out. Every possible factor will have a **positive** and a **negative** effect and a diverse portfolio should always provide assets with a positive and negative correlation. Unsystematic risk can therefore be diversified away.

> ### KEY TERM
>
> **Systematic risk** is also called **market risk**. It is the risk that an asset has as a result of its sensitivity to market wide factors, eg the capital value of all gilts will increase when interest rates fall, and fall if they rise.

2.25 There are two main ways to **limit exposure** to **systematic risk**. One is to ensure that the portfolio contains assets from a number of different classes, eg equities, gilts cash, property etc. Different asset classes vary with different factors, which should, in most cases, stop the whole portfolio from moving with a single asset class. However, although all asset classes are affected in different ways by different factors, occasionally these factors will conspire to move the markets together.

2.26 The other way is to adopt one or more risk models to make a **portfolio** more **efficient**. An efficient portfolio is one where the level of risk taken for any expected investment return is no more than it has to be. In effect, this minimises the risk and, the more effective this is, the more successful the investment manager is against his peers. However systematic risk cannot be diversified away.

2.27 **Risk**

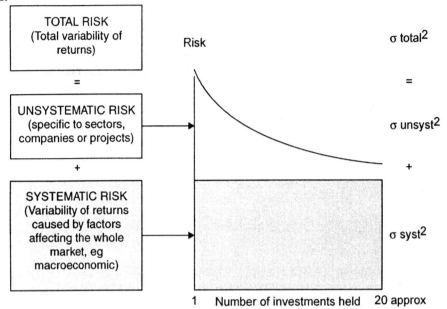

The diagram above illustrates the effect of diversifying an equity portfolio upon risk. Once a portfolio contains about 20 shares in different companies in different sectors, most (but not all) of the unsystematic risk is diversified away. However, systematic risk is not affected by the level of diversification.

The risk return trade off when diversifying

2.28 **Diversification** reduces risk. It will also affect return. The return of a two asset portfolio will be a simple weighted average of the returns of the constituents:

$$r_{ab} = w_a r_a + w_b r_b$$

where r = return
    w = % of the fund invested

2.29 For example if Sam invests 50% of his portfolio in share A giving a 10% return and 50% in share B, giving a 5% return his returns will be:

$$r_{ab} = 50\% \times 10\% + 50\% \times 5\%$$
$$r_{ab} = 7.5\%$$

2.30 The risk of a two asset portfolio is given by the following formula.

$$\sigma_{ab} = \sqrt{\sigma_a^2 x^2 + \sigma_b^2 (1-x)^2 + 2x(1-x)p_{ab}\sigma_a\sigma_b}$$

where:

σ_{ab} is the standard deviation of a portfolio of two investments, A and B

σ_a is the standard deviation of the returns from investment A

σ_b is the standard deviation of the returns from investment B

σ_a^2, σ_b^2 are the variances of returns from investment A and B (the squares of the standard deviations)

x	is the weighting or proportion of investment A in the portfolio
p_{ab}	is the correlation coefficient of returns from investment A and B

$$= \frac{\text{Covariance of investments A and B}}{\sigma_a \times \sigma_b}$$

2.31 Modern Portfolio Theory shows that as long as the return on assets in a portfolio are not perfectly positively correlated, ie have a correlation of less than 1, the risk of a portfolio will be less than a simple weighted average of the risk of the constituents of the portfolio. The lower the correlation, the lower the risk of the portfolio. Ideally, negatively correlated assets should be chosen, but in practice shares are not negatively correlated. However, diversification will still reduce risk.

2.32 Assuming the risk of A is 20% and the risk of B is 15% and that the correlation coefficient is 0.8, then the risk of the portfolio would be as follows:

$$\sigma_{ab} = \sqrt{0.2^2 \times 0.5^2 + 0.15^2 \times 0.5^2 + 2 \times 0.5 \times 0.5 \times 0.8 \times 0.2 \times 0.15}$$

$$= \sqrt{0.01 + 0.0056 + 0.012}$$

$$= 0.166 \text{ or } 16.6\%$$

2.33 This is less than a simple weighted average risk of 17.5%. In other words there is a beneficial trade off between risk and return when diversification takes place.

Question 13.4

Briefly explain how a portfolio invested in both equities and gilts can cancel market risk to a certain extent.

KEY TERM

Modern portfolio theory concludes with the development of the **Capital Market Line** which links total risk as measured by standard deviation and required return. A linear relationship is established when we introduce risk free returns as illustrated below.

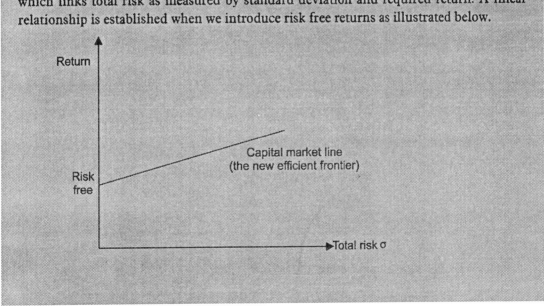

2.34 This model can be used when the investor is undiversified, because they then face total risk as measured by standard deviation, σ. However as mentioned above, when an investor diversifies, risk is reduced. Diversified investors do not therefore face total risk - only systematic risk. We therefore need a new model - the Capital Asset Pricing Model.

3 THE CAPITAL ASSET PRICING MODEL

3.1 The **Capital Asset Pricing Model (CAPM)** develops MPT and provides a model to **estimate** whether the expected **returns** from the **portfolio** are adequate given the level of **risk** being taken. It is a linear model linking risk and return.

KEY TERM

The principle of the **CAPM** is that investors will be fully diversified and hence will face systematic risk only. The CAPM identifies a measure of this systematic risk (beta) and establishes a linear relationship between beta and required return.

Systematic risk and security characteristic lines

3.2 Systematic or market risk has been defined as the impact of changes in market factors, for example interest rates, upon an asset or an asset class. This relationship can be identified simply by plotting a scatterdiagram of asset returns and market returns over time. When the market rises by 10%, what happens to returns on the asset. The data used for the scatterdiagram can be fed into a regression analysis generating a line of best fit. This line is called the security characteristic line, illustrated below.

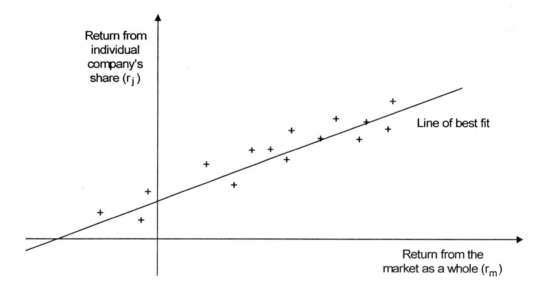

3.3 The gradient of this line is known as the beta or β factor. The greater the gradient, the more sensitive the asset is to market changes, ie the greater the systematic risk.

3.4 Beta factors can be measured for any asset where price and return data are available. The investment banks and organisations like the London Business School, Reuters and Bloomberg all provide beta factor statistics for quoted shares.

3.5 The higher the beta factor the higher the required rate of return. The precise relationship between beta and systematic risk is given by the CAPM formula.

CAPM formula

3.6   The equation for it is:

$$E(R_i) = R_f + ß_i[E(R_m) - R_f]$$

$E(R_i)$ = the expected return from the investment
R_f = the risk free return
$ß_i$ = the beta of the investment
$E(R_m)$ = the expected return from the market

Risk free return

3.7   The model uses a '**risk-free return**' figure to provide a base, which is the return that can be achieved without taking any risk. It provides the **starting point** for the **relationship** between **risk** and **return**, ie for returns at or below the risk-free return there is no risk to capital, but where the expected return is greater, then some risk must be taken.

3.8   In order to find a level for **risk-free return**, it is first necessary to find an investment that provides a totally risk-free return. The most risk free assets in the UK are those issued by the British Government, as they provide a guaranteed return in terms of income and capital and the risk of them defaulting is fairly negligible. However, gilts and other long term instruments are subject to a number of other risks, such as inflation, so, in order to minimise this, the basis for risk-free return is usually the current return on Government Treasury Bills.

Calculating the expected return for an investment

3.9   To see the **CAPM** in action, it is important to look at some examples.

> ### Exam focus point
> CAPM often appears in the G70 examination, particularly the calculations based on it, and candidates would be well advised to become familiar with them.

3.10 EXAMPLE: CAPM

As an example, let us look at JKH plc shares. These shares have a ß of 2. The markets are expected to grow at 8% for the next year. In order to find out the expected return, we also need to know the risk free return. If we assume 4% (as the rate for a 3-month Treasury bill) then to calculate the expected return for JKH Plc. we use the CAPM equation:

$$E(R_i) = R_f + ß_i[E(R_m) - R_f]$$

The expected return on this investment as part of a portfolio would be:

$$E(R_i) = 4\% + 2 \times [8\% - 4\%] = 12\%$$

This figure can be used as a point of comparison against others in the portfolio.

3.11 EXAMPLE: CAPM

Joseph has shares in Sam plc. Joseph thinks that these shares will provide returns of 10%. Sam plc shares have a β of 1.3. The market return is 8% and the risk free rate is 4%. Evaluate whether Sam plc is correctly priced.

The expected return on Sam plc is:

$$E(R_i) \quad = 4\% + 1.3\,(8\% - 4\%)$$
$$= 9.2\%$$

10% exceeds 9.2%, hence Sam plc will outperform if Joseph is correct. Otherwise it will underperform relative to his expectations. If he is right, this means that Sam plc is currently underpriced. The market may realise this eventually and buy Sam plc, forcing the price up until it generates a return of 10%.

One of the assumptions of the CAPM is that this market price change will take effect quickly, ie that the market is efficient.

KEY TERM

The **security market line (SML)** describes the relationship between systematic risk as measured by beta and return.

3.12 The security market line

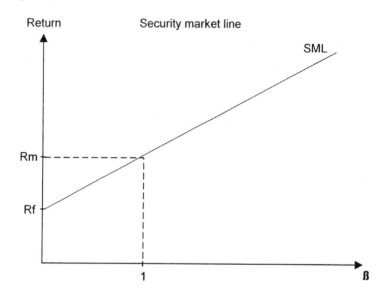

3.13 The diagram above of the SML is the graphical representation of the CAPM formula. When $\beta = 1$ (ie the risk of the market) the return is Rm, the return on the market. The difference between the SML and the CML described previously is the measure of risk used. The SML assumes diversified investors and employs β, the measure of systematic risk. The CML assumes undiversified investors and employs σ, the measure of total risk.

Exam focus point

In the examination, you may be asked to calculate the expected market return and risk free rate of return based on the CAPM equation. In order to calculate these figures you would normally need two securities that are on the market line. Typically in the examination, one of them will have a ß of 1. Where this is the case, it should be a very simple task to calculate the risk free return.

3.14 EXAMPLE: SECURITY MARKET LINE 1

XYX Plc has an expected return within a portfolio of 15% and a ß factor of 1.
ZXZ Plc has an expected return within the portfolio of 10% and a ß factor of 0.5.

The first thing is to calculate the expected market return. This will give the risk free rate by substitution (or *vice versa*).

First, substitute the known figures into the CAPM equation, starting with the security with the ß factor of 1.

$$E(R_i) = R_f + ß_i[E(R_m) - R_f]$$

In this case

$$15\% = R_f + 1[E(R_m) - R_f] \text{ or } 15\% = R_f + E(R_m) - R_f$$

R_f and $- R_f$ cancel each other out so $15\% = E(R_m) =$ expected market return.

These figures can be substituted with the second security:

$$E(R_i) = R_f + ß_i[E(R_m) - R_f] \text{ or } 10\% = R_f + 0.5[15\% - R_f]$$

Therefore $10\% = R_f + 7.5\% - 0.5R_f$ or $10\% - 7.5\% = R_f - 0.5R_f$

Or $2.5\% = 0.5\ R_f$

Therefore $R_f = 5\% =$ Risk free rate.

Exam focus point

It is possible for an exam question to ask for a calculation where the ß of one of the shares was not 1. This is complex, but is possible using simultaneous equations.

3.15 EXAMPLE: SECURITY MARKET LINE 2

ZXZ Plc has an expected return within the portfolio of 10% and a ß factor of 0.5.
YZY Plc has an expected return within the portfolio of 12.5% and a ß factor of 0.75.

In order to calculate the risk free return in this case, create a pair of simultaneous equations.

$$10\% = R_f + 0.5[E(R_m) - R_f]$$
$$12.5\% = R_f + 0.75[E(R_m) - R_f]$$

To solve this, get the answers the same by multiplying the first equation by 5 and the second by 4.

$$5 \times (10\% = R_f + 0.5[E(R_m) - R_f])$$

therefore $50\% = 5R_f + 2.5[E(R_m) - R_f]$ or $50\% = 5\ R_f + 2.5E(R_m) - 2.5R_f$

$$4 \times (12.5\% = R_f + 0.75[E(R_m) - R_f])$$

therefore $50\% = 4R_f + 3[E(R_m) - R_f]$ or $50\% = 4\ R_f + 3E(R_m) - 3R_f$

Both equations now equal 50% and can be combined.

$$5R_f + 2.5E(R_m) - 2.5R_f = 4\ R_f + 3E(R_m) - 3R_f$$

Gather all of the R_f figures on one side and the R_m on the other.

$$5R_f - 2.5R_f - 4R_f + 3R_f = 3E(R_m) - 2.5E(R_m) \text{ or } 1.5R_f = 0.5E(R_m)$$

Therefore $3R_f = E(R_m)$.

$E(R_m)$ can now be expressed in terms of R_f and substituted into either equation:

$$10\% = R_f + 0.5[E(R_m) - R_f]$$
or $\quad 10\% = R_f + 0.5[3R_f - R_f]$
or $\quad 10\% = R_f + 1.5R_f - 0.5R_f$

or $\quad 10\% = 2R_f$

Therefore $R_f = 5\%$ = the risk free rate.

Based on $3R_f = E(R_m)$, the expected market rate = 15%

CAPM and portfolio construction

3.16 When constructing a **portfolio** with **specific investment objectives** in mind, the **CAPM** can help, providing we have the **risk free return** and the ß for each individual investment. In many cases, the questions ask candidates to determine whether the expected returns for an equity are realistic.

3.17 EXAMPLE: CAPM AND PORTFOLIO DESIGN

The risk free return is 4%, and the expected market return is 10%. Share XYZ has a beta factor of 2 and an estimated return of 12%. Comment on whether this estimated return figure is too optimistic.

Using the equation, $E(R_i) = R_f + ß_i[E(R_m) - R_f]$:

$E(R_i) = 4\% + 2[10\% - 4\%] = 16\%$, the estimated return on the investment using the CAPM figures is 16%. The estimated return quoted is low.

Question 13.5

What is the expected return of an investment with a risk free return of 2%, ß of 0.9 in a market with an expected return of 6.5%?

Limitations with the CAPM model

3.18 In order for the **CAPM** to work, the following assumptions must be made.

- Investors are inherently **risk adverse** and invest based on risk.

- The markets are **efficient** at reproducing prices.

- All investment returns are calculated over the **same time period.**

- The effects of **transaction costs** are ignored by investors.

- Investors invest irrespective of the individual **tax treatment** of the investment.

- All investors have access to the **same market intelligence.**

- All investors have **unlimited amounts of money,** or can borrow it at interest rates equivalent to the risk free rate.

3.19 Most of these assumptions are flawed in one way or another.

- Investors do not always consider **risk** alone when investing.

- The markets are **not always efficient** at reproducing prices and anomalies exist.

- It is possible to calculate investment returns over the same time period.

- Investors do not ignore transaction costs.

- Investors do not invest irrespective of the tax treatment of the investment.

- Some investors are better informed than others, because the information provided by the various information systems varies widely. In addition, some investors trade, directly or indirectly, on inside information, although this is illegal.

- Clearly not all investors have unlimited funds of cash!

3.20 Every model must use assumptions to reduce complexity. The **CAPM** relies on three variables to calculate a fourth, but all are flawed. Establishing a totally risk free rate can be very difficult, and should be different for each asset class.

3.21 The **expected market returns** is also a very difficult figure to estimate and probably the best figures for this are given by the **Barclays Capital Equity-Gilt Study**. According to the study, the past **average returns** generated by **gilts** in **real terms** were 2.3% over the period from 1918 to 2003. In comparison, **equities** produced a return of 6.2%. If we look more recently, over the last 20 years, real returns on gilts were 6.1 per cent, UK equities 8 per cent, and cash 4.4 per cent. Both figures would be reasonable for an expected market return and yet the figures are quite different.

3.22 The figures calculated for **betas** are all based on historic information. They will not necessarily apply in the current or future years.

3.23 **CAPM** is still used today, but as methods and computer systems for analysing models and the variables upon which they are based improve, it is becoming increasingly outdated. Newer and more complex models, such as the Arbitrage Pricing Model, are gradually taking over.

4 ARBITRAGE PRICING THEORY

4.1 One of the possible **objectives** of a model is to **reduce** the **variables** down to a manageable and measurable number. The other is to accurately model whichever piece of behaviour is being studied.

4.2 As discussed earlier in the chapter, the price of every security is influenced by thousands of different factors. The **CAPM** model assumes unsystematic risk is divesified away and that systematic risk can be measured by one factor - β. The CAPM is a good model, but there are more efficient models.

> ### KEY TERM
>
> **Arbitrage Pricing Theory** provides a model that is significantly more complex and accurate. It uses 180 different factors which are analysed weekly against 30,000 shares. Each quarter, the best 20 of all the factors recorded, are used to provide pricing estimates for the next quarter. Every quarter, a new group of 20 factors is selected. This model can effectively adapt to factors increasing and reducing their influence over time. The APT is a multi factor model. The CAPM is a single factor model.

4.3 As computing power and information networks continue to increase, models for **reducing the risk of portfolios** are likely to become even more complex.

Question 13.6

Why is it that financial models can never be totally accurate?

5   ASSET ALLOCATION AND THE ROLE OF THE INVESTMENT MANAGER AND ADVISER

5.1   The **allocation of assets** in the appropriate mix to achieve the desired objectives of the customer is one of the most important tasks for the fund manager or adviser. It is central to performing their role effectively and the skill with which this task is performed separates the good manager from the rest.

The role of the investment manager

5.2   Where a **manager** or **adviser** is to act on behalf of a customer in an advisory or discretionary capacity, it is vitally important that they understand the **needs and investment goals of the investor**. This is a **regulatory requirement** for all private customers. In some cases, the manager or adviser may also be required to help the customer to **identify** their needs and investment goals. This information must be recorded on the customer file and regular reviews must be carried out to ensure that they have not changed.

5.3   Once the **requirements of the portfolio** are fully understood, the manager must construct an appropriate **investment strategy** to meet the requirements ascertained from the client information and recorded on the file. This should achieve or exceed the desired objectives, providing it can be done so with the **minimum risk**.

5.4   The **selection of the asset types** and **distribution of asset** within an individual class is an important foundation for the **portfolio**. However, in order to achieve above average returns for the investor, the selection of the underlying assets is very important.

5.5   Having **constructed a portfolio,** it is vital that the manager monitors the performance of each investment to ensure the objectives are met and will continue to be met. This **monitoring process** should highlight selected assets that are under-performing, so they can be changed, and provide prior warning for the manager if any of the objectives cannot be met, so that remedial action can be taken.

5.6   Even when the portfolio is achieving the objectives set, the investment manager is still required to periodically contact the customer to ensure that circumstances have not changed and that the **portfolio** is still appropriate. As part of the annual review, it may be necessary to make new investments into the many tax-exempt schemes as new limits become available, for example ISAs, pensions and NS&I Savings Certificates.

Identify the needs and goals of the investor

5.7   A **corporate client** is able to identify clearly what they want to achieve within the portfolio. **Private customers** are likely to be different and may need some coaxing. Either way, RITA should be considered.

   R - Risk
   I - Investment objective
   T - Timescale
   A - Accessibility

Risk tolerance

5.8 A manager must first establish the level of **risk** the investor is prepared to take. This will need to be discussed with the client to ensure that their understanding is the same as that of the adviser.

Question 13.7

Should a portfolio manager accept a customer's objectives without questioning them?

5.9 The **measures of risk** are categorised by firms in different ways. These can vary from the four main definitions to scales of ten or more different levels as defined by the relevant firm. The main four levels are as follows.

- No-risk
- Low-risk
- Medium or moderate-risk
- High-risk

5.10 Where a customer asks for '**no risk**', it is important that they understand what this means, for example that no reduction in the capital value of the portfolio is acceptable. Many customers will ask for **no risk**, but it is important that the consequences of this choice are fully explained because the risk level requested by the customer restricts the choices of investments available to the manager. For a **no-risk portfolio**, the manager will be restricted to cash, deposits, treasury bills and gilts with a short-term to maturity, held to maturity. A portfolio set up on this basis will have limited returns, however skilful the manager and in high inflation years will be affected by inflation and may decline in value in real terms. In many cases, customers are seeking '**no risk**' investment combined with above average investment returns. This is not achievable and the manager should manage the customer's expectations accordingly.

5.11 **Low-risk investment** means that a low level of fluctuation in the value of the portfolio is acceptable, providing that there is the potential for greater gain than cash investments over the medium to long term. A portfolio set up on this basis will need to have a wide diversification of asset types to avoid the down turn of an asset affecting the whole portfolio. The gains should be better than cash investments, but there is no guarantee, and a truly '**low risk**' portfolio will not provide returns as high as equities over the longer term.

5.12 With a **medium-risk profile**, customers must be prepared to accept fluctuation in the value of the portfolio in return for the potential for good medium to long term capital growth.

5.13 Investors who are prepared to accept **high risk** should expect their portfolio to fluctuate in exchange for the potential for good gains over the medium to long term.

5.14 There are many other definitions of risk and firms specify their own. One definition that cuts across low, medium and high risk is '**balanced**'. A '**balanced' portfolio** will have **medium risk** on average, but the assets making up the portfolio can be low, medium or high. This definition gives the manager greater leeway to use his skills to invest than when just specifying 'medium' risk, which may lead to greater gains for the same risk levels.

Investment objectives

5.15 The next most important factor after risk is the type of **investment return** the investor is looking for from the portfolio. This could be one of the following.

- Income (a minimum or expected level may be specified)
- Growth (a time period may be specified, eg medium or long term)
- A combination of the two

5.16 The customer may also specify other **investment objectives** apart from these, such as minimising taxation or protection from inflation. In either case, this will affect **portfolio design** and will probably result in the use of one or more of the tax exempt investment types, or the use of index linked assets.

Time scale

5.17 The reasons for investing, for example retirement, will impact on the **time scale of the proposed investment**. The money invested may be required at a particular age (to buy an annuity) or, alternatively, the investment objective of the portfolio may change from capital growth to income. As an alternative, a private customer may be saving for a particular event, such as a cruise, school fees or a future business venture.

Accessibility

5.18 An important point to cover when dealing with private customers is that they have a sufficient **emergency fund** of instantly accessible cash. The **level of liquidity** required for each customer will vary, but a reasonable amount for most would be 25 to 50% of annual income.

Question 13.8

If the customer objective is funding for retirement, what time scale will the investment need to work on?

Constructing an appropriate investment strategy

5.19 The requirements of the customer will have a significant impact on the **chosen strategy** for each portfolio.

Risk

5.20 Depending on the **level of risk** the investors are prepared to take, the contents of the portfolio will change.

Risk level	Portfolio contents
No-risk	Should typically invest in cash and short term deposits, but gilts held to maturity could be included if the time-scale allows, as would index linked investments in the form of gilts or National Savings Certificates.
Low-risk	Might include cash, deposits, and fixed interest stocks including index linked investments. It could also allow some investment into guaranteed income or growth bonds or unitised with-profits to provide good growth over the longer term with a very small potential for risk.
Medium-risk	Could invest in a variety of medium-risk pooled investments. If there was sufficient cash available, a selection of blue chip shares from the FTSE 100 Index could also be included. Gilts and other fixed interest stocks could also make up a proportion of the portfolio together with some cash and deposits.
High-risk	Could easily take some of the higher risk pooled investments, such as unit trusts or investment trusts from overseas, or even a small amount in emerging economies. One would also expect to find direct investment in a range of listed equities, providing there was sufficient capital to allow diversification. There might even be some room for a small amount in unlisted equities, but only through recognised EIS or VCT schemes.

Investment objective

5.21 Where the objective is for the portfolio to provide a **fixed level of income**, this should always be guaranteed. Gilts held to maturity, guaranteed income bonds and deposits could be used to generate this income on a reliable basis. Where the income level is easily achievable within the portfolio, or where a steadily increasing income is required, dividends from a portfolio of listed equities could be used. This strategy also works well where a combination of income and growth is required.

5.22 In order to achieve '**real**' growth over the medium to long-term, equity investment will be needed. This can be achieved directly, through a portfolio of shares, or indirectly via a pooled investment with equities as the underlying investment. Fixed interest stocks and cash are unlikely to achieve this objective over the longer term.

5.23 If the investor wishes to **save tax**, this can be achieved by a variety of means, but it is also very important to ensure that their risk requirements are also met. There are several vehicles which are tax-efficient in different ways.

- ISAs
- National Savings & Investments products
- EIS and VCTs
- Life assurance bonds, by use of the deferred tax treatment
- Offshore roll-up funds (also for tax deferral)
- Use of equities and collective investments up to the CGT exemption

5.24 An objective to **minimise** the **risk of inflation** would result in the choice of index linked fixed interest investments or NS&I Certificates.

Time scale

5.25 The timescale specified by the investor will impact on the choice of investment.

Timescale	Choice of investment
Short-term investment	Up to five years and would tend to be restricted to deposits or, where the customer was prepared for a little more risk, gilts and other fixed interest investments. Depending on the investment objectives, insurance investments such as guaranteed growth bonds, guaranteed income bonds, or with-profit bonds could be used.
Medium-term investment	5-15 years which considerably improves the scope of underlying investments to include collective investments and equities in addition to the above.
Long-term investment	A minimum of 15 years. Few investments are restricted by these time periods, giving the portfolio manager a wide choice of assets for the portfolio.

Accessibility

5.26 The only investment that provides truly instant access would be some form of **instant access account**. The appropriate amount of this investment should be built into every portfolio.

Select the appropriate investments

5.27 So far, we have considered the objectives of the customer and the ways in which these might restrict the portfolio manager's choice of underlying asset. We will now go on to consider the **selection** of **appropriate investments** by looking at each of the main asset classes and, subsequently, at strategies for selecting investments from within them.

Cash/deposits/cash instruments

5.28 The choice of underlying assets for this asset class will be largely based on interest rates offered. **Portfolio managers** may seek **higher rates** available from the money markets or treasury bills where appropriate, providing there is sufficient in the portfolio to meet the **minimum requirements**. Offshore accounts may provide higher returns providing they are safe. This class of asset can be used to reduce the overall risk of a portfolio, or increase the income levels available to higher fixed or variable amounts.

Gilts/fixed interest investments

5.29 Selection of **gilts** and **fixed interest investments** for private customers may well be influenced by their tax position. The use of gilts trading at below par can give a taxpayer gains which are free of tax at redemption, but it is very likely that the redemption yields of such stocks will be lower to compensate. Other considerations will be the extent to which each would react to **interest rate changes**, and what the anticipated interest rate changes are. The **time scale** of investment will also have a bearing, as long-term interest rates will differ to short-term ones.

5.30 This class of asset can be used to **reduce the risk** of the **portfolio**, as gilts and fixed interest investments are less volatile than equities, or to **increase** the levels of **income** available for the customer, as the returns are higher than for equities.

5.31 **Diversification** within this asset class can be achieved by investing in a variety of yields and terms to maturity.

Question 13.9

What types of gilt would give higher rate taxpayers the biggest tax advantage?

Equities

5.32 **Equities** have a place in many portfolios and, in some cases, will be the only underlying asset class. They represent the **highest risk** of all of the asset classes discussed to date. It is important to diversify that risk away by spreading the portfolio over a number of different shares.

5.33 The **asset class** could be broken down and diversified across:

- Business sectors
- Market capitalisation
- Geographical spread

5.34 The main reason for investing in UK or overseas equities as part of the **asset allocation of a portfolio** is to increase risk and to increase the potential for future long-term gains.

5.35 The selection of **individual equities** within the allocated asset class and business sectors is a decision that will have a big impact on **portfolio returns**. There are two basic methods of selecting shares.

(a) **Fundamental analysis** is the most popular. Shares are selected on the basis of the underlying value of the shares and by an examination of the companies' accounts and the various ratios derived from them.

(b) **Technical analysis** is the selection of shares based on the movement of price by graphing or statistically analysing trends.

5.36 The technical analyst is using past performance as an indication of future performance. Many managers now use technical analysis to support decisions made based on fundamental analysis.

Derivatives

5.37 **Derivatives** are specialist investments and, in many cases, separate portfolios are set up specifically dealing in them. They are occasionally used as part of a broader based portfolio for **hedging** or **risk reduction**. Increasing a proportion of this asset will significantly increase the potential returns from a portfolio and the risk. The **highly geared** nature of these investments allows a very small proportion of the portfolio invested to reap the benefit of far larger investments. Providing the right derivatives are used, the levels of risk can be managed.

Pooled investments

5.38 Most **portfolios** will be based on the **direct investment** into assets or **pooled funds**, but few mix the two. Many issues will affect the selection of pooled investments, such as risk, past performance, the skills and reliability of the fund managers, and the tax treatment of the investment. For certain classes of pooled investment, such as investment trusts, the level of premium or discount of an investment trust to its net asset value will also be a factor.

5.39 Within a portfolio, **pooled funds** have the effect of **reducing risk** by providing additional diversification. Careful selection of funds can provide global coverage across most asset forms based on a relatively small number of individual investments.

Monitor investment performance

5.40 Having **agreed a strategy** for the proportion of each asset class and picked the assets underlying each class, it is important for managers and advisers to carefully **monitor the performance** of the portfolio. One of the difficult factors in doing this is to produce an appropriate benchmark for the performance. Indices perform this role exceptionally well.

5.41 The **FTSE 100 Index** is a good benchmark for a portfolio-based on the top shares, whereas the **FTSE All-Share Index** is more appropriate for a broader based portfolio. There are indices for every sector of every class of asset which can be used in combination to benchmark the appropriate proportions of the underlying asset allocation.

5.42 **FTSE International** has published three private investor indices in conjunction with **The Association of Private Client Investment Managers and Stockbrokers (APCIMS)** for monitoring portfolio performance. They reflect the main investment objectives and provide a benchmark for investment portfolio performance. The current allocations and their respective indices are as follows.

Asset type	Income portfolio	Growth portfolio	Balanced portfolio	Representative index
UK shares	47.5%	60%	55%	FTSE All-Share
International shares	7.5%	25%	20%	FTSE World ex-UK Index, in sterling
Bonds	40%	10%	20%	FTSE Gilts All Stocks Index
Cash	5%	5%	5%	7-day LIBOR –1%
Total	100%	100%	100%	

Exam focus point

It is important for the examination that you can state the asset allocations for each portfolio and that you know the relevant benchmarks.

Investment objective

5.43 Managers of pension funds can compare their performance with that of other pension fund managers through statistical data provided by specialist information providers such as Bacon & Woodrow or Russell/Mellon Caps.

Regular reviews

5.44 The **regulatory requirements** for all assets specify a period for discussing the performance of the portfolio to demonstrate how it has met the agreed objectives. There is a further requirement to check with the customer that their personal situation has not changed in a way that could affect the objectives of the portfolio.

Portfolio trading strategies

5.45 So far, we have examined the portfolio and the ways in which asset allocation can achieve the desired objectives of the customer. The **trading strategies** adopted by the manager will also have an impact.

5.46 Large funds will contain very large holdings of assets. Any attempt to sell them to purchase another will have the result of depressing the price. As a result of this, most of the larger funds tend to be **passively managed**, either by sticking to a fixed asset allocation (buy and hold strategy), or by replicating an index to a greater or lesser extent. In the case of the latter, this can be admitted publicly, by calling it a **tracker fund**, or, informally, by adopting the strategy without necessarily adopting the name. **Tracker funds** tend to have **lower management charges** as they simply **track an index,** significantly reducing the need for investment staff to make decisions. Informally following an index gives the benefit of a stable and well-diversified portfolio, with a passive management style without the need to lower charges. This is consistent with the fact that many of the larger funds are not seeking to massively outperform the market, simply match it, or improve on it slightly by using a more effective asset allocation.

5.47 Typically, **smaller funds** will adopt a much more **active investment strategy**. They can buy and dispose of assets without having an effect on the market, making it much easier for them. In many cases, this active strategy is used to try to achieve returns in excess of the market benchmark. There are **two main strategies** for **active management**:

   (a) To select assets from the underlying categories on the basis that, if a category does well, so does the asset within it, in a 'top down' strategy. For example, investing in EU shares because European equities are likely to do well.

   (b) To pick individual stocks using fundamental or technical analysis suggest and invest in them, irrespective of the category they are in, using a 'bottom up' strategy.

5.48 Portfolios of **pooled funds** are far more suited to **passive management**, mainly because of the charges. The funds are managed twice and the cost of this management has to be paid for, so a change of fund can cost anything from 2-6%. If an active management policy were pursued, the charges would erode the effect of any improved performance.

Question 13.10

Why is it that large portfolios are less able to follow an active management strategy?

---

6 PORTFOLIO OPTIMISATION

MPT and portfolio design

6.1 Modern Portfolio Theory can be employed to generate efficient portfolios for investors. If the manager has data on the returns, risks and correlations of available asset classes, an efficient frontier may be generated (see paragraph 2.15 of this chapter).

6.2 EXAMPLE

The following example is for illustrative purposes only. You need to be able to describe portfolio optimisation and correlation matrices, but you do not need to perform calculations.

Returns and risks

Asset class	Return	Risk
Shares	13%	18.5%
Bonds	8%	6%
Treasury Bills	6%	0.4%

Correlation coefficients

	Shares	Bonds	Treasury Bills
Shares	1	0.2	-0.15
Bonds	0.2	1	-0.12
Treasury Bills	-0.15	-0.12	1

This data may be used to generate optimal portfolios for a given required rate of return using quadratic programming. Such an optimum portfolio will be that where the asset allocation weightings generate the required return, but at the lowest possible risk.

In our example we wish to obtain returns of 6%, 9% and 12%. The asset allocations and portfolio would be as follows.

Return	Risk	Asset Allocation		
		Shares	Bonds	Treasury Bills
6%	0.4%	0%	0%	100%
9%	6.552%	24.8%	64.2%	10.9%
12%	15.142%	80.3%	19.7%	0%

The return risk coordinates would all lie on an efficient frontier.

7 EQUITY RESEARCH METHODOLOGY

7.1 While it is not the purpose of this Study Text to advocate a particular method of equity (share) selection for investors, it is important that the factors considered by investors, intermediaries and portfolio managers alike are understood.

Top down, bottom up

7.2 **Top down investment** involves selecting geographical or business sectors which the investor believes will do well, basing investment decisions on that fact by investing in strong companies in those sectors. **Bottom up investment** involves picking individual companies which the investor believes will do well irrespective of their sector. In dealing with equity selection, we are often dealing with the latter.

7.3 There are two very different forms of analysis used in stock selection: **fundamental analysis** and **technical analysis**.

Fundamental analysis

7.4 **Fundamental analysis** looks at the underlying financial position of the company. It looks, for example, at earnings, cash flow, cash reserves, dividend levels, sales and stock. It looks at the economic and financial fundamentals of the company and the way it is run, the size of the order book and features of the market in which it operates. Analysts using this approach hope to find companies that have either been undervalued or have a potential to increase in value through growth. They also hope that in time this will be realised by other investors and the value of the company will rise.

7.5 Investors seeking hidden value are often termed **value investors**, while those seeking exceptional growth prospects are termed **growth investors**.

7.6 Important sources of data for the fundamental investor will be the company's published accounts and official stock exchange announcements from a news service such as Reuters.

7.7 Fundamental analysis can be used gradually to build up portfolios but it can take time, depending on the equity selected. Shares in the FTSE-100 Index have usually been well researched by the large investment banks, which means that there is much research available and little chance of finding something new. The smaller the company, the better the chance of finding hidden value. Consequently there could be more chance of finding value in the FTSE-250, the 'Small Caps' (companies with a relatively small capitalisation) or the AIM. However, with smaller companies it will probably take more time for others to find and recognise this value.

7.8 The effectiveness of fundamental analysis can be somewhat variable as market sentiment can often be a significant driver of prices and price volatility. With stock market sentiment at an all-time low, even companies with a lot of hidden value can suffer share price falls. The hope of the fundamental analyst is that the strength of the company will make it fall less when sentiment is against it and rise further when it is with it.

Technical analysis

7.9 **Technical analysis** seeks to determine both what to buy and when to buy it. As such it tends to be used for short-term results.

7.10 An important principle of technical analysis is that all that is known about an asset is reflected by the price, which reflects the buying and selling habits of individuals with the knowledge. Herd instincts determine what is being bought, how quickly and up to what levels. Technical analysts (or **'chartists'**) use a variety of graphs to make assumptions about a particular asset such as whether the price is increasing, decreasing and where the price resistance and support levels are.

7.11 A wide variety of charts can be used, from the conventional line graphs to 'point and figure' charts, candlestick charts and bar charts showing the opening, closing, high and low values over a time period. For each of these charts there are various ways of interpreting the information. For example, with a line chart we might be looking for formations such as 'head and shoulders', or 'double tops'. Users of Japanese candlestick charts use names such as 'the shaven head' as well as 'the morning star' and the 'hanged man' for their formations, each of which is used to predict the future movement of the asset price.

7.12 In addition to looking at price movements, technical analysts can study volume of trade and the momentum (rate) of movements. You will often see other smaller graphs at the base of a price chart, which can show a range of different things including oscillators (which have a value between 0 and 1) such as Moving Average Convergence Divergence (MACD) or overbought/oversold indicators.

7.13 To try to gain an advantage, some technical analysts have taken the art a little further by applying a range of additional techniques to the above, such as genetic pattern selection using 'neural networks' and strategies such as 'Digital Signal Processing'.

7.14 If any of the above systems worked with a high degree of accuracy then it should be possible to make regular profits. However, paradoxically, if such profits were exploited widely by investors, then the anomalies which the method seeks to exploit should tend to disappear. Most serious investors do not use technical analysis alone, but will apply fundamental principles as well.

8 RESEARCH INFORMATION SOURCES

8.1 Asset analysis requires reliable sources of information. Fundamental analysts use company reports and, for them, access to the full company reports on the shares they wish to research is essential. A news source will also be required to provide details of Stock Exchange announcements for individual shares and for more general news that could affect prices. Technical analysts will want to have the most up-to-date information for their graphs and the majority get their information from one or more internet-based systems. Some still get their data via a daily data file sent by email.

Summary of information sources

Source	Notes
General news	Periodicals such as the Financial Times or the money sections of other newspapers and websites. There are a number of bulletin boards and internet forums including iii.co.uk and Hemscott's 'Information Exchange' for the discussion of news. Unregulated bulletin boards are susceptible to rumour-mongering and it is important to verify information as appropriate.
Specific news	Specialist magazines such as the Investor's Chronicle or Shares magazine.
Real time price data	This can be accessed via the internet and this will usually be in the form of a subscription website such as Interactive Investor (iii) or ADVFN.
Technical analysis	This is available over the internet, for example via the iii website, but more complex packages tend to use internet data with additional software that must be installed, such as Updata or Sharescope.
Company reports	Hemscott has for some time provided a great deal of fundamental data for research via their Refs Online system.

8.2 There are now so many sources of information that it is necessary to be selective to avoid information overload.

Chapter roundup

- **Modern Portfolio Theory (MPT)** allows investment managers to assess investment portfolios.

- MPT shows that diversification will generate a portfolio with returns equal to the weighted average of returns of constituent investments. The risk of a portfolio will be less than or equal to the weighted average risk of the portfolio components.

- The risk of a portfolio will be determined by the correlation coefficients between investments.

- A linear efficient frontier may be generated by introducing risk free assets - this is the **Capital Market Line**, showing the relationship between total risk and return.

- Risk can be distinguished as **systematic and unsystematic risk**. The latter can be diversified away leaving only systematic risk.

- Systematic risk may be measured by the beta factor of an investment.

- The linear relationship between beta and return is the **Security Market Line (SML)**. The CAPM is the formula for the SML being $E(R_i) = R_f + \beta_i (E(R_m) - R_f)$.

- The various deficiencies of MPT and the CAPM are products of the simplicity of the models. The **Arbitrage Pricing Model** develops a more sophisticated model with more practical aspects for investment management.

- MPT and CAPM are employed to generate efficient portfolios. Investment managers must also have regard to risk, investment objective, timescale and accessibility (RITA).

Quick quiz

1   What are the two main factors that modern portfolio theory correlates within the efficient frontier?

2   List the three main types of statistical average.

3   What is the ß of an equity, or any other security?

4   What does it mean if an asset is negatively correlated to a specific factor and how can this be used to reduce risk in a portfolio?

5   What is systematic risk?

6   How does the Capital Asset Pricing Model, model non-systematic risk?

7   What is the risk free return?

8   What is the Capital Market Line?

9   Given the beta factors and expected market returns for assets on the security market line, how many assets are required to be able to calculate the risk free return and the expected market rate?

10 Why is it that CAPM often fails to model accurately?

11 What is the main difference between CAPM and Arbitrage Pricing Theory?

12 What are the main tasks a portfolio manager must perform to run a portfolio for a private customer?

13 List the four main risk levels recognised by all portfolio managers.

14 As part of a customer's portfolio, what would be a reasonable fund of instantly accessible money for emergencies?

15 What investment vehicles might be used as part of a portfolio to improve to reduce the overall tax liability for a customer?

16 How might a portfolio manager allocate assets within the gilt class?

17 Into which categories could the asset class of equities be further divided?

18 What are the names of the three private investor indices published by FTSE International?

The answers to the questions in the Quick Quiz can be found at the end of this Study Text. Before checking your own answers against them, you should look back at this chapter and use the information in it to correct your answers.

Answers to Chapter Questions

13.1 The expected return would be $(15 + 10 + 8 + 14 + 12 + 14 + 13 + 12)/8 = 12.25\%$

13.2 Standard deviation for PQR Co Ltd.

Return %	Difference from mean (12.25)	Difference squared	Difference squared multiplied by the probability (12.5% - 1 in 8)
15	2.75	7.5625	0.945313
10	–2.25	5.0625	0.632813
8	–4.25	18.0625	2.257813
14	1.75	3.0625	0.382813
12	–0.25	0.0625	0.007813
14	1.75	3.0625	0.382813
13	0.75	0.5625	0.070313
12	–0.25	0.0625	0.007813
		Total	4.6875

Standard deviation = square root of $4.6875 = 2.16506$.

13.3 In the region of 12% (answer in the range 10-15% acceptable).

13.4 When equities are performing poorly, many portfolios switch to gilt investments, driving up the price. As a result, a portfolio with both has protection from a drop in equity markets.

13.5 $2\% + 0.9 \times [6.5\% - 2\%] = 2\% + 4.05\% = 6.05\%$

13.6 Financial markets are exceptionally complex and move in line with a number of different factors, some of which are measurable and others such as emotion and sentiment are not. All of the factors act on share prices to a greater or lesser extent. To accurately model financial systems, it would be necessary to use all the factors and understand exactly how each affects the market.

13.7 The role of the portfolio manager is to ensure that the customer's objectives are consistent with their personal circumstances.

13.8 This would really depend on the time the money is needed. For an individual of 40, this would be a minimum of 10 years, but if the individual were 50, it would be a question of discussing appropriate time scales with the customer.

13.9 Gilts trading significantly below par would give the biggest tax advantage, as the capital growth is not subject to tax.

13.10 The main reason is that the fund is likely to have large holdings of individual shares. When these are disposed of, or new shares purchased, they will influence prices in the market. Large portfolios shift their position more slowly by dividing their holdings into a number of smaller transactions.

PRACTICE QUESTION 13

Norman Smedley has asked you to review his investment portfolio to ensure that the risks he is taking are appropriate for the returns he is expecting. Using the Capital Asset Pricing Model (CAPM), he would like you to analyse his portfolio.

Shares	Expected returns	Beta co-efficient
Unum Plc	10.0%	1.00
Dos Plc	15.0%	1.50
Tress Plc	15.0%	2.00
Quattro Plc	17.5%	3.00
Quince Plc	25.0%	4.00

Unum Plc and Quince Plc both lie on the Security Market Line for the portfolio.

(a)   What is the CAPM formula?   (6)

(b)   Use the CAPM formula to calculate:

    (i)   The expected return from the market   (6)
    (ii) The risk free return that has been assumed   (4)

(c)   Determine whether you feel the returns estimated for Dos, Tress and Quattro are correct based on their Beta coefficients.   (9)

(d)   State the two main approaches to active management and explain briefly the strategy for each.   (6)

Chapter 14

FUND MANAGEMENT SERVICES

Chapter topic list	Syllabus reference
1 Portfolio investment management	8.1
2 Investment objectives	8.1
3 Portfolio investment management services	8.1
4 Portfolios based on direct investments	8.2
5 Portfolios based on pooled investments	8.2
6 Pensions	8.3
7 ISAs and PEPs	8.4
8 Funds supermarkets and wrap accounts	8.5
9 Pensions simplification proposals	8.6

Introduction

In this chapter, we will be examining the role of the investment manager and the main features of portfolios as a form of investment. We will go on to consider the responsibilities of investment managers with the main types of investment portfolios. We will also consider the management of portfolios of packaged investment and pension products and the strategies for investment of the underlying investments.

A radical overhaul of the pensions regime is expected to be implemented in April 2006: these are the so-called 'pensions simplification proposals'.

1   PORTFOLIO INVESTMENT MANAGEMENT

1.1 An **individually managed portfolio** is that it can cater for a wide range of needs. Portfolios can be set up for private or institutional customers, to deal with any form of investment and the **flexible** nature of the make-up of a portfolio can cater for most investment objectives.

The roles of investment managers and advisers

1.2 The **main role of investment managers or advisers** is to **help their clients to achieve their investment objectives**. Some clients are not always aware of their own priorities and needs so the role can extend to helping the client discover these.

1.3 The four main **stages of the portfolio management process** are as follows.

- Determine investment objectives of client
- Formulate the investment policy and strategies to meet the objectives
- Choose the funds or stocks for the portfolio
- Review the portfolio and measure performance against benchmarks

1.4 The **key factors** a portfolio manager should consider when **designing a portfolio** for private clients are as follows.

- Investment objectives
- Liquidity needs
- Tax status
- Time horizon
- Risk tolerance
- Cost

Exam focus point

As in the 2004 exams, you may be asked to identify the above 'main stages' and 'key factors'.

1.5 **Regulatory requirements for private customers** dictate the following.

(a) Advisers must record (in writing) the objectives identified, together with the acceptable levels of risk, and the strategy proposed for dealing with it. Getting the customer to understand the concept of the risk they are taking, and to quantify the levels they are prepared to accept, can be a difficult task but it is also part of the role of investment management.

(b) The investment manager has a **duty of care** to **manage** the portfolio in the **best interests** of the customer, using their skills and relevant experience in a proficient manner.

(c) The advisor must **review** the objectives on a regular basis to ensure they remain in keeping with the customer's personal circumstances. Changes in objectives may require changes in the investment strategy.

(d) Investment managers must have **sufficient knowledge** of the investments in which they are dealing and are required to maintain their knowledge. However, for many this is more than a regulatory requirement because the success of an individual, or the firm they work for, as a portfolio manager will be dependent on the results achieved and the consistency with which they are achieved. In order to do this a portfolio manager must be able to allow for the fluctuating financial and economic conditions.

1.6 The **investment manager** is also responsible for the necessary administration and paperwork for the portfolio and ensuring that the customer receives the appropriate information relating to their accounts. These requirements are quite different for private and institutional investors. The subject will be examined in detail in Chapter 16, together with the different regulations for each type of investment.

1.7 The **administration requirements** will also vary significantly depending on the underlying investments of the portfolio such as unit trusts, equities, properties, and also with the tax status, eg pension and ISA funds, which have an advantageous tax treatment. **Management of the tax strategy of a portfolio** can have a big impact on net returns and it is important that this is considered in the overall running of the portfolio.

Types of portfolio

1.8 **Investment managers** need to cope with a **variety** of **portfolio requirements** depending on whether the portfolio is being managed on behalf of a **private investor** or an **institutional investor**.

Private investors	Institutional investors
Income (retirement) portfolios	Income portfolios
Growth portfolios	Growth portfolios
Trust investments	Surplus capital (money market investments)
ISA funds	Investment trusts
SIPP and SSAS funds	Unit trusts
Investment clubs	Trust investments
	Pension funds
	Charity funds

Question 14.1

Why will the portfolio management of a charity fund be different from any other growth or income portfolio?

Investment markets

1.9   When talking about **portfolio management**, most people automatically think of **equities** as being the chief underlying investment. It many cases it will be, but **any investment** can be managed as part of a portfolio. It is highly likely that, in each case, the manager will be different, as the required expertise to manage a portfolio is tied into the underlying investment. As we discussed in Chapter 10, investments can be anything from vintage cars to derivatives and each will require specific expertise to manage.

1.10 **Gilts** and fixed interest investments are the biggest UK investment by capitalisation and the skills to manage a **gilt portfolio** will be quite different to those for equities. The underlying financial instrument is quite different and responds to deferent economic and financial circumstances.

1.11 The third main class of investment is **cash** and there is a requirement for managed **cash portfolios**. This could be for life assurance, unit trust or pension funds or even on behalf of a private or business customer. Large companies and institutions often have substantial amounts of money floating around in many different accounts and most use the services of a manager to invest the money in a variety of different money market investments and cash instruments, depending on time scales. Where the companies deal in a variety of different currencies, the management issues are further increased.

1.12 The fourth group of investments includes **derivatives**. Many of the required skills are transferable from the equities market, but considerable additional knowledge and experience will be required. **Futures** and **options** operate in different ways and require different knowledge and skills.

1.13 The 'other' class of investments covers many different investments each requiring **highly specialised knowledge**, such as antiques, bicycles, cars, coins, comics, jewellery, lawnmowers, racehorses and stamps. The investment characteristics of each will be quite different.

2 INVESTMENT OBJECTIVES

2.1 There are a **variety** of **investment objectives** and the requirements for these will vary from investor to investor. The main requirements will centre around:

- The **type of return** the investor is looking for, **income** or **growth**
- The **measure of risk** the investor will be prepared to take to achieve it
- **Accessibility**
- **Term of investment**
- **Saving tax**
- Having an **ethical and environmentally friendly portfolio**
- Producing a **suitable cash flow**

All of the issues will vary considerably between the private and the institutional investor. These have already been considered briefly in Chapter 13 using the mnemonic **RITA**.

Return

2.2 One of the main **objectives** for any **portfolio** is the requirement for the **investment return** in terms of the provision of income, capital growth or a measure of the two. **Private investors** might be seeking **income for a specific reason**, for example in retirement, or may simply be looking for capital growth. **Institutional investors** could also seek the same, but for different reasons.

2.3 Companies or institutions with substantial sums may just be looking for **capital growth** and it is possible to set a portfolio up with this objective in mind. However, as new investment opportunities come along many will wish to take advantage of them. A fund invested on the basis of **capital growth** will need to **sell investments** in order to **release money**. In addition to everything else, this could cause **tax implications**. One way around this is to achieve the **growth objective** by investing in investments that **produce income** and **reinvesting the income** as it is produced.

Question 14.2

How has the removal of the ability to reclaim dividend credits altered the return objectives of investors not liable to UK tax?

Risk

2.4 In order to have the prospect of achieving their **return objectives**, investors must be prepared to accept **realistic levels of risk**. It would be unreasonable to expect high investment returns in the form of income or capital without being prepared to accept some risk. On the other hand, the fact that there is risk implies that the investment may fail to achieve high returns.

2.5 As mentioned earlier in this section, it may be necessary to ensure that clients know what each **level of risk** means. When doing fact finds as part of a financial review, it is not uncommon to find clients whose attitude to investment risk does not match their investments, eg their attitude to risk is low and yet they hold warrant funds, unlisted equities, or Far East unit trusts.

2.6 Different levels of risk tolerance are discussed in Chapter 13, section 5.

Accessibility

2.7 The requirement to have **access to funds**, either immediately or within a time frame, may well be an objective of the customer. It is important that the manager structures the portfolio to cater for this.

Timescale of investment

2.8 Ultimately the money from a portfolio will be used for something. This usually dictates the **timescale of investment**. With individual pension funds, the money is required to grow until retirement, at which stage it must produce an income. Although the rules have changed, allowing facilities to draw on these funds until 75, at that time the money is required to purchase an annuity. This determines the **term** of the investment strategy that the manager has for the underlying fund.

Case example: SIPP

In this case, the situation is actually more complex. If an individual is 55 now and wishes to draw an income from his Self-Invested Personal Pension at 65 and will need to buy an annuity at 75, there are two separate investment phases. The first is a ten-year term requiring a growth investment strategy and the second, a ten-year term where the strategy is to produce the income required by the customer (within the overall framework of the limits allowed). This can be achieved by investing in an equity based fund with phased investment into bonds and cash, as the investor approaches age 65. The individual can then use the income drawdown facility and place capital into a portfolio containing equities, bonds and property to maintain the capital value and provide income for ongoing withdrawals.

Tax

2.9 For the **private investor**, use of **tax-efficient investments can** give an **advantage** over using **taxable investments**, which often need to produce a greater overall return to match the performance of their exempt relatives.

2.10 **Portfolio managers** can also **reduce** the **tax liability** on a portfolio by making effective use of **capital gains tax** and **income tax allowances** and **exemptions** to improve **net returns**. It may also be possible to use unused allowances or lower rates of income tax effectively. For those benefiting from increased allowances, such as age allowance, the levels of income produced can be tailored to ensure that they do not exceed the limit above which the allowance is reduced.

2.11 For institutions, the considerations are quite different. **Charities**, for example, have enjoyed **tax free investment** until recently but, although they currently still have the ability to reclaim dividend credits, transitional arrangements are underway to remove this advantage. This will change the strategy that needs to be used for their portfolios. **Pension funds** were prevented from reclaiming tax credits on dividends in the Finance Act 1997. As a result, some pension funds changed their portfolios, although only marginally, moving to gilts from equities. **PEPs**, on the other hand, were given a reprieve for five years, as with **ISAs**. Depending on the investments chosen, there may be other tax benefits, such as that with life assurance bonds. Offshore bond gains can be offset against business losses, but an onshore bond cannot.

2.12 **Investment managers** of **trust portfolios** need to take into account the different tax rules that apply to the four main types of trust (**bare, accumulation and maintenance, discretionary** and **interest in possession**) each of which may necessitate a different investment strategy.

Question 14.3

What aspects of a private client's tax situation could a portfolio manager use to gain a tax advantage?

Ethical and environmental factors

2.13 **Ethical** considerations an **increasingly important factor** in some portfolios. Many large bodies and **charities** have money to invest, but would not wish to project the wrong image. For these, and any other individuals who wish to help reduce the impact we have on the planet, the make-up of investments within their **portfolios** needs to be **sensitive** to this. Some institutions and many private individuals, have significant amounts of money to invest. A suitable portfolio would not include investment in arms companies, companies that pollute the environment and companies that support dictatorships around the world would. The list of **ethically unfriendly companies** is a long one and in addition to research on investment performance, **ethical fund managers** need access to information on the **ethical and environmental** issues of the companies for potential investment. There are two basic strategies with ethical investment: a **passive** or an **active** approach. Passive investments do not do harm; active investments will be in companies that do good.

Cash flow

2.14 Some portfolios need a steady stream of **cash** which affects the **investment strategy**. Large pension funds often need **cashflow** to provide transfer values, possibly death benefits (if uninsured) and lump sums to purchase annuities or pay pension benefits. In the past, this could have been achieved by high yielding shares, but the removal of the ability to reclaim dividend credits above has modified this approach.

2.15 **Charities** need to **pay out money** on a regular basis, so **cashflow** is also important to them. The **reclaim of dividend** credit issue will also affect them when their rights to reclaim dividend credits are removed.

Legal constraints

2.16 In some cases, **portfolio managers** may have additional **legal constraints** placed on their investment choice. The best example of this are those that are **'tax exempt'**, such as ISAs and EIS schemes. In exchange for the preferential tax treatment, there are restrictions on the underlying investments. Whichever type of fund that is being managed, the restrictions will have an impact on the investment strategies and choices available to the manager. These choices often increase the risk and restrict the underlying choice of investment to those that do not produce significant amounts of income.

2.17 **Pension funds** are also subject to **legal restrictions**. Most of these are as a response to the **tax exemptions**, but further ones may be imposed as pensions are written under trust and the investment powers laid out in the trust deed will specify precisely which asset classes and investment vehicles may be employed.

2.18 Any other **trust investments** can also be affected. The investment powers of the trust are either given to it by the trust deed itself, or by the **Trustee Act 2000** (which superseded the Trustee Investment Act 1961). The later act allows for trusts to invest in a wider range of assets. Many trusts have wide powers of investments written in to them, but may still exclude certain forms of investment.

2.19 Managers of **portfolios of shares** within a **trust** may also be subject to other legal influences. Where there is a life interest as well as a final beneficiary, the trustees must not favour one class of beneficiary over any other. The effect of this is that the investment strategy must produce income for distribution to the life interest and still maintain the value of the capital for the final beneficiary.

Question 14.4

How do the restrictions on the available investments of an EIS affect the potential investment strategy of a fund manager?

3 PORTFOLIO INVESTMENT MANAGEMENT SERVICES

3.1 The **services** provided by **portfolio managers** will vary depending on the nature of the agreement between manager and client. The two main **types of agreement** are for **'advisory'** or **'discretionary management services'**.

Advisory investment management

3.2 With **advisory investment management,** the manager is required to suggest a course of action that is appropriate to the personal circumstances of the client. The manager contacts the client with the advice and, if they want to go ahead, authorises the manager to make the transaction.

3.3 This type of service has been popular in the past, but is much reduced in popularity for a number of reasons.

(a) It is **expensive** to provide.

(b) It is **labour-intensive** in that the clients must be contacted to discuss the advice.

(c) Since the Financial Services Act 1986, there has been far more **accountability** on the shoulders of the fund manager than previously as a result of having to 'know the customer' and offer 'best advice'.

(d) There are many **other sources of advice** for those who wish to make their own investment choices, advice newsletters, the Internet, Ceefax, newspapers etc.

(e) The service appears **expensive from the customers' perspective.**

Question 14.5

Why is advisory investment advice expensive to provide?

Discretionary investment management

3.4 With **discretionary investment management,** the investment manager is required to 'know the customer' and create a set of objectives that are suitable to the client's personal circumstances. As part of the customer agreement, the manager is given the right to buy and sell assets on the client's account without consultation.

3.5 Discretionary management is on the increase at the expense of advisory management. The system allows the manager to move quickly into situations without too many other people knowing about it. The **discretion** is **limited** to the **investment strategy** (including risk limits) agreed with the client at the start.

Requirements for reporting to clients

3.6 The full **legal requirements** for client information are discussed in Chapter 16 and depend on the investments being managed and the regulator of the adviser.

3.7 Details of the **reports** that will be provided for the clients will be discussed in advance with the customer and will be specified in the terms of business letter or client agreement. This will include details of the **frequency of contact** and will give some idea of the level of detail of information provided in the reports.

3.8 Depending on the underlying investments and the regulator of the firm, the **minimum frequency** of reports may vary from **monthly** with derivatives, to **annually** for life assurance policies. Where the underlying investments are securities, there is a legal requirement to provide contract notes covering the transactions within clearly defined timescales.

Question 14.6

What information must be provided on a contract note?

3.9 The **summaries** issued should contain the following information.

- The **date** of the last summary (to ensure continuity)
- The **value of the portfolio** at the last summary
- Details of the portfolio's **holdings**
- **Movements** of cash in or out
- **Investment transactions** (full details)
- **Income payments** from the underlying assets
- **Changes in value** in percentage terms

3.10 **Client reports** may also contain recommendations for a change in strategy together with any reasons and, possibly, an authority letter to implement it. In addition to this, **certificates of income paid**, in terms of dividends, coupon payments from fixed interest investments and any interest paid by the portfolio bank account, will be sent periodically to allow the individual to complete their self-assessment forms.

Charging structures for investment portfolios

3.11 The **charging structure** will often be different for **discretionary** and **advisory management** portfolios.

Discretionary fund management

3.12 There are a number of **alternatives** for the **payment of fees** on a **discretionary management agreement**. These will vary with the type of investment being managed.

3.13 A **flat fee** can cover the discretionary management of most variations of underlying investment (paid quarterly or annually). Where this is the case, the transaction charges will usually remain the same. This method of charging means that the manager is paid, irrespective of the frequency of investment transaction. An **alternative** to this is to **charge a fee** based on a **flat percentage** of the value of the fund.

3.14 In some cases, where the manager is also a **broker**, a **higher commission** may be charged for each transaction. In these cases, the greater the activity on the account, the greater the reward for the manager.

3.15 Where the manager is an **intermediary** of some form, the products being bought and sold may generate commission. In some cases, the adviser will keep all or a proportion of the commission generated. In these cases, managers should document the reasons for making each transaction to avoid any possibility of them being accused of '**churning**', which is prohibited. Some product managers opt for a fee or flat percentage of the fund to avoid any such accusations.

Advisory fund management

3.16 Every time the manager contacts the customer to advise them, it is costing the firm **time** and **money**. This form of advice is best suited to **transaction based charges**. For securities, this will typically be in the form of an additional commission percentage or dealing charge.

3.17 Where the underlying product is a commission generating product, the adviser may keep all or part of the **commission** generated. **Commission structures** are far more flexible today than they ever were. It is not unusual for intermediaries to work on a fee basis, either paid up front or deducted from the commission, the rest of which is diverted back into the investment in the form of an increased allocation.

4 PORTFOLIOS BASED ON DIRECT INVESTMENTS

4.1 The range of assets underlying each portfolio will have an impact on the way it operates. The different assets have been discussed at length in Chapters 6, 7, and 8. In the next sections, each will be examined in more detail as an **investment within a portfolio**.

4.2 **Portfolios** may be invested in one or more classes of **security** as their underlying asset. In this case, the manager will use his professional skills to pick appropriate investments to achieve the **customer's objective** for the portfolio.

4.3 One of the main factors with any portfolio is the **reduction of risk**. As discussed previously, there are two main forms of risk, **systematic (market)** and **non-systematic (specific)**. With a direct investment portfolio, investing in a wide range of equities can **reduce non-systematic risk**. However, this can only be done where there is sufficient money, a minimum investment of £1,000 to £1,500 should be invested in each share, and a reasonable spread of shares is 25 to 50. In view of this, many portfolio managers have a minimum limit of £50,000 or more for portfolios of direct investments.

4.4 To reduce systematic risk in a directly invested portfolio, it will be necessary to **spread the investment** over a number of different classes of security, eg equities, gilts and fixed interest, cash. The principle behind this is that not all classes of direct investments perform badly at the same time. To get a **reasonable spread** across more than one class of securities will require an even greater minimum investment.

4.5 Direct investment portfolios, providing they are of sufficient size, are likely to be **less expensive** to run than a portfolio using **pooled investments** because they are likely to be subject only to a **flat fee**, or an **enhanced stockbroker's fee** of some 1-2% over normal on transactions. This follows through when a change of strategy is required and the investments are sold and others are repurchased. However, even if a portfolio is small, the management costs will still need to be paid and, where a fee rather than a percentage on each transaction is charged, the costs could be high.

4.6 Direct investment portfolios (particularly advisory) can give the customer a measure of **personal involvement**, which some investors enjoy. It is relatively easy to keep track of small numbers of shares. However, where larger numbers of shares are involved, or where the customer does not want any involvement, this can be a problem.

4.7 Direct investment portfolios are easy to **tailor** to the client's requirements for **investment objectives, risk, environmental or ethical issues** and **cash flow**. Funds directly invested in **single asset portfolios** are unlikely to provide ready access to money without **compromising** the **investment strategy** of the portfolio and a **minimum investment** term of five years would be advised.

4.8 The **taxation** considerations of each portfolio will **vary** with the underlying asset classes.

Question 14.7

How can a portfolio manager reduce systematic risk with a directly invested portfolio?

5 PORTFOLIOS BASED ON POOLED INVESTMENTS

5.1 It is possible to **invest** in a **portfolio** based on **pooled funds**. Put simply, a pooled fund is any fund where the money of more than one investor is mixed together in a pool. Examples of pooled funds include final salary pension funds, Small Self-Administered Scheme funds, Unit Trusts, Investment Trusts and Open Ended Investment Companies, Life Assurance Bond Funds and all forms of Offshore Fund.

5.2 The benefits of pooling are:

(a) Professional fund management of assets

(b) The reduction of risk by:

    (i)   Spreading money across a greater range of asset numbers
    (ii)   Spreading money across asset types
    (iii)   Spreading money across different commercial and geographical areas

(c) By dealing in bulk, the costs of dealing may be reduced

5.3 This method of investment gives access to investment areas that would not normally be available, for example direct equity investment for those with small amounts of money.

Pooled investment portfolios

5.4 Generally, **pooled investment portfolios** will have access to a **wider range** of **underlying assets** than one that is directly invested. In many cases, they provide access to markets that might not be accessible by a directly invested portfolio, such as **emerging markets**. It can be easier to achieve **investment objectives** using **pooled investments** because the range of funds available is so wide. They can provide a geographical spread, across the different types of security, and can even provide for specialist needs, such as high income.

5.5 Where the **objective** of the **customer** is to **reduce tax**, the range of different financial structures of pooled funds allows greater flexibility than with direct investments, and still keeps a choice of underlying investment. In some cases, they may also allow an active management policy without being hindered by tax considerations.

5.6 With pooled funds, the **portfolio administration** is considerably **simpler** than with direct investments because there are often fewer holdings underlying the portfolio. However, the **costs** of **pooled fund portfolios** are generally **higher** than direct investment. The reason for this is that there are two layers of management, which will need to be paid for.

5.7 Underlying investments will determine the **charges** and **tax treatment** within the portfolio and the relative **advantages** and **disadvantages** of each investment.

5.8 Where a manager is authorised by the FSA they must provide **'best advice'**, and they will also need to complete a **suitability letter** (formerly called a **'reason why' letter**), justifying the investments and/or funds used. They will also be expected to justify their choice of provider for the investment in terms of investment performance, charges, and administration and company strength.

Unit trusts and OEICs

5.9 Unit trust /OEIC portfolios are particularly suitable for investors with less money available, as much of the **diversification** is achieved within the **pooled funds** rather than by the diversification of the pooled investments themselves. Each pooled investment will have a number of **underlying investments**. Equity based unit trusts must invest in a minimum of 16 different equities.

5.10 Unit trusts can provide a range of **risk profiles** from low-risk, such as with gilt and fixed interest funds, to **high-risk**, as with geared futures and option funds. They cannot provide 'no-risk' investment as the underlying investments cannot include cash or deposits although future developments will change this.

5.11 To cater for the customer's **income requirement**, unit trusts come in two forms, **accumulation** and **distribution**. **Distribution units** provide the customer with income without the need to encash investments.

5.12 With respect to **taxation**, the assets underlying the unit trust can be switched without tax liability, allowing the manager of the unit trust to adopt an **active management policy**. **Managers** of a unit trust portfolio can make use of the **customer's personal annual CGT exemption** to reduce the tax liability for the customer on portfolio transactions. Income produced by the underlying assets is taxable whether the units are accumulation or distribution.

5.13 In terms of charges, **initial investment costs** for a unit trust can be in the region of 3-6%, payable each time a trust is bought. **Portfolio managers** may refund part of this. If the portfolio manager wishes to **change strategy**, funds are sold and new ones purchased resulting in further charges. The manager of the portfolio may charge a flat fee, a percentage of the fund, or take all or part of the commission from the unit trust investments. The unit trusts will also have **annual management charges** in the region of 0.75-1.5% in addition.

Question 14.8

How do the charges on a unit trust portfolio compare with those for a direct investment?

Offshore funds

5.14 In many cases, **offshore funds** can give the portfolio access to an even wider range of underlying investments than UK based funds, providing excellent opportunities for **diversification**. Funds available can range in **risk** from **low** to **high**. Some companies even offer funds that provide guaranteed returns, and others work on a ratchet mechanism so that fund gains are locked in periodically. Further variations include funds denominated in currencies other than sterling. These can provide additional opportunities, but come with additional risks that the changes in values of the assets and currency may combine to increase a loss or cancel out a gain.

5.15 From the tax perspective, there are two types of fund, those with **distributor status** and **non-distributor status**.

    (a) **Distributor funds** must distribute 85% of the income generated and be registered with the FSA. Distributor funds are taxed in a similar way to unit or investment trusts. Income tax is payable on income payments and CGT is payable on gains.

    (b) Funds that do not distribute 85% of their income or are not registered with the FSA are **non-distributor funds**. Non-distributor funds are taxed on an arising basis, which means that all income and gains are taxed as they arise for UK resident investors. Both income and gains are taxed as income. This can have tax planning advantages for a portfolio manager, as tax is deferred until the money is withdrawn.

5.16 Depending on where the fund is based, some or all of the income produced by the underlying shares may be subject to **withholding tax**, which may **not** be **reclaimable**.

5.17 With respect to **charges**, the **offshore funds** may be subject to **initial investment charges** in the region of 3-6%. **Annual management charges** of 1-2% will typically be payable and these are typically more expensive than with UK funds. There are two main reasons for this, firstly, there will be more work in investing offshore, and secondly, because, if the underlying income is not taxable, then the charges cannot be set against it. Costs will be incurred when funds are sold and new funds purchased.

Exam focus point
Examiners' reports highlight a lack of knowledge of offshore funds among candidates.

Funds of funds

KEY TERM

A fund of funds is a pooled fund that is made up of a number of other pooled funds, such as a unit trust where the underlying investment is other unit trusts.

5.18 There are two main types of **funds of funds**:

    (a) Those where the underlying investment funds are all from the same investment groups

    (b) Those where the underlying funds are from different investment groups

5.19 The advantage of this type of investment is that it lowers risks by spreading the underlying investment over a wider range of asset types, over a wider geographical area or across a range of investment managers.

5.20 Prior to a reclassification of funds by AUTIF and AITC, 'fund of funds' were a class in their own right.

5.21 **Advantages of funds of funds**

  (a) Reduced risk through wide diversification

  (b) Professional management

  (c) Tax planning: disposals within the fund of funds do not crystallise capital gains

  (d) Convenience and reduction of paperwork, with a wide range of underlying holdings being represented by a single fund

5.22 **Disadvantages of funds of funds**

  (a) An element of double charging as there are two or more layers of professional management

  (b) Funds of funds from a single group will often contain funds that are performing as well as those that are not (this is less of a problem for funds that cover a range of investment groups)

OEICs

5.23 **OEICs** can provide a wide spread of investment as a **portfolio asset**, with the possible underlying assets being the same as with a unit trust. Because of this, the risk levels are the same with funds available offering low to high risk investment.

5.24 The taxation of **OEICs** is the same as with a unit trust. **Capital** gains on encashment are subject to **CGT** but can benefit from any remaining exemption. Income is in the form of a **dividend income**, taxed at source at the dividend income rate or as savings income where the fund assets are 60% in interest bearing investments. The portfolio manager has the same flexibility for tax planning as with a unit trust.

5.25 **Costs of buying and selling** may be **lower** than an equivalent unit trust because charges are more transparent when deducted/added to the single price. There will still be an initial charge and possibly a dilution levy as well. **Portfolio management charges** are likely to be on top, in the form of a flat fee or a percentage of the fund.

Question 14.9

Are the costs of running an OEIC portfolio likely to be more or less than with a directly invested portfolio?

Investment trusts

5.26 Where the investment objective is for income, **investment trusts** can provide **higher yields** than a similar portfolio of shares under a directly invested portfolio. This arises from the fact that many investment trusts operate at a discount and this means that the **underlying**

assets have often been purchased at a **discount**. This gives a greater pool of assets to provide the income at lower capital cost, which increases the yield.

5.27 **Investment trusts** can provide a wider range of risks than the other pooled investments we have discussed mainly because of a special type of investment trust called a **split capital investment trust** (discussed in detail in Chapter 7). By splitting an investment trust into different classes of share, a range of different investments are produced giving access to little or no risk, up to very high levels of risk, with some of the highly geared classes of share.

5.28 The **tax treatment** of an investment trust is broadly similar to a unit trust. Transactions within the fund do not give rise to a tax charge, but the sales of the investment may. The portfolio manager may make use of any of the customer's remaining **CGT exemption** to aid for **tax planning**. Distribution of income is in the form of a dividend and will be taxed as such.

5.29 **Charges** on a **portfolio of investment trusts** tend to be **low**. Most are purchased or sold via a **stockbroker** for the usual commission fees of an equity of 1-2% plus stamp duty of 0.5% on sales. Increasingly, **independent intermediaries** are getting involved in these investments, supplying direct to customers or managing part of a portfolio. A further initial charge of about 3% is then also levied on the customer and portfolio management charges may be on top of this.

Question 14.10

How can investment trusts provide portfolio managers with a wider range of risks than other pooled investments?

Life assurance funds

5.30 The main form of life assurance fund portfolio is the **life assurance bond**. It is not effectively a portfolio in its own right, but is a vehicle that has **access** to **life assurance funds**. These funds may be managed to achieve set objectives. An intermediary may manage any number of bonds for a customer. It is increasingly common for life companies to offer a 'multi fund manager' approach to investment, allowing investors a choice of funds from different investment houses as well as the life company's own.

5.31 A variation on the straightforward life assurance bond is the **broker bond**. With this type of investment, the manager actively manages the composition of funds to achieve the agreed objective. The broker funds are made up of different proportions of the life assurance funds, which are themselves managed by the life assurance company. Some companies have a very wide range of investment fund links and, under these circumstances, a wide range of objectives and risk levels can be achieved.

5.32 Life assurance products do not produce income in the true sense of the word, but the investment can generate a stream of money if required. This is achieved by the **encashment** of the **life assurance units**. The money cannot be defined as income as it is effectively a combination of capital and reinvested income. Care should be taken by the portfolio manager to avoid **erosion of capital** where such an income is taken. In respect of this form of withdrawal, customers have a cumulative allowance, allowing them to take 5% per annum of the original investment without immediate tax consequences. The **allowance** is **cumulative** as any of the 5% not used in one year can be used in the next. A maximum of 100% is allowed in this manner in total.

5.33 Managers of a **life assurance fund** can switch investments with little or no charge and without a tax liability being produced. This enables them to follow an **active investment policy**. Where the manager feels that a particular investment company is no longer suitable, the investment must be sold and a new one purchased. This will involve initial charges that the manager may or may not reduce by giving up part of their commission. Extra care must be taken in these circumstances to avoid any question of **churning**.

5.34 The underlying funds of UK life assurance funds are themselves **subject to income tax** and **corporation tax** at the life assurance company's rate, which is **not reclaimable** in any way by the policyholder or their portfolio manager. As a result of this, gains are not subject to tax at basic and lower rates. The tax treatment of gains for higher rate taxpayers in respect of full encashments, partial encashments and withdrawals of regular payments is complex and it is possible for considerable amounts of tax to be saved by a portfolio manager who plans the transactions carefully. Where the investor is 65 or over, even more care must be taken to **avoid unnecessary tax** as a result of losing age allowance. In this case a portfolio manager can add significant additional value.

5.35 **Offshore** variations of life assurance bonds have even greater potential for **saving tax**. The underlying investments of the life assurance are **not subject to income tax** or **corporation tax** like the UK bonds (they may suffer a small withholding tax). These investments are only taxed when a chargeable event occurs and there are significant tax planning opportunities using the timing of the encashments.

5.36 Whether dealing with a life assurance fund, or a broker bond, the manager is often remunerated by taking all, or part of, the **commission** produced as a result of the sale of the product. Typically, initial costs will be up to 5% in the form of a **bid-offer spread** or in some cases there may be an establishment charge with single priced units. In addition to this, an **annual management charge** is levied on the fund in the region of 0.75-1.5%. **Multi manager arrangements and broker bond funds** effectively have an additional level of management and, as a result, the annual management charges may be 1-2% higher.

6 PENSIONS

6.1 The **pensions market** is probably one of the **largest** for **investment portfolio management**, both directly and indirectly. Most large final salary schemes have their own managers to invest the money, others use third party investment management which operate directly, or indirectly, as managers of an underlying pension fund. Many pension schemes such as, money purchase, personal pensions, Additional Voluntary Contributions (AVCs), Free Standing AVCs (FSAVCs), Executive Pensions Plans (EPPs), typically invest in pension funds which are portfolios in their own right and require managing. In addition to this, there are a number of types of pension where the investments will need to be managed on a far more personal basis. These may or may not use the skills of a manager, such as Self-Invested Personal Pensions (SIPPs), Small Self-Administered Schemes (SSAS) or even Funded Unapproved Retirement Benefit Schemes (FURBS).

6.2 The advent of **pension fund withdrawals** (sometimes erroneously called 'income' drawdown) has increased the need for **management** in these cases. This allows individuals to vest their pension rights (ie, take the tax-free cash and start drawing an income) but leave the fund invested in assets rather than taking a **Compulsory Purchase Annuity (CPA)**. This facility was initially only available for use with personal pensions but has now been extended to (FS)AVCs, buyout schemes and occupational schemes.

Self-Invested Personal Pensions (SIPPs)

6.3 A 'self-invested' personal pension (SIPP) is a personal pension plan that allows the member to **control the underlying investments**. The scheme is subject to a number of restrictions designed to stop policy holders personally benefiting from the investments of their pension (except in the approved form).

SIPP providers

6.4 From the investor's perspective, **SIPPs** are available from a number of sources. Some **life assurance companies** effectively provide the framework of the **SIPP** as part of their own **personal pension plan**. Discounted **online SIPPs** providing dealing on an execution-only basis (without advice) have also become available in recent years.

Qualifying SIPP investments

6.5 **SIPPs** are also available from independent firms such as firms of **trustees, specialist investment companies** and **stockbrokers**. A **SIPP** from one of these sources should not have to invest in any particular fund and will benefit from the **full range** of qualifying **SIPP investments**.

6.6 **Permitted SIPP investments (2005/06)**

   (a) Quoted shares, including AIM shares
   (b) Futures and options (if traded on a recognised exchange)
   (c) Collective investments such as unit trusts, OEICs and investment trusts
   (d) Insurance company fumds
   (e) Traded endowment policies
   (f) Commercial property

   Investments not permitted in SIPPs (2005/06)

   (a) Residential property (with minor exceptions, eg in the case of a caretaker's flat in a commercial building)

   (b) Loans

   (c) Unlisted shares

   (d) Chattels such as antiques, paintings, fine wines

   (e) Gold bullion

   (f) NS&I Premium Bonds

6.7 A SIPP can **borrow** to buy and develop commercial property, to a maximum of 75% of the purchase price or development cost.

6.8 While the above investment rules currently apply, an overhaul of the permitted investments will take place along with the other major pensions changes being introduced from 6 April 2006. SIPPs appeal to those who wish to control the investment decisions made, either personally or through an adviser such as a broker. SIPPs could be relatively high risk, depending on the investments chosen. The availability of low-charging on-line schemes makes SIPPs viable for those making relatively low contributions.

Small Self Administered Schemes (SSASs)

6.9 This is a form of **executive pension plan**, where there is considerable **flexibility** in the **investment** and **lending** facilities of the scheme. It is an **occupational scheme** available to companies, typically set up for controlling directors or very senior employees (the rules state there must be less than 12 members). Typically, all of the members will be trustees of the scheme, and there will be additional investment restrictions where this is not the case.

6.10 The main objective of this type of scheme is to allow individuals to use their **pension scheme** as an **asset** of the business. A **SSAS** achieves this by allowing the trustees **access to investments** and **control** over them.

> **Exam focus point**
> The legal aspects of SSASs are detailed and complicated. These aspects are outside the scope of this examination, which focuses on the portfolio management aspect of the schemes. Details on the above can be found in the Study Text for G60.

Question 14.11

What are the main reasons for having a SSAS?

Permitted SSAS investments

6.11 As with a **SIPP**, a **SSAS** provides many opportunities for members and their families to benefit. As a rule, any investment or transaction that confers a benefit on the member or anyone connected with them will not be possible. The list of acceptable investments is as follows.

- Company shares
- Copyrights
- Deposit accounts
- Financial futures
- Commodity future
- Traded options

6.12 The following investments/transactions are permitted, but the **SSAS administrators** must advise HMRC in writing within 90 days of when they take place. This allows HMRC to ensure that **no benefit** has been conferred to a member or a person connected to them.

(a) **Loans** to the employer or associated companies

(b) The **purchase or sale of property**

(c) **Borrowing money** (within the fund, for example for property purchase)

(d) Buying or selling **unlisted shares in the employer or an associated company**

(e) Buying, selling or leasing **other assets** from or to the company or an associated company

6.13 **Residential property** is specifically listed as not appropriate, on the basis that it is difficult to ensure that no benefit is conferred. These rules and those related to the purchase of commercial property are examined in more detail in the BPP Study Text for G60 *Pensions*.

6.14 HMRC also has a specific list of investments that are unacceptable, known as **'pride in possession items'**. These are investments where the member will receive some benefit from owning them, typically on an aesthetic level.

- Antiques
- Works of art
- Rare books
- Rare stamps
- Jewellery
- Gem stones
- Oriental rugs

- Furniture
- Fine wines
- Vintage cars
- Yachts
- Gold bullion
- Krugerrands

As with SIPPs, a radical overhaul of permitted investments is expected to take place from April 2006.

Question 14.12

What is the principal reason for the investment restrictions on a SSAS scheme?

Pension fund withdrawals

6.15 These facilities were introduced with the 1995 Pensions Act. Prior to this time, **pension funds** (after tax-free cash) had to be used to purchase a **Compulsory Purchase Annuity (CPA)**. These are taxed as earned income and must provide an **income for life**. This legislation introduced the option for personal pensions (or transfers in from occupational schemes) to remain invested in the underlying pensions investments until the age of 75, at which time a **CPA** had to be bought. One of the key reasons for this introduction was the diminishing annuity rates available. New **pensions simplification rules** due to be introduced in April 2006 will allow the pension fund to remain invested after age 75.

Income levels

6.16 The **pension fund withdrawal system** requires the individual to draw a pension of between 35% and 100% of the amount they would have received by buying an annuity. The assumed rates are based on a **single life level annuity** and use the current yield of the long Gilt as the underlying rate. The tables are produced for all ages by the **Government Actuary Department (GAD)** and are known as the **GAD** rates. The member can choose their level of income between 35% and 100% of the **GAD** levels, and can vary it if they wish, providing the minimum level is paid each year. The proposed pensions simplification rules will allow the income to be reduced to 0% if required.

Starting withdrawals

6.17 To bring the **pension fund withdrawals** into effect, the member has to vest their pension rights, ie take the tax-free cash and start drawing an income. The **rules** relating to pension fund withdrawals in payment are based on the **post vestment rules** applicable to personal pensions, ie the income must be taxed as earned income.

6.18 Once **withdrawals** have started, it is now possible to transfer the fund. Previously it was only possible to purchase an annuity on the open market, using the **Open Market Option (OMO)**. For this reason, many used to choose a **SIPP** based product that allowed them the greatest flexibility of investment.

Phasing pension segments

6.19   A **personal pension** is usually made up of a **number of segments**. There is no requirement for all segments to be in the **withdrawal phase** at the same time. It is possible to have combinations of **unvested pension** (ordinary personal pension segments) and **vested pension** (segments that have moved into withdrawal). Once a **pension segment** has started **withdrawals**, further contributions are not permitted. Having some **unvested segments** allows **contributions** to **continue**. This **mixing** and **matching** between **vested** and **unvested** pension rights is known as **phased retirement** and works whether a CPA is purchased, or the pension moves into the withdrawal phase.

The benefits of withdrawals

6.20   One of the **key benefits** is that an **annuity** does not need to be purchased to start receiving an income, which can be particularly advantageous in the current situation where annuity rates are relatively low. Using **pension fund withdrawals** allows the member to wait until 75 before **buying an annuity**. The theory is that **annuity rates** should be considerably better at 75 than they were at 60 or 65, but there is no guarantee of this, particularly as life expectancies are increasing and interest rates are still falling. Once an **annuity** is **purchased**, that **level of income** is **fixed for life**, but **pension fund withdrawals** allows the member to wait for **annuity rates** to improve. The pension simplification rules will allow annuity purchase to be delayed after 75.

6.21   Where the money is **invested** and **effectively managed**, the final **pension** could be **larger** than it would have been with an annuity, providing the withdrawals up to retirement have been reasonable. The opposite is also true, which makes the **role of the investment manager** very important in these cases.

6.22   Many **intermediaries** recommend this **form of pension** to improve the **death benefits** for the spouse or surviving children, as one of the options available on the death of the member is to take a cash lump sum less 35% tax. It is beyond the scope of this session to look at this in any further detail. The pension simplification rules will allow withdrawals to continue after 75, but no lump sum death benefits will be available.

6.23   Before recommending a **pension fund withdrawal facility**, a full **financial fact find** will need to take place, looking at the client's attitude to risk, other assets and liabilities, expected retirement dates and state of health, to ensure that they are consistent with the investment objectives of the client.

Question 14.13

What was the main reason for the introduction of pension fund withdrawals?

Investment under a pension fund withdrawal scheme

6.24   The **investment decisions** made under this type of scheme can have a significant impact on the final pension, so it is important for the manager of the investment to have a thorough understanding of the factors that will affect the returns in order to make the right decisions. A wrong decision on the underlying investments could make the member considerably worse off at retirement than if he had purchased an annuity.

6.25 In making **investment recommendations**, a number of factors will need to be taken into account.

- Charges
- Mortality drag
- Pound cost averaging
- Annuity rates
- Risk/reward

Charges

6.26 When a member elects to draw their pension via **pension fund withdrawals**, they will be involving themselves in **additional charges**, but there would be none if they drew it from an annuity. For some, the personal pension that the fund is in may not have the facility for pension fund withdrawals, so the first thing required is a **transfer** to a suitable plan. This will involve **additional cost** as part of the transfer of up to 5% of the fund. However, this could be **reduced** by the **rebate of commission**. In addition to this, there will be **ongoing plan and management charges**. In some cases the transfer will be to a **SIPP**, which may involve **additional fees**, but could **save annual management fees** if some of the money is to be invested in direct investments.

6.27 Before considering a **transfer** to a **withdrawal arrangement**, a judgement will have to be made as to whether the term is long enough to overcome the effect of the charges to retirement. Where there is a longer period, such as 10 or 15 years, it should be easier, but there are no guarantees and the investment strategy of the manager will have an impact on the result.

Mortality drag

6.28 This is an advantage of an **annuity** over **continuing investment** as part of a **pension fund withdrawal** scheme. As the member gets older, the chance of dying increases. The **annuity rate** is based on the **life expectancy** of an **annuitant**, as this will determine the period over which the capital invested in the annuity can be returned. There is another factor relating to annuities that changes with the age of the annuitant. The younger the annuitant is, the larger the proportion is of the annuity paid that is based on cross subsidy of capital from those expected to die.

> **KEY TERM**
>
> **Mortality drag** describes the fact that when an individual takes pension fund withdrawals there is no cross subsidy.

Case example: mortality drag

To demonstrate the principle, take five people aged 60, and assume that by the time they reach 65 one will have died. With annuities, no money is returned to the estate of the individual, so this windfall is used to subsidise the annuity rates of the survivors, ie the money left in the pot of our deceased annuitant provides more money in the pot of the survivors. This keeps annuity rates higher than they would otherwise be.

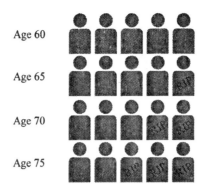

Age 60

Age 65

Age 70

Age 75

6.29 Typically, **annuity rates** are based on the **yield** of the **long gilt**, but are subsidised by this **mortality drag**. With a **pension fund withdrawal arrangement**, this subsidy does not take place because the pot of the member exists in isolation of other investors. The level of mortality drag has been estimated at between 0.5 to 2% per annum, and some even deny its existence. However, if it does exist, it becomes an additional factor that must be overcome by the investment fund.

6.30 In the early days of **pension fund withdrawals**, the **long gilt** was suggested as a **suitable investment** for a **pension fund withdrawal arrangement**. The main reason for this recommendation was that the value of a fund invested in **long gilts** will vary inversely with the interest rates in the economy. If interest rates went down, the value of the long gilts in the fund would increase, and if they went up, they would reduce. The fact that **annuity rates** move in line with economic interest rates means that the buying power of the fund in terms of the annuity would remain constant. However, the two factors we have just examined, **charges** and **mortality drag**, would reduce annual investment returns by 2-3% or more, so if a **long gilt fund** was used there would be a **guaranteed reduction** in the **purchasing power** of the fund.

Question 14.14

What would probably happen to annuity rates and the value of a fund invested in the long gilt if the Bank of England were to reduce interest rates?

Pound cost averaging

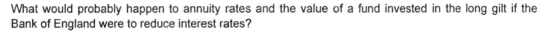

KEY TERM

The principle of **pound cost averaging** is that regular payments made into an investment produce a larger fund if the fund is volatile than one that is not, based on the same average fund value. With pension fund withdrawals, the reverse is happening because a lump sum is being used to produce a regular payment. In reverse, the more volatile the fund, the more the capital will be eroded.

Case example: pound cost averaging

The following example demonstrates this.

Pound cost averaging

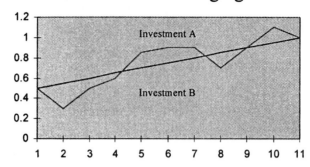

Investment A is a volatile investment, while investment B grows in value steadily.

The scale along the bottom represents regular payments, in this case they are payments out, and the scale up the side, the price of the units.

In order to make withdrawals from a pension fund withdrawal arrangement we must cancel or dis-invest units. If we dis-invest £30 per payment from each investment at the prevailing price we can see the number of units cancelled in each case.

It is important to note that the prices start and finish at the same level and the average is the same in each case.

Payment	Selling price of units in Investment A in £	Units sold for a £30 payment	Selling price of units in Investment B in £	Units sold for a £30 Payment
1	0.50	60.00	0.50	60.00
2	0.30	100.00	0.55	54.55
3	0.50	60.00	0.60	50.00
4	0.60	50.00	0.65	46.15
5	0.85	35.29	0.70	42.86
6	0.90	33.33	0.75	40.00
7	0.90	33.33	0.80	37.50
8	0.70	42.86	0.85	35.30
9	0.90	33.33	0.90	33.33
10	1.10	27.27	0.95	31.58
11	1.00	30.00	1.00	30.00

Average price 8.25   Total units 505.41   Average price 8.25   Total units 461.27

As you can see if you had made withdrawals from investment A, you would have cancelled 505.41 units. If you had made withdrawals from investment B, you would have cancelled 461.27. On the assumption we started with the same number of units in each case, the holder of the more volatile investment would be worse off.

6.31 This effectively introduces another factor for the investment manager to take into account. If they use a **volatile fund** to produce a **higher return** to overcome the effect of charges and mortality drag, the effects of **pound cost averaging** are increased. If they use a **less volatile fund** to **reduce the effect** of **pound cost averaging**, they are unlikely to overcome the effects of **charges** and **mortality drag,** creating an interesting dilemma.

Annuity rates

6.32 Pension fund withdrawals defer the need to purchase an **annuity,** which may be an advantage as annuity rates typically increase with age. The current trend for interest rates to reduce overall, has caused a real threat in the short-term that **rates will not increase with age.** Over the longer term, many suggest that interest rates cannot continue to fall and will stabilise, or may even increase in the future. However, this is another one of the many factors the adviser must consider when recommending a pension fund withdrawal arrangement.

6.33 Under a **pension fund withdrawal arrangement**, the fund must currently provide an **income** of between 35% and 100% of **GAD limits**, from the time the pension is vested to the time the annuity is finally purchased. One of the main considerations for the **investment manager** is the extent to which the fund can support the income. If the member draws the minimum, **35% of GAD**, it is likely that the growth on the fund will pay this income and maintain the value of the fund. Where the member is drawing **100% of GAD**, this could be as high as 14% of the fund, which if investment performance was not good, in combination with charges, mortality drag and the negative effects of pound cost averaging, will lead to a year on year reduction of the fund.

Question 14.15

What level of income withdrawals should be recommended to an individual aged 50 when withdrawals start?

Risk/reward

6.34 Where an individual is approaching **retirement**, the **risk aspects** of the **portfolio** need to be taken into account. However, as we have seen, with charges, mortality drag, the negative effects of pound cost averaging, and ever decreasing annuity rates, unless a **higher risk/higher return** strategy is made, the client may be worse off than with an annuity.

6.35 We have already mentioned the use of **long gilts** investments as a strategy to combat this but this can be flawed. A further strategy would be to use an **investment fund** based on **equities** which, according to the Barclays Gilt/Equity study, have over longer periods of time out performed gilts. The problem with this strategy is that **equities** may give a **higher return**, but it is given with **higher risk** to the portfolio. The capital value of the portfolio may fluctuate which could leave the member in a worse position when the annuity needs to be purchased.

6.36 A further possible strategy may be to use **with-profit investments**. This removes the **pound cost averaging risk** and can out-perform **gilts** on a regular basis. The strategy can work for funds where the member is withdrawing the **minimum pension**, but has successively less chances of working as the income increases. A further issue with this is that, even with the benefits of with-profits investments, many companies have a **Market Value Reduction (MVR)**, which they reserve the right to use if the market falls. With this, it is clearly a case of reading the small print as many companies allow encashment at particular dates without applying an MVR.

6.37 A final investment option is to use some form of **protected equities** or **tracker fund**. These funds are **protected** from **downward movements** by the use of **derivatives** and many companies now offer them. The protection is typically only effective on specified dates. The overall performance will not be as good as a non-protected fund as part of the investment is used to purchase the guarantee.

6.38 None of the **investment strategies** discussed above can guarantee the member will not be in a worse position as a result of taking pension fund withdrawals, but there are several steps that **advisers** and **investment managers** can take to reduce the risks. Most companies offering **pension fund withdrawal arrangements** can offer an illustration that includes a 'critical yield' figure. This yield, if it is achieved by the underlying investments, should result in the level of income quoted not reducing. It is important to ensure that the terms of the arrangement allow for a **critical yield** that can realistically be met by the investment performance of the proposed underlying investments. Where they do not, there are three choices: to accept the reduction in the value of the fund; to reduce the percentage of GAD payable to the member; or to recommend buying an annuity instead.

Question 14.16

What sort of funds can give most of the benefits of equity investment, without the risk of loss?

Unit-linked pensions investments

6.39 The size of pension produced by a **money purchase fund** is dependent on the performance of the underlying fund. **Investment managers** looking after such an arrangement must be aware of a number of important factors.

6.40 There will be a trade off between **risk** and **return**. The use of a **low-risk fund** should mean that a drop in investment markets near to retirement would not affect the pension income too much. However, if the investment into the low risk fund happens too soon, the investment returns achieved will be significantly lower. A **high-risk strategy** would allow the member to benefit from market movements right up until retirement, but sudden downward movements in the market could dramatically reduce the pension payable.

6.41 Many managers use a '**lifestyle' investment models** with pensions to get around these problems. The basis of **lifestyling** is that the closer to retirement a customer gets, the less risk they should take. A typical model would operate on the basis that, if the member were more than ten years from normal retirement date, they should be fully invested in equities. Once they get to ten years from retirement, a greater and greater proportion of the fund should be invested in gilts, eg 10% at 9 years 20% at 8 years and so on.

6.42 This **programmed approach** gives the member the best of both worlds. Some life assurance companies offer the facility for the switch to be made automatically, without the intervention of the manager or adviser.

Individual Pension Accounts

6.43 Individual Pension Accounts are simple pension accounts, available from April 2001, that allow pension investors to save for retirement via unit trusts, open-ended investment companies (OEICS) and investment trusts. The name is similar to the 'ISA' and is designed to invoke a similar image of simplicity. However, there has been little market activity in this area.

6.44 IPAs are essentially the wrapper in which a variety of investments can be placed, but this in itself is not new. Self-Invested Personal Pensions (SIPPS) have been available for some time and allow a considerably wider range of investments, but generally only suit sophisticated investors with large sums to invest. The IPA was designed to open up the wrapper concept to a far wider range of individuals at low cost, with the facility for further low cost products such as tracker funds to be their main investment asset.

6.45 A key factor with the IPA concept was that they are designed to give more flexibility than a normal personal or stakeholder pension, in that they are not tied to a single investment house. With the IPA wrapper, the choice of provider and investment could in theory be different. HMRC sought to enhance this ability to choose and vary investments by exempting such schemes from the 0.5% stamp duty normally applicable to the purchase of unit trust and OEIC investments.

6.46 Investment fund managers were given a choice of three methods to operate the new exemption:

(a) By offering entire unit trusts and OEICs which are restricted to holdings within IPAs

(b) By providing separate share classes within OEICs which are restricted to holdings within IPAs

(c) By operating unit trusts with a mixture of IPA and non-IPA unit holders, provided that:

(i) Systems are in place to identify all of the units of the unit trust which are held within IPAs, and

(ii) None of the SDRT charged in respect of surrenders of non-IPA units is charged to IPA holders

7 ISAS AND PEPS

Individual Savings Accounts

7.1 An ISA is an **Individual Savings Account,** a form of tax-efficient savings plan. ISAs came into existence from 6 April 1999, as a replacement for Personal Equity Plans (PEPs) and TESSAs. The Government has indicated that ISAs are to be available until April 2010, at least. An **ISA manager** must have HMRC approval.

Eligible ISA investors

7.2 An eligible ISA investor is anyone who:

- Is aged **18 or over,** or **aged 16 or over in the case of a cash ISA**

- Is resident and ordinarily resident in the UK for tax purposes, or is a Crown employee working abroad and subject to UK tax on earnings, and

- Has not subscribed to any maxi ISA, or any mini ISA of the same type as is to be applied for, in the same tax year

7.3 If the ISA holder ceases to be resident and ordinarily resident in the UK, the ISA can remain open and retain the UK tax benefits, but no new contributions can be made. There may be tax to pay in the foreign jurisdiction to which the investor emigrates. It is not possible to hold an ISA jointly or as a trustee for someone else.

Types of ISA

7.4 There are (since April 2005) **two** types of 'component' in an ISA, namely **cash** and **'stocks and shares'.** An ISA may offer both components (a **'maxi ISA')** or just one of them (a **'mini ISA').** Separate **mini ISAs** (one for each component) may be taken out during each tax year, or a maxi ISA may be taken out, but a mini ISA and a maxi ISA cannot be taken out in the same year.

7.5 From 6 April 2005, the separate **insurance component** was abolished and that component was merged with the stocks and shares component. From 6 April 2005, the stocks and shares component is able to hold eligible life insurance products and **medium-term stakeholder products** (explained further below).

7.6 A **TESSA-only ISA (TOISA)** may only accept a cash component and this must be from the capital proceeds (not the interest) from a maturing TESSA (Tax Exempt Special Savings Account). TESSAs no longer exist, and the last possible date for transfers from maturing TESSAs into a TOISA passed in October 2004. Therefore, all existing TOISAs have already received the transfer-in of funds from the TESSA.

7.7 **CAT standards** are **withdrawn** for **new ISAs,** with effect **from 6 April 2005.** Existing CAT standard ISAs will continue to operate under the same terms. However, providers will no longer be able to market ISA products using the CAT standard. The CAT standards have been withdrawn for ISAs because of the introduction of the new range of **risk-controlled stakeholder** suite of products available from 6 April 2005.

ISA investment limits

7.8 The annual ISA contribution limits are summarised in the Table below. The limits for the tax year 2005/06 are expected to apply unchanged until 5 April 2010.

	ISA component	2005/06 to 2009/10 annual limit
Mini ISA	Cash only	£3,000
	Stocks and shares only	£4,000
Maxi ISA	Cash component	£3,000
	Stocks and shares component	£7,000 *less* amount invested in cash component

7.9 Once funds are withdrawn from an ISA, they cannot be paid back in without counting as a new subscription. The ISA subscription limits apply to the total **payments in** to the account during the tax year.

7.10 Shares acquired from an approved profit-share scheme, share incentive plan or all-employee share option scheme may be **transferred directly** into the stocks and shares component of a maxi ISA or a stocks and shares mini ISA. The value of the shares at the date of transfer will count towards the normal stocks and shares annual limit. They must be transferred within 90 days of the exercise of the option or release from the profit-sharing scheme.

7.11 Other subscriptions to ISA managers must generally be in the form of cash rather than, for instance, by means of existing shares. (If an investor wants to continue to hold shares he or she currently holds, but within the ISA wrapper, it is necessary to sell the shares, and then re-purchase within the ISA. This will normally incur dealing costs, although some providers may waive some of the costs.) Subscriptions can be either lump sum or via regular savings schemes.

Cash component

7.12 The following can be included in the **cash component** of a maxi ISA or a cash mini ISA.

 (a) Cash deposited with building societies, credit unions and UK or European banks. Such accounts will have interest credited gross.

 (b) Units in a money market fund holding cash deposits, or in a qualifying 'fund or funds' which invests solely in money market funds

 (c) Funds and (from 6 April 2005) life insurance and stakeholder products qualifying for the cash component by passing the '5% test' – see below

 (d) The National Savings & Investments cash mini ISA

Stocks and shares component

7.13 The following may be held in the stocks and shares component of an ISA.

 (a) **Shares** issued by a company (other than an investment trust or fund - see below for rules on collective investment schemes) which are listed on a recognised stock exchange. (Shares on the Alternative Investment Market (**AIM**) **cannot** be held in an ISA.)

 (b) **Corporate bonds** (secured or unsecured loan stock) issued by a company incorporated anywhere in the world, with a residual term of at least five years when first held in the ISA. Either the securities themselves must be listed or the company issuing them must be listed.

 (c) **Gilts and government bonds**, including strips, from any country in the European Economic Area (EU plus Norway, Iceland and Liechtenstein) with a minimum residual term of five years when first held in the ISA.

 (d) UK authorised **unit trusts and OEICs**. Money market funds, futures and options funds, geared futures and options funds, property funds and feeder funds are specifically excluded.

 (e) Shares in UK-listed **investment trusts** that do not have any property income.

 (f) Shares acquired from an **approved profit-share scheme, share incentive plan** or **all-employee share option scheme**, if transferred within 90 days of the exercise of the option or release from the profit-sharing scheme.

 (g) From **6 April 2005**, medium-term **stakeholder products** and **life assurance products** qualifying for the stocks and shares component under the 5% test.

 (h) **Cash**, but only **for the purposes of investing** in qualifying 'stocks and shares' (interest received on cash within the 'stocks and shares' component being subject to a 20% charge).

Stakeholder products and the 5% test

7.14 From 6 April 2005, expanded ranges of risk-controlled **'stakeholder'** products, which can be sold with a **simplified advice regime**, have become available. Some of these can be held in ISAs.

7.15 Medium-term stakeholder products and life assurance products are permitted in the stocks and shares component. To qualify, these products must be similar to equity investments (shares) rather than cash investments.

7.16 The **5% test** is applied to decide whether a **fund** or **stakeholder or life assurance product** is more like a cash investment (qualifying for the **cash component**) or like an equity investment (qualifying for the **stocks and shares component**).

- Investments guaranteeing a return of at least 95% of the original capital invested qualify for the cash component
- Others qualify for the stocks and shares component of an ISA or PEP

7.17 **Collective investment schemes** and **linked long-term funds** meeting stakeholder requirements must be single-priced. They must have no more than 60% of their value in listed equities, and must be appropriately diversified.

ISA tax advantages

7.18 Income received from investments in an ISA is free of income tax. (But see below regarding interest on cash.) The 10% tax credit attached to UK dividends on shares held within an ISA cannot be reclaimed.

7.19 There is a tax credit of 20% reclaimable on bond interest paid in the stocks and shares component of an ISA or an insurance ISA.

7.20 **Interest** in the **cash component** of an ISA is tax-free. Interest paid on cash held temporarily in a **stocks and shares** or **insurance** ISA component is subject to a flat rate 20% charge before being credited to the account, but higher rate taxpayers will suffer no further liability to income tax.

7.21 Disposal of ISA investments is **exempt from capital gains tax**. However, the other side of the coin is that there is no allowance for ISA losses to be offset against gains made elsewhere.

7.22 There is **no minimum holding period** to obtain the tax advantages. There is **no requirement to declare** ISA income or capital gains on a tax return to the Inland Revenue.

7.23 The tax advantages of stocks and shares ISAs are less attractive now that tax credits on dividends can no longer be reclaimed. The main tax advantages of such ISAs are for:

- Higher rate taxpayers, who are liable to additional tax on dividends received outside the tax-advantaged ISA wrapper

- Those whose capital gains exceed, or would otherwise exceed, the annual CGT allowance. (Remember that such people will include some basic rate taxpayers, as well as some higher rate taxpayers.)

Transfers between ISA managers

7.24 ISA managers are required to allow transfers, although a manager is not required to accept a transfer in. The investor may transfer an ISA to a different manager in the year of subscription, but then the entire ISA subscription for that year must be transferred. After the first year, partial (or full) transfers between ISA managers are permitted.

7.25 Securities within the ISA can be re-registered in the new manager's name. They do not have to be sold and re-purchased. If a manager returns ISA proceeds to the investor, this will be treated as a withdrawal.

7.26 Transfers between different investment components are not allowed at any time. It is not possible to transfer individual investments between a maxi ISA and a mini ISA or *vice versa*. However, an ISA from previous years' subscriptions can be transferred to a different type of ISA. For example, a maxi ISA can be transferred to a mini or maxi ISA, or *vice versa*. The component parts of the ISA must retain their identity after transfer.

7.27 No transfers are allowed between a Personal Equity Plan and an Individual Savings Account (ISA).

Charges

7.28 The following charges may apply to ISAs.

(a) **Unit trust and OEIC/ICVC** funds held in ISAs may carry initial charges of up to 5%, but commonly this charge is discounted, down to zero in some cases.

(b) **Investment trust** ISAs may carry a management charge in addition to the charges internal to the trust.

(c) Charges on **direct investments** in an ISA may be paid to the manager separately from and on top of the ISA subscription. Dealing commissions and stamp duty must come out of the invested subscriptions.

(d) **Annual charges** of 0.5% to 1.5% of the fund value are typical. Some managers make a fixed charge, for example £25 plus VAT per half year, irrespective of the value of the investments.

(e) There may be a charge on **termination** or on **transfer** of the ISA.

(f) Purchase and sale of shares, including shares in investment trusts, will generally incur **broker's commission**, which may be at a percentage rate, possibly with a minimum and maximum charge per deal, or it may be at a fixed rate per deal.

(g) There are charges for **dividend collection** in some self-select ISAs.

(h) Many managers levy a charge if holders of ISAs with direct shareholdings wish to receive copies of **annual reports** via the manager or want to vote in or attend shareholders' meetings.

Question 14.17

How can an ISA investment help a fund manager with an overall portfolio favouring the UK and US, seeking global investment?

Personal Equity Plans

7.29 **Personal equity plans (PEPs)** were introduced in 1986 to encourage investment in UK quoted companies. Subsequent amendments to the legislation increased the subscription levels and extended greatly the number of qualifying investment that could be held within the plan.

7.30 The Finance Act 1998 announced that from 6 April 1999, **no new investment** in PEPs would be possible. However, any PEPs in existence at 5 April 1999 generally retain their tax-free status indefinitely. In addition, transfers can continue to be made between approved PEP managers. It is possible to transfer part of a PEP (as well as the whole of a PEP) to another manager.

7.31 Any individual, aged 18 or over, who was resident and ordinarily resident in the UK, could invest up to £6,000 (by lump sum or instalments) per tax year in a general PEP. In addition, he could invest up to £3,000 per tax year in a single company PEP, which invests only in the shares of one company. Since 6 April 2001, there has been no distinction between general and single company PEPs and existing holdings can be merged.

Eligible PEP investments

7.32 Since 6 April 2001, the rules on qualifying investments have been aligned with those for ISAs. So, an existing PEP can be used to hold equities, unit trusts, OEICs/ICVCs, permitted government stocks and corporate bonds. As with ISAs, 'self-select' PEPs are available.

PEP tax reliefs

7.33 Provided that a PEP meets all the necessary conditions, the investor is entitled to the following **reliefs on gains and income** arising from a PEP. These are the same as for ISAs, except in respect of interest paid on cash (see later below).

- All capital gains on disposals are free of tax.
- All withdrawals of capital are free of capital gains tax.

7.34 All dividends and interest payments are exempt from further income tax. The 10% tax credit on dividends cannot be reclaimed. The tax reliefs will continue to apply if a UK-resident PEP holder becomes **non-UK resident**. Disposals of PEP assets at a loss do not give rise to allowable losses for capital gains tax purposes.

7.35 As with ISAs, PEPs can be advantageous to those who expect to have fully used their annual capital gains tax exemption, and to higher rate taxpayers, who have to pay additional tax on dividends received outside PEPs and ISAs.

7.36 The rule on **interest paid** on cash held in **PEPs** is different from the rule for **ISAs**. Interest on cash in a PEP is credited without deduction of tax. The investor may withdraw up to £180 in interest each year without a tax charge. If this limit is exceeded, all of the interest is taxable at 20%. However, this is unlikely to occur in practice as proceeds of share sales can normally be withdrawn ahead of interest income.

7.37 Cash is only allowed to be held for re-investment purposes, and the PEP manager should check that uninvested cash is not being held for excessive periods. On the **death of the investor,** the PEP ceases to be exempt from tax as from the date of death. The account must be encashed and forms part of the deceased's estate.

Question 14.18

Can PEP funds be transferred into an ISA, or will they need to be kept separate?

8 FUNDS SUPERMARKETS AND WRAP ACCOUNTS

Fund supermarkets

8.1 **Fund supermarkets** are a concept in internet-based financial services (**e-commerce**). Funds supermarkets offer funds from various different providers, particularly for holding in an **Individual Savings Account (ISA)**.

8.2 A full online fund supermarket may provide:

(a) The ability to '**mix and match**' funds from different providers within a single ISA or other account without incurring the extra charges normally associated with self-select ISAs. However, only **unit trusts** and **open-ended investment company** investments can be held, so that investors wanting a selection of individual shares or investment trusts will still need to choose a self-select ISA

(b) The facility to **deal online** by credit card or debit card in real time without the need to download and print an application form

(c) The facility to **track and manage** the account online

(d) The ability to switch between funds within the service at minimal cost

8.3 IFAs selling products from fund supermarkets may waive or reduce the initial charge for setting up the fund while the investor would not normally have commission refunded if buying direct from a fund management company.

8.4 **Discount brokers** run on an execution only basis are sometimes referred to as fund supermarkets, but they do not normally offer the mix and match facility and switches.

8.5 **Companies** offering a 'mix and match' supermarket facility include:

(a) Fidelity's Funds Network
(b) Cofunds, whose funds are available through IFAs

8.6 With funds supermarkets, it is possible to invest with several different fund managers and have all transactions summarised on a single statement, electronic or paper. Distributions can be aggregated and paid by a single cheque and in many cases, regular withdrawals of capital from the whole portfolio can be automated to 'simulate' an 'income'. As well as having a wide choice of funds it is possible to switch between funds at low cost and avoid a high proportion of the initial charge.

8.7 Most fund supermarkets specialise in unit trusts and OEICs, but there are offerings from Skandia Life that provide a similar service for on and offshore life assurance funds and also pension funds.

8.8 **Fund supermarkets features**

Feature	Notes
Fund manager links	This can vary from three or four to fifty or more.
Fund links	For each fund manager, there may be access to some or all of the funds of that manager. This can mean the difference between access to 16 funds in total to 1,000 or more.

BPP
PROFESSIONAL EDUCATION

Feature	Notes
Contribution options	Some offer lump sum investments only, whereas others will allow regular monthly contributions. Regular contributions offer the advantage of pound cost averaging.
Contribution limits	For each company, there will be different lump sum minima and (if offered) different regular premium minima.
Income options	Many funds produce an income in the form of distributions. Most schemes offer the facility for these to be aggregated and sent as a single cheque, or re-invested into other units/shares.
Access	Some of the supermarkets are only accessible via an intermediary. Others are available directly to the public. This could be a relative advantage for an adviser or investor in different circumstances.
Internet access	Many of the supermarkets are accessible via the internet and again this may be perceived as an advantage or disadvantage depending on the investor's point of view.
Charges/discounts	Each firm can negotiate discounts with the managers and decide any discount it will pass on to the client. Where the firm has greater buying power, discounts are likely to be greater. It may be possible to buy funds from a fund supermarket cheaper than going direct to the manager. However, using some funds with very low charges (eg tracker funds and fixed interest funds) could be more expensive due to charges levied by the fund supermarket itself.
Added value	Most provide basic access to information on the funds accessible. Some go further, providing a full charting package and in some cases a full portfolio tool analysing a portfolio by asset class, investment sector or geographical distribution.
Aggregation	A funds supermarket may allow existing holdings to be aggregated together in a single account.

8.9 When choosing which fund supermarket to use, there are a number of factors to take into account:

- The number of fund managers accessible
- The number of funds accessible
- Costs involved in switching funds
- Whether access is available on a regular premium basis
- Any minimum premium
- How income is taken from the funds. Some funds allow a programmed series of monthly withdrawals to allow a larger and more regular income (particularly effective to make use of the annual CGT exemption)
- Additional services are available (such as data and information or access to make switches and make new contributions via internet)

Wrap accounts

8.10 A further development is the introduction of 'wrap' accounts. These take the concept further and allow a wider range of assets to be held including:

- Unit trusts/OEICs – based on a supermarket-type arrangement
- ISAs and PEPs
- Pension investment from a SIPP or SSAS
- Life Assurance Bonds
- Shares, held in a nominee account

8.11 The ability to analyse all these assets from a single source allows the portfolio manager an to reduce administration and to manage the funds under a range of different arrangements as part on a single portfolio.

8.12 Whilst these are relatively new arrangements, initial signs are that they could become very popular.

9 PENSIONS SIMPLIFICATION PROPOSALS

9.1 In recent years, the Inland Revenue and the Department for Work and Pensions have put forward proposals for reform of pension arrangements. These proposals have led to legislation for **pensions simplification** which is contained in the Finance Act 2004. The pensions simplification proposals are expected to be brought into force on 6 April 2006. However, because the decisions people make now will sometimes be affected by the impending changes, it is important for advisers to know about the expected changes. It is also important to appreciate that not all of the changes have been finalised yet.

9.2 There is also a new **Pensions Act 2004**. The changes arising from this legislation concern such matters as the funding of schemes, the security of benefits and contracting-out requirements.

9.3 The pensions simplification proposals and pension reforms as they are currently envisaged will lead to a number of changes from 6 April 2006, as described in the following paragraphs. There will be a **single tax regime** for all pension schemes, to replace the currently different arrangements for different types of scheme.

9.4 Under the new unified scheme, there will be a single structure of limits. There will be a **lifetime allowance** limit on the total value of funds or benefits at retirement, covering benefits from all pension sources. The lifetime allowance will be on a rising scale, starting at £1.5 million per person in 2006/07 and increasing as follows over a five year period.

Tax year	Lifetime allowance £m
2006/07	1.5
2007/08	1.6
2008/09	1.65
2009/10	1.75
2010/11	1.8

9.5 For the purpose of checking whether this limit is breached, the value of a pension benefit in a final salary (defined benefit) scheme is converted to an equivalent fund value at a factor of 20:1, with annual pension increases being converted at a rate of 10:1. Thus, a pension benefit of £30,000 per year will be valued at £600,000.

9.6 If the value of a person's accumulated funds and benefits exceeds the lifetime allowance, a tax charge called the **recovery charge** will apply at the time that benefits are taken. The recovery charge will be at a rate of 25% of the excess fund, where benefits are taken in the form of income. The individual is permitted to take excess funds as a lump sum, in which case the recovery charge will be 55% of the excess.

9.7 If a person already has pension funds exceeding the lifetime allowance at 6 April 2006 ('A-Day'), he may register the value of the funds and then the registered fund will become that person's **personalised lifetime allowance**. The personalised limit will be increased annually in line with the increases in the normal lifetime allowance. This type of arrangement is called **primary protection**.

9.8 Through **enhanced protection** arrangements, it is possible to avoid any recovery charge on benefits accrued by 'A-Day' (6 April 2006), but only if the individual makes no further contributions and accrues no further benefit under registered pension arrangements.

9.9 From 6 April 2006, there will be a new basis for the annual limit of contributions to pension schemes. Contributions will generally be limited to the greater of £3,600 (gross) per year and 100% of annual earnings, with an overriding limit called the **annual allowance**. The annual allowance will be set at £215,000 for 2005/06, rising on a pre-set five-year scale as follows.

Tax year	Annual allowance
	£
2006/07	215,000
2007/08	225,000
2008/09	235,000
2009/10	245,000
2010/11	255,000

9.10 For all schemes, it will be possible to take a **tax-free lump sum of 25%** of the funds, when benefits are taken and a pension is obtained. This follows the current rules for personal and stakeholder pension schemes. This is a major change for occupational pension schemes. The new rule will also apply to Additional Voluntary Contribution schemes, for which there is not currently the possibility of taking a 25% tax-free lump sum.

9.11 Retirement income will be provided by purchase of an **annuity,** or by **secured income** provided by an occupational scheme, or by **unsecured income** – this last option probably applying only to a money purchase scheme. The unsecured income is similar to the income withdrawals that are currently possible. However, with the new arrangements there will be no minimum withdrawal as at present, so an individual could take the 25% tax-free lump sum but defer taking any income benefit until later. The maximum unsecured income will be 120% of the annuity that would otherwise be available. The limits must be reviewed only every five years (as compared with every three years as is currently required).

9.12 There will be a lifting of restrictions on drawing benefits from occupational schemes while employed by the same employer, and the concept of normal retirement age will be abolished. The minimum age for drawing benefits will be raised from **50 to 55**, although this change will not be introduced until **6 April 2010**.

9.13 The general rule that an annuity must be taken by age 75 at the latest will remain under the new regime. However, there will be an additional basis available only at age 75 for money purchase schemes known as **Alternatively Secured Income (ASI)** or Alternatively Secured Pension. The ASI arrangement is designed for members of certain religious groups for whom the mortality basis of annuities is unacceptable. Under ASI, the need to purchase an income is removed. The ASI basis does however carry restrictions on the death benefits that can be made available.

9.14 There will be the possibility of **commutation of trivial pension rights** for cash where the total value of such rights does not exceed 1% of the lifetime allowance. Commutation will only be available between ages 60 and 75. If benefits have not yet been taken, a 25% lump sum will be tax-free and the remainder will be taxable. If benefits have already been taken, the lump sum will be fully taxable. A full tax-free commutation of pension rights is possible before age 75 if medical evidence of **serious ill health** is provided.

9.15 A funding test specific to the scheme will replace the **Minimum Finding Requirement** for occupational schemes.

9.16 A new pensions regulator will be established to replace the current **Occupational Pensions Regulatory Authority (OPRA).**

9.17 A number of features of current pensions legislation will disappear, including the earnings cap, restrictions on concurrent membership of different schemes and restrictions on transfers between different types of pensions.

Chapter roundup

- The main role of **investment managers** is to help clients achieve investment objectives. Investment managers must also satisfy regulatory, general administration and taxation administration requirements.

- **Investment objectives** are determined by risk, return, accessibility, term, taxation, cashflow and ethical factors.

- Investment management services may be split between **advisory and discretionary management**.

- Although there are substantial funds managed on a segregated/direct basis, most funds are managed on a collective or pooled basis. The most important **pooled funds** are unit trusts, OEICs, life funds and pension funds.

- The growth of funds managed under existing PEPs and new ISAs is likely to continue due to the tax-efficient nature of these vehicles.

- New facilities for portfolio management continue to be developed such as **funds supermarkets** and **wrap accounts**.

- The **pensions simplification proposals** will radically overhaul the pensions regime from April 2006.

Quick quiz

1   Should a portfolio manager always accept the decision made by a customer on the risk strategy to be followed?

2   Why is the management of portfolios of gilts and fixed interest investments fundamentally different from management of portfolios of equities?

3   List five different investment objectives.

4   What factors relating to the term of investment do managers of SIPP funds for pension withdrawals need to take into account?

5   Why do portfolios of investments for large pension funds need to produce a reasonable cash flow?

6   What are the two main types of portfolio management? Briefly, explain the difference.

7   What is the typical frequency for the generation of client reports?

8   Why is it that the minimum investment requirements for directly invested portfolios tend to be high?

9   How is it possible to get a greater diversity of investment from a pooled fund investment portfolio rather than one based on direct investments?

10 How many different underlying securities must a single unit trust have as a minimum?

11 Why might offshore funds as the underlying investment for a portfolio provide more opportunities for a manager to plan the tax situation?

12 Which pooled investment provides the fund manager with the greatest potential to influence the customers tax position by varying the size and timing encashments?

13 How might the investments be restricted where a SIPP is purchased from a life assurance company?

14 Why might the use of with-profit investment funds not be appropriate for a pension fund withdrawal arrangement?

15 List the investments that a SIPP may invest in.

16 How much income can be withdrawn from a personal pension fund withdrawal arrangement?

17 What factors will affect the size of the fund and hence the pension paid after the end of the pension fund withdrawal period?

18 What is mortality drag?

19 What factor will affect the degree to which a fund will be affected by the negative effects of pound cost averaging?

20 What is the annual limit for stocks and shares ISA investment?

The answers to the questions in the Quick Quiz can be found at the end of this Study Text. Before checking your own answers against them, you should look back at this chapter and use the information in it to correct your answers.

Answers to Chapter Questions

14.1 The tax-exempt status of charities means that the strategy will need to be altered to maximise the returns within the tax framework. The strategy will be quite different from that for a private or business investor.

14.2 The investment strategy is likely to favour an objective of growth rather than income, as the income is now automatically taxed, but the growth may not be.

14.3 The private investor may wish a manager to make use of tax exempt investments.

- They may wish the manager to use their capital gains exemption effectively
- They may wish to make use of allowances or lower rates of income tax
- They may need increased allowances to be taken into account such as age allowance

14.4 EIS investments are limited to investment in unlisted shares that are high-risk, which will compromise the investment strategy of the manager. Recent changes in legislation also restrict EIS investment to shares that do not generate high levels of regular income, further reducing the manager's choice.

14.5 It is expensive to provide because the fund manager must take the time out to contact the customer and discuss the advice with them. The main cost is the time of the fund manager. In some cases, the customer will not want to effect the recommended transaction and, depending on the nature of the charging agreement, this may result in no commission for the firm.

14.6 Contract notes must contain the following information.

- The bargain number (to identify the deal)
- The date and time the bargain was struck
- The customer and/or account the bargain was made for
- The full name of the security purchased
- The number of securities (contracts/shares etc) bought or sold
- The price the bargain was struck at
- Full details of commission payable
- Stamp duty payable (on purchases)
- The settlement terms and the date that payment is required

14.7 With a directly invested portfolio, a measure of reduction of systemic risk can be achieved by investing in a number of different asset classes.

14.8 Charges on a unit trust portfolio are considerably higher because of the initial charges on the unit trust and the ongoing management charges will, in some cases, have to paid in addition to the cost of managing the portfolio. The initial cost can be in the region of 3-6% and will arise every time a trust is sold. A management charge of 0.75-1.5% per annum will also apply. This is compared to 1-2% in total with a direct investment plus, possibly, a flat fee or a percentage of each transaction.

14.9 Although the costs of running an OEIC portfolio are likely to be less than with a unit trust, they will be higher than with a directly invested portfolio. There will still be initial charges and possibly additional costs in the form of a dilution levy on purchases or sales.

14.10 A portfolio based on investment trusts has access to a special type of 'split capital' investment trust. These are trusts where the share capital has been split down to provide a number of different classes of share, each with a different level of risk. These different classes of share range from the very safe to the very speculative.

14.11 The reason for having a SSAS is to permit firms to use their pension scheme, as an asset of the business by allowing access to investments and control over them.

14.12 The principal reason for restrictions on a SSAS are to avoid conferring any benefits on the member as a result of the investments made by the pension scheme, other than providing benefits at retirement.

14.13 The main reason for the introduction of pension fund withdrawals was to remove the need for members to lock themselves into low annuity rates to draw their pension benefits. The pension fund withdrawal system allows them to put this off until 75 when the annuity rates should be higher as a result of the higher age.

14.14 If interest rates were reduced, annuity rates would reduce and the capital value of a fund invested in long gilts would increase.

14.15 For an individual aged 50 when withdrawals start, the income may be required over a long period. To avoid any possibility of erosion of the capital, it would be wise to recommend the lowest income possible, preferably the minimum 35%, until the sustainable income for the portfolio had been ascertained (unless the objective is to strip out as much cash as possible from the fund).

14.16 A protected equities or tracker fund gives exposure to upward movements, but is protected from downward movements by the use of derivatives.

14.17 The portfolio manager could use the ISAs to represent assets from geographical areas other than the UK or US allowing more portfolio assets to be invested in the UK.

14.18 PEPs cannot be transferred into ISAs.

PRACTICE QUESTION 14

(a)   List the main types of portfolio an institutional investor may be interested in.   (8)

(b)   What are the main investment objectives that a private investor may have?   (5)

(c)   Explain the principle of discretionary portfolio management. Is it more or less popular than advisory management? Go on to explain how the service might be charged for and any legal requirements before an adviser can start to give advice.   (6)

(d)   Explain the term 'mortality drag'. What effect will it have on pension fund withdrawals relative to just using an annuity?   (4)

(e)   What is the maximum contribution to equities in ISAs in the current fiscal year?   (2)

(f)   What types of gilt can an ISA include as part of its stocks and shares component?   (2)

Part G
Performance assessment

Chapter 15

PERFORMANCE ASSESSMENT

Chapter topic list	Syllabus reference
1 Time value of money	9.1
2 Benchmarks and indices	9.2
3 Understanding and using statistical data	9.3
4 Investment criteria	9.4
5 Switching	9.4
6 Risk indicators	9.5

Introduction

Financial calculations are vital to understanding investments and making decisions about them. In this chapter, we will look at all aspects of financial calculations with respect to the assessment of investment performance. We will examine the time value of money and the principles of the calculation of benchmarks and indices. We will move on to look at the use of statistical data for the measurement of the returns from the main types of investment. Finally, we will discuss investment criteria for the original selection of funds and for subsequent switching before looking at the statistical methods of measuring risk.

1   TIME VALUE OF MONEY

1.1   One of the underlying **principles** of making any **financial plans** is understanding what **money** will be worth at any stage **in the future**. Whether it is calculating the size of a pension fund at retirement or the amount of money that will need to be invested today to provide £20,000 for a world cruise in five years time, the ability to do this is fundamental to all areas of financial services.

1.2   **EXAMPLE: TIME VALUE OF MONEY**

In each of these cases, the relationship is simple. As an example, if there is £10,000 in our pension fund today, then to calculate the value at retirement, we will need two further pieces of information, the time to retirement and the rate at which the money will grow between now and then. If we assume ten years to retirement and a return between now and then of 10% we can do the calculation. It is simply a matter of compound interest. At the end of the first year the fund will be worth £11,000, which is the £10,000 + 10% of £10,000 (£1,000). At the end of year 2, the fund will be worth £11,000 plus 10% of £11,000 (£1,100) giving a total of £12,100. We could continue the calculation in this manner, but the mathematics of compound interest will come to our aid. In order to do the full calculation in one go, we can use the following calculation.

Present value (PV) $\times (1 +$ interest rate (i)$)^{\text{Number of years (n)}} =$ Future value (FV)

BPP

PROFESSIONAL EDUCATION

$$£10,000 \times (1 + 10\%)^{10} = £25,937.42$$

The formula can be used for any calculation of a future value given the present value, the interest rate and the time between them.

Question 15.1

An investor has a £10,000 National Savings Certificate (5 year term) which pays 4.5% per annum, what will it be worth at maturity?

1.3 This calculation can be used for simple projections of **lump sum investments** but, in many cases, the **effects of inflation** can make the calculation meaningless.

1.4 EXAMPLE: EFFECTS OF INFLATION

Taking the previous calculation, the pension fund may be £25,937.42 in ten years time, but what would this be worth if **price inflation** were running at an average of 4%? One way to look at this would be to say that if inflation is running at 4% and the investment is growing at 10%, then the net growth is 6%. However this is an oversimplification.

The true relationship between nominal and real returns is given by the formula

$$(1 + r)^n = \frac{(1 + nom)^n}{(1 + i)^n}$$

where   r = real rate
               nom = nominal rate
               i = inflation rate
               n = number of years

Using the above example

$$(1 + r)^{10} = \frac{(1 + 10\%)^{10}}{(1 + 4\%)^{10}} = \frac{(2.593)}{(1.480)} = 1.752$$

$$1.752 - 1 = r = 0.752$$

Please note that this is the real return over 10 years 75.2%. In the G70 exam, you will often be asked to calculate this figure in annual terms. To calculate this, raise your answer to the power of one divided by the number of years. The real annual rate of return = $(1.752)^{1/10}$ = 1.058 or 5.8%.

1.5 **Compound interest** calculations can be used to find more complex values, such as the amount of money that needs to be put away today to achieve a figure in the future. If we take our earlier example of the amount of money that will need to be invested today to provide £20,000 for a world cruise in five years time, a small modification to the calculation should allow us to calculate this.

$$FV/(1 + i)^n = PV$$

Where   FV = **Future value**
               PV = **Present value**

Assuming an interest rate of 6%

$$£20,000/(1 + 6\%)^5 = £14,945.16$$

1.6   The **compound interest calculation** can be used for even more complex financial situations.

1.7   EXAMPLE: COMPOUNDING INTEREST

An investor wants to know the size of lump sum contribution he would need to put into his pension today to get a retirement fund in ten years time of £100,000, if a growth rate of 10% is assumed. What size lump sum would be required to achieve the same in five years time?

Using the formula $FV/(1 + i)^n = PV$

In ten years

$£100,000/(1 + 10\%)^{10} = £38,554.32$

Or in five years time:

$£100,000/(1 + 10\%)^5 = £62,092.13$

This provides an important example of the need to invest for retirement earlier rather than later.

Question 15.2

An investor has a requirement to pay his first years school fees for his child in five years time. He would like you to tell him how much he would need to invest into National Savings & Investments Certificates paying 4.5% per annum, to cover the fees of £6,000?

1.8   It is important when comparing two different investments that the comparison is on a like-for-like basis.

1.9   EXAMPLE: COMPARING LIKE WITH LIKE

As an example, suppose that an investor has a choice of two building societies, one paying 6% annually and another paying 5.8% per annum in two half-yearly payments. Compound interest can be used to calculate which is the better. The account receiving 6% in one payment per annum will achieve a return of 6%, but this does not automatically mean it is a better return than that from the other account. Based on an investment of £1,000, this would give £60 in interest. The account paying interest half yearly will pay half of 5.8% (2.9%) in 6 months, on £1,000 this would be £29 and a further 2.9%, but for the second payment it will be on £1,029 @ 2.9% = £29.84. In total, this adds up to £1,058.84, less than the other account, but more than 5.8%. The 5.8% figure is the **nominal rate of interest** and 5.884% is the **effective rate of interest**. This calculation is used for Annual Equivalent Rate (AER) figures on deposit accounts and mortgages.

1.10   To calculate different compounding periods, we use the following calculation.

$I/YR = (1 + (i/n))^n - 1$, where i is the interest and n is the number of compounding periods.

Using the example above, 5.8% per annum:

$(1 + (5.8\%/ 2))^2 - 1 = 5.884\%$ per annum

PROFESSIONAL EDUCATION

1.11 EXAMPLE: USING A BUSINESS CALCULATOR

To do the same calculation with a business calculator (HP 10B), the parameters would be as follows.

P/YR   Payments per years = 2

Nom %   Nominal interest rate = 5.8% .

Pressing (or solving for EFF%) Effective interest rate = 5.88410

Question 15.3

A customer is considering two investment accounts, one pays 6% half yearly, the other pays 5.8% on a monthly basis. Which will give the greater return?

1.12 **With-profit funds** increase in value daily, based on a fixed percentage rate. A slight variation on the above method can be used to calculate the value of this.

1.13 EXAMPLE: WITH-PROFIT FUNDS

An investor has £10,000 in a unitised with-profit fund. The fund increases at 6% per annum, but interest is added on a daily basis. What will the investment be worth in one year's time?

$$£10,000 \times (1 + (6\%/365))^{365} = £10,618$$

1.14 The compound interest values we have been calculating so far have used some of these parameters.

- Present value (PV), the starting value
- Future value (FV), the final value
- Annual Interest Rate (I/YR), we have used 'i' to denote this in calculations so far
- Number of years (N), we have used 'n' to denote this in calculations so far

1.15 Given any three of these values it is possible to calculate the fourth.

1.16 EXAMPLE: TIME VALUE OF MONEY

An investor had a pension transfer 20 years ago of £100,000. The value of the pension fund today is £400,000. What is the annual return they received on their investment?

$$(FV/PV)^{1/N} = I/YR$$

$$(£400,000/£100,000)^{1/20} = 7.18\%$$

Using business calculators

1.17 Whichever calculator you are using, the buttons should be the same, but a quick reference to the manual should iron out any differences. For the **time value of money calculations** in the examinations, the main parameters are the ones we have already seen.

- Present value (PV), the starting value
- Future value (FV), the final value
- Annual Interest Rate (I/YR)
- Number of years (N)

Plus

- Amount of payments in or out during the year (PMT)
- Number of payments per year (P/YR)
- The nominal percentage rate (NOM%)
- The effective percentage rate, APR (EFF%)
- Whether interest is added at the beginning or end of the payment period (BEG/ END)*

  *   This should normally be set to END.

1.18 Using the calculator, the calculations we have performed so far become relatively straightforward (**saving time in the examination**), but it is possible to calculate even more complex scenarios which we will look at later in the chapter. Using the calculator makes any variation on compound interest calculation easy to achieve with a few keystrokes.

1.19 EXAMPLE: USING A BUSINESS CALCULATOR

An investor has £10,000 in an account paying 6.5% annually in one interest payment. He wishes to know how long it will take the fund to grow to £15,000. By inputting these parameters, the calculation is relatively straightforward.

PV   = –£10,000 the minus sign in front of the figure, this represents £10,000 paid out
FV   = £15,000
I/YR   = 6.5
P/YR   = 1 (number of times per year interest is paid)

The answer is 6.43853 years. It may be useful to run a very quick, rough, double check in exam conditions to ensure that this is correct £10,000 × (1 + (1.065)$^{6.4}$) = £14,963

Question 15.4

The trustees of a pension scheme have calculated the cash equivalent pef Roger Smith's pension, which is £388,045.13. They feel that they could get a return of 7% on the money between now and his retirement in 20 years time. How much would they need to put aside today to produce this and how much should they offer him as a transfer value?

1.20 Calculations using the **time value of money** are frequently used to calculate, monitor and predict past or future returns on investments. Examples that are more complex will come up later in the chapter.

2 BENCHMARKS AND INDICES

2.1 When measuring the performance of **individual securities** or **whole portfolios** it is important to have a basis of comparison. For most markets there is an appropriate stock market index allowing comparisons to be made, the difficult task is to use an appropriate index that provides a valid basis of comparison. Indices can cover different types of securities in different countries, with different levels of market capitalisation. There are three main categories of index from the UK perspective:

(a) **UK indices,** covering all aspects of the UK market

(b) **Overseas equity indices,** covering the major indices from other countries markets

(c) **Crossborder indices,** which can be indices of shares from different countries markets, or may even be indices of indices covering the world's main financial centres

UK indices

2.2 There are a variety of indices used in the UK to cover many situations at home and abroad. **FTSE International** is an independent company wholly owned by the Financial Times and the London Stock Exchange which produces the following indices.

- FTSE-100
- FTSE-250
- FTSE-250, excluding investment trusts
- FTSE-350
- FTSE-350, excluding investment trusts
- FTSE-350 higher yield
- FTSE-350 lower yield
- FTSE-Small Cap
- FTSE-Small Cap, excluding investment trusts
- FTSE-TechMARK All-share

- FTSE-TechMARK 100
- FTSE-All-share
- FTSE-All-share, excluding investment trusts
- FTSE-Fledgling
- FTSE-Fledgling, excluding investment trusts
- FTSE-All-small
- FTSE-All-small, excluding investment trusts
- FTSE-AIM
- FTSE4Good – indices for ethical investment
- Individual indices for each sector

2.3 Each index has a **different composition** and there is a sufficient range that **portfolio managers** should be able to find an appropriate benchmark to match their portfolios. There is even more flexibility if two or more indices are used in combination. Benchmarks are also very important to provide performance comparisons for individual shares.

2.4 The **FTSE** UK indices do not assume reinvestment of dividend income. Adjustments can be made for this, but the result is that the actual return for the underlying shares, including income, will not match the index.

FTSE 100

2.5 The FTSE 100 (the 'Footsie') is the most followed and probably the **best known UK index**. The index covers **shares** of the **top 100 UK companies** ranked by market capitalisation. The index is an arithmetic weighted index, weighted by market capitalisation and is re-weighted every day. During the day, it is calculated every minute.

2.6 Constituent reviews are carried out quarterly. Additions and deletions are performed strictly in accordance with a set of rules supervised by the **FTSE Actuaries Share Indices Steering Committee**, an independent body.

2.7 The **base date** of index was the 31 December 1983. The base number was 1,000.0.

Question 15.5

How is the FTSE-100 index calculated?

FTSE 250

2.8 This covers the next **250 companies** ranked by **market capitalisation**. There is a variation on the **FTSE-250**, which excludes investment trusts. The index operates in real-time and includes companies with a market capitalisation of between £250m and £1.5bn.

FTSE 350

2.9 This index is a combination of the **FTSE 100** and the **FTSE 250** and covers the **UK's top 350 companies** by market capitalisation. There are three variations on this index, one of which is the index excluding investment trusts. The other two splits are on the basis of yield and are called the higher yield and the lower yield.

FTSE Small-Cap

2.10 This index has about **430 constituents** capitalised at around £40 million to £250 million and represents the **smallest by market capitalisation** of the **FTSE All-share index**. As with the others, there is a variation that excludes investment trusts.

2.11 The **Small Cap index** is calculated in real time.

FTSE All-Share

2.12 This index is made up of **shares** covering the **whole market place**. As with the others, there is a version that excludes investment trusts.

2.13 The index is considerably **less volatile** than the **FTSE 100** and this makes it a useful index for a **tracker fund**. It is also very good as a benchmark as it provides the ultimate representation of the diversified UK share portfolio.

FTSE Fledgling

2.14 This is made up of **companies** which are **newly listed** and listed companies not included in the other indices, some of which are too small to qualify for inclusion in the **FTSE All-Share index**. There is also a version that excludes investment trusts.

FTSE-AIM

2.15 This covers **companies** from the **Alternative Investment Market**.

FT 30

2.16 This is the **oldest UK index** and is known as the **FT Ordinary Share Index,** but is often called the **FT 30.** It was established in 1935 by the Financial Times and reflects the share prices of 30 of the largest companies in the UK. It started with a base price of 100 and is an un-weighted index with each share counting equally rather than in proportion to its market capitalisation. It is calculated by way of a geometric mean.

2.17 The **FT 30** is rarely quoted as a market barometer these days, because it represents such a small proportion of the market, but it is used as an economic barometer since the constituents generally reflect industrial, commercial and service sectors.

Question 15.6

How does the calculation of the FT-30 index differ from that of the FTSE-100?

FTSE TechMARK Allshare

2.18 This index includes technology companies from across the main market. It includes high growth medium and small cap technology shares.

FTSE TechMARK 100

2.19 This index includes the top 100 technology companies with a market capitalisation of less than £4 billion at the launch of the index. Both TechMARK indices provide a useful benchmark for fund managers tracking technology stocks.

Other UK indices

2.20 **FTSE International** also has other indices covering index-linked and fixed-interest securities markets. These are very useful where the portfolio has an asset allocation outside equities.

2.21 All forms of security have **benchmarks** published by various interested parties. Some other forms of investment also have their own indices, such as the Nationwide or the Halifax House Price Index, which looks at residential property prices nationally and by area of the UK.

Overseas equity indices

2.22 For each geographical area, there will be **one or more indices** relating to a variety of different levels of market capitalisation and sectors.

2.23 For most countries in the world, there is usually at least **one index** to represent **equity movements** in their domestic market. The most well known are listed below.

France

2.24 France has a similar selection of indices to the London market. The **CAC 40 index** is the main real-time indicator, but is a subset of the newer **SBF 120 index,** calculated in real-time. The **SBF 120** is, in turn, a subset of the **SBF 250,** which replaces the old **CAC General index**. The series of indices is published by the Societe des Bourses Francaises.

With the **CAC 40**, the base date of the index is 31 December 1987 and the base number is 1,000.00. The index is calculated every minute. It is weighted by market capitalisation.

Germany

2.25 The **DAX** is the principal real-time **German share index** and is published by the **Frankfurt Stock Exchange**. It contains 30 stocks from the main German stock markets.

2.26 The **DAX** is a **total return index,** meaning that it measures the price movements of its constituents in conjunction with the return provided by the dividends paid to shareholders. Most other major indices are based on capital movements only, with total return shown as an additional calculation. The DAX now publishes a calculation based on the late-afternoon close of the **IBIS electronic trading system**, as well as the earlier close of the physical market.

2.27 The **base date of the index** was 30 December 1987 and it started at 1,000.00. It is calculated every minute.

Question 15.7

What is the main difference between the calculation of the FTSE-100 and the DAX?

Japan

2.28 The **Nikkei 225**, once known as the **Nikkei-Dow index,** is the original Japanese share index published by Nihon Keizai Shimbun, Tokyo. Like the Dow-Jones Industrial Average, on which it was modelled, it is a **price-weighted index**. Movement in the share price of a small company may have as great an influence on the day's price movements as a comparable move in the price of a large one. With the **Nikkei,** this effect is heightened by the presence in the index of a number of old-line manufacturing firms, many of which are now considerably less important than they used to be.

2.29 The Tokyo authorities have, for some time, attempted to promote global markets to look at other, broader, more modern indices weighted according to market capitalisation, such as the **TOPIX** and the **Nikkei 350**, but global attention still tends to focus on the **Nikkei 225**.

2.30 The **base date of index** was 16 May 1949 and the base price 100. The index is calculated every minute.

USA

2.31 **Dow-Jones and Co, New York** publish four of the main indices of stock (share) prices in the US, the best known of which is the Dow-Jones Industrial Average (DJIA or 'the Dow'). It also produces indices relating to US bonds, transportation stocks and utilities.

2.32 The **Dow-Jones Industrial Average** is globally the best known of all share price indices. It was first calculated on 12 stocks in January 1897, but now contains 30 stocks, chosen by Dow-Jones and the *Wall Street Journal,* which are designed to represent a balanced selection of **blue chips**. In recent years, the constituents have been gradually altered, to reflect the shift in the US economy away from old-line manufacturing towards computers and service industries.

2.33 The **index** is **price-weighted**, so a move in the share price of a company with relatively modest market capitalisation will have as great an influence on the day's price movements as a comparable move in the price of a large one. With the **Dow**, this factor is reduced by the selection of very large companies, and by the tendency for US companies to manage the nominal value of their shares to ensure market prices that fall into a roughly comparable range, between $30 and $100. The original base number was 100 and the index is calculated every minute.

2.34 **Standard and Poors (S&P)** produce a range of indices covering a wide range of US securities, the most widely known of which is the **S&P 500 Index**.

2.35 The **S&P 500 Index** is a weighted, composite index covering 500 shares listed on the New York Stock Exchange. The shares represent some 80% of the total market capitalisation and, as such, are very representative of the US market. The index is seen globally as the main measure for US shares.

2.36 There are also indices covering the technology-weighted NASDAQ, such as the **NASDAQ Composite Index**, and the **NASDAQ 100 Index**.

Question 15.8

What do the Nikkei 225 and the Dow Jones Industrial Average indices have in common?

International indices

2.37 Some indices are made up of the shares of a number of different countries. The largest series of these is **FT/S&P**, which has over 40 indices covering most countries and a number of geographical regions, eg Pacific Basin, Pacific Basin including/excluding Japan, Europe including/excluding UK, Euro Pacific etc.

2.38 They also produce **world indices** covering equities from across the globe including the world index, world index excluding UK, world excluding Eurobloc, world index excluding US and the world index excluding Japan.

2.39 Europe is very well covered with indices including the **FTSE Eurotop 100**, a weighted index based on shares of 100 leading European companies, expressed in Euros, €. The index is composed in such a way as to be considered representative of trends on the major European stock exchanges. In order to guarantee that it is representative, the **FTSE Eurotop 100** includes only stocks from countries which meet minimum exchange capitalisation requirements.

2.40 The **Eurotrack 200 index** is a composite. It contains both shares of 100 companies from Continental Europe, and those of the FTSE 100 Index. The index is a market capitalisation-weighted index. However, stocks from each country reflect that country's proportionate share of total European stock market capitalisation. The weighting of the 100 shares from the UK are adjusted so as not to take up an inappropriate proportion of the index. The **FTSE Eurotrack 200** is calculated every minute using real-time prices provided by the quote-driven **SEAQ International system**.

2.41 The arrival of **economic monetary union** is also influencing indices and there are now indices such as the **Eurobloc100** and **300** (the **FT-E100** and **E300**). Eurobloc indices cover the countries participating in **European Economic and Monetary Union**.

3 UNDERSTANDING AND USING STATISTICAL DATA

3.1 In order to **manage** portfolios of investments **effectively** it is essential that **fund managers** can measure the performance in **absolute** and **relative** terms, both for the underlying assets and the overall portfolio.

Statistical data for the measurement of investment performance

3.2 Obtaining **statistical data** relating to the **investment performance** of any regularly traded investment, has never been **easier**. The increased popularity of the **Internet** has seen an explosion in the number of sites offering all forms of financial data, often free of charge. **Internet sites** such as those run by MoneyAM and Interactive Investor provide access to prices for UK life, pension and unit trust funds, as well as UK and overseas shares.

3.3 These **sites** can present the **data** in a number of different ways, eg the highest and lowest performers in each type of investment, investment category, geographical focus, over terms of 1, 3, 5 or 10 years and so on. Many sites even offer their own **rating** for each **fund** in terms of performance or consistency. Most of the sites give fund rank by category or overall. They can also graphically represent the absolute or relative fund performance of any fund against any other, or against the average fund performance. In many ways, this makes investigation of fund performance much simpler than it used to be.

3.4 The original source of the data is in many cases the same. For equities, the main sources are **Reuters, Bloomberg, Standard and Poors** and, for funds, it will tend to be **Micropal** (owned by Standard and Poors) or **HSW (Harvard Stafford Wright)**. For pooled funds, the service offered by Morning Star is very popular.

Statistical measures

3.5 Traditionally, in assessing **investment fund prices, absolute performance** is less important than relative performance. In a sense, it does not matter if a fund loses 10% in value, providing all of the others in the same category have lost more. There is a sound reason for this, in that funds within the same category have access to the same investments and exposure to the same market risk. Better performance in these circumstances will be as result of the choice of investments made by the fund manager.

3.6 In addition to beating **rival funds**, it is also important to beat them on a **regular basis**. Most funds and marketing groups use basic statistics to demonstrate their performance.

Average or mean

3.7 The main aim of fund managers is to be **above the average**. Analysis of most fund categories will usually include the average performance of all funds in the category.

Case example: Anonymous Mutual

The example given below shows the performance of the Anonymous Mutual European Pension Fund and its performance over a period of ten years. The row marked 'Europe' is the average performance of all funds in the European pension fund category. The bottom row shows the fund's rank out of all funds in the category.

	88-89	89-90	90-91	91-92	92-93	93-94	94-95	95-96	96-97	97-98
Anon Mutual European	33.14	−5.26	10.08	11.79	28.05	0.32	10.47	17.67	19.65	24.00
Europe	38.15	−7.78	7.01	7.59	36.54	4.14	15.04	15.39	19.34	21.07
Rank	45 / 69	22 / 77	31 / 86	18 / 95	90 / 101	80 / 103	84 / 106	42 / 111	67 / 118	38 / 119

From the statistics, we can see that the fund outperformed the average in 89-90, 90-91, 91-92, 95-96, 96-97 and 97-98, six out of the ten years selected.

3.8 Many managers **rank their funds** on their performance relative to the other funds in the category, rather than relative to the average performance. Statistically we can look at a number of other significant figures, the **median** and the **upper and lower quartiles**.

Median

3.9 The **median** is the **halfway point**, the point where half of the sample is higher and the other half lower. If we look back at our table at the 97-98 year, we can see the fund was ranked 38 out of 119. The **median performance** would be the performance of the fund ranked 60 out of 119. This would be the point where 59 funds had performed better and 59 funds had performed worse. In this case, the fund is above the median.

3.10 If we look at the 1996-97 year, the fund performed above average, but was ranked 67 out of 118. In this case, the **median** would be a ranking of half way between 59 and 60. The fund in this case was below the median, having been outperformed by 66 funds and outperforming 51 funds.

Quartiles

3.11 Performance against the median is a good measure, but for many, a more detailed analysis is required. To do this, funds are **ranked by quartile**. If there were 120 funds, those ranked 1-30 would be in the upper (or first quartile) and those ranked 91-120 would be in the lower (or fourth) quartile. This leaves the two quartiles either side of the median, the one above it is generally termed the second quartile and that below it is the third quartile. Let us go back and rank the performance of the fund by quartile.

3.12 EXAMPLE: QUARTILES

	88-89	89-90	90-91	91-92	92-93	93-94	94-95	95-96	96-97	97-98
Anon Mutual European	33.14	–5.26	10.08	11.79	28.05	0.32	10.47	17.67	19.65	24.00
Europe	38.15	–7.78	7.01	7.59	36.54	4.14	15.04	15.39	19.34	21.07
Rank	45 / 69	22 / 77	31 / 86	18 / 95	90 / 101	80 / 103	84 / 106	42 / 111	67 / 118	38 / 119
Quartile	3	2	2	1	4	4	4	2	3	2

If we average the quartile rankings, we get a figure of 2.7. This effectively means that on average over the 10 years the manager has been beaten by 67.5% (2.7/4) of other fund managers in the same category. This is not promising performance.

3.13 This **method of analysis** can be used for any financial instrument, but tends to be used mainly for funds. For **individual securities** there are a very wide range of different measures that can be used as an alternative such as Sharpe, Jensen and Treynor measures.

Question 15.9

If a fund is ranked 34 out of 132, what quartile ranking does it have?

Rates of return

3.14 In order to **measure** and **compare** the **performance of an asset** with others of the same, or even different types, the **manager of a portfolio** must be able to accurately calculate the investment return it provides, whatever form that return may take.

Money Weighted Return (MWR)

3.15 The simplest way to look at an **investment return** is to look at the difference in the value of the portfolio at the start and the end of the period of time being measured, and express this as a percentage of the original sum invested. This will give the increase in **capital value** over the time and, as a calculation, is fine for investments that produce no income. A simple way to allow for the income is to add it into the total.

> **FORMULA TO LEARN**
>
> Return (R) = (Final Value (V^1) – Initial Value (V^0) + Accrued income (I))/V^0

3.16 EXAMPLE: MONEY WEIGHTED RETURN (1)

The value of the portfolio on the 1 January 2004 was £100,000. On 1 January 2005, it was £121,000 and the income distributed during the year was £8,000.

Using $R = (V^1 – V^0 + I)/V^0$

$R = (121,000 – 100,000 + 8,000)/100,000$

$= 29,000/100,000 = 0.29$ or 29%

3.17 The **MWR calculation** is quick and straightforward, but not necessarily accurate, as it makes no allowance for the timing of the income, or the proportion of any return that is attributable to the re-investment of that income. With an **investment return** comprised wholly of capital appreciation, this would not make a difference, but the greater the return is, in the form of income, the greater impact it will have.

3.18 In order to get an accurate figure of **investment return**, a new calculation must be done whenever income is produced.

3.19 A further complication is the **addition** or **removal** of **investment capital** part way through the term, which will reduce the accuracy of the MWR. Again, additional calculations every time money is added or taken away will rectify the problem.

3.20 **Calculating returns** every time income or capital is added or taken away will be a complex and tedious task for all but the simplest of calculations. Fortunately, **computers** can take care of the calculation work in most cases. The calculation to do this is called the **Time Weighted Return**.

Question 15.10

Mr Jones invested £10,000 into shares valued at £1 on 1 January 2004. On 1 January 2005, the share price was £1.24 and the shares had produced dividend income of £760. Calculate the Money Weighted Return.

Time Weighted Return

3.21 The **Time Weighted Return** of an investment is not a single calculation, but a **series** of **MWR calculations** multiplied together. Every time the value of the portfolio changes, a further calculation is performed, providing an exact figure for the investment return.

3.22 EXAMPLE: TIME WEIGHTED RETURN

As an example, a portfolio had the following investments:

The initial investment was £20,000 into ABC co. shares at £2.00 on 1 January 2004.

On 1 February 2004, the price of share ABC Co. was £2.10.

On 1 March 2004, a 10p dividend was paid on ABC Co., which stood at a price of £2.15.

On 1 April, a further £10,000 was invested into shares of BCD Co. shares, at a price of £1.00 (10,000 shares). The price of ABC Co. at this time was £2.20.

On 1 May, the price of ABC Co. was £2.40 and BCD Co., £1.05.

On 1 June, the price of ABC Co. was £2.45 and BCD Co., £1.10.

On 1 July, the price of ABC Co. was £2.50 and BCD Co., £1.15.

This effectively cuts the investment period into slices of one month, with all significant cash flows occurring at the beginning of each month (for convenience). To calculate the TWR, a MWR calculation must be performed for each month.

February	V^0 = £20,000
	V^1 = ABC Co. 10,000 × £2.10 (£21,000)
	I = £0
	R = (£21,000 – £20,000 + £0) / £20,000
	= £1,000/£20,000 = 0.05 or 5%
March	V^0 = £21,000
	V^1 = ABC Co. 10,000 × £2.15 (£21,500)
	I = £0
	R = (£21,500 – £21,000 + £0)/£21,000
	= £500/£21,000 = 0.02380 or 2.380%
April	V^0 = £21,500
	V^1 = ABC Co. 10,000 × £2.20 (£22,000)
	I = £1,000 from dividend (10,000 × 10p = £1,000) – Taken out of the calculation (spent)
	R = (£22,000 – £21,500 + £1,000)/£21,500
	= £1,500/£21,500 = 0.06977 or 6.977%
May	V^0 = £22,000 + £10,000 additional investment
	V^1 = ABC Co. 10,000 × £2.40 (£24,000) + BCD Co. 10,000 × £1.05 (10,500)
	I = £0
	R = (£34,500 – £32,000 + £0)/£32,000
	= £2,500/£32,000 = 0.07813 or 7.813%
June	V^0 = £34,500
	V^1 = ABC Co. 10,000 × £2.45 (£24,500) + BCD Co. 10,000 × £1.10 (11,000)
	I = £0
	R = (£35,500 – £34,500 + £0)/£34,500
	= £1,000/£34,500 = 0.02899 or 2.899%
July	V^0 = £35,500
	V^1 = ABC Co. 10,000 × £2.50 (£25,000) + BCD Co. 10,000 × £1.15 (11,500)
	I = £0
	R = (£36,500 – £35,500 + £0)/£35,500
	= £1,000/£35,500 = 0.02817 or 2.817%

The overall return over the six-month period can be calculated by multiplying the percentages together. For the calculation to work it is necessary to add one to each figure and deduct one from the result:

$(1.05000 × 1.02380 × 1.06977 × 1.0781 × 1.02899 × 1.02817) – 1 = 0.3117$ or 31.17% return.

3.23 Although complex, this method is **more accurate** than **MWR** and the use of a **computer spreadsheet** would speed it up considerably.

3.24 This calculation will only be **totally accurate** providing the **major cash flows** occur on the **first of each month**. On the assumption that cash flows could occur on any day, a repeat of this calculation on a daily basis would be fully accurate whenever they occurred. This would involve considerably more calculations but a dedicated computer program copes with it easily.

3.25 EXAMPLE: MONEY WEIGHTED RETURN (2)

Taking the information from the above example, the MWR would be:

V^0 = £30,000 (£20,000 + £10,000 invested)

V^1 = ABC Co. 10,000 × £2.50 (£25,000) + BCD Co, 10,000 × £1.15 (£11,500) = £36,500

I = Dividend on ABC Co. 10,000 × 10p = £1,000

R = (£36,500 − £30,000 + £1,000)/£30,000

= £7,500/£30,000 = 0.25 or 25%

This is not a bad approximation, but does not represent the full picture. A difference of over 5% in fund performance over six months would be very important to a portfolio manager.

Question 15.11

What factor has the main influence on the accuracy of a Time Weighted Return?

Uses and limitations of performance measurement

3.26 Calculating **rates of return** is useful to measure the performance of the assets underlying a portfolio and the portfolio itself. Measurement of the **absolute return** from a portfolio is used to ensure that the manager is meeting objectives but, as we have seen, relative performance is more important. A customer might be happy with a return on their portfolio of 15%, unless they were to realise that three quarters of the other managers in the same sector were performing better. When selecting a **fund manager, relative performance** and the **ability to consistently perform well** will be important.

3.27 **Evaluation** of the **performance of a portfolio manager** can be broken down into two areas, their ability to select the correct asset allocation to achieve the investment objectives of the customer and the selection of individual securities within those asset groups that will outperform the average.

Asset allocation

3.28 The **asset allocation** chosen by the **fund manager** should be tailored to meet the **investment objectives** for the **portfolio** and the relevant proportions invested in each asset should reflect them. The choice of assets will have a significant impact on the overall risk of the portfolio, the potential returns and the income produced.

3.29 For each **investment objective**, measured in terms of **risk/reward** and **income/capital growth**, there will normally be a **typical asset allocation**. In some cases, a portfolio manager will use the asset allocation specified by the investment company for the portfolio objective, in others, the fund manager will create the mix specifically.

3.30 Where the requirement is for **income**, the fund manager will choose a greater proportion of **gilts/fixed interest** or **high yielding equities** and a low-risk portfolio would also contain more gilts/fixed interest and cash than equities. If the customer is looking for **long-term capital growth**, a greater proportion of **equities** may be chosen.

3.31 In order to assess the **manager's skills** in **asset allocation** we must look at two main criteria.

(a) The performance of the portfolio against the asset allocation chosen
(b) The performance of the portfolio against a portfolio with the typical asset allocation

3.32 As mentioned in an earlier Chapter, the Association of Private Client Investment Managers and Stockbrokers (APCIMS) publishes a set of standard benchmarks that can be used in the assessment of portfolios run by investment managers. These may be used to determine a suitable benchmark asset allocation or measure performance.

	Income portfolio %	*Growth portfolio* %	*Balanced portfolio* %	*Representative index*
UK shares	47.5	60	55	FTSE All-Share Index
International shares	7.5	25	20	FTSE World Ex-UK Index calculated in Sterling
Bonds	40	10	20	FTSE Gilts All Stocks Index
Cash	5	5	5	7-day LIBOR – 1%
Total	100	100	100	

3.33 The CII often use these portfolios for assessment of performance. In a number of questions, there has been a requirement to know the asset allocations of one or more of the above portfolios.

3.34 Let us assume that the appropriate asset allocation for the portfolio we are looking at is that for the income portfolio.

Asset type	*Typical allocation % for portfolio objective*
UK shares	50
International shares	5
Bonds	40
Cash	5
	100

3.35 In order to calculate the **performance** of the **typical portfolio** over the chosen period, it will be necessary to choose **appropriate benchmarks** to **represent the performance** of each of these assets. If the UK equities were mainly in shares with a larger market capitalisation, the **FTSE-100** might be appropriate, or alternatively, if the equities were more broadly based the **FTSE All-Share** index. APCIMS provides a list of suitable benchmarks.

3.36 To calculate the performance of the **typical portfolio,** it is necessary to calculate the **performance** of the chosen **benchmark**. In the examination, these may need to be calculated first using the benchmark index figures at the start and finish of the measurement period using MWR or TWR if appropriate. For the purposes of the example, the performances of the benchmarks are shown below.

Asset type	Performance of benchmark % over period
UK shares	15.0
International shares	10.0
Bonds	7.5
Cash	5.0

3.37 To calculate the **performance** over the **specified period** of the **typical portfolio**, the contribution of each asset to the total performance must be calculated. Multiplying the asset allocation by the performance of each asset gives a figure for this.

Asset type	Typical allocation % for portfolio objective	Performance of benchmark % over period	Contribution to overall portfolio performance %
UK shares	47.5	15	7.125
International shares	7.5	10	0.750
Bonds	40	7.5	3.000
Cash	5	5	0.250
	100		11.125

3.38 Based on the figures given, the **typical portfolio** would have performed at 11.125% over the specified period. If the portfolio manager is exceeding this level of performance and achieving the investment objectives then it is reasonable to assume he is doing a good job. Where the **asset allocation** he is using is different to this, it is also important to ensure that he is also **outperforming the benchmark** based on his own asset allocation. As an example, let us assume that his asset allocation is as follows and the portfolio has performed at 12.35%, exceeding the performance of the typical portfolio.

Asset type	Typical allocation % for portfolio objective
UK shares	50
International shares	40
Bonds	5
Cash	5
	100

3.39 The portfolio is **overweight** in UK and overseas equities, and **underweight** in fixed interest (bonds). Based on the benchmark results, it is possible to calculate the 'benchmark' returns for a portfolio with this asset allocation.

Asset type	Typical allocation % for portfolio objective	Performance of benchmark % over period	Contribution to overall portfolio performance %
UK shares	50	15.0	7.500
International shares	40	10.0	4.000
Bonds	5	7.5	0.375
Cash	5	5.0	0.250
			12.125

3.40 The **benchmark performance** for a portfolio with this asset allocation is 12.125%. It is essential to ensure that our manager is outperforming this, as well as the performance of the model portfolio. As it happens, our manager's portfolio increased by 12.35%, out performing the benchmark by 0.225%. The fund manager in this case has outperformed both the benchmark for the typical portfolio and that for his own asset allocation.

Selection of individual investments

3.41 Having determined the **investment manager's performance** on asset allocation, we will now examine his ability to pick investments from within each asset class. To do this, we must assess the manager's performance in each investment class of asset against the appropriate benchmark. To calculate this, the difference between the benchmark performance and the manager's performance is multiplied by the managers selected asset allocation.

Asset	*% invested*	*Benchmark performance*	*Managers performance*	*Effect on return (% invested × difference) %*
UK shares	50	15	17	+ 1.000
International shares	40	10	8	– 0.800
Bonds	5	7.5	8	+ 0.025
Cash	5	5	5	0.000

3.42 From these figures, we can see that the manager's stock selection for **UK equities** is good and has added to the performance of the portfolio. His selection of **overseas equities** detracted from the performance of the portfolio. His performance in **fixed interest** improved portfolio performance slightly, but his **cash and gilt selection** were neutral, not least because very little of either asset was selected.

> ### Exam focus point
> From the perspective of the examination this analysis goes into sufficient depth. This topic is regularly examined and you should ensure that you are competent in performing the computations. For a full analysis of a portfolio, it would be necessary to further break down each category of asset. The UK equities should be further broken down by sector and the overseas equities should be analysed by region and sector.

Limitations of performance measurement

3.43 As we have seen, **measurement of portfolio performance** can provide a lot of information about the performance of a **fund manager** against benchmark averages. Managers are also measured against each other in absolute terms which also provides relative comparisons. However, performance measurement does have its limitations and these should not be overlooked.

3.44 One of the most important factors to take into account when comparing the performance of one manager to another is that the figures have been calculated on a like-for-like basis. **Differences** could arise as the result of a number issues, such as a portfolio having a different investment objective, eg comparing one manager's growth portfolio with another's income portfolio.

3.45 Levels of cash flow, in and out, can seriously affect the performance of a portfolio if the information is not measured in the right way, ie **time weighted**. Equally important is the **'phase'** of a portfolio. A portfolio in its **'growth'** phase, where there is a net inflow of money, can use the new money to invest in new opportunities and to take up new positions. A fund in a **'steady state'** will need to sell to attain liquid assets to take advantages of the same opportunities. A fund in **'decline'** will regularly need to sell assets, which could, at best, be inconvenient and, at worst, compromise the investment strategy of the portfolio.

3.46 The **type of fund** being managed is also relevant to the above points. A **unit trust** or **OEIC**, for example, will have money flowing in and out because of the purchase and sale of units. **Investment trusts**, on the other hand, have a limited capital base, requiring assets to be sold before new ones can be purchased.

3.47 The **size of the portfolio** is also important. **Smaller portfolios** are more **flexible** and can react more quickly to changing market conditions. **Larger portfolios**, on the other hand, can be significantly **more difficult** to change direction. Size will certainly have an impact on both the risk and the volatility of a portfolio.

3.48 A particular portfolio manager may be turning in **top performances** now, but how long has this been happening? Was the time of measurement just in a **bull market**, and would that change if the market turned down? The **consistency of performance** over a range of market conditions could be considered more important than sporadic, but spectacular, performance under some circumstance.

3.49 The only way to reduce the effect of market conditions, as a factor in performance, is to **compare** a peer group of **fund managers** against a set **range of portfolio objectives**. However, as we have seen this will introduce problems of its own. Comparisons of the managers of collective investments are quite straightforward as there is significant market intelligence on the funds, but statistics on individually managed portfolios are less easy to come by. For collective investments, statistical tables of performance are regularly published, showing the rank order of funds and determining quartile performance within each pooled fund sector. The companies often quote these figures over a variety of periods and funds to demonstrate the consistency of their performance.

Question 15.12

What is the main problem incurred when performing a peer comparison of two portfolio managers?

Sharpe ratio

3.50 The **Sharpe ratio** is a measure of the risk-adjusted return of an investment or a portfolio of investments. The ratio was derived by Professor William Sharpe of Stanford University. The underlying principle of the Sharpe ratio is to compare the returns on an investment or portfolio with the 'risk-free' rate of return, which is generally taken to be the rate of return on government-backed securities such as undated gilts.

3.51 To calculate the ratio:

- Calculate the average monthly return over some number of months, for example 24 months, by averaging the returns for the 24 month period

- Calculate the standard deviation of the monthly returns over the same period

3.52 Then, to annualise these numbers:

- Multiply the average monthly return by 12
- Multiply the standard deviation of monthly returns by the square root of 12

3.53 The **excess return** is then calculated. This is the annualised return achieved by the investment in excess of the available risk-free rate of return. This excess return is the risk premium earned for assuming some risk. The standard deviation or variability of the returns is a measure of the risk.

Excess return = Annualised annual return – Risk-free return

3.54 The **Sharpe ratio** of the returns over the past 24 months is then calculated as:

Sharpe ratio = Excess return / Annualised standard deviation of returns

3.55 For the investor, the higher the Sharpe ratio, the more favourable is the relationship between risk and return. If the returns are high for a portfolio or investment with relatively low risk, then the Sharpe ratio will be relatively high.

3.56 The Sharpe ratio can be a useful measure for investors and advisers. However, it should be borne in mind that it is based on historic data. Furthermore, the Sharpe ratio for a particular investment can vary widely when calculated for different time periods.

4 INVESTMENT CRITERIA

4.1 Whether a customer is looking for a personally managed portfolio of direct investments or to invest in a single pooled investment, the quality of the investment management is of vital importance. A number of **investment criteria** could be used to choose a manager but, before investing, it would be wise to consider all of the following.

- Administration
- Costs and charges
- Experience and skill in the relevant investment area
- Funds under management
- History
- Investment strategy/style
- Past performance
- Quality of service and staff
- Resources

Administration

4.2 The **portfolio manager** is responsible for a number of administrational items, such as reports and valuations of the investment. Depending on the service being provided, this can also be extended to cover things such as tax summaries or even returns. It is very important from the point of view of an individual seeking **portfolio management** that these aspects are effectively taken care of. It is even more important where an intermediary is recommending the service to one of his or her own clients.

Costs and charges

4.3 It is important that **charges** and **costs** are taken into account. For smaller portfolios, it can be uneconomic to use direct investments. Under those circumstances, one or more pooled investments could be used to achieve the investment objective at lower cost. For larger portfolios, this effect is reduced and in some case, management costs for large portfolios can be proportionately less than using pooled investments.

4.4 When making **comparisons** between **managers**, charges will affect performance. **High charges** can quickly **reduce** the **effective investment performance**. **Tracker funds**

typically have **low charges** compared to their actively managed counterparts. Many consider that the **difference in cost** is **difficult to justify** where there is **no extra investment performance**.

Experience and skill in the relevant investment area

4.5 It is important to use a **management company** that has both **experience** and **skill** in your chosen market. When considering a portfolio of options and futures, it would be wise to choose a firm or individual experienced in the area rather than a management firm specialising in gilts.

Funds under management

4.6 If the requirement is to **invest** a lot of money then it is essential to deal with a **firm experienced** in handling **large portfolios** as the investment strategies will be quite different from a smaller one. Similarly, there is little point in going to a firm experienced in large portfolios when what you are seeking a small, specialised portfolio.

History

4.7 This is tied in with **reputation** and **performance**. Many large firms of intermediaries will only use investment management from houses that have been operating for a minimum period, for example 10 years. This demonstrates stability and, in many cases, will be supplemented by a reasonable amount of **investment history**. This information can demonstrate the **management skills** in **bull** and **bear markets** and the consistency of returns against a known benchmark. A company called Lipper provides an assessment of preservation of capital and consistency of return for all UK funds on its website.

Investment strategy/style

4.8 **Different management firms** and funds use **different strategies** and **styles** of investment. A good example of this could be firms that invest in 'value' stocks (stocks which appear underpriced), and those that invest in 'growth' stocks (stocks which are likely to grow rapidly). Other strategies may pivot on whether the managers 'buy and hold' or adopt an 'active' management strategy.

4.9 Each investment firm will have a view as to the way to structure a portfolio for each investment objective. The extent to which this is enforced by the management can make a significant difference to individual results. Houses with less control allow their managers greater flexibility to meet the needs of their investors.

Past performance

4.10 **Past performance** is not necessarily an indication of future performance, but this does not stop it being one of the most important factors as to which investment manager to use. Few intermediaries will actively recommend a company that has turned in fourth quartile performances for ten years on the basis that they could get better. On the other hand, it can be dangerous selecting a company with top quartile performance without looking at their history to see if they are consistent.

4.11 A company that regularly puts in top quartile performances may not always be the best recommendation. It is important to ensure the **performance** is **properly monitored** and that the company can be changed if the levels drop. In this case, choosing on past performance is a reasonable strategy.

4.12 Care should be taken to ensure that the factors causing the **good performance**, such as individual fund managers and overall group management, remain the same, or at least the situation should be monitored for any change.

Question 15.13

Why is it that a company that puts in regular top quartile performance is not necessarily the best recommendation?

Quality of service and staff

4.13 For many with significant funds to invest, the **quality of the interaction** with the company is of great importance. It does not matter if the fund management abilities of the company are the best in the world, if they do not answer the telephone or carry out instructions accurately this will be of little use. For many, the **quality** of the **front line staff** in a company will often be a **good indication** of the **quality** of the **back office staff**, the ones that make the investment decisions.

4.14 In the same way, unhappy or unsettled investment staff will not always make for the best performance. The stability of the investment management team can have a significant influence on fund performance.

Resources

4.15 An **investment house** is only as good as the **market intelligence** it receives and it is important to ensure that the managers have access to the most up-to-date information and data feeds. As markets become increasingly reliant on computers, market activity is happening faster than ever before and it is important that investment managers can deal with it.

5 SWITCHING

5.1 On occasions, an **investment strategy** will not work out in quite the way that was expected. In these circumstances, it is important to evaluate whether a **change in strategy** and, consequently, a switch of the investments is necessary. This is even more important because of the charging and taxation implications of such a course of action. A **change of investment** can cost a lot of money to arrange and it is essential that the client, or their representative, can see that it was in their interest to pursue such a course of action.

5.2 It is vitally important to ensure that the **reason** for the **change of investment** is **fully documented**, particularly where additional costs for the customer are involved. Where investments are regularly switched for no apparent reason, it is conceivable that the accusation could arise that this was **churning**, switching carried out in order to increase charges or commission. Regulators are keen to ensure that this does not happen with their members and have included various rules in their training and competence requirements to reduce the incidents of **churning**. Trading or switching more than is necessary is prohibited under FSA rules.

Question 15.14

What two costs might a customer incur during the switch of one investment to another?

Reasons for switching

5.3   Providing it is in the customer's best interest there should be no problem in **switching** their investments. Good reasons for switching might be where:

- The customer has given **clear instructions**
- The **client's objectives** have changed
- The **client's attitude** to risk has changed
- The **market conditions** have changed
- An investment has regularly **under-performed** its benchmark
- The **tax treatment** of the investments has changed

5.4   Where the client has given clear instructions for a **switch** there should be no problems associated with carrying out the instruction. However, it would be advisable to get the **instruction in writing**, or at least make a file note, in case the client develops memory problems at a later stage.

5.5   The clients may **change** their **investment objective** from **capital growth** to **income**, or vice versa. In these cases, it may be necessary to **sell** and **repurchase** investments. With equities or gilts this could involve selling shares with lower yields and buying those with higher yields. With unit trusts, this could involve a **switch** from **accumulation** to **distribution** units. Most unit trust companies will effect this switch free of charge.

5.6   When the client's attitude to **risk** changes, this may involve the sale of higher risk assets and the purchase of lower risk assets or vice versa, for example with equities, smaller companies could be sold and blue chip equities could be purchased. With a unit linked life assurance bond this may be achieved by switching funds, usually at no cost.

5.7   As market conditions change, it may be necessary to take action with a portfolio to **avoid under performance**. A good example of this could be where the market moves from a **bull market** to a **bear market**. In these circumstances, the '**top down**' approach stops working and a switch to '**bottom up**' investing may improve matters. Another strategy that is useful if the market turns, is to switch from cyclical to the counter cyclical shares.

5.8   For **pooled investments**, a **switch** to funds that are less influenced by market movements would be a good idea to avoid them following the market down, for example a move from UK equity to UK managed.

5.9   **Investment under-performance** can cause problems as, in many cases, the investments were chosen by the investment portfolio manager. However, providing it is possible to establish a reason for the investment not performing and ascertain whether the effect will continue into the future, a change of direction could be justified. In these circumstances, the **reasoning** behind the **switch** should be **fully recorded** to avoid the possibility of this being perceived as **churning**.

5.10 It is essential when considering a switch that the **tax issues** are considered.

Type of investment	Tax implications of a switch
Equities	Capital Gains Tax liability could be incurred
Cash/deposits	Not usually a liability unless currency dealing
Distributor fund	Capital Gains Tax liability could be incurred
Gilts/qualifying fixed interest	No CGT liability, but accrued income gains will be chargeable to income tax
Investment trusts	Capital Gains Tax liability could be incurred
Life assurance bond UK and offshore	No liability on switching
Non-distributor fund	Could give rise to offshore income gains where money is withdrawn
Unit trusts	Capital Gains Tax liability could be incurred

5.11 It is important that the **disruptive effects** on any **tax planning** that has already taken place, is taken into account, as well as the main reason for **switching**. There may be the possible advantage of being able to offset losses against existing gains, or to use up the CGT exemption limits where the investment being switched is of an appropriate size.

Defining appropriate benchmarks

5.12 This subject has been examined in some detail in a number of different chapters. It is important that when using **benchmarks** to **measure performance**, the appropriate ones are used. In addition to the various indices, which we have discussed at length together with their use as benchmarks, the *Financial Times* and other bodies publish a number of benchmarks looking at different types of tradeable asset, for example, the Halifax House Price Index.

Exam focus point

As part of the examination, you should be able to quote a suitable benchmark for each of the main types of asset. The benchmark should be appropriate for the asset being invested, from the perspective of the type of asset, market capitalisation, market sector, geographical area and yield. As an example, the FTSE-100 could be used for larger UK shares, the FTSE-All-share for a broader base of shares, the FTSE-Sector indices different sectors, the Dow Jones for US Blue Chips, the 15 Year gilt for long term gilts and so on.

Question 15.15

Which benchmark would be most appropriate for a portfolio of unlisted shares?

Exam focus point

In his report on the October 2002 exam, the examiner commented that few candidates could explain benchmarking.

6   RISK INDICATORS

6.1   The **understanding of risk** is fundamental to **good portfolio management**. It is an issue that has been widely researched and there are numerous ways of quantifying it, categorising it and measuring it which all have the objective of reducing it.

6.2   In this book we have examined the **definition of risk** in terms of the standard deviation of investment performance, and examined the use of **Beta factors** in portfolio construction. We have discussed methods of **reducing specific (non-systemic) risk** by diversifying the investments within an asset group. We have also looked at ways of **reducing market (systemic) risk** by using different types of asset within a portfolio.

6.3   We have examined the **risk assessment** that uses the standard deviation of performance to measure risk. It works on the basis that some of the shares will follow the normal distribution curve for risk. This assumes that, statistically, the chance (or risk) of the return of the investment being within one standard deviation of the mean is 68%. The risk of the return for that investment being within two standard deviations is 95%. However, this still means that 5% of the time it will be outside. Even this fact presumes that the assumptions made are correct, whereas recent research implies that it is not.

6.4   The **calculation of risk** is an exercise in statistics based on historic information. It makes no allowance for what is happening now or what could happen. As a result of this, measurement of risk is not always effective for an individual share. A portfolio of 1,000 different shares will not be affected if one or two go out of business and this is the reason why **diversification reduces risk**. However, there is no protection to the buyer of an individual share. Statistically, it may be very unlikely for shares in the **FTSE All-Share index** to go out of business, but when dealing with an individual share, it either will or it will not. The **Beta factor** calculated for the share may give an indication of the potential returns, but again this is based on historical information and research suggests they do not tend to be that accurate.

6.5   Most **risk models** look at the behaviour of investments over a long period of time. As a result, applying these measures to **short-term investment** is not valid and even applying them to the **longer-term investment** is equally dangerous, as the past gives no indication of the future. A company may perform consistently for ten years under the guidance of a particular management team. If that company is bought out, and the management team is changed, things could progress quite differently, but all of the risk statistics will still be referring to the time before.

6.6   All of the **risk models** used are based on the market continuing on as we know it, but there is nothing to say that **radical reforms** could not change the way the market operates and render existing risk models useless.

6.7   Effectively the **measurement** and **reduction of risk** will only ever work 'on average'. Any individual choosing not to follow the **line of average investment** is exposing themselves to different risks. Even those taking the **low-risk** approach, open themselves up to **inflation risk**. Ultimately 'no risk' may not be what it seems. We have, in this text, described deposit accounts as no risk, but this has also been quantified by mentioning the compensation scheme. An investor with £100,000 invested in BCCI will have got back £18,000, a loss of original capital of 82%. If they had placed their money in shares, they could have quadrupled it, or lost it all, depending on their choice.

6.8 The search to find the ultimate risk model will continue as long as people are investing. The most active area for research at the moment is in the area of **derivatives**. As we know, the returns are potentially spectacular. However, the search for a **perfect risk model** is driven by the fact that if the risk of investment in derivatives can be measured, it can be avoided. Traders can make more money by avoiding risk rather than better trading. As a result, a number of complex '**value at risk**' models have been developed. Examples are:

- Closed form
- Monte Carlo
- Historical
- Delta-Gamma

6.9 These range from **complex to ultra complex** and are not suitable for discussion here, but many consider that each methodology has strengths and weaknesses.

6.10 **Risk** is a fundamental factor of dealing in any investment market. Understanding and being able to control it is the key to successful investment. As things stand, all models for risk are flawed, but many can provide an edge, which will, over time, provide greater returns for the portfolio manager.

6.11 From the **customer's perspective**, the most important factor is to ensure that they understand the **levels of risk** involved with the investments made on their behalf. This means the adviser objectively informing them of the worst case scenario, the expected outcome and the potential upside of the risk they are taking. Providing the customer understands the risk, and is prepared to accept it, then his expectations have been managed whatever the outcome.

Chapter roundup

- The performance of funds is the key indicator in assessing the efficacy and efficiency of an investment manager.

- A key principle in performing such an assessment is the time value of money. For the exam you must learn the following formulae and other equations based on it.

    $$FV = PV(1 + i)^n$$
    eg $PV = FV/(1 + i)^n$

- Performance of a fund is normally measured by reference to a benchmark, such as an index. The index must be appropriate and relevant.

- When assessing a fund it is common to rank performance against competitors and identify the quartile placing.

- Returns may be calculated by means of the money-weighted or time weighted return basis. The latter is preferred since it is not distorted by the timing of cashflows into and out of the fund.

- Performance assessment should allow the investor to evaluate the asset allocation and stock selection skills of the manager.

- Modern evaluation techniques assess the risk-adjusted returns of a fund.

Quick quiz

1   What is the calculation to get the future value of a lump sum investment, given the original investment, the interest rate and the term?

2   What is the calculation to get the size of investment needed to produce a fixed sum of money at a fixed time in the future based on a known rate of interest?

3   From the UK perspective, what are the three main types of index?

4   List the three variations on the FTSE-350 index

5   What is the name of the new French index?

6   List the two main publishers of US share price indices.

7   What is a crossborder index?

8   Name an original source for data on life assurance, pension or unit trust funds.

9   In order for a fund manager to perform better than the median in a fund category, what must they do?

10   What is the formula for calculating Money Weighted Return?

11   Why is a Time Weighted Return more accurate than a Money Weighted Return?

12   What are the two main aspects of fund manager's performance for an investment portfolio?

13   How does cash flow within a fund affect the validity of a comparison of the performance of the manager?

14   What are the main considerations when selecting a fund manager?

15   To what extent will a 'house style' affect a portfolio?

16   Why is it that calculated values of risks are not always accurate in practice?

The answers to the questions in the Quick Quiz can be found at the end of this Study Text. Before checking your own answers against them, you should look back at this chapter and use the information in it to correct your answers.

Answers to Chapter Questions

15.1 $£10,000 \times (1 + 4.5\%)^5 = £12,461.81$.

15.2 $£6,000 / (1 + 4.5\%)^5 = £4,814.70$.

15.3   Half yearly - $(1 + (6\% / 2))^2 - 1 = 6.09\%$ per annum, Monthly - $(1 + (5.8\% / 12))^{12} - 1 = 5.96\%$ per annum. In this case, it is the account that pays half yearly.

15.4   This can be calculated using a business calculator.

FV = - 388,045.13 (negative because it will be a payment out)
I/YR = 7%
P/YR = 1
N = 20 years

We could solve for PV = £100,278.24.

This could be calculated using a scientific calculator using the following formula.

$PV = FV/(1 + i)^n$

Putting the above figures in $PV = 388,045.13/(1 + 0.7)^{20} = £100,278.24$

15.5 • It is a weighted index by market capitalisation.
   • It covers the top 100 UK companies by market capitalisation.
   • It is calculated every minute while the market is open.

15.6 The FTSE 100 is a weighted index, whereas the FT 30 is an un-weighted index calculated by way of a geometric mean, where each share counts equally regardless of market capitalisation.

15.7 The movement of the DAX also includes an allowance for the income produced by the underlying shares.

15.8 Both indices are price weighted.

15.9 It is in the second quartile.

15.10 Using $R = (V^1 - V^0 + I)/V^0$

   $R = (12,400 - 10,000 + 760) / 10,000$

   $R = 3,160/10,000 = 0.316$ or 31.6%

15.11 The size of the time slice determines the accuracy of a 'Time Weighted Return'.

15.12 The main problem is getting sufficient accurate information to allow a like for like comparison.

15.13 It may not be the best recommendation if one or more of the factors that were responsible for its good performance have changed.

15.14 They may incur additional charges for encashment and reinvestment and in some circumstances a charge for tax.

15.15 The FTSE AIM Index would probably be the best choice.

PRACTICE QUESTION 15

(a) A gilt pays a coupon of 6.5% every half year. What is the effective interest rate on this investment, assuming it was purchased at par? (2)

(b) Ronald Small is saving for his retirement in ten years time and wishes to know to what extent a lump sum of £10,000 will grow between now and then. Ronald is planning to invest for five years in equities, and the remaining five in gilts. Assuming equities grow at 9% on average and gilts at 6%, calculate the lump sum Ronald will have using a Time Weighted Return. (6)

(c) Explain the two main methods for calculating benchmark indices. Which gives the more accurate representation of the market? (4)

(d) List the main benchmark indices for the French, German, Japanese and New York stock exchanges. (6)

(e) Show the formula for Money Weighted Return. (4)

(f) Explain how a Time Weighted Return differs from a Money Weighted Return. (2)

(g) Patrick Newman has a portfolio of shares with an investment manager. The asset allocation on the portfolio is as follows.

UK equities	45%
Overseas equities	45%
Gilt	0%
Fixed interest	0%
Property	0%
Cash	10%
	100%

The benchmark for this type of portfolio would normally be as follows.

UK equities	50%
Overseas equities	40%
Gilt	5%
Fixed interest	0%
Property	0%
Cash	5%
	100%

The benchmark return for UK equities was 15%, for overseas equities 10%, for gilts 7.5% and for cash 5%. The portfolio manager produced an overall return on the portfolio of 13%.

(i)   Did he outperform the benchmark portfolio?   (6)

(ii) Did he outperform the benchmark for his own asset allocation?   (6)

Part H

The regulatory environment

Chapter 16

THE REGULATORY ENVIRONMENT

Chapter topic list		Syllabus reference
1	UK financial services regulation	10.1
2	Application of FSA Conduct of Business rules	10.1
3	Financial promotion	10.2
4	Accepting customers	10.2
5	Advising and selling	10.2
6	Product disclosure	10.2
7	Dealing and managing	10.2
8	Client assets	10.2
9	Periodic statements	10.2
10	Complaints and compensation	10.1
11	Money laundering and insider dealing	10.1
12	The Investment Services Directive	10.3

Introduction

In this chapter, we will examine the regulation of investment business affecting investment managers and advisers, including the ways it applies to their responsibilities and the expertise required to perform their role. We will go on to examine the Insurance Services Directive in relation to all aspects of investment business.

1 UK FINANCIAL SERVICES REGULATION

FSA as overall regulator

1.1 On 30 November 2001, the **Financial Services Authority (FSA)** became the single statutory regulator for the financial services industry under the **Financial Services and Markets Act 2000 (FSMA 2000)**, which replaced the Financial Services Act 1986. **Mortgage business** came under FSA regulation from 31 October 2004 and **general insurance business** came under FSA regulation from 14 January 2005.

From self-regulation to statutory regulation

1.2 Before the FSA 1986, a system of self-regulation prevailed in the UK financial sector. The FSA 1986 brought a new system of **'self-regulation within a statutory framework'**, with financial services firms authorised by Self-Regulatory Organisations (SROs).

1.3 When the Labour Party gained power in 1997, it wanted to make changes to the regulation of financial services. A series of financial scandals had added weight to the political impetus for change.

The FSA: single statutory regulator

1.4 The FSA as single statutory regulator:

(a) Brings together regulation of investment, insurance and banking
(b) Brings a move from contractual to statutory regulation
(c) Makes the UK the only major developed country with such a system

1.5 The FSA is not a government agency. It is a private company limited by guarantee, with HM Treasury as the guarantor. It is financed by the financial services industry. The Board of the FSA is appointed by the Treasury.

1.6 The FSA:

(a) Is the authorising body for those carrying on regulated activities
(b) Is the regulator of exchanges and clearing houses operating in the UK
(c) Approves companies for listing in the UK
(d) Is a rule making body
(e) Undertakes supervision
(f) Has powers of enforcement

1.7 With the implementation of FSMA 2000, the FSA became responsible for:

(a) Prudential supervision of all firms, which involves monitoring the adequacy of their management, financial resources and internal systems and controls, and

(b) Conduct of business regulations for those firms doing investment business. This involves overseeing firms' dealings with investors to ensure, for example, that information provided is clear and not misleading

1.8 **Regulatory structure post-N2**

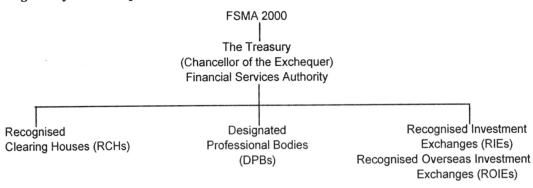

FSMA 2000

The Treasury
(Chancellor of the Exchequer)
Financial Services Authority

Recognised Clearing Houses (RCHs)

Designated Professional Bodies (DPBs)

Recognised Investment Exchanges (RIEs)
Recognised Overseas Investment Exchanges (ROIEs)

Question 16.1

What category of body has been replaced by the category 'Designated Professional Bodies'. Give two examples.

The FSA's statutory objectives

1.9 The FSA's **four statutory objectives**, as set out in FSMA 2000, are in substance as follows (with BPP comments in brackets).

(a) To **maintain confidence** in the UK financial system. (The FSA is concerned with the **stability of firms** and the **stability of markets**.)

(b) To promote **public understanding** of the financial system, including: awareness of the benefits and risks associated with different kinds of investment or other financial dealing, and providing appropriate **information and advice**. (The emphasis is on consumers protecting themselves.)

(c) To secure the appropriate level of **protection for consumers**, bearing in mind:

(i) The different levels of risk that come with different kinds of investment or other transaction

(ii) The differing experience and expertise of consumers

(iii) Consumers' needs for accurate advice and information, and

(iv) The principle that consumers should take responsibility for their decisions. (This marks a move towards the principle of caveat emptor - 'let the buyer beware'.)

(d) To continue to **reduce financial crime** (by reducing the possibility for a regulated person to carry on a business whose purpose is connected with financial crime).

The FSA's risk-based approach to regulation

1.10 The FSA seeks to adopt a **'risk-based' approach** to regulation for the future. This means that it will focus its attention on those institutions and activities that are likely to pose the greatest risk to consumers and markets. The approach is intended to recognise the responsibilities of consumers themselves and of firms' management. The FSA considers it both **impossible and undesirable to remove all risk and failure** from the financial system.

FSA enforcement powers

1.11 The FSA *Enforcement Manual* details the FSA's powers of:

(a) **Investigation.** If you are the subject of an investigation, you do not have a **right to silence**. However, because of human rights legislation, your answers are not admissible in human rights or market abuse proceedings.

(b) **Varying permission** to carry out regulated activities.

(c) **Redress for consumers.** The FSA can require firms to compensate consumers.

(d) **Discipline,** through fines, warnings or censure.

(e) Specific powers in relation to **market misconduct.** In relation to **market abuse**, the FSA can act against anyone.

1.12 The FSA adopts a **'top-down'** approach to enforcement. It will first look to **senior management** before going down the organisation to the person who has apparently acted wrongly.

FSA PRINCIPLES FOR BUSINESS

1:	**Integrity**	A firm must conduct its business with integrity.
2:	**Skill, care and diligence**	A firm must conduct its business with due skill, care and diligence.
3:	**Management and control**	A firm must take reasonable care to organise and control its affairs responsibly and effectively, with adequate risk management systems.
4:	**Financial prudence**	A firm must maintain adequate financial resources.
5:	**Market conduct**	A firm must observe proper standards of market conduct.
6:	**Customers' interests**	A firm must pay due regard to the interests of its customers and treat them fairly.
7:	**Communications with clients**	A firm must pay due regard to the information needs of its clients, and communicate information to them in a way which is clear, fair and not misleading.
8:	**Conflicts of interest**	A firm must manage conflict of interest fairly, both between itself and its customers and between a customer and another client.
9:	**Customers: relationships of trust**	A firm must take reasonable care to ensure the suitability of its advice and discretionary decisions for any customer who is entitled to rely upon its judgment.
10:	**Clients' assets**	A firm must arrange adequate protection for clients' assets when it is responsible for them.
11:	**Relations with regulators**	A firm must deal with its regulators in an open and cooperative way, and must disclose to the FSA appropriately anything relating to the firm of which the FSA would reasonably expect notice.

FSA Principles for Business

1.13 The 11 **Principles for Business** of the FSA are very important for advisers in retail financial services. In 2004 and 2005, the FSA has been putting special emphasis on **treating customers fairly,** which is covered by Principle 6.

Market abuse

1.14 The new regulatory regime under FSMA 2000 brought with it the new offence of **market abuse,** complementing legislation covering insider dealing and market manipulation. The FSA's **Code of Market Conduct** applies to any person dealing in certain investments on recognised exchanges and does not require proof of intent to abuse a market.

1.15 Section 123 of FSMA 2000 gives statutory powers to the FSA to impose unlimited fines for the offence of **market abuse. Section 165** gives the FSA powers to require information, and requires anyone to cooperate with investigations in to market abuse. As a civil offence, market abuse will be assessed on **a balance of probabilities.** The criminal law requires proof of guilt and, in the past, criminal convictions for insider dealing and financial fraud have been few.

1.16 **Market abuse** could consist of:

(a) Knowingly buying shares in a takeover target before a general disclosure of the proposed takeover (an example of **insider dealing**, which we discuss later in this Chapter)

(b) Market distortion: dealing on an exchange just prior to the exchange closing with the purpose of positioning the share price at a distorted level in order to avoid having to pay out on a derivatives transaction

(c) Posting an inaccurate story on an internet bulletin board in order to give a false or misleading impression

Section 150, FSMA 2000

1.17 **Section 150** of FSMA 2000 gives a **right of action by a private person** (an individual not carrying an investment business, or a business not acting in the course of business of any kind) to sue for breaches of **Conduct of Business (COB) rules.** Unlike the case of suing for negligence, or for breach of contract, to establish that there is a claim it is only necessary to show that there has been a **rule breach** and a **loss.**

1.18 **Any person** (not just private persons) has a right of action under Section 150 FSMA 2000 in relation to:

(a) COB rules prohibiting an authorised person from seeking to exclude or restrict any duty or liability

(b) COB rules seeking to ensure that investment transactions are not based on unpublished price-sensitive information

---

Question 16.2

A journalist working for an investment magazine discovers that a financial services firm on which he is writing an article is in breach of the FSA's Conduct of Business rules. Can the journalist bring an action under Section 150 FSMA 2000?

FSA Handbook

1.19 The **FSA Handbook** (available online at **www.fsa.gov.uk**) applies to all regulated firms. The Handbook contains both **high level requirements** applicable to all firms and **specialist sourcebooks** for particular types of firms.

Authorisation of firms and approval of individuals

1.20 The regulatory regime is mainly directed at **firms**. Firms carrying on regulated activities are required to have **authorisation** to do so. However, firms' ability to maintain appropriate standards depends on the quality of the individuals it has performing key roles. Under FSMA 2000, the FSA is responsible for a single regime for **approval** of individuals carrying out **controlled functions** for **authorised firms**. As well as covering senior management, the **approved persons regime** importantly covers those giving **investment advice**. First, we look at the authorisation process for firms before going on to look at the approval of individuals.

Regulated activities under FSMA 2000

1.21 Section 19 of FSMA 2000 provides that a person (firm) must not carry on a **regulated activity** in the UK unless either:

(a) **Authorised**, or

(b) **Exempt**

Potential consequences of breaching this provision are:

(a) Criminal charges

(b) Contracts becoming voidable

(c) Claims for damages

1.22 In deciding whether **authorisation** is required, the following need to be considered:

Regulated activities

↓

Exceptions

↓

Exemptions

1.23 The scope of **regulated activities** is determined by the Regulated Activities Order and covers:

(a) Dealing in investments

(b) Arranging deals in investments

(c) Managing investments

(d) Advising on investments

(e) Establishing or operating a collective investment scheme

(f) Establishing or operating a stakeholder pension scheme (SHP)

(g) Safekeeping of and administering investments

(h) Lloyds insurance business

(i) Carrying out contracts of insurance

(j) Accepting deposits

(k) Regulated residential mortgages (excluding buy-to-let mortgages)

1.24 **Investments** covered by regulated activities are also listed in the Order:

(a) Deposits

(b) Contracts of insurance

(c) Shares

(d) Government and local authority securities

(e) Instruments giving title to investments

(f) Units in collective investment schemes

(g) Options, futures and contacts for differences

(h) Lloyds syndicate capacity and membership of syndicates

Exceptions

1.25 By exception, the following are not regulated activities:

(a) **Dealings as principal** - ie, dealing in investments for yourself

(b) **Newspapers and the media** - however, 'tipsheets', whose primary purpose is to tip shares, are not an exception

(c)   Acting as an **unremunerated trustee**

(d)   **Employee share schemes**

(e)   **Certain overseas persons**, for business solicited in the UK

Exempt persons

1.26   The **Exempt Persons Order** exempts from authorisation:

(a)   **Appointed representatives**, such as self-employed persons selling insurance under a contract for services with the product provider to whom they are tied, where the provider firm takes full responsibility

(b)   Certain institutions, including **central** and **National Savings banks**, and **local government authorities**

(c)   Certain **members of professions**, such as lawyers, accountants and actuaries. Formerly, Recognised Professional Bodies (RPBs) such as the professional accountancy institutes and the Law Society provided authorisation. The RPBs became 'Designated Professional Bodies' (DPBs) at N2. Member firms of these bodies require **FSA authorisation** if they recommend the purchase of specific investments, such as pensions or listed company shares to clients, approve financial promotions or carry out corporate finance business. If their activities are **'non-mainstream' investment** business, only assisting clients in making investment decisions as part of other professional services, they are exempt from FSA authorisation but must obtain a **licence** from the DPB, under which they are subject to a light form of regulation.

(d)   **Members of Lloyd's** (The Society of Lloyd's, in respect of insurance business).

Permissions

1.27   Firms must apply to the FSA for **permission** to carry out any regulated activities as set out in the legislation. A bank, for example, will need to apply for permission to accept deposits. Limitations or requirements may be imposed by the FSA, for example over whether it may deal with private customers, or over the level of financial resources it must have. Firms will each have one permission for all their regulated activities. Authorisation by the FSA gives permission (often called a **Part IV permission**, after the relevant Part of FSMA 2000) to carry on one or more regulated activity.

Authorisation routes

1.28   **Routes to authorisation** for a firm are:

(a)   Direct, or
(b)   'Passporting'

Passporting

1.29   The process of **passporting** allows European firms to operate branches and to sell across borders throughout the European Economic Area (EEA) without the need for licensing in each separate jurisdiction. The **EEA** comprises the countries of the **European Union** plus **Norway, Iceland** and **Liechtenstein**. See the section later in this chapter on the European **Investment Services Directive (ISD)**.

BPP
PROFESSIONAL EDUCATION

1.30 For passported activities, responsibilities are divided between home State and host State as follows.

(a) **Home State responsibilities**

- Authorisation
- Capital adequacy
- Fitness and prosperity
- Conduct of Business in the home state
- Client assets

(b) **Host State responsibilities**

- Conduct of Business in the host state

Question 16.3

A bank X based in France and authorised by French authorities offers investment products to UK citizens through a website. A UK-based firm Y operates branches in Germany through which it offers non-protection life policies.

To which does 'passporting' apply?

Approved persons regime

1.31 **Individuals** who carry out **controlled functions** must have FSA approval to do so, and are subject to **Statements of Principles for approved persons** and a **Code of Conduct**.

1.32 **Controlled functions** include:

(a) Governing body functions (eg directors)

(b) Required functions (eg Money Laundering Reporting Officer)

(c) Systems and controls (eg senior personnel in internal audit)

(d) Significant management functions (eg heads of business units in larger firms)

(e) Customer functions including:

(i) Advisory functions

(ii) Customer trading and investment management functions

1.33 The new regime places significant emphasis on **senior management responsibilities,** and it can be expected that the new regulator will look to senior management in holding firms accountable for failures.

1.34 Importantly, **customer functions** include the activities of **most personnel advising customers** under the category of **advisory functions**.

1.35 Advisory functions include:

(a) Those who provide **investment advice** (or **financial advice,** as it is often known), including those not yet assessed as competent

(b) Advice to clients relating to corporate finance business

(c) Advice on pensions transfers and pension opt-outs

(d) Advice to underwriting members of Lloyd's

Question 16.4

Give at least two examples of personnel in the financial services industry who are not subject to the approved persons regime.

Statements of Principle for approved persons

1.36 Failure to comply with the **Statements of Principle for approved persons** constitutes an act of misconduct which may result in disciplinary action, but only where there is **personal culpability**.

1.37 Principles 1 to 4 apply to all approved persons. Principles 5 to 7 apply to senior management ('significant influence' functions) only. The seven Principles are set out below.

STATEMENTS OF PRINCIPLE FOR APPROVED PERSONS

Statement of Principle 1

An approved person must act with integrity in carrying out his controlled function.

Statement of Principle 2

An approved person must act with due skill, care and diligence in carrying out his controlled function.

Statement of Principle 3

An approved person must observe proper standards of market conduct in carrying out his controlled function.

Statement of Principle 4

An approved person must deal with the FSA and with other regulators in an open and cooperative way and must disclose appropriately any information of which the FSA would reasonably expect notice.

> 5 to 7 apply to senior management only

Statement of Principle 5

An approved person performing a significant influence function must take reasonable steps to ensure that the business of the firm for which he is responsible in his controlled function is organised so that it can be controlled effectively.

Statement of Principle 6

An approved person performing a significant influence function must exercise due skill, care and diligence in managing the business of the firm for which he is responsible in his controlled function.

Statement of Principle 7

An approved person performing a significant influence function must take reasonable steps to ensure that the business of the firm for which he is responsible in his controlled function complies with the relevant requirements and standards of the regulatory system.

1.38 The FSA's **Code of Conduct** sets out examples of conduct which is seen by the FSA as contravening the **Principles for approved persons**. Some of the most important examples for the first four Principles are set out below.

Principle	Examples of non-compliance
1	Misleading or attempting to mislead a customer, the firm or the FSA, eg falsification of documents, misleading customer about risks of an investment.
2	Failing to give a customer, the firm, its auditor or its actuary information which the person knew or should have known they should have provided, eg failing to disclose charges or surrender penalties.
3	Market abuse (see Paragraph 1.14 to 1.16).
4	Failure to report relevant matters internally, where internal reporting procedures exist in the firm.

Disciplinary sanctions

1.39 For non-compliance with any of the Principles, the FSA may:

(a) Issue a public statement of misconduct ('naming and shaming')

(b) Impose a fine

(c) Withdraw approved person status, if fitness and properness are concerned, and thus prevent the person from carrying out controlled functions. The process is subject to a warning and decision notice procedure with a right of referral to the Financial Services and Markets Tribunal by the individual.

Prohibition orders against individuals

1.40 Under Sections 56 to 58 FSMA 2000, the FSA can prohibit an **individual** who is not fit and proper from the whole industry or part of it.

(a) A prohibition order under s56 FSMA 2000 leads to **criminal sanctions**

(b) Authorised firms must take reasonable care to avoid employing **prohibited persons**. If they **fail** to do so, a **private person** who suffers loss has a right of action against the firm.

2 APPLICATION OF FSA CONDUCT OF BUSINESS RULES

Purpose of the Conduct of Business rules

2.1 The **Conduct of Business Sourcebook (COB)** forms part of the **FSA Handbook**. The full Handbook can be found on the FSA website at www.fsa.gov.uk. The COB rules deal with the protection of the customer, and differentiate between types of customers, with the purpose of enabling greater protection to be given to the most vulnerable.

Application of the rules

2.2 COB applies to **all authorised firms**. An **exception** is that COB does not apply generally to **authorised professional firms** (such as firms of solicitors, accountants and actuaries) in respect of their **non-mainstream regulated activities**.

2.3 COB applies to firms in respect of **regulated activities**, except where specifically excluded. This covers **designated investment business** generally.

2.4 Designated investment business includes:

- **Advising on investments**
- **Dealing in investments**

2.5 The COB rules do not apply to **deposits,** such as bank deposit accounts. Such accounts are covered by the banks' own voluntary codes. If these codes are seen to fail in the future, FSA rules could be extended to cover such deposits.

2.6 COB applies to activities carried out **in the UK** and also covers **business brought into the UK,** for a client in the UK.

Electronic media

2.7 Where the COB rules require a communication, notice or agreement to be given **in writing** or where they refer to a **document,** a firm can comply with the rule using **electronic media.**

Clear and fair communication

2.8 'When a firm communicates information to a customer, the firm must take reasonable steps to communicate in a way which is clear, fair and not misleading.' (COB 2.13)

Question 16.5

Which FSA principle does the above rule restate?

2.9 This important rule restates one of the FSA Principles (Principle 7). Restating the Principle in COB enables a private customer to bring an action for damages under **FSMA 2000 Section 150** to recover a loss resulting from a **breach of the rule** by a firm.

Inducements and commission rules

2.10 The purpose of the rules on **inducements** is to ensure that firms' business arrangements do not conflict with its **duty to customers,** whom it must treat **fairly.**

2.11 A firm should take reasonable steps to ensure that inducements are not offered, given, solicited or accepted by the firm itself, or by anyone acting on the firm's behalf, if this is likely to inflict with the firm's duty to customers.

2.12 Many firms will have explicit **policies** covering gifts which might be seen as inducements in certain circumstances. Giving or receiving certain **indirect benefits** such as gifts, hospitality and promotional competition prizes, is permitted.

KEY TERM

A **packaged product** is:

(a) A life policy (other than a pure protection policy)
(b) A unit in a regulated collective investment scheme
(c) An interest in an investment trust savings scheme, or
(d) A stakeholder pension scheme

whether or not (in the case of (a), (b) or (c)) held within a PEP or an ISA.

Packaged products and 'soft commission'

2.13 Firms should not enter into the following types of **commission arrangements** for **packaged products** where commission must be disclosed.

(a) Commission on several transactions that is more than a single multiple of commission payable on a single transaction (**'volume overrides'**)

(b) Commission in excess of that disclosed to the customer, unless due to higher contributions

(c) Arrangements to indemnify payment of commission where the recipient benefits if the commission becomes repayable

(d) Arrangements to pay commission other than to the seller firm, unless:

(i) The firm has passed on the rights to commission, or

(ii) Another firm has given advice to the customer, or

(iii) The firm is a provider firm involved in a direct offer financial promotion involving an independent intermediary, who receives the commission

> **KEY TERM**
>
> A **soft commission agreement** is an agreement which permits a firm to receive certain goods or services from another person in return for transacting designated investment business with or through that other person.

Conflicts of interest

2.14 **Chinese walls** are internal arrangements - for example, physical arrangements or organised structures - restricting the movement of information within a firm. For example, in a securities firm the corporate finance department might be located on a different floor from the sales department.

2.15 Chinese walls are a legitimate way for a firm to **manage conflicts of interest**. The arrangements must be **effective** and they must be **monitored**.

Exclusion of liability

2.16 The FSA's Principle 6 *Customers' interests* requires a firm to pay due regard to the interest of customers and to treat them fairly.

2.17 A firm may not exclude the **duties it owes** or the **liabilities** it has to customers **under FSMA 2000** or the **regulatory system**. This means that customers cannot sign away their rights under the COB rules.

3 FINANCIAL PROMOTION

3.1 **Financial promotion** is a concept designed to encompass more fully a wider range of media, including the internet, than the old FSA 1986 regime, which focused on **investment advertisements** and **unsolicited calls**. The newer FSMA 2000 rules also cover **solicited calls**.

3.2 The rules governing financial promotion:

(a) Are directed at **regulated activities,** although they only affect deposits and general insurance to some extent

(b) Are **media-neutral,** ie applying to all media of communication, including the internet

> **KEY TERM**
>
> **Financial promotion:** an invitation or inducement to engage in investment activity communicated in the course of business. (FSMA 2000, s21(1))

3.3 **Financial promotions** may be communicated in:

(a) Product brochures
(b) General advertising (eg newspapers, television, websites)
(c) Mailshots (including by fax or email)
(d) Telemarketing, eg from call centres
(e) Written correspondence, telephone calls and face to face discussions with advisers
(f) Sales aids
(g) Presentations
(h) Tip sheets (tipping shares or investments)
(i) Other publications containing non-personal recommendations

3.4 Section 21 of FSMA 2000 contains a **general prohibition on financial promotion,** except where they are issued or approved by an **authorised person.**

Exemptions

3.5 Exemptions from the financial promotion and other COB rules cover a number of types of promotions issued by an unauthorised person, including **generic promotions** (eg for **Investment Trusts** generally), one-off communications, 'sophisticated investors' and high net worth individuals in respect of unlisted securities.

3.6 Regulated firms must ensure that communications are **clear, fair and not misleading** even for the following, which are **exempt** from the detailed promotion rules:

(a) Financial promotions to market counterparties (such as another firm, or a government body) and intermediate (ie non-private) customers

(b) One-off non-real time or solicited real-time communications

(c) Short form advertisements giving brief facts about a firm or product

(d) Personal quotations or illustrations

(e) A takeover promotion

3.7 COB distinguishes the following.

(a) A **real time financial promotion** is communicated in an interactive dialogue.

Examples: personal visit, telephone call.

(b) A non-**real time financial promotion** is non-interactive. The recipient of the promotion is not required to respond to it immediately.

Examples: newspapers, television.

3.8 **Non-real time financial promotions** must be **checked and approved** by the firm before they are used. Details must be given of:

   (a) The **firm**
   (b) An **address,** or a **contact point** from which the address can be obtained

Specific non-real time promotions

3.9 A specific non-real time promotion is one which promotes a particular investment or service, and must include details of:

   (a) The **nature of the investment or service**
   (b) The **commitment** required
   (c) The **risks** involved
   (d) The **service provider** (if not the firm approving the promotion)

3.10 If **past performance** is detailed:

   (a) Suitable text for the target audience must be shown, and
   (b) Attention must be drawn to the fact that past performance will not necessarily be repeated
   (c) A relevant and sufficient period must be covered
   (d) Past data should not suggest that it constitutes a **projection**

3.11 For **packaged products:**

   (a) The past performance data must cover the previous **five years,** or the whole period if the product has been offered for less than this.

   (b) Comparative performance data should be stated:

      (i) On an offer to bid basis, or

      (ii) On an offer to offer, or offer to bid basis for comparisons with an index or movements in prices of units, or

      (iii) A single pricing basis, with allowance for charges

---

Question 16.6

Identify which of the following could communicate a financial promotion, and if so identify each as 'real time' or 'non-real time'.

   (1) Solicited phone call
   (2) Unsolicited telephone call
   (3) Internet 'chat' facility
   (4) A website showing an email address for contact

Real-time financial promotions

3.12 The firm must try to ensure that an individual making a real-time financial promotion on the firm's behalf:

   (a) Does not make **untrue** claims

   (b) Identifies himself, the firm and the purpose of the financial promotion

   (c) If the time and form of communication were not agreed:

      (i) Checks that the recipient wishes to proceed (stopping, if not)

   (ii) Respects the recipient's wishes to end communication

 (d) Provides a contact point to a client with an appointment

 (e) Does not communicate at unsocial hours (before 9.00am or after 9.00pm or all day Sunday) unless agreed

 (f) Does not use an unlisted telephone number, unless agreed

Direct offer financial promotions

> **KEY TERM**
>
> A **direct offer financial promotion** is a non-real-time financial promotion offering or inviting someone to enter into an agreement which specifies the manner of response or includes a form in which any response is to be made (for example by providing a tear-off slip).

3.13 A direct offer financial promotion must contain:

 (a) Sufficient information to enable an informed assessment of the investment or service

 (b) A statement that the firm is FSA-authorised

 (c) A statement that anyone with doubts about suitability of the product should seek advice from the firm, or from an independent financial adviser if the firm does not offer advice

 (d) The full name of the person offering the investment or service

 (e) Details of charges or expenses

 (f) Commission or remuneration to third parties

Unsolicited real-time financial promotions

3.14 These are restrictions on uninvited calls, visits or interactive dialogue. Financial promotion by such methods is only permissible:

 (a) For recipients with an established existing customer relationship with the firm, where such unsolicited promotions are envisaged by the recipient

 (b) For investments not involving high volatility funds

 (c) In cases where the general exemptions from financial promotions by regulated firms apply (see Paragraph 3.5 above)

Financial promotions and the internet

3.15 As already mentioned, the FSA adopts a media-neutral approach, to cover all media whether electronic or not, in its rules. Therefore, internet communications and moving images are governed by similar provisions to print-based media.

3.16 Specific issues affecting internet **'e-commerce'** communications especially are as follows.

 (a) Access to **key features** and **terms and conditions** is important. This could be provided by a clear hypertext link, not hidden in the body of the text. Perhaps a better approach would be to ensure that applicants must scroll through the relevant information.

    (b) Care must be taken in promoting **unregulated CISs,** possibly by use of passwords to limit access to those to whom they may be promoted.

    (c) Firms are encouraged to include a hyperlink to the **FSA's website** www.fsa.gov.uk, which includes pages of specific relevance to customers.

4   ACCEPTING CUSTOMERS

4.1   The level of **regulatory protection** provided is differentiated by type of customer, based partly on their **size** and **knowledge.** Clients are classified as:

    (a) **Market counterparties** (eg governments, other firms)
    (b) **Intermediate customers** (eg large businesses, experts)
    (c) **Private customers** (eg individuals, small businesses)

4.2   There are provisions for:

    (a) **Opting up** to a status offering a lower level of protection (eg private customer to intermediate customer), or

    (b) **Opting down** to a status offering a higher level of protection (eg market counterparty to intermediate customer)

4.3   Think of **opting up** as climbing a ladder. The higher you climb, the more risk you take on. **Opting down** is like descending the ladder. For what reasons might 'opting up' be chosen?

    (a) **Price.** Reduced compliance costs may reduce the level of commission.

    (b) **Prestige or kudos.** For example, a treasury department of a large company with considerable trading expertise might wish to be treated as a market counterparty.

4.4   **Market counterparties** include:

    (a) Governments
    (b) Central banks
    (c) Supranational bodies (eg IMF, World Bank)
    (d) State investment bodies
    (e) **Another firm,** or overseas financial services firm
    (f) An associate of the firm (with consent), but not if an occupational pension scheme
    (g) A large intermediate customer classified as a market counterparty

4.5   **Intermediate customers** include:

    (a) Local or public authorities
    (b) Large companies listed on a stock exchange
    (c) Body corporates or partnerships with share capital or net assets of at least £5 million
    (d) Trusts with assets of at least £10 million
    (e) **Another firm acting for an underlying customer,** if it is so agreed
    (f) Unregulated collective investment schemes
    (g) **Expert private customers** re-classified as intermediate customers

4.6   An **expert private customer** is:

    (a) An experienced knowledgeable private customer

    (b) Who, having received a warning

(c) Consents to treatment **as an intermediate customer** after having been given sufficient time to consider

4.7 The category of **private customer** covers clients who are not market counterparties or intermediate customers. This category includes **individuals** who are not firms.

4.8 **A firm may treat any client** (other than a firm), who would otherwise be a market counterparty or an intermediate customer, **as a private customer**. The client should then be notified that he may not have rights under ombudsman or compensation schemes.

Question 16.7

Why do you think a firm (such as a bank) might choose to classify all its customers as private customers?

Differentiation of customer by service level

4.9 Different protections are given to customers depending on the **level of service (discretionary, advisory** or **execution only,** in descending order of protection level) they receive as well as their classification as **private** or **intermediate.**

Agents

4.10 An **agent** should be treated as **principal**:

(a) If it is another firm

(b) If it is not a firm, as long as the arrangement is not designed to avoid duties to the underlying client

4.11 *Example.* An IFA ('C1') has a private customer ('C2') and, acting as agent for C2, does business with a broker firm 'F'. Then, the IFA (C1) is a client of F.

4.12 The above provision will not apply if the firm ('F') has agreed with C1 in writing to treat C2 as its client.

Terms of business and customer agreement

4.13 Note that:

- Terms of business are one-way (unsigned)
- A customer agreement is two-way (signed)

4.14 Where a private customer has made an **oral offer** to enter into an **ISA** or **stakeholder pension** agreement, a firm must provide a private customer with its terms of business **within five business days** of the offer. In other cases, the firm must provide a **private customer** with its **terms of business before** conducting designated investment business with the customer.

4.15 Terms of business must be provided to an **intermediate customer** within '**a reasonable period**'.

4.16 The **terms of business** must take the form of a **client agreement** for a UK-resident private customer in the case of:

(a) Discretionary investment management

(b) Contingent liability investment

(c) Stock lending

(d) Underwriting

4.17 The terms of business and client agreement requirements do not generally apply to:

(a) **Execution only** transactions (where no advice is given)

(b) Transactions resulting from **direct offer financial promotions**

(c) **Life policies**

4.18 The **terms of business** may comprise **more than one document.**

4.19 The firm must give **ten business days'** notice to the customer before conducting business on **amended terms.**

4.20 **Contents of terms of business**

The **terms of business** (including a **client agreement**) should include provisions about:

(a) **Commencement** of terms of business

(b) The fact that the firm is **regulated or authorised by the FSA**

(c) Customer's **investment objectives**

(d) Any **restrictions** of the investments or markets the customer is seeking to use

(e) **Services** the firm will provide

(f) **Payment** arrangement for the firm's services

(g) For **packaged products** with **private customers**, disclosure of **polarisation status** (see Section 5 below)

(h) Where the firm acts as an **investment manager**

   (i) The arrangement for giving and acknowledging instructions
   (ii) The initial value and composition of the managed portfolio
   (iii) The period of account for periodic portfolio statements

(i) **Accounting arrangements**

(j) The **right to withdraw,** in the case of non-packaged ISAs or PEPs

(k) Whether the firm may communicate **unsolicited real time financial promotions**

(l) Whether the firm may **act as principal**

(m) How **fair treatment** will be ensured if there is **material interest** or **conflict of interest**

(n) If the firm acts as a **broker fund adviser** for a private customer, a statement explaining the firm's dual role as adviser to the **customer** and adviser to the **life office or operator**

(o) **Soft commission agreements**

(p) **Risk warnings** where relevant, eg for warrants or derivatives

(q) Any services relating to **unregulated collective investment schemes**

(r) Rights to realise a **private customer's assets,** if applicable

(s) **Complaints** arrangements, including a statement that the customer may subsequently complain to the **Financial Services Ombudsman**

(t) **Compensation scheme** arrangement

(u) Arrangements for **termination** of terms of business, stating that:

    (i) Termination is without prejudice to transactions already initiated, if this is the case

    (ii) The customer may terminate by written notice, and when this takes effect

    (iii) The form has termination rights, if so, and what the minimum notice period is

(v) Arrangements for waiving the **best execution** rule, if applicable

Additional terms of business for discretionary management

4.21 In respect of discretionary management, terms of business (including a **client agreement**) should also include some provision about:

(a) The extent of the discretion to be exercised by the firm, including any restrictions on:

    (i) The value of any one investment, and

    (ii) The proportion of the portfolio which any one investment or any particular kind of investment may constitute

(b) The frequency of any **periodic statements** whether those statements will include some measure of performance, and if so, the basis of measurement

(c) The basis on which assets comprised in the portfolio are to be **valued**

(d) The circumstances in which the firm may supplement the funds in the portfolio, including borrowing on his behalf and details of limits to this

(e) If the firm may commit the customer to any obligation to underwrite or sub-underwrite any issue or offer for sale of securities with details of any relevant restrictions or limits

Record keeping

4.22 The general rule is that firms must keep records for the following periods:

(a) Indefinitely for pension transfers, pension opt-outs and FSAVCs

(b) Six years, for life policies and pension contracts

(c) Three years in other cases

5 ADVISING AND SELLING

Depolarisation

5.1 **Polarisation** rules have dictated, in the past, that a retail financial adviser dealing with the general public must either give advice on **a single product provider's** products, or they must be **independent financial advisers**, advising on the different products available across the **whole market**.

5.2 In **Policy Statement 04/27** released in November 2004, the Financial Services Authority announced its new rules which reform polarisation. These rules abolish polarisation and introduce new rules designed to improve disclosure to consumers.

5.3 The new rules took effect on **1 December 2004**. There is a six-month transition period up to 31 May 2005, during which time firms may either continue to be regulated under the present rules or notify the FSA that they wish to adopt the new rules. If they choose the new rules, they must comply immediately, which will include providing customers with new-style **key facts documents** (see below). From 1 June 2005, all firms must follow the new rules and polarisation will be complete. The introduction of Keyfacts documentation for advice on **packaged products** follows the introduction of similar disclosures for **mortgages** on 31 October 2004 and for **general insurance** on 14 January 2005.

5.4   Firms wishing to be regarded as independent advisers must offer advice encompassing the whole market or a whole market sector. Clients must be given the option to pay by **fee**. If charging only by fee, the adviser can only retain minimal amounts of annual **trail commission**.

5.5   **Distributors** or '**multi-ties**' are able to emerge under the new regime, forming a new 'middle ground'. These are firms entering into agreements with two or more providers to sell the products offered or adopted by them. **Appointed representatives** will continue to have a **single principal**.

'Key facts' documents: the menu and IDD

5.6   The following new 'key facts' documents are required (since 14 January 2005):

- A **menu**, and
- An **Initial Disclosure Document**

5.7   When a firm's representative makes initial contact with a private customer with the intention of advising on packaged products, the representative must give the consumer an information document, known colloquially as a **menu. Packaged products**, remember, comprise life policies, personal pensions and collective investments. The menu must also be given to a customer whenever the customer requests it.

5.8   The **menu** includes:

- A section on the FSA, and the purpose of the required menu
- A section in which the firm gives details of 'Our services'
- The payment options offered
- The maximum commission the firm is likely to receive for a transaction
- An indication of the market average commission

5.9   The **market average (MA)** is designed to give consumers a benchmark for what might be a competitive level of commission.

5.10   An adviser should not start charging until after the customer has been given a menu and has agreed the **payment option** for the client.

5.11   It is acceptable for a firm to have different 'menus', and firms are free to offer different charging structures to different groups of clients.

5.12   The **Initial Disclosure Document (IDD)** must also be given on first making contact with a private customer. The **IDD** must be separate from the menu and:

- States that the firm is regulated by the Financial Services Authority

- States whether advice is given only for a single provider's products, for a limited number of providers, or for the whole market

- Invites clients to ask for a list of products on which advice is offered

- Indicates whether a product provider has a shareholding of 10% or more in the advising firm

- Tells customers what to do if they have a complaint

- Gives detail of compensation arrangements through the Financial Services Compensation Scheme

5.13 A firm may want to show its remaining **terms of business** on the back of the IDD.

5.14 Both the menu and IDD must carry the **keyfacts logo** as prescribed by the FSA, and this logo must not be used where its use is not mandated under FSA rules. The FSA provides downloadable templates on its web site which firms can use for a **menu** and both a **retail investment IDD** and the **combined IDD (CIDD)**.

5.15 With the new initial disclosure requirements introduced on 14 January 2005, firms must also provide the client with a **statement of his demands and needs** (except where these points are otherwise covered, in the **suitability letter**).

The **statement of demands and needs**:

- Should state simply and clearly why the personal recommendation is viewed as suitable, having regard to the client's demands and needs

- Is presented in a way which is for the firm to decide (Simplicity and plain language, and concise and clear messages, are recommended.)

Know your customer

5.16 Someone giving advice to a private customer (or acting as an investment manager for a private customer) must:

(a) Obtain relevant personal and financial information before acting: this process is often known as **'fact-finding'**

(b) **Warn** of adverse consequences, if the customer refuses to provide the necessary information

(c) Conduct regular **reviews**, depending upon the client's particular stage of life and circumstances

5.17 **Records** of the fact-find must be kept for the following periods after the information is obtained:

(a) Indefinitely for pension transfers, pension opt-outs and FSAVCs
(b) Six years for life policies and pension contracts
(c) Three years in other cases

5.18 A **firm** acting as a **discretionary investment manager** for a **private customer** should also ensure that before acting in the exercise of discretion it has sufficient information about its **private customer** to enable it to act in a suitable way for that **private customer.**

Suitability

5.19 A firm must take reasonable steps to ensure that it does not make a **personal recommendation** to a private customer to buy or sell a designated investment unless the recommendation or transaction is **suitable** for the customer having regard to information disclosed by him and other facts of which the firm is or ought reasonably to be aware.

5.20 A firm which acts as an **investment manager** for a **private customer** must take reasonable steps to ensure that the **private customer's** portfolio or account remains suitable, in the light of the facts disclosed by the customer and other relevant facts about the customer.

5.21 Where, with the agreement of the customer, a firm has pooled his funds with those of others with a view to taking common **discretionary management** decisions, the firm must take reasonable steps to ensure that a discretionary transaction is suitable for the fund, having regard to the stated investment objectives of the fund.

5.22 A **provider firm** making a personal recommendation to a private customer on a **packaged product** must seek to ensure that the product is the most suitable available from the products of the marketing group or the products adopted by the firm.

5.23 An **independent intermediary:**

(a) Must **not** recommend a generally available product if he is aware of a more appropriate alternative, and

(b) Must **not** recommend the product of an associated person, such as his own firm's products, if he ought reasonably to be aware of another generally available product which can satisfy the customers needs as well.

5.24 In order to meet the rules in the previous paragraph, the intermediary should have adequate knowledge of the packaged products available in the market as a whole. This means that an independent adviser employed by a provider firm can only recommend his own company's products if he can be sure that they are **better than the best** otherwise available on the market. In practice, this often means that such an independent adviser usually will not recommend his own firm's products, because it is unlikely that those products stand out as significantly better than the rest of the market as required to satisfy this rule.

Suitability letter (formerly 'Reason Why') letter

5.25 A firm must take reasonable steps to ensure that it does not make a **personal recommendation** to a private customer to buy or sell a designated investment unless the recommendation or transaction is suitable for the customer having regard to information disclosed by him and other facts of which the firm is or ought reasonably to be aware. A **suitability letter** (called a 'reason why' letter under pre-N2 rules) is required following a personal recommendation to a private customer on:

(a) **A life policy**
(b) **A stakeholder pension scheme (SHP)**
(c) Certain **pensions** transactions
(d) Regulated collective investment schemes

5.26 The **suitability letter** explains why the firm has concluded that the transaction is suitable, given the customer's circumstances. The suitability letter must specifically justify any recommendation of:

(a) A personal pension scheme instead of a SHP
(b) A Free-Standing AVC scheme instead of an in-house AVC

The suitability letter must be issued as soon as possible, or no later than the issue of the post sale notice of the customer's right to cancel in the case of life policies or SHPs.

5.27 The suitability letter might form part of:

(a) A financial report to the customer, or

(b) A fact find document

Suitability of broker funds

5.28 A firm acting as a broker fund adviser for a private customer must:

(a) Take account of the characteristics of the fund, including all charging arrangements, when assessing the suitability of the arrangements

(b) Review on a regular basis the customer's current investment objectives and strategies relative to those at the time of any previous periodic report

(c) Follow up the review with a recommendation in writing to the customer at least annually, either to continue with the investment or to withdraw, with reasons

(d) Provide the customer with an alternative recommendation if the broker fund arrangement is no longer suitable

(e) Notify any significant known change in the investment strategy of the fund to the customer in advance together with confirmation why the fund continues to be suitable, or an alternative recommendation

Customers' understanding of risk

5.29 There is a **general obligation to disclose risks,** in accordance with the FSA's Principle 7 *Communications with clients* and Principle 9 *Customers: relationships of trust.*

5.30 There are also particular specific obligations to warn private customers of the risks of certain transactions, including **warrants and derivatives,** and **non-readily realisable investments.**

Excessive charges

5.31 Principle 6 *Customers' interests* requires a firm to pay due regard to the interests of customers and to treat them fairly. Therefore charges to a private customer must not be **excessive.**

5.32 What is 'excessive'? The firm should consider:

(a) Charges on similar products in the market

(b) Whether charges could be an abuse of the customers' trust

(c) The extent to which charges are disclosed

Disclosure of charges and commission

5.33 There is an **obligation to disclose** to private customers:

(a) The basis or amount of charges

(b) Before business is transacted

5.34 When a firm is a **broker fund adviser,** disclosure should include any fees payable to the firm or its associate in connection with that activity by a provider firm.

5.35 For **packaged products,** the following must also be disclosed:

(a) Any remuneration payable to employer or agents

(b) Any remuneration or commission received by the firm

Basic advice on stakeholder products

5.36 The **Sandler Review** proposals have been put into effect in legislation and in changes to the FSA Handbook which came into force on 6 April 2005. These rules allow for firms to provide a **basic level of advice** on a range of stakeholder products. **Stakeholder products** are intended to provide a relatively simple and low-cost way of investing and saving.

5.37 The range of stakeholder products include:

(a) Stakeholder pension schemes
(b) Stakeholder Child Trust Funds (CTFs)
(c) Stakeholder-compliant deposit accounts
(d) Stakeholder-compliant collective investment schemes (CISs)
(e) Stakeholder-compliant linked long-term contracts

5.38 **Child Trust Funds** were introduced in April 2005 and, for children born after 31 August 2002, provide an account started by an initial Government contribution of £250 (or £500 for lower income families). There is no access to the account until the child reaches age 18.

5.39 To be a stakeholder product, a **deposit account** must have a minimum deposit amount set no higher than £10 per occasion. Interest must accrue at a rate not less than the Bank of England base rate minus 1 per cent per annum. The interest rate must be increased within one month of a change in the base rate. Withdrawals must be paid within 7 days, with no limit on frequency of withdrawals.

5.40 To meet stakeholder requirements, **collective investment schemes** and **linked long-term funds** must have no more than 60% of their value in listed equities, and must be appropriately diversified. The minimum contribution must be set no higher than £20. The scheme must be **single-priced** – with no spread between the buying and selling price of units.

5.41 Linked long-term contracts are assurance-based contracts. Where such contracts have **smoothed investment returns**, additional requirements apply. The fund must seek to meet a target range of investment return, which must be notified to the investor at the outset. However, no guarantee will be given. Full information must be made available about the policy and charges. The **basic level of advice cannot be provided** on smoothed linked long term products.

5.42 Medium term and pension stakeholder products have a **cap on charges** at 1.5% per year for the first ten years that the investor holds the product. After that, a cap of 1 per cent applies. The charge caps will be reviewed by the Government in 2008.

5.43 The new requirements on **basic advice on stakeholder products** is designed to enable firms to provide **simple, quick and limited** advice to people interested in buying stakeholder products. The requirements include the following.

(a) An **Initial Disclosure Document (IDD)** is to be provided, and explained to the customer.

(b) The advice should be based on either a limited number of stakeholder product providers, or a single provider.

(c) The range of products should not include more than one of each of:

(i) A collective investment product or linked life products

(ii) A stakeholder pension

(iii) A stakeholder Child Trust Fund

(There can be more than one deposit-based product in the range. Also, a firm may operate with more than one range of stakeholder products. Proper records of the ranges must be kept, for six years.)

(d) Representatives are not to recommend one particular fund, and they are not to give advice on products outside the range while advising on stakeholder products. The firm must not hold itself out as giving **independent advice** when it is giving only basic advice on stakeholder products.

(e) Remuneration of representatives must not be likely to influence them to give unsuitable advice or induce them to refer customers to another firm.

(f) The sales process for basic stakeholder advice must use **scripted questions** put to the customer. Unless excluded at the preliminary stage, the customer must be sent a copy of the completed scripted questions and answers.

6 PRODUCT DISCLOSURE

6.1 Chapter 6 of the COB rules covers **product disclosure and the customer's right to cancel or withdraw**.

Packaged product and ISA disclosure

6.2 FSA Principle 7 *Communications with clients* states that due regard must be paid to the information needs of customers. The disclosure rules on packaged products and ISAs are intended to enable the **customer** to make a **comparative analysis** of **different packaged products**. Note the emphasis on the customers themselves making comparisons between products, in an environment in which the general level of charges is being driven down in order to give better value to customers.

6.3 There are disclosure rules covering:

(a) Packaged products – **Key Features Document (KFD)** required

(b) Cash deposit ISAs – **information document** required

(c) Variations on life policies

(d) Income withdrawals from pension schemes

6.4 **Key Features Documents**

(a) May be in electronic form only, if the firm conducts the business solely through electronic media.

(b) Must be produced to **at least the same quality** as associated sales and marketing material

(c) Must be separated from other material, except for collective investment schemes or SHPs where it may be incorporated within other material if given due prominence

(d) Must comply with the COB rules in content and format

The rationale of Key Feature Documents (KFDs)

6.5 A consumer review carried out by the FSA found that 48% of customers recalled being given a Key Features Document, and only 8% had actually read the document - hence the perception that the KFD requirement should be reviewed.

6.6 Although originally designed to facilitate comparison between products of different providers, the purpose of KFDs has become more like that of summarising features of a particular product in easily readable form. As detailed in the previous section, new **Key facts documents** are also now required.

Broker funds

6.7 At the same time as providing a **private customer** with a **suitability letter**, the **broker fund adviser** must inform the private customer in writing of:

(a) The proposed investment objectives, and the policies and strategies which are to be followed to achieve the objectives

(b) The relevant published index or other indicator with which comparison of the performance of the fund or scheme may fairly be made

(c) A published index or sector average which the firm must identify as appropriate to the investment objectives and strategy of the fund or scheme under comparison

(d) The name of any person providing advice under the arrangement

6.8 Firms acting for **broker funds** are required to provide **extensive information** to the customer on an **ongoing basis**, as detailed later in this chapter. This is considerably **more detailed** than that required for **life assurance investment** and is far closer to the **provision of information requirements** for a **discretionary managed portfolio of securities**. These include the requirement for regular publication of fund prices notifying customers prior to any significant change in investment strategy. These regulations have arguably reduced the volume of broker bond business.

Question 16.8

Who is responsible for ensuring that the systems for running and administering broker funds are in place?

Cancellation and withdrawal

6.9 **Cancellation** and **withdrawal** rules apply to:

(a) Life policies
(b) Unit trusts and open-ended investment company (OEIC) units
(c) Long-term insurances
(d) Cash ISAs
(e) Stakeholder pension schemes
(f) Pension contracts

6.10 For life policies, pension contracts and (if advice is given) ISA or PEP investments, there is a **pre-sale right to withdraw,** with the investment being made at the end of the period of reflection (7 to 30 days, depending on the product).

6.11 More usually, firms will give a **post-sale right to cancel**, although such rights do not apply to a non-unit based ISA. The money is invested throughout the period of reflection (14 to 30 days, depending on the product), during which time the customer may suffer loss of capital due for adverse market movements.

6.12 **Pre-sale notice: example**

'You will be able to cancel your [investment]/[contract] during a two-week period after concluding the agreement and receive a refund [in full/less a deduction for shortfall to reflect any fall in the markets in the interim]. You will be told of this right in more detail (including when it begins and ends, and how to exercise it) in documents that we will send you at the relevant time.'

6.13 The pre-sale notice summarises information in the **post-sale notice**, which must be sent by post or electronically. The post-sale notice is accompanied by a slip or form, or electronic equivalent, enabling the customer to exercise the right to cancel.

With-profit guides

6.14 Section 6.9 of the COB covers **with-profits guides**, whose purpose is explained in the following introductory text to such guides as prescribed by the FSA.

'All insurance companies, and the larger friendly societies, which market with-profits policies in the United Kingdom, are required to make available a guide containing information about the company or society and its with-profits fund. This is because the benefits under such polices depend in part, and sometimes to a considerable extent, on bonus additions which are made by the company or the society from time to time and which cannot be known in advance. It is therefore important that potential policyholders and their advisers should have access to information about the most important factors influencing such bonuses.'

'However, investors are advised that, in comparing a policy marketed by one company or society with other policies, it is unwise to place too much importance on any one factor. An over all view of all relevant elements will usually give a more realistic comparison: in particular, an examination of the history of a fund over a period of years will usually give a fuller picture than can be obtained from looking at the figures for just one year'.

7 DEALING AND MANAGING

7.1 **Best execution** rules are covered in Chapter 7 of the COB rules, entitled **Dealing and managing**.

7.2 COB Chapter 7 also covers:
- Dealing rules
- Conflicts of interest

Conflicts of interest

7.3 A firm must not **knowingly** deal or advise if the firm has a **material interest** or **conflict of interest** unless reasonable steps are taken to ensure fair treatment of customers.

Question 16.9

Which FSA Principle is re-stated in the COB rule stated in Paragraph 7.3?

7.4 The purpose of re-stating the FSA's Principle 8 in this context is to make it **actionable under Section 150 of FSMA 2000.**

7.5 A firm may **manage a conflict of interest** by:

(a) Disclosing the interest to a customer
(b) Relying on a **policy of independence**
(c) Establishing **internal arrangements** ('Chinese walls')
(d) **Declining to act** for the customer

KEY TERM

A **policy of independence** is a 'Chinese wall of the mind' - a policy of disregarding in your mind a material interest or a conflict of interest.

Broker fund advisers

7.6 A **broker fund adviser** acting for a **private customer** must obtain the customer's acknowledgement that he understands the firm's dual role as **adviser to the private customer** and **adviser to the long-term insurer or operator** of the fund.

Churning and switching

7.7 The following are prohibited when conducting investment business with or for a customer.

(a) For investments generally: **churning** - ie, dealing too frequently in the circumstances

(b) For packaged products: **switching** between packaged products, **unless** the dealing or switching is in the client's best interest. Note that recommending the surrender of a life policy in order to switch into a new one could be against a client's interests because the surrender value could be relatively low compared with the expected maturity value, and there will also be charges on the new policy.

7.8 **'Churning'** refers to dealing or switching excessively, with the objective of increasing commissions earned. Interpretation of what constitutes churning will depend on the circumstances: no definition of churning, for example in terms of the rate of dealing, is provided in the COB rules.

Question 16.10

Why do you think that the FSA does not define 'churning' in the COB rules?

Dealing ahead

7.9 Firms which issue recommendations to customers, for example in newsletters, are prohibited from **dealing ahead**. No 'own account' transactions are permitted before customers have had time to react.

7.10 **Exceptions to the prohibition on dealing ahead**

    (a) If the information is **not price sensitive** (for example, merely confirming others' research, or if the market size is too large to be influenced by the recommendation)

    (b) In the case of fulfilment of an **unsolicited customer order**

    (c) Buying (eg by a broker firm) to fulfil anticipated demand (termed '**stock up**')

    (d) Where the dealing is **disclosed**

Best execution

7.11 The requirement to carry out **best execution** especially affects broker firms, and is the requirement to obtain the **best price for a transaction of its type and size.**

7.12 Exceptions to the rule are:

    (a) Units in collective investment schemes
    (b) Life policies

7.13 **Intermediate customers** may waive the right to receive best execution. They may wish to do this because obtaining stock at a particular time, for example when dealing in futures, may be of more importance than the price.

7.14 Firms must also carry out **timely execution.** In other words they must deal as soon as is reasonably practicable.

7.15 **Aggregation of deals** may only be undertaken if:

    (a) Each customer is not likely to be disadvantaged
    (b) Each customer is informed orally or in writing of the possible disadvantage

7.16 There are rules which seek to ensure that customers are not disadvantaged by **personal dealing** carried out by employees of an FSA-regulated firm. The **firm** must seek to ensure that its duties to customers are not compromised.

8 CLIENT ASSETS

8.1 The COB rules on **client assets** (COB Chapter 9) are designed to answer the question: How do we protect clients if firms go insolvent? There are the following way of providing such protection:

    (a) Putting assets into trust
    (b) Segregation of assets
    (c) Ensuring adequacy of the firm's resources
    (d) Procedures to reconcile assets held

8.2 The FSA's **Principle 10** *Clients' assets* states that a firm must arrange adequate protection for clients' assets for which it is responsible.

Custody rules

8.3 Custody rules apply to a firm when it is **safeguarding and administering investments:**

    (a) **Registration and recording.** Firms are expected to register and record the legal title of safe custody investments so as to provide appropriate protection to the client.

(b) **Assessment of custodian.** Firms must undertake an appropriate **risk assessment** of any custodian with whom safe custody investments are to be held.

(c) **Client agreements.** Clients must be notified of terms and conditions applying to safe custody services provided to a client.

(d) **Custodian agreements.** Terms and conditions must be agreed with any custodian.

> **KEY TERM**
>
> A **safe custody investment** is a designated investment that a firm receives or holds on behalf of a client. A safe custody investment is not the firm's but the firm is accountable for it. Custody assets include designated investments and any other assets that the firm holds in the same portfolio as designated investments held for or on behalf of the client.

Reconciliation

8.4 **Reconciliations** must be carried out at least:

(a) **Every 25 business days,** for assets not held by the firm but for which it is accountable
(b) **Every six months,** for assets held by the firm

8.5 Reconciliations must be completed within 25 business days and errors corrected 'properly'.

Client money rules

8.6 **Client money rules** cover money which the firm looks after and which is not its own. (Intermediate customers and market counterparties may **opt out** of these rules).

8.7 The FSA generally requires a firm to place **client money** in a **client bank account** with an **approved bank.** Many Independent Financial Advisers (IFAs) have **no authority to handle client money.** In that case, they do not need to maintain client money accounts and they should ensure that the client makes cheques payable direct to the product provider.

8.8 **Key concepts**

(a) **Segregation** of money into separate client accounts

(b) **Trust** arrangements: for example, the bank at which a client account is held should confirm in writing that money in the client account is legally owned by the firm, but that the firm is not the beneficial owner of the money.

8.9 Client bank accounts may be:

(a) **Designated** - holding the money of specific client(s), or
(b) **General**

8.10 **All interest payments** must go to the client, unless the firm has notified the customer that different arrangements will apply.

Client money calculation

8.11 **Each business day,** the firm must:

(a) Check that:

Client money resource ≥ Client money requirement

(b) Ensure that any **shortfall** or **excess** on the account is adjusted by the close of business on the day that the calculation is performed.

9 PERIODIC STATEMENTS

9.1 **Periodic statements** of a portfolio of investments held for a private customer should normally be provided every six months unless agreed otherwise, within 25 business days of the end of the statement period.

9.2 The statement should show:

(a) The number, description and value of each designated investment held
(b) The amount of cash held
(c) The total value of the portfolio
(d) The basis of valuation

9.3 **Additional information for a discretionary managed portfolio**

(a) Details of any assets loaned or charged
(b) Transactions and changes in composition
(c) Charges and remuneration

9.4 **Additional information for a broker fund**

(a) Details of holdings worth more than 5% of the fund value

(b) Comparison figures with managed funds of the long-term insurer, in the case of unit-linked life policies

(c) A price comparison, with published index or sector averages

(d) Investment objectives and strategies

(e) The cash value of benefits and rewards received by the broker fund adviser and any associate

10 COMPLAINTS AND COMPENSATION

Complaints

10.1 The FSA's **complaints rules** are similar to the pre-existing requirements.

10.2 There must be effective **written complaints handling procedures:**

(a) Availability of the procedures must be referred to in writing at the point of sale

(b) A copy of the procedures must be provided to a complainant on request, or when complaint is received

10.3 Complaints must be dealt with by a **designated complaints handler** who must be:

(a) Competent
(b) Uninvolved
(c) With authority to settle the complaint

10.4 **Complaint handling timescales**

(a) Complaints must be acknowledged within **five days.**

If a complaint is not settled within eight weeks, the complainant must be informed of his right to take the complaint to the **Financial Ombudsman Service (FOS)**

(b) By **four weeks** after receipt of the complaint, the firm should send a **final response** or a **holding response**.

(c) By the end of **eight weeks**, the firm must have sent a **final response**, or a letter explaining:

    (i)   Why a final response still cannot be given

    (ii)   When such a response is likely

    (iii) The fact that the complainant may go to the FOS if dissatisfied with the delay

10.5 A **final response** is a response from the firm which either:

(a) Accepts the complaint and where appropriate offers redress or offers without accepting the complaint, or

(b) Rejects the complaint and gives reasons for doing so, and contains information about the right to refer the complaint to the FOS.

10.6 The **final response** 'starts the clock' in respect of the six month limitation period on the complainant taking the matter to the FOS.

10.7 Note that a '**closed complaint**' - one for which a **final response** has been issued - is not the same as a resolved complaint.

Records and reports

10.8 **Records** must be kept of all complaints for **three years** from the date of receipt. **Reports** must be made to the FSA on a semi-annual (twice yearly) basis.

10.9 There should be a **complaints log**, even if there are no complaints!

Financial Ombudsman Service (FOS)

10.10 The following complainants are eligible to refer a complaint to the new integrated Financial Ombudsman Service if the complaint is not resolved after eight weeks:

(a) Private individuals

(b) Businesses, charities or trusts with turnover of less than £1,000,000

10.11 The FOS does not cover **intermediate customers** or **market counterparties**.

Question 16.11

What is the explanation of the fact that the FOS cannot be used by intermediate customers or market counterparties?

10.12 There is a maximum award of £100,000, plus costs and compensation for any distress, suffering, damage to reputation, and inconvenience. The awards aim to restore the position customers could have been in if things had not gone wrong. The FOS is required to take into account such matters as are 'fair and reasonable in all the circumstances'.

Compensation

10.13 There is a single compensation scheme for investors, known as the **Financial Services Compensation Scheme**. This scheme is the final 'safety net' for eligible claimants of failed authorised UK firms. Private customers, except larger companies and partnerships, can claim.

10.14 The scheme comprises four sub-schemes. The compensation limits for these are as under previous arrangements except in the case of deposits, for which the limits are increased.

10.15 **Financial Services Compensation Scheme limits**

(a) **Insolvency of investment business firm** – 100% of the first £30,000; 90% of the next £20,000, ie £48,000 maximum (as formerly under the Investors Compensation Scheme).

(b) **Insurance company default** – compensation of at least 90% of the policy value for long-term insurance contracts. For general insurance contracts: 100% of first £2,000 and 90% of remainder of the claim, or 100% of the claim in full if subject to compulsory liability insurance (compensation formerly available through Policyholders Protection Board)

(c) **Loss of deposits following default by bank or building society** – 100% of the first £2,000; 90% of the next £33,000, ie £31,700 maximum (formerly the Banks' and Building Societies' Deposit Protection Schemes, which had lower limits)

11 MONEY LAUNDERING AND INSIDER DEALING

> **KEY TERM**
>
> **Money laundering** can be defined as the conversion of money derived from criminal activities into legitimate funds. Methods used for laundering such dirty money can be extremely complex and involve trusts, companies (both offshore and onshore) and could involve the use of relatively complex bank instruments.

11.1 **Money laundering** legislation is included in the **Criminal Justice Act 1993 (CJA 1993)**. The FSA is responsible for ensuring that authorised firms have controls which limit opportunities for money laundering.

11.2 The **CJA 1993** places an obligation on all areas of the financial services sector to assist in the prevention of laundering the proceeds of drug trafficking or other serious criminal activities.

11.3 The **Money Laundering Regulations 2003** apply to banks, building societies, insurance companies and all firms and individuals authorised under the **Financial Services and Markets Act 2000**.

There is a legal requirement for organisations and individuals, including investment managers and financial advisers, to take the following actions.

(a) To set up procedures and establish accountabilities for senior individuals to take action to prevent money laundering

(b) To educate staff and employees about the potential problems of money laundering

(c) To obtain satisfactory evidence of identity where a transaction is for more than €15,000 or £10,000

(d) To report suspicious circumstances (according to the established procedures)

(e) Not to alert persons who are or might be investigated for money laundering

(f) To keep records of all transactions for five years

11.4 Note the following possible penalties:

(a) 14 years imprisonment, for knowingly assisting in the laundering of criminal funds

(b) 5 years imprisonment, for failure to report knowledge or the suspicion of money laundering

(c) 5 years imprisonment for 'tipping off' a suspected launderer. In this context, note that suspicions must be reported to the firm's **Money Laundering Reporting Officer (MLRO)**, who will decide whether to report to the **National Criminal Intelligence Service**. The suspected launderer must not be alerted.

Question 16.12

Why should an adviser not give a warning to a client whom he suspects of money laundering?

11.5 **The role of the FSA**

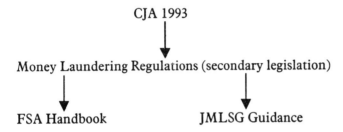

CJA 1993

Money Laundering Regulations (secondary legislation)

FSA Handbook   JMLSG Guidance

11.6 The **FSA Handbook** and the **Joint Money Laundering Steering Group (JMLSG)** guidance include similar, and therefore parallel but separate, rules and guidance.

11.7 The **FSA Handbook** contains the following added provisions.

(a) The **MLRO** must prepare an **annual report** for senior management

(b) **Training**

(i) Training must be carried out on a regular basis

(ii) The nature of the training must be recorded

(iii) Names of staff and dates of training must be recorded

Financial exclusion and identity checks

11.8 The FSA has issued guidance on the risks of **financial exclusion** of those without detailed evidence of their identity. If a person does not have a passport or driving licence, and does not have their name on utility bills, a firm may accept a letter from someone in a position of responsibility who knows the client to confirm the client's identity and permanent address, if they have one.

Proceeds of Crime Act 2002

11.9 The **Proceeds of Crime Act 2002** ('the Act') extends provisions about money laundering and crime proceeds in ways that can affect regulated financial firms.

11.10 Under the Act, it is a criminal offence for anyone to be involved in arrangements that they suspect facilitate (in any way) someone else in acquiring, retaining, using or controlling the proceeds of crime.

11.11 It is also a criminal offence under the Act for anyone working in a regulated financial firm not to report any dealing that they suspect, or ought to suspect, involves the proceeds of crime. This would include tax evasion. The report should be made to the firm's **money laundering reporting officer**, who must report appropriate cases to the **National Criminal Intelligence Service (NCIS)**.

11.12 In most cases, this will be after the transaction has taken place. Where the firm has advance notice of the transaction, it is protected against an allegation of '**assistance**' if it gets consent, or 'deemed' consent, from NCIS before it carries out the transaction.

It is a criminal offence for anyone to do or say anything that might '**tip-off**' someone else that they are under suspicion of acquiring, retaining, using or controlling proceeds of crime. That applies whether or not any report has been made to NCIS.

11.13 This means that a financial firm:

(a) Must not, at the time, tell a customer that a transaction is being delayed because a report has been made under the Proceeds of Crime Act, and

(b) Must not later (unless NCIS agrees) tell a customer that a transaction was delayed because a report had been made under the Proceeds of Crime Act.

Assets Recovery Agency (ARA)

11.14 The **Assets Recovery Agency (ARA)** was set up under the Proceeds of Crime Act 2002 in order to confiscate the proceeds of crime from criminals.

11.15 The ARA can obtain a court order giving them the power to sell a defendant's assets.

11.16 The ARA has wide powers to obtain financial information. The Agency could, for example, require trustees or managers of pension schemes to pay to the Agency the value of pension rights. The ARA's powers will override any scheme rules prohibiting the surrender or commutation of a pension. The member would lose rights under the scheme, following the payment to the ARA.

11.17 The ARA also has powers to **tax** gains from criminal conduct, taking over the function of the Inland Revenue in respect of capital gains tax, corporation tax, national insurance contributions and inheritance tax in the cases involved.

The European Savings Directive

11.18 Agreement was reached during 2003 on the EU's **European Savings Directive**. This Directive requires EU member states to exchange information automatically on the financial affairs of residents of other EU countries, or to levy a withholding tax. These measures are designed to prevent individuals from illegally concealing investments and savings from the proper legal authorities.

11.19 The European Savings Directive will affect EU citizens who hold investments offshore within the EU, or in Switzerland, a country that remains outside the EU and has been well known for having a banking system offering high levels of secrecy to account holders.

11.20 Two different mechanisms were established from the beginning of 2005:

- Most EU countries, including the UK, plan to introduce **automatic exchange of information** between their respective tax authorities.

- Switzerland together with the three EU members Belgium, Luxembourg and Austria will instead introduce a **withholding tax** on cross-border interest payments via banks and paying agents responsible for crediting interest. The tax retained will increase in steps from 15% in 2005 to 20% in 2008 and 35% in 2011.

11.21 The rules do not cover interest payments originating outside the EU and Switzerland, and they cover individuals but not **legal entities**.

11.22 The Directive covers bank accounts, interest bearing investments including investment funds whose assets are made up of at least 40% of bonds, money market instruments, government securities or corporate debt. Investments that pay a dividend or capital gains, such as shares, are currently exempt.

11.23 It would be legitimate for a person to neutralise the effects of the Directive by selecting **managers** to administer investments through an offshore company or trust, for example in conjunction with a tax exempt life wrapper to hold assets on a personalised basis.

Insider dealing

11.24 The facts of the following case are an example of what is now called **insider dealing**. Note that the directors purchased the share when they (as directors) knew and the vendor shareholders did not know that there was the possibility of a takeover bid at a higher price.

> *Percival v Wright 1902*
> *The facts:* The claimants asked the company whether it could find buyers for their shares, which they valued at £12.50 each. The directors purchased the shares at that price. At the time the directors knew that a third party was interested in buying the entire issued share capital at a higher price than £12.50. In fact nothing came of these negotiations. But the claimants demanded that their sale to the directors should be rescinded for non-disclosure of the possibility of re-sale by the directors at a higher price.
>
> *Decision:* The directors owed no duty to members individually which obliged the directors to disclose what they knew.

11.25 Part V of the **Criminal Justice Act 1993** includes the following on insider dealing.

(a) S 52 describes **the offence** as dealing in securities while in possession of inside information as an insider, the securities being **price-affected** by the information.

The prosecution must prove that the possessor of inside information:

(i) **Dealt** in **price-affected securities**
(ii) **Encouraged another** to **deal** in them
(iii) **Disclosed** the **information**

(b) S 55 defines **dealing** as **acquiring or disposing** of or **agreeing** to **acquire** or **dispose** of relevant securities whether **directly** or **through an agent** or nominee or a person acting according to direction.

(c) An offence is also committed if an individual, having information as an insider, **encourages another person** to deal in price-affected securities in relation to that information, **knowing** or having reasonable cause to believe that **dealing** would **take place**.

(d) It is also an offence for an individual who is considered an insider to **disclose** the **information** to another person otherwise than in the proper performance of the functions of his employment, office or profession.

(e) S 54 states that the securities covered by the Act include shares, debt securities and warranties.

(f) S 56 defines inside information as '**price sensitive information**' relating to a **particular issuer** of **securities** that are price-affected and not to securities generally. It must, if made public, be likely to have a **significant effect on price** and it must be **specific or precise**. Specific would, for example, mean information that a takeover bid would be made for a specific company; precise information would be details of how much would be offered for shares.

(g) S 57 states that a person has information as an insider if it is (*and* he **knows** it is) inside information, and if he has it (*and* **knows** he has) from an inside source:

   (i)   Through being a **director, employee** or **shareholder** of an issuer of securities
   (ii) Through access because of **employment, office** or **profession**
   (iii) If the **direct** or **indirect source** is a **person within these two** previous **categories**

(h) S 53 gives a **general defence** where the individual concerned can show that:

   (i)   He did **not expect** there to be a **profit** or avoidance of loss
   (ii) He had **reasonable grounds** to **believe** that the **information** had been **disclosed widely**
   (iii) He would have **done** what he did **even** if he did not have the **information**, for example, where securities are sold to pay a pressing debt

(i) Maximum **penalties** given by s 61 are **seven years' imprisonment** and/or an **unlimited fine**. Contracts remain valid and enforceable at civil law.

Problems with the laws on insider dealing

11.26 The courts may have problems deciding whether information is specific or precise. S 60(4) states that information shall be treated as relating to an issuer of securities which is a company not only when it is about the company but also where it may affect the business prospects of the company.

11.27 The requirement that price-sensitive information has a significant effect on price limits the application of the legislation to fundamental matters such as an impending takeover, or profit or dividend levels which would be out of line with market expectations.

Market Abuse Directive

11.28 In 2005, the FSA published new rules and guidance for implementation of the **Market Abuse Directive (MAD)**, which is part of a common EU approach for prevention and detection of market abuse.

11.29 MAD includes the following measures.

* **Insiders' lists:** firms must keep lists of persons with access to inside information

- **Disclosure of managers' dealing:** managers working for an issure must provide details of **personal dealing**

- **Suspicious transactions reporting:** firms must report transactions to the FSA if there is a reasonable suspicion of **market abuse.**

12 THE INVESTMENT SERVICES DIRECTIVE

12.1 **Firms** that are **not authorised** to **transact business** by the FSA may not transact investment business in the UK. However, these may be **authorised** through a **licence** issued under the **Investment Services Directive (ISD)**, which became effective in 1996.

12.2 The **ISD** allows **investment firms** to **trade** within the **European Economic Area (EEA)**, subject to authorisation by their own regulatory body, providing they can satisfy the terms of the **Capital Adequacy Directive (CAD)**. All EU member states were required to have brought in compliant local legislation by the effective date of the directive to allow this. The fundamental concept of the **ISD** is contained in Article 14 of the directive, which provides that each member state must allow firms authorised in other member states to conduct investment business in their own jurisdictions without any further authorisation requirement, or imposing local capital rules. Such business can be conducted through a branch office or on a cross border basis, but there is no automatic right to set up a subsidiary company.

12.3 Under the **ISD,** all investment firms conducting relevant financial services activities will need to be **authorised** in their **home state.** They will need to assess both new local rules and the extent to which their crossborder activities will require prior approval and be affected by new marketing, authorisation and conduct of business rules in other EU States in which they have customers.

Question 16.13

Does an authorised UK firm have an automatic right to transact business in another EEA country?

The services and instruments covered by the ISD

12.4 The **ISD** authorises the firm to deal with the following **financial instruments** in relation to the services listed below.

Financial instruments	Services
• Financial futures contracts	• Reception and transmission of orders, on behalf of investors, in relation to one or more of the relevant financial instruments or the execution of such orders other than for their own account
• Forward interest rate agreements	
• Money market investments and related instruments	
• Swaps in interest rates, currencies and equities	• Dealing in any of the relevant instruments for their own account
• Transferable securities, shares, debentures, government and public securities, instruments entitling to shares, and securities and certificates representing shares	• Managing portfolios of investments in accordance with mandates given by investors on a discretionary, client by client basis where such portfolios include one or more of the instruments

Financial instruments	Services
• Units in collective investment undertakings	listed to the left
	• Underwriting in respect of issues of the listed instruments and/or the placing of such issues

12.5 Firms conducting the **core services** listed above must, if required, be permitted to conduct certain related **non-core services** including the following.

(a) **Safekeeping** and administration in relation to one or more of the listed instruments

(b) **Safe custody services**

(c) **Granting loans** or credits to an investor to allow him to carry out a transaction in one or more of the listed instruments, where the firm granting the credit/loan is involved in the transaction

(d) **Advice** on capital structure, industrial strategy and related matters and mergers and acquisitions

(e) Services related to **underwriting**

(f) **Investment advice** concerning one or more of the listed instruments

(g) **Foreign exchange services** where these are connected with the provision of investment services

Authorisation under ISD

12.6 The **terms of the ISD** apply to all firms authorised in their own state. For the UK, this will include firms authorised by the FSA. The **SRO** is a '**competent authority**' under the legislation. A firm wishing to transact business outside their home state, by establishing an office elsewhere in the EEA, must apply to competent authority in writing. The authority is required to consider the application from the UK perspective and contact the relevant overseas regulator in the host country within three months. The **host regulator** has two months to respond and, after this time, if the application is successful, the firm may transact business there.

12.7 **Firms** wishing to **operate** from their own country by **remote means**, eg telephones, the Internet, or some other form of computer system, must also **apply** to their **regulator**. The regulator must consider the application and reply within one month. The **host regulator** is **not given** a **time period** within which to respond and the **firm** may **transact business** as soon as it receives **authority** from their **regulator**. The provision of the right to trade in this manner is '**passporting**'.

12.8 The terms of the **ISD** also include **minimum authorisation** and **ongoing supervision requirements** that must be applied to all companies seeking to trade. It is the responsibility of the '**competent authority**' to ensure that these requirements are met. For UK firms, most of the requirements are met under the terms of their authorisation from the FSA. Under the full list of requirements, firms must comply with the following.

(a) Have their head office and registered office in the same member state

(b) At all times comply with the capital requirements of the Capital Adequacy Directive (see later)

(c) Have managers with sufficient experience

(d) Produce a business plan or equivalent programme of proposed operations and an organisational structure

(e) Have sound administrative and accounting procedures, including internal control mechanisms (eg, in relation to personal account dealings by employees) and control and safeguard electronic data processing

(f) Have arrangements for safeguarding customer assets and keep such assets segregated from the firm's own assets

(g) Keep adequate transaction records

(h) Be structured and organised so as to minimise conflicts of interests

(i) Comply with local conduct of business rules covering both the core and non core services, which contain principles designed to ensure honesty and fair dealing in the best interests of clients and the integrity of the market

(j) Act with due care, skill and diligence

(k) Have sufficient resources and procedures for their business

(l) Seek sufficient information from customers regarding their financial position, experience and objectives

(m) Make adequate disclosure of material information

(n) Attempt to avoid conflicts of interest and, where these arise, customers must be treated fairly

12.9 **Firms** executing **transactions,** as opposed to investment managers, must treat the ultimate customer as their client (as opposed to an introducer or order passer) for the purpose of **complying** with **suitability requirements.**

Question 16.14

How long does it take to get authorisation for a firm to deal on a crossborder basis and does the local authority have any jurisdiction to stop a firm conducting business in this way?

Regulation and compliance with local rules

12.10 A combination of 'home state' (UK) rules and those of the 'overseas state' govern firms operating under the **ISD** (host state).

(a) The **home state** is responsible for the **initial authorisation** of the company and for the rules relating to supervision and reporting of transactions.

(b) The **host state** is responsible for the **rules** relating to the **conduct of business.**

Capital Adequacy Directive (CAD)

12.11 To **qualify** to **trade** under the **ISD,** investment firms will be required to comply with the **minimum base capital requirements** for the services that the individual firm provides.

12.12 Banks and other substantial financial institutions do not have a problem **meeting** and **maintaining compliance** with these rules but smaller fund managers and brokers in most jurisdictions encounter difficulties. This will particularly be the case if they hold client money and/or deal for their own account, which attracts the highest level of base capital.

12.13 In addition to the **base capital requirements**, the **CAD** contains detailed **capital provisions** in relation to position risk, large exposures, consolidated supervision and reporting requirements.

Exemptions from the ISD

12.14 Certain UK investment firms are **exempt** from becoming ISD authorised firms and can automatically deal in the EEA. These include:

   (a) Collective investment schemes and their operators

   (b) Company pension schemes

   (c) Group treasurers

   (d) Investment trusts

   (e) Professional advisers giving advice that is incidental to the investments, eg accountants and solicitors

12.15 Firms specialising in **receiving** or **transmitting investment orders** to **ISD** firms, **BCD** firms or **non-EEA** firms on behalf of investors would usually be exempt, providing that their core service relates to orders in transferable securities or collective schemes and that they do not hold client's money or assets.

European firms without ISD authorisation

12.16 Not all firms will **qualify** to **transact business** under the **ISD firms** if their regulatory system does not mirror the **ISD regulations,** or if they cannot meet the **CAD minimum capital requirements.** For these firms it is possible to transact business elsewhere in Europe by obtaining a separate licence in each country that they wish to operate.

Non-EEA firms

12.17 **Investment firms** from **outside the EEA** can establish an operation in the UK under a different arrangement called a **Financial Information Sharing Memorandum of Undertaking (FISMOU)**. This agreement is established between the firm's home country regulator and the UK regulator.

12.18 Where an **overseas firm** is **not covered** by the **ISD** or a **FISMOU,** as in the case of a firm from outside the EEA, the only way they can trade in the UK is to set up a UK subsidiary and get it authorised by the appropriate authority.

Chapter roundup

- The conduct of investment business is regulated under the Financial Services and Markets Act 2000.

- A major overhaul of the regulation of the whole of the financial services was fully implemented with effect from 1 December 2001. The FSA took over responsibility for the following, bringing the overall regulation of the financial services industry under the FSA:

  - The regulation of investment business under the Financial Services Act 1986
  - The supervision of banks under the Banking Act 1987
  - Regulation of investment business

- New rules have been released to encompass the old ones and provide an overall standard across all areas of the financial services industry

- The previous ombudsman schemes have been amalgamated under the Financial Ombudsman Scheme (FOS)

- There is now a single Financial Services Compensation Scheme

- The ISD provides for EEA investment business and allows investment firms authorised within the EEA to undertake investment business elsewhere within the EEA, upon receipt of automatic authorisation by the host country regulatory authorities.

Quick quiz

1   What is the overall regulatory structure for the financial services industry?

2   What are the FSA's four statutory objectives, as set out in FSMA 2000?

3   State three types of market abuse.

4   What are the potential consequences of carrying out a regulated activity without the appropriate authorisation or suitable exemption?

5   What are the two main authorisation routes?

6   What additional principles apply to senior management in addition to the four required for 'approved persons'?

7   Under what circumstances can a firm deal through an intermediary under a 'soft commission agreement'?

8   What is a Chinese Wall?

9   To what types of communication does the concept of financial promotion under the FSA regime extend?

10   What are the three main classes of client under the FSA regulatory regime?

11   What is the difference between a 'one way' customer agreement and a 'two way' customer agreement?

12   What are the basic rules for disclosure of charges and commission?

13   What happens where a client has opted to use their cancellation rights on a policy where there has been a significant loss in the underlying investment?

14   What is 'best execution'?

15   How often must a firm reconcile assets held on behalf of their clients in 'safe custody'?

16   Where a complaint is not settled within eight weeks a firm must provide details of the client's right to take the complaint to an external body. What is this external body called and what is the maximum award they can make?

17   What is the minimum compensation available under the Financial Services Compensation Scheme (FSCS) for an individual with £50,000 in a deposit account with an institution that has gone out of business?

18   What is the maximum punishment for knowingly assisting in the laundering of criminal funds?

19   List the services that an ISD authorised firm may offer.

20   How long does it take for a company get authorised under the ISD to set up a branch in another EEA Member State?

21   Which state is responsible for the rules relating to the conduct of business?

The answers to the questions in the Quick Quiz can be found at the end of this Study Text. Before checking your own answers against them, you should look back at this chapter and use the information in it to correct your answers.

Answers to Chapter Questions

16.1 Recognised Professional Bodies.

Examples include the Law Society (solicitors) and professional accountancy bodies, such as the Institute of Chartered Accountants in England and Wales.

16.2 Unless the journalist has suffered a loss - and there is no evidence that he has - then there is no right of action.

16.3 To both firms, X and Y.

16.4 Those dealing with execution-only transactions or merely introducing a customer to a firm would not be carrying out 'customer functions'.

Also a bank cashier who accepts deposits from a customer is probably not carrying out an advisory function.

16.5 Principle 7 *Communications with clients*.

16.6 All could be used to communicate a financial promotion.

(1), (2) and (3) are 'real time'. (4) is non-real time: response is not required immediately.

16.7 In order to simplify its procedures.

16.8 The life assurance company issuing the facility.

16.9 This rule effectively re-states Principle 8 *Conflicts of interest*.

16.10 The rate would vary for different types of investment, and if limits were specified, there would be a risk that the limits would be seen as targets.

16.11 This is because the FOS is intended to benefit the consumer, ie private customers.

16.12 Tipping off a suspected money launderer is an offence. Alerting the suspect would be likely to hamper any subsequent investigation by the authorities.

16.13 EEA member states must allow firms authorised in other member states to conduct investment business in their jurisdictions without any further authorisation requirement or the imposition of local capital rules, but there is no automatic right to set up a branch.

16.14 The competent authority has a month to reply to an application to transact cross border business. The local authority cannot stop a firm operating in this way.

PRACTICE QUESTION 16

Your firm is looking to employ two new investment advisers.

(a) What information would be required by the FSA's Individual Registration and Vetting Department? (9)

(b) The FSA requires candidates to be fit and proper. On what criteria do they assess this? (3)

(c) The FSA's code of conduct has four principles for 'approved persons'. Give an example of a breach of each of these. (4)

Firms regulated in the UK can apply to trade in other member states in the European Economic Area under the provisions of the Investment Services Directive.

(d) List the financial instruments in which a firm may transact business under the terms of the ISD. (7)

(e) Briefly, explain the action that a firm must take to get permission to transact cross border business under the terms of the ISD. (4)

(f) List the non-core investment services that can be carried out in conjunction with core investment services under the terms of the ISD. (7)

(g) Briefly explain the relevance of the Capital Adequacy Directive (CAD) in relation to the 'passporting' of financial services. (1)

Part I

Sitting the G70 examination

Chapter 17

SITTING THE G70 EXAMINATION

Chapter topic list

1   The G70 examination

2   AFPC marking and re-marking

3   Examination technique

4   G70 questions

5   Conclusion

Introduction

In this chapter, we look at a range of techniques to help you to prepare for and maximise the marks you can achieve in the G70 examination.

---

1   THE G70 EXAMINATION

The pass mark

1.1   One of the most important aspects of this examination, as with all AFPC examinations, is the pass rate. Information from the CII indicates past pass rates of between 33% and 44%. The pass marks are not published but the CII does set a nominal pass mark of 55% which can be adjusted to suit the circumstances of the paper. Of those that fail, many are within a narrow margin of 10% of the pass mark. This 10% can easily be earned through efficient and effective preparation for the exam and basic exam technique skills.

Examiner's comments

1.2   For many, the loss of crucial marks could be avoided by better time keeping, reading the instructions for the examination, reading the questions properly and generally not allowing the examination to stress them to the point where they may make mistakes. Areas commonly mentioned in examiner's report are as follows.

- Calculations (not showing method and workings)
- Examination technique
- Failing to read examiner's report
- Poor layout
- Poor time allocation
- Not taking account of numbers of marks (answers too brief)
- Knowledge/answers too basic
- Not reading (understanding) the question
- Writing irrelevant information

1.3 Most people who have worked through this Study Text should be capable of achieving at least an X grade (narrow fail). This chapter concentrates on techniques for ensuring they get the extra few marks required to turn a narrow fail into a pass.

G70 Investment portfolio management

1.4 The first sitting of the new G70 examination was in October 1997. The assumed knowledge for this examination is that of Papers 1 and 2 of the Financial Planning Certificate (now replaced by the Certificate in Financial Planning) and paper G10 Taxation and Trusts. It is considerably different from G20 (Personal Investment Planning), as it concentrates on the principles of portfolio construction using a wide range of investments. In contrast, G20 concentrates more on the construction of portfolios with a smaller range of investment vehicles: those which a financial adviser is likely to come into contact with on a regular basis. G70 does, however, build on knowledge gained by studying for the G20 paper.

1.5 The G70 examination was effectively created at the request of the industry. Surveys had sought views about future subjects on which the CII should produce examinations. Many members were interested in an advanced investments paper such as this.

1.6 The G70 examination is similar in many ways to those set by the Securities and Investment Institute, but with a slant more towards the financial adviser. As such it is an excellent alternative for those with an 'Investments' bias.

1.7 G70 is a specialist examination. The ground covered should certainly meet the needs of those financial advisers working with stockbrokers, or in conjunction with other departments of their company offering portfolio management services. It will also be of considerable use to those working in a portfolio management environment, combined with G10 and G20. In addition to this, some individuals working more on the investment side of the business may be taking this exam as an interesting and more relevant alternative to the other non-compulsory subjects.

1.8 It is important not to under-estimate the standard of this examination. The case studies are designed to demonstrate a more sophisticated level of advice than in G20 and there is a requirement for attention to detail in the answers.

1.9 The examination is based on the **syllabus**, which is reproduced at the fron of this book. This Study Text contains sufficient information to pass without referring to any additional material, but to ensure that you can answer every possible question that may be asked, you would be advised to do some extra reading of journals and periodicals such as *Investors Chronicle* and *Professional Investor* (published by the IIMR).

Practice examination papers

1.10 The Examination Guide (available from the CII) contains a full specimen examination with model answers. Examiner's Reports for all exams held to date are available from the CII.

1.11 With G70, as with all examinations, you should attempt at least one practice exam under simulated exam room conditions. You will find a practice examination at the end of this Study Text.

If you decide to mark your own paper, you will need to make an assessment which is as objective as possible. If you have a friend or colleague who is studying or has studied this paper, you might ask him or her to mark your paper for you, thus gaining a more objective assessment. Remember however that you and your friend are not trained or objective markers, so try to avoid complacency or pessimism if you appear to have done very well or very badly.

2   AFPC MARKING AND RE-MARKING

2.1   AFPC examinations are marked positively. This means that if you have written down information that is in the examiner's marking scheme you will get marks for it irrespective of incorrect information you may also have put down, so long as you do not directly contradict yourself.

2.2   All of the examinations are marked to a marking scheme. This means that you will normally only get the marks if you have the answer on the schedule. Occasionally there will be some 'floating' marks, but not normally more than 5%.

2.3   Typically the distribution of candidates' marks will be 'peaked' in statistical terms. Many candidates achieve similar marks to each other, with smaller numbers getting higher or lower marks. This gives you an opportunity, as relatively little additional effort is required to improve your score, and good examination technique can really make the difference.

2.4   Individuals who score a narrow fail can request that the paper be re-marked. In the CII's words, 'if you do apply (for a re-mark), it is most unlikely that your grade will be changed, but you will receive a report indicating areas of weakness in your performance'. Unofficial estimates suggest a success ratio of 1 in 40.

2.5   The CII does not normally issue information relating to a candidate's marks. However you can request a 'Data Protection Print' from the CII. This will cost £15 (administration fee) and will tell you your mark. A judgement can then be made as to whether to pay £60 for a re-mark.

3   EXAMINATION TECHNIQUE

What the examiner is looking for

3.1   Above all, **the examiner is looking for facts**. Typically, there is one mark available for each 'fact'. Note well that all questions itemise the number of marks available.

3.2   You do not have to write in perfect English or give an essay for each answer. Structuring your answer, for example by using short sentences and bullet points, will help to show the examiner the number of separate points you are making.

Allocate your time

3.3   There are a possible 200 marks to gain during the 180 minutes of the exam. This equates to 54 seconds per mark (just under one minute per mark). I suggest that you use these maximum timings accurately on each part of every question. Count the number of marks and multiply by 0.9 to give the number of minutes you should spent. Avoid giving shorter answers to heavily weighted questions.

3.4   To have a reasonable chance of passing the examination, you need to attempt all questions and therefore it is imperative to keep to these timings.

3.5   You will normally collect the most marks in the first few minutes of starting a new question or subsection. If you reach the end of your allotted time for each question or subsection, it is

BPP)))
PROFESSIONAL EDUCATION

advisable to leave the question part-finished and move on to the next one, leaving space to allow you to return to the incomplete question afterwards (if you have time).

Read the instructions

3.6 The question paper will include a page of instructions at the beginning. This can vary slightly from examination to examination, but it will be largely similar to that shown in past papers.

Reading the question

3.7 As with all examinations, you should read and understand the whole question before attempting to answer any part. (You may wish to use a highlighter pen to mark key points for later reference.)

3.8 A mistake sometimes made by candidates is to attempt answer separate sections of a question more than one at a time, for example, in answering the following type of question.

   (a) List the facts relating to Mr Smith's tax position.....
   (b) Identify any problems with Mr. Smith's proposed course of action......
   (c) Recommend an appropriate course of action to achieve the desired objectives....

If the sections (a), (b) and (c) are run together as a single answer instead of being answered separately, the examiner will have the problem of unravelling the answer and you may risk losing marks as a result.

Writing technique

3.9 Write clearly, concisely and legibly. Although marks are not taken off for poor handwriting, it does make the answers harder to find, and increases the chances of a correct answer being missed by the examiner.

3.10 The candidate instructions for all papers include the following statement:

'Subject to providing sufficient detail, you are advised to be as brief and concise as possible, using note format and short sentences on separate lines wherever possible.'

For a question requiring a list, aim to write at least one answer for each mark available.

3.11 When asked to compare two types of investment, it may be best to write two parallel lists and to ensure that every point you make has a point of comparison in both lists.

> ### Exam focus point
> Here is an example.
> Compare the tax treatment of shares and gilts.
>
> **Shares**
> - Dividends are subject to tax of 10% at source.
> - Higher rate taxpayers will be liable to a further 22½% taxation via self assessment.
> - CGT is payable on the gains.
> - Lower and basic rate taxpayers have no further income tax liability.
>
> **Gilts**
> - Coupons on gilts are paid free of tax at source.
> - Basic rate taxpayers are liable to a 20% tax charge, higher rate taxpayers 40%.
> - There is no CGT payable on gains.

Calculations

3.12 Calculations form a part of the examination that is totally objective. It is possible to score full marks on a calculation question.

(a) It is worthwhile practising the common calculations and getting to know the way calculations should be laid out.

(b) Show all calculations. In some cases, there are more marks available for workings than for the final answer.

(c) You may not take a programmable calculator into the exam. If you normally use one, you should practise using a different calculator, as functions you are expecting to have may not be there.

(d) If your calculator is battery powered, take spare batteries into the exam. If it is a solar powered calculator, check that it has a battery backup.

(e) For the G70 examination, you should use a 'business calculator'. The Hewlett Packard 10B or 10B II is recommended. Of course, you need to know how to use it and how apply it to the questions that are likely to come up in the examination.

4 G70 QUESTIONS

4.1 It is essential that you cover **all subjects** in this Study Text to maximise your chances of passing.

4.2 **Section A** is likely to try to cover as much ground as possible and there is no shortage of theories, concepts and calculations that could be covered in a 4-10 mark short question. Expect to see at least one financial calculation question and probably a regulation question appearing in this section.

4.3 **Section B** is the main area to pull knowledge together. A portfolio might well be provided as part of the case study, with a requirement to comment on the portfolio, to explain the underlying theories and make suggestions and recommendations on future courses of action.

4.4 **Section C** allows the examiner to concentrate more fully on three areas, from which you are required to select two questions. With a syllabus covering this much ground, there is a wide choice for the examiner and no obvious clues for the candidate.

5 CONCLUSION

5.1 G70 can be a very rewarding subject to study and, if you understand the key concepts and theories and know the basic information, you should be able to pass. However, it is always disappointing when candidates know the material but fail because of poor technique. While knowing the subject is half the battle, communicating it to the examiner represents a good proportion of the rest of it. Good technique will allow you to structure your questions to maximise the marks available. It will also make the examiner's job considerably easier - a very useful thing when crucial marks could easily go either way.

Chapter roundup

- Poor exam techniques such as not reading the question and not allocating the marks properly, cause candidates to lose marks.

- AFPC examinations are marked 'positively'. Marks will be given for correct information and will not be deducted for incorrect information (unless it is directly contradictory).

- The examiner is looking for facts - approximately one for each mark given.

- Structuring your answer allows you (and the examiner) to monitor your marks more easily.

- Timing is vital. Allocate 0.9 minutes per mark.

- Practice the layout of the main calculations in the syllabus.

- Read the examination instructions.

- Read the questions carefully.

- Write clear concise answers.

- When asked to 'compare', aim to have a comparison point on each subject.

Appendix:
Tax tables

TAX TABLES

Income tax rates

2005/06		2004/05	
Rate	Band	Rate	Band
%	£	%	£
10	1 – 2,090	10	0 -2,020
22	2,091 – 32,400	22	2,021-31,400
40	Over 32,400	40	Over 31,400

National Insurance contributions: 2005/06 rates

	Weekly	Monthly	Yearly
Class I (employee)			
Lower Earnings Limit (LEL)	£82.00	£356.00	£4,264.00
Upper Earnings Limit (UEL)	£630.00	£2,730.00	£32,760.00
Earnings Threshold (ET)★	£94.00	£408.00	£4,895.00

Employees' contributions – Class 1

Total earnings £ per week	Contracted in rate	Contracted out rate
Below £94.00★	Nil	Nil
£94.01 - £630.00	11%	9.4%
Excess over £630.00	1%	1%
		1.6% rebate on earnings between LEL and ET

Employer's contributions – Class 1

Total earnings £ per week	Contracted-in rate	Contracted-out rate	
		Final salary	Money purchase
Below £94.00★	Nil	Nil	Nil
£94.01 - £630.00	12.8%	9.3%	11.8%
Excess over £630.00	12.8%	12.8%	12.8%
		3.5% rebate on earnings between LEL and ET	1% rebate on earnings between LEL and ET

★ Earnings threshold below which no NICs payable. There is a zero band between the lower earnings limit (£82 pw) and the earnings threshold (£94 pw) to protect lower earners' rights to contributory state benefits such as basic state pension.

Class 1A (employer's contributions on most benefits) 12.8% on all relevant benefits

Class II (self-employed)   Flat rate per week £2.10 where earnings are over £4,345 pa

Class III (voluntary)   Flat rate per week £7.35

Class IV (self-employed)   8% on profits £4,895 – £32,760; 1% on profits above £32,760

Income tax reliefs

		2005/06 £	2004/05 £
Personal allowance	– under 65	4,895	4,745
	– 65 – 74	7,090	6,830
	– 75 and over	7,220	6,950
Married couple's allowance	– 65 – 74 (see note 1)	5,905	5,725
	– 75 and over (see note 1)	5,975	5,795
	minimum for 65+	2,280	2,210
Age allowance income limit		19,500	18,900
Blind person's allowance		1,610	1,560
Enterprise investment scheme relief limit (see note 2)		200,000	200,000
Venture capital trust relief limit (see note 3)		200,000	200,000

Notes

1 Either spouse must be born before 6 April 1935. Relief is restricted to 10%.

2 EIS qualifies for 20% relief.

3 VCT qualifies for 40% tax relief.

Working and child tax credits

Working tax credit	2005/06 £	2004/05 £
Basic element	1,620	1,570
Couple and lone parent element	1,595	1,545
30 hour element	660	640
Childcare element of WTC		
Maximum eligible cost for 1 child	175 per week	135 per week
Maximum eligible cost for 2 children	300 per week	200 per week
Percent of eligible child costs covered	70	70
Child tax credit		
Family element	545	545
Baby addition	545	545
Child element	1,690	1,625
Tax credits income thresholds and withdrawal rates		
First income threshold	5,220	5,060
First withdrawal rate	37%	37%
Second income threshold	50,000	50,000
Second withdrawal rate	6.67%	6.67%
First threshold for those entitled to CTC	13,910	13,480
Income disregard	2,500	2,500

Personal Pension Contributions (PPCs) and Retirement Annuity Premiums (RAPs)

Age at beginning of tax year	% of Net Relevant Earnings	
	PPCs %	RAPs %
35 or less	17.5	17.5
36 – 45	20	17.5
46 – 50	25	17.5
51 – 55	30	20
56 – 60	35	22.5
61 or more	40	27.5

Earnings limit (PPCs only)		
	2005/06	£105,600
	2004/05	£102,000
	2003/04	£99,000
	2002/03	£97,200
	2001/02	£95,400
	2000/01	£91,800
	1999/00	£90,600
	1998/99	£87,600

Maximum contribution without evidence of earnings (2005/06) £3,600 gross (£2,808 net)

Car and fuel benefits

Company cars Lower threshold CO_2 – 140g/km: 15% of list price (max £80,000 including VAT)

2005/06 Increase by 1% for each 5g/km (round down to nearest multiple of 5g)
3% supplement for diesel cars (maximum 35% of list price)
To maximum: 35% of list price (max £80,000 including VAT)

Car fuel £14,400 × % used for car benefit

Further information:

(a) **In most cases, accessories** are included in the list price on which the benefit is calculated.

(b) **List price** is reduced by employee's capital contributions (maximum £5,000).

(c) **Car benefit** is reduced by the amount of employee's contributions towards running costs, but **fuel** benefit is reduced only if the employee makes good **all** the fuel used for private journeys.

Fixed profit car scheme (authorised mileage rates)

2005/06 rates

Car or Van		Motorcycle	24p
Up to 10,000 miles	40p	Cycle	20p
Over 10,000 miles	25p	Passenger payments	5p

Inheritance tax

Death rate %	Lifetime rate %	Chargeable 2005/06 £'000	Chargeable 2004/05 £'000	Chargeable 2003/04 £'000
Nil	Nil	0 – 275	0 – 263	0 – 255
40	20	Over 275	Over 263	Over 255

Inheritance tax reliefs

Annual exemption	£3,000	Marriage	– parent	£5,000
Small gifts	£250		– grandparent	£2,500
			– bride/groom	£2,500
			– other	£1,000

Reduced charge on gifts within 7 years of death

Years before death	0 – 3	3 – 4	4 – 5	5 – 6	6 – 7
% of death charge	100%	80%	60%	40%	20%

Main Social Security benefits

		From 11.4.05	From 12.4.04
		£	£
Child benefit	– first child	17.00	16.50
	– subsequent child	11.40	11.05
Incapacity benefit	– short term lower rate	57.65	55.90
	– short term higher rate	68.20	66.15
	– long term rate	76.45	74.15
Attendance allowance	– lower rate	40.55	39.35
	– higher rate	60.60	58.80
Retirement pension	– single	82.05	79.60
	– married	131.20	127.25
Widowed parent's allowance		82.05	79.60
Bereavement payment (lump sum)		2,000.00	2,000.00
Jobseekers allowance		56.20	55.65

Value added tax

Standard Rate	17½%
Annual Registration Limit – from 1 April 2005	£60,000
Deregistration Limit – from 1 April 2005	£58,000

Corporation tax

Financial Year	2005 to 31.3.06	2004 to 31.3.05
Full rate	30%	30%
Small companies rate	19%	19%
Starting rate	0%	0%
Profit limit for starting rate	£10,000	£10,000
Effective marginal rate for starting rate	23.75%	23.75%
Profit limit for starting rate	£50,000	£50,000
Small companies limit	£300,000	£300,000
Effective marginal rate for small companies	32.75%	32.75%
Upper marginal limit	£1,500,000	£1,500,000

There is a minimum 19% corporation tax charge on distributed profits.

Capital allowances

	First year allowance	Writing down allowance pa
Plant and machinery	40% * 50% **	25% (reducing balance)
Information and communication technology	100% ***	not usually applicable
Motor cars	–	25% (reducing balance) (max £3,000)
Motor cars – low emission (not more than 120gm/km)	100%	not usually applicable
Industrial buildings	–	4% (straight line)
Agricultural buildings	–	4% (straight line)
Hotels	–	4% (straight line)
Enterprise Zones	100%	–
Scientific research	100%	–
Patents, know-how	–	25% (reducing balance)

* For small and medium sized enterprises from 2 July 1998

** For small enterprises in the one year period commencing 1.4.04/6.4.04 (companies/unincorporated businesses)

*** For small enterprises from 1 April 2000 to 31 March 2004

Small/medium sized enterprises

	Turnover (not more than)	Balance sheet total (not more than)	No of employees (not more than)
Small enterprise	£5.6 million	£2.8 million	50
Medium sized enterprise	£22.8 million	£11.4 million	250

Capital gains tax

	2005/06	2004/05
Rate	Gains taxed at 10%, 20% or 40%, subject to level of income	Gains taxed at 10%, 20% or 40%, subject to level of income
Individuals-exemption	£8,500	£8,200
Trusts-exemption	£4,250	£4,100

Taper relief (for disposals on or after 6 April 2002)

Gains on business assets		Gains on non-business assets *	
Complete years after 5 April 1998	% of gain chargeable	Complete years after 5 April 1998	% of gain chargeable
0	100.0	0	100
1	50	1	100
2 or more	25	2	100
		3	95
		4	90
		5	85
		6	80
		7	75
		8	70
		9	65
		10 or more	60

* Non-business assets held on 17 March 1998 given additional year of relief.

Retail prices index

	Jan	Feb	Mar	Apr	May	Jun	Jul	Aug	Sep	Oct	Nov	Dec
1982			79.4	81.0	81.6	81.9	81.9	81.9	81.9	82.3	82.7	82.5
1983	82.6	83.0	83.1	84.3	84.6	84.8	85.3	85.7	86.1	86.4	86.7	86.9
1984	86.8	87.2	87.5	88.6	89.0	89.2	89.1	89.9	90.1	90.7	91.0	90.9
1985	91.2	91.9	92.8	94.8	95.2	95.4	95.2	95.5	95.4	95.6	95.9	96.0
1986	96.2	96.6	96.7	97.7	97.8	97.8	97.5	97.8	98.3	98.5	99.3	99.6
1987	100.0	100.4	100.6	101.8	101.9	101.9	101.8	102.1	102.4	102.9	103.4	103.3
1988	103.3	103.7	104.1	105.8	106.2	106.6	106.7	107.9	108.4	109.5	110.0	110.3
1989	110.0	111.8	112.3	114.3	115.0	115.4	115.5	115.8	116.6	117.5	118.5	118.8
1990	119.5	120.2	121.4	125.1	126.2	126.7	126.8	128.1	129.3	130.3	130.0	129.9
1991	130.2	130.9	131.4	133.1	133.5	134.1	133.8	134.1	134.6	135.1	135.6	135.7
1992	135.6	136.3	136.7	138.8	139.3	139.3	138.8	138.9	139.4	139.9	139.7	139.2
1993	137.9	138.8	139.3	140.6	141.0	141.0	140.7	141.3	141.9	141.8	141.6	141.9
1994	141.3	142.1	142.5	144.2	144.7	144.7	144.0	144.7	145.0	145.2	145.3	146.0
1995	146.0	146.9	147.5	149.0	149.6	149.8	149.1	149.9	150.6	149.8	149.8	150.7
1996	150.2	150.9	151.5	152.6	152.9	153.0	152.4	153.1	153.8	153.8	153.9	154.4
1997	154.4	155.0	155.4	156.3	156.9	157.5	157.5	158.5	159.3	159.5	159.6	160.0
1998	159.5	160.3	160.8	162.6	163.5	163.4	163.0	163.7	164.4	164.5	164.4	164.4
1999	163.4	163.7	164.1	165.2	165.6	165.6	165.1	165.5	166.2	166.5	166.7	167.3
2000	166.6	167.5	168.4	170.1	170.7	171.1	170.5	170.5	171.7	171.6	172.1	172.2
2001	171.1	172.0	172.2	173.1	174.2	174.4	173.3	174.0	174.6	174.3	173.6	173.4
2002	173.3	173.8	174.5	175.7	176.2	176.2	175.9	176.4	177.6	177.9	178.2	178.5
2003	178.4	179.3	179.9	181.2	181.5	181.3	181.3	181.6	182.5	182.6	182.7	183.5
2004	183.1	183.8	184.6	185.7	186.5	186.8	186.8	187.4	188.1	188.6	189.0	189.9
2005	188.9	189.6	190.5	191.6								

Indexation relief was frozen at 5 April 1998 and replaced by taper relief for individuals and trustees.

Practice examination

PRACTICE EXAMINATION

G70 Investment Portfolio Management

Time Limit: 3 Hours

The exam is based on English law and practice. Questions will be based on the 2005/06 tax year except where it is explicitly stated otherwise.

You should assume that all individuals are UK resident and UK domiciled, except where the question explicitly states otherwise.

You may use a non-programmable calculator. You may not use any reference materials other than the tax tables.

You should attempt all the questions in parts A and B of this paper, and two of the three questions in part C. The time limit is 3 hours.

Section A carries 45 marks.

Section B carries 75 marks.

Section C carries 80 marks.

Subject to providing sufficient detail, you are advised to be as brief and concise as possible using note format and short sentences on separate lines wherever possible.

SECTION A

This section carries 45 marks and you should answer all questions

1   List the factors you would take into account when investing in shares on a non-UK stock market.   (5)

2   State the principal characteristics of a Zero Dividend Investment Trust.   (5)

3   List the main tax reliefs on an Enterprise Investment Scheme (EIS) and briefly state the conditions it must meet in order for it to gain them.   (8)

4   Graham Waller is considering investing part of his recent inheritance in a portfolio of antiques.

   (a)   What are the likely costs of such an investment?   (6)

   (b)   How might the returns and potential risks vary with that of a portfolio of Unit Trusts?
                                                                                              (3)

5   Every firm must have written procedures for dealing with complaints. What are the key points that should be covered in those written procedures?   (4)

6   Calculate the expected price of the shares of XYZ Ltd., whose shares currently stand at £2.00, after a 1 for 4 rights issue with a subscription price of £1.50.   (5)

7   UVX Ltd. has capital reserves of £100 million and long term debts of £40 million. The company has 100 million ordinary shares in issue and £10 million in preference shares. Calculate the gearing of UVX Ltd in percentage terms.   (3)

8   Briefly, explain the principles of the Capital Asset Pricing Model.   (6)

SECTION B

This section contains one compulsory question, carrying 75 marks

9   Nigel Banks is aged 48 and married to Marcia with two children, Sophie and Michael, aged 7 and 10. Nigel has accumulated a relatively diverse portfolio of investments over the years by investing his quarterly bonus, mostly on the advice of the journalists of his regular Sunday paper. Six months ago his mother died and the estate has just been settled. Nigel has received £200,000 in cash. It is the need to invest this money, combined with concern over his existing portfolio, that has prompted him to seek your advice. The existing portfolio, as at 30 April 20X4 is as follows. (Year 20X4 follows year 20X3, which follows 20X2, etc. 20Y6 is the year which is ten years after 20X6.)

Number or amount	Asset	Annual yield	Acquisition price/date	Current price	Current value
10,000	Blue Chip PLC ordinary shares	3.5%	£4.50 1-6-20X1	£9.50	£95,000
6,000	Murky Water ordinary shares	5.0%	£2.00 1-9-20X1	£4.75	£28,500
10,000	Explorer Oil ordinary shares	0.5%	£0.50 1-3-20X2	£0.25	£ 2,500
£8,000	Treasury 7% 20X5		£95 1-12-20X2	£1.03	£ 8,240
£8,000	Treasury 10% 20X7		£107 1-3-20X3	£1.09	£ 8,720
£8,000	Treasury 9% 20Y6		£111 1-6-20X3	£1.11	£ 8,880
5,000	Points West Bank - Far East Equity Unit Trusts	0.5%	£1.00 1-9-20X1	£0.40	£ 2,000
10,000	Beard Investments - Unit Trust FTSE tracker	0%	£1.80 1-11-20X1 FTSE @ 6170.4	£1.26	£12,600
10,000	Points West Bank – North American Equity	2.0%	£1.50 1-3-20X2	£3.00	£30,000
5,000	Irish National Split investment Trust Capitals	0%	£5.00 1-6-20X2	£2.39	£11,950
5,000	Irish National Split investment Trust Warrants	0%	£0.50 1-9-20X2	£0.15	£ 750
				Total	£209,140

Nigel has no other investments and Marcia has no investments of her own. He is not averse to putting a proportion of his portfolio in joint names.

He explains that his objective for the portfolio together with the £200,000 inheritance is to provide mostly capital growth, but that he would also like to provide some money to put towards the children's school fees. He estimates that £12,000 per annum should be sufficient. Nigel's attitude to risk is moderate and he would definitely like to steer clear of high-risk investment, as his experiences of investment in the Far East have been disastrous.

Nigel intends to retire in 12 years time at the age of 60 and he has requested that the portfolio should start to produce an increasing income from that time. He would like the level of risk to reduce in five years time.

Nigel is also keen to reduce his tax liabilities wherever possible. He is a higher rate taxpayer. He has not made use of his Capital Gains Tax Allowance yet this year; neither has Marcia. He also informs you that they have sufficient emergency money in the building society, so there is no need to make an allowance for that.

He states that he would like you to manage the portfolio on a discretionary basis.

Show all calculations. Answers should be expressed to two decimal places.

(a) (i)   On the assumption that the portfolio value was calculated on 30 April 20X4 when the FTSE 100 index stood at 4489.1, calculate how accurately the Beard Investments tracker fund has tracked the FTSE 100.   (3)

(ii)   Taking the investment term as two years and six months, express the loss in annual percentage terms of the decline in the FTSE 100 Index and the decline in the tracker fund.   (2)

(iii)   Briefly, explain why there is a difference in the performance of the tracker fund and the FTSE-100.   (4)

(iv)   Explain how the FTSE-100 index is made up.   (3)

(b) (i)   The Treasury 9% 20Y6 gilt has a current market price of £121 and pays its coupons twice a year. It is due to be redeemed at par in thirteen years' time. Calculate the running yield and redemption yield (approximate only) based on the original purchase price.   (10)

(ii)   The Treasury 9% 20Y6 has a current market price of £121, whereas the Treasury 10% 20X7 has a market price of £119. Explain possible reasons for the difference in price, despite the similarity in yield.   (5)

(iii)   How well do you feel the Gilts would fit in with the portfolio based on Mr Banks's investment objectives? Would you recommend keeping them?   (5)

(c) Blue Chip PLC has a beta factor of 0.95, Murky Water 1.05 and Explorer Oil 2.

(i)   Briefly explain the nature of a beta factor, giving an example.   (3)

(ii)   Which of these shares is most in keeping with Mr Banks's investment objective and why?   (9)

(iii)   Suggest how a portfolio manager could improve Mr Banks's tax situation in keeping with his stated objectives   (6)

(iv)   Blue Chip PLC has just announced a rights issue of 1:5 for £8 per share. What would be the cost of subscribing to the new shares?   (4)

(v)   Having a beta of 2, the Capital Asset Pricing Model suggests that the Explorer Oil share should have increased by more than the rate of increase in the market (up 38%) and yet it has reduced by 50%. How can this be?   (3)

(d) The price of the Irish National Split Capital Investment Trusts has increased by a factor of 10, whereas the warrants have increased by a factor of 30 in 9 months.

(i)   How can the split capital shares have performed so badly?   (3)

(ii)   How can the warrants have performed even worse?   (3)

(iii)   List three other classes of share that may be present in a split capital investment trust   (3)

(iv)   Discuss briefly the investment return from each of those listed in (iii)   (9)

SECTION C

Answer two of the three questions in this section. Each question carries 40 marks.

10   Martin Fraser inherited a portfolio of Accumulation Unit Trusts from his father exactly five years ago. He has asked you to examine the portfolio to determine whether you think it is suitable to provide him with an increasing income in retirement.

Number or amount	Asset	Annual yield	Price at the date of inheritance	Current price	Current value
20,000	Pilkington - UK Growth	2.0%	£1.50	£2.20	£44,000
20,000	Lipton - UK Income	6.0%	£2.15	£3.00	£60,000
20,000	Homeway - UK Equity	4.5%	£1.75	£2.50	£50,000

Martin has not touched the portfolio since he inherited it. Inflation has averaged 2.5% per annum over the time Martin held the investments. According to the documentation, the Lipton - UK Income unit trust uses historic pricing, whereas the other two use forward pricing.

(a) State the formula for calculating the money-weighted rate of return from a portfolio and calculate it for this portfolio. (10)

(b) Calculate the real annual rate of return on the portfolio. (5)

(c) (i) What would be a suitable benchmark for this portfolio? Explain the reason for your selection. (3)

   (ii) Describe how the benchmark listed in (i) is made up and calculated. Explain how often it is changed. (3)

(d) State whether you feel this portfolio would provide Martin with an increasing income and explain why. (5)

(e) (i) Explain the way that unit trusts are priced. Refer specifically to the differences between forward and historic pricing. (4)

   (ii) What complications are there for units on a historic pricing basis if the value changes significantly? (2)

   (iii) Explain how the maximum offer price would be calculated by the fund managers. (6)

   (iv) Under what circumstances is the unit trust fund manager likely to move the prices onto a 'bid' basis? (2)

11   Amanda Tucker has a portfolio of shares and would like you review it to ascertain whether the level of risk taken is appropriate for the returns she is expecting. Amanda has been told that portfolio theory, and the Capital Asset Pricing Model in particular, will help to determine this. Her portfolio is as follows.

Shares	Expected return	Beta coefficient
Vortex Plc ordinary shares	12%	1.00
Wainwright Plc ordinary shares	10%	0.80
Xenor Plc ordinary shares	10.5%	0.75
Yang Computers Plc ordinary shares	16%	1.60
Zeta Plc Ordinary shares	18%	2.0

Vortex Plc and Xenor Plc both lie on the Security Market Line for this portfolio.

(a) Using the CAPM formula:

   (i) Calculate the expected rate of return for the portfolio (4)
   (ii) Calculate the expected rate of return for risk free assets (6)

425

(b) (i) What are the assumptions made by the CAPM formula? (6)

  (ii) Do you feel that these assumptions are realistic? If so, does this invalidate the model? Give reasons for your answer. (4)

(c) Using the information given above, calculate whether Amanda's expected returns are realistic given the beta coefficients of the shares concerned. (9)

(d) (i) What is unsystematic risk? (2)

  (ii) How can it be reduced? Give an example. (3)

(e) What is a counter-cyclical security? How can the systematic risk on a counter-cyclical security be reduced? (2)

(f) Amanda would like you to manage her portfolio on a discretionary basis.

  (i) What are the responsibilities of a discretionary fund manager? (3)

  (ii) What form are the charges for discretionary fund management likely to take? (1)

12 Your company provides a portfolio management service across all types of UK assets via all of the regulated markets. The company specialises in portfolios related to new share issues. As an adviser to clients, you are frequently asked questions about the way the UK stock market works and occasionally, how this might compare with other markets.

The following questions are typical of those asked by clients.

(a) (i) How does the London Stock Exchange operate for equities in the main market? (3)

  (ii) List the other markets through which the London Stock Exchange carries out its operations. (4)

  (iii) Explain briefly the differences between a primary and a secondary market and highlight any relationships that exist between them. (4)

(b) (i) What are the key requirements for a company to obtain a listing on the main market? (6)

  (ii) What obligations are placed on companies as a condition of their listing? (4)

  (iii) How do the requirements of an AIM listing differ to one for the main market? (4)

(c) (i) What is the normal settlement period on the London Stock Exchange? (2)

  (ii) What are the normal settlement periods on the Frankfurt, Paris, New York and Tokyo stock exchanges? (4)

(d) (i) How does the London Gilt Edged market operate? (2)

  (ii) What is an inter-dealer broker (IDB)? (2)

(e) (i) What types of securities are traded on the Stock Exchange Alternative Trading Service? (2)

  (ii) What type of information is listed on the system for each company? (3)

Answers to practice examination

SECTION A

1.
- The currency of the shares and the potential exchange rate risk
- The liquidity of the shares (ability to buy and sell them)
- The systematic issues of the country, for example political risk, inflation and interest rates
- The specific risk of the shares, gearing levels, earnings, dependency on any other industries
- Accountancy standards: these vary from country to country and some are more accurate than others, but this information is essential for fundamental analysis
- The taxation of the securities within the country and the presence of a double taxation agreement

2.
- It is an investment trust that produces no dividend income.
- It is a split of a larger investment trust.
- The security has a nominal repayment value at a fixed time in the future.
- The repayment at this level is dependent on the underlying performance of the company's assets.
- Zeros often have first call on the assets of trust.
- Zeros produce their investment return in the form of a capital gain and as such are subject to CGT.

3. **EIS tax reliefs**
- Tax relief of up to 20% on investments up to £200,000 per annum.
- Capital gains can be deferred by reinvesting them into an EIS using reinvestment relief.
- Gains on the EIS are free of CGT.
- Losses can be offset against income (less the 20% tax relief).

Conditions for tax reliefs
- The shares underlying the EIS must be in unlisted companies.
- Qualifying companies must carry on a trade for at least three years.
- The investor must not hold, directly or indirectly more than 30% of a company.
- The investor must hold the shares for at least three years.

4. (a)
- Acquisition and disposal costs such as auctioneers' or antique dealers' mark-ups
- Travel to and from auctions, information and research costs, books etc
- VAT if buying from a dealer
- Insurance costs
- Storage costs
- Repairs/restoration

(b)
- The returns could potentially be significantly higher (discovering a valuable rarity), but will certainly be more volatile than unit trusts.
- The return will be in the form of capital gains. Items under £6,000 will be covered by the chattels exemption, but the excess will also benefit from the option of taxation of $^5/_3$rds.
- The risks are likely to be significantly higher: the risk of buying a fake, or paying too much for an item.

429

5   •   Each employee should be made aware of the customer complaints procedure.

      •   Complaints should be investigated by a senior member of the firm.

      •   Copies of written complaints and responses should be kept on file together with a record of action taken.

      •   The customer should be informed of details of the appropriate ombudsman or arbitration services available to him.

6   Original holding 4 shares @ £2.00 = £8.00.   (1)

    New rights shares 1 @ £1.50 = £1.50.   (1)

    Post rights issue expected price: 5 shares held, acquisition cost £9.50 = £9.50/5 = £1.90.

        (3)

7   The calculation for gearing is long term debt plus any preference shares, all divided by capital reserves. In this case it would be:

$$\frac{£40 \text{ million} + £10 \text{ million}}{£100 \text{ million}} = 0.5,$$ (2) to get this into % terms we multiply by 100 = 50%.

        (1)

8   •   The CAPM separates the diversifiable risk in a portfolio from the undiversifiable risk or systematic risk.

      •   The principles of the model are based on a series of assumptions related to perfect capital markets.

      •   The model suggests that the systematic risk can be represented by the ratio by which the share rises and falls in relation to the rest of the market.

      •   The ß of the shares is used to represent this movement relative to the market.

      •   The contribution to the portfolio of each asset is defined as:

        Risk free return + ß [Market return – Risk free return].

SECTION B

9   (a) (i)   •   The decrease in the FTSE 100 Index was $1 - (4489/6170.4) = 27.25\%$

              •   The decrease in the unit price over the same period was $1 - (£1.26/£1.80) = 30.00\%$

              •   The tracking error over the period was 3.54%.

      (ii)   •   FTSE annual growth = $(1.2725)^{1/2.5} = 1.1012 = 10.12\%$ per annum loss.

              •   Tracker annual growth = $(1.300)^{1/2.5} = 1.1107 = 11.07\%$ per annum loss.

      (iii) •   The most likely cause of the difference is charges.

              •   There are several methods of tracking an index and these can introduce tracking errors.

              •   Stratification is less accurate than the full replication method, as assumptions are made as to which equities would best reflect the index.

              •   Optimisation uses computer based statistical models to calculate the relationship with the index. In reality the relationships are very complex and this method is not always accurate.

      (iv) •   It is an index of the top 100 shares listed on the UK Stock Exchange.

              •   It is weighted by market capitalisation.

              •   It is continuously updated during trading hours (every minute).

   (b) (i)   Running yield $= \dfrac{\text{Coupon or nominal yield}}{\text{Price}} = \dfrac{9\%}{1.21} = 7.44\%$ or 0.0744

Redemption yield requires the use of internal rates of return. The Hewlett Packard HP 10B allows this figure to be calculated relatively simply.

    •   Future Value: FV = £100 return on redemption.

    •   The current cost, or present value: PV = –£121 (a negative figure to represent a cash outflow)

    •   Interest payments: PMT = £4.50 (2 per year = £9).

    •   Number of payments due: N = 26 (2 per year over 13 years).

    •   There are 2 payments per year: P/Yr.

This should give an answer of 6.57%, which is a nominal yield. The effective rate should be 6.68%.

An approximation would be allowed, for example:

    •   The stock was bought for £121 and will be redeemed at £100: this represents a loss of £21 over 13 years

    •   This equates to a loss of $21/121 = 0.1736$ over 13 years or $(1.1736)^{1/13} = 1.0124$ or 1.24%

    •   When this (negative figure, a loss of 1.24%) is added to the running yield of 7.44%, this gives us an approximation of the redemption yield, which should be in the region of 6.20%

      (ii) •   The main issue here is not the yield, it is the redemption date.

              •   Long-term interest rates have been relatively low.

              •   A factor such as the potential for the UK joining the rest of Europe in economic monetary union could be the cause. A poorer economic outlook could also depress long-term interest rates.

- Investors seeking a reasonably safe long-term return (12 years) will get it with the Treasury 20Y6, but the Treasury 20X7 will be redeemed in 3 years time with any re-investment subject to prevailing interest rates.

- Purchasers of the longer gilt are prepared to pay more, despite a lower return, because that rate will be guaranteed for 12 years.

(iii)
- Mr Banks is seeking growth and is prepared to take a moderate risk.

- Within the profile of this portfolio, some Gilt investment may be required depending on the asset allocation determined by the manager.

- Maintaining these Gilts would be an option rather than buying more.

- A factor in this decision would be future estimates of inflation, as one of the risks with fixed interest investments is that where inflation rates increase, the real rate of return can reduce and could even be negative.

- I would recommend keeping them.

(c) (i)
- A beta factor is a measure of volatility of a share relative to the rest of the market.

- The beta factor relates to the movement above the risk free return.

- It indicates the likely level of movement of a share relative to the market.

(ii)
- Blue Chip has a beta of 0.95 and has a similar volatility to the market. It is likely to meet Mr Banks's investment objective on the grounds of risk.

- It also has the potential for growth, another of Mr Banks's objectives.

- In respect of tax, there is likely to be an issue as the share has a dividend of 3.5%, which on £95,000 is not inconsiderable, and he will be liable to income tax at 40%, which may not meet his objective of tax minimisation.

- Murky Water is also suitable on risk, having a beta of 1.05.

- It also has the potential for growth.

- It does however have a large dividend which will be taxable at 40%.

- Explorer Oil is way above Mr Banks's risk tolerance.

- It has the potential for growth, but this is of less importance than the risk issue.

- The dividend income is at a minimum and will not be a problem. However this is also less important than the risk issue. The loss in capital value can be offset against future capital gains.

(iii)
- Selling the Explorer Oil shares would create a capital loss, which can be offset against gains realised in the current year.

- The portfolio manager could 'bed and ISA' Nigel's shares up to his maximum of £7,000 into stocks and shares ISA.

- He could do this for both Mr Banks's and Marcia's ISA allowances.

- He could put the total portfolio in joint names, transferring the shares as well, giving two CGT allowances.

- He could also use some of the tax-exempt NS&I products.

(iv) The number of shares to purchase would be 10,000 / 5 = 2,000.

At £8, this would be £16,000.

(v) • The CAPM assumes that the specific element of an asset's price variation can be represented by its performance relative to the market.

• In reality, this will not always work as there are many other factors to take into account.

• Oil exploration companies are notoriously volatile and their prices can vary widely with the results of their exploration.

• Beta factors are based on past performance and cannot predict the future.

(d) (i) • Split Capital Investment Trusts are highly geared investments.

• They are the split of an investment trust that gets all the capital growth from the others such as the Zero Dividend and the Stepped Preference splits.

• When markets fall, this gearing increases losses to well above market levels.

(ii) • Warrants may be even more highly geared than capitals.

• The warrants give a right to buy, probably the capital shares at a fixed price.

• The performance of the underlying share is poor and this has affected the performance of the warrant.

(iii) • Income shares
• Zero dividend shares
• Stepped preference shares

(iv) *Income shares*

• Receive all of the income paid after payment of any preference shares.

• The income tends to be fairly high as it comes from a large pool of underlying assets.

• The shares will be redeemed at fixed date in the future for a fixed price.

• Neither the income nor the return of capital is guaranteed.

• Risk levels can vary from moderate to low risk depending on the growth required in the underlying asset to repay the share's nominal value (the hurdle rate).

Zero dividend preference shares

• The return is in the form of an increase in the value of the shares at a fixed date in the future.

• The future return is not guaranteed, but depends on the performance of the underlying investment trust assets.

• No income is produced.

• Risk levels can vary from moderate to low-risk depending on the growth required in the underlying asset to repay the shares' capital value (the hurdle rate). These are high up in the priority order for payment.

• Even greater risk levels can occur where the shares are based on other zeros rather than a properly constructed split of shares

Stepped preference shares

• The return is in the form of an increasing dividend.

• A nominal value is repaid at a fixed date in the future.

• Preference shares have first call on the assets of the investment trust.

• Risk levels tend to be low because of the priority of this share class over the others.

SECTION C

10   (a) •   Return, $R = (V_1 - V_0 + I)/V_0$.

          • V_1 = Value of the portfolio at the end of the period.

          • V_0 = Value of the portfolio at the beginning of the period.

          •   I = The income or capital distribution during the period.

      For this portfolio:

          • V_1 = £154,000

          • $V_0 = (20,000 \times 1.5) + (20,000 \times 2.15) + (20,000 \times 1.75) = £108,000$

          •   I = 0. As these are accumulation unit trusts no distribution has been made of income and Martin has not touched the portfolio since he inherited it.

          •   Therefore, the money weighted return = (154,000 − 108,000)/108,000 = 42.59%

    (b) •   The money weighted return is 42.59% over five years.

          •   Annualised, this would be $(1.4259)^{1/5} = 1.0735$ or 7.35% per annum.

          •   Inflation has averaged 2.5% per annum, therefore the real rate of return would be $\dfrac{1.0735}{1.025} = 1.047 = 4.7\%$.

    (c) (i) •   FTSE All Share Index

              •   Because it tracks UK shares, which is where the majority of this Unit Trust Money is invested

              •   There is a mixture of income and growth stocks as well as the UK equities. This is likely to give a wide spread of UK shares, ruling out the FTSE-100

        (ii) •   The FTSE-All-Share Index is made up of the shares in the FTSE-100, the FTSE-250 and a further 500 plus quoted companies representing some 96.8% of the market value.

              •   It is a real-time index.

              •   The constituents are reviewed quarterly (March, June, September December).

    (d) •   Yes - on balance the portfolio should provide for an increasing income.

          •   The UK Equity Unit Trusts should mirror the yield on the FTSE All Share index at some 3.0%.

          •   The yield should continue to be the same as the value of the index rises increasing the return.

          •   The growth trust has a smaller yield to start with, but overall this should rise as the companies, which are investing for growth grow and their incomes increase.

          •   The income trust produces a good income, but it is not likely to grow very quickly. This should be offset by the growth trust.

    (e) (i) •   The price of unit trusts is calculated at a specific time each day.

               •   The price is based on the value of the shares within the trust divided by the number of units.

               •   With forward pricing, units purchased will get the next price fixed by the company.

- With historic pricing, units will be purchased at the previously fixed price until a new price is fixed.

(ii) Where the managers believe the unit price to have changed by more than 2% since the last price was fixed, they must switch to a forward pricing basis.

(iii)
- The total value of the securities underlying the trust is calculated.

- The dealing costs of purchasing those assets are added in, for example, stamp duty and brokerage.

- Any other trust assets are added in, such as any un-invested cash, accrued income that has not yet been distributed and the balance of any charges and expenses.

- The total of the assets is added up and divided by the number of units.

- The initial charge will then be added on.

- Prices are rounded to four significant figures.

(iv)
- Where demand is low
- Where more units are being redeemed than sold

11 (a) (i) As Vortex and Xenor are both on the Security Market line, we can calculate the portfolio return using substitution.

The CAPM equation is: Return = $R_f + ß(R_m - R_f)$

With Vortex, $12\% = R_f + 1(R_m - R_f)$ $12\% = R_m + R_f - R_f$ so $12\% = R_m$

As the ß of Vortex is 1 and it is on the Market Security Line for the portfolio, the expected rate of return on the portfolio is 12%.

(ii) If we use the R_m figure calculated above and assuming Xenor is also on the Market Security Line:

$10.5\% = R_f + 0.75 (12\% - R_f)$
$10.5\% = R_f + 9\% - 0.75R_f$
$10.5\% - 9\% = R_f - 0.75R_f$
$1.5\% = 0.25 R_f$

Therefore $R_f = 1.5\%/0.25 = 6\%$.

(b) (i)
- That investors are naturally risk-averse

- That all investments have the same holding period

- That the market is liquid

- That there are no transaction costs and taxes on the returns

- That market intelligence is freely available

- That unlimited amounts of money can be borrowed at the risk-free rate by the investors

(ii)
- No. All of these assumptions are wrong to a greater or a lesser extent.

- Not all investors are naturally risk-averse. Not all investments have the same holding period. The market is not totally liquid, although liquidity is high for listed shares. There are transaction costs. Market intelligence is not freely available and there is certainly not unlimited amounts of money that can be borrowed by investors at the risk free rate.

- However, these points do not invalidate the model entirely. Markets are very complex and any attempt to model them will involve assumptions.

(c) *Wainwright*

R = 6 + 0.8 (12 − 6) = 10.8%

Her expectation is low. The share is underpriced.

Yang

R = 6 + 1.6 (12 − 6) = 15.6%

Her expectation is high. The share is overpriced.

Zeta

R = 6 + 2.0 (12 − 6) = 18%

Her expectation is correct. The share is correctly priced.

(d) (i)
- Unsystematic risk is risk inherent in the share itself.
- It is the level of risk that is not related to the market.

(ii)
- Unsystematic risks can be reduced by diversification, by buying other shares that cancel out the risk.

- An example could be an ice cream manufacturer. When the weather is bad, ice cream sales are likely to drop.

- This could be diversified out by an umbrella manufacturer, which will increase production in bad weather. They also cancel each other out over the summer/winter cycle.

(Any reasonable pair of companies will do as an example.)

(e)
- This is a security that does well when the economic cycle is in decline. It will normally perform less well when the market is booming.

- By purchasing a security that is in phase with the economic cycle.

(f) (i)
- To make investment transactions on the investor's behalf without consulting her

- To take care of the administrative issues relating to the portfolio

- To produce regular reports

(ii) Any one of the following.

- A fixed annual fee.

- An annual fee based on a percentage of the fund.

- The commission may just be retained.

- Extra charges may be levied for administration, safe custody, and distributions.

12 (a) (i)
- It is a quote-driven market for the majority of shares using the SEAQ system.

- An order-driven system called SETS has been in operation since the end of 1997 covering the FTSE 100 shares plus other liquid shares.

(ii)
- International equity market
- Gilt-edged market
- Other fixed interest markets

- Alternative Investment Market

(iii)
- Primary markets are a facility for companies, governments and other international organisations to raise new capital.

- Secondary markets provide investors with the means to buy and sell securities that they already own.

- Primary markets are dependent on secondary markets as, without them, it is highly unlikely new issues would be taken up, because there would be no means for selling the securities on.

- Secondary markets rely on primary markets to provide them with a good stream of quality stock.

(b) (i)
- The market value of the securities must be at least £700,000 for shares (£200,000 for other securities).

- The security must be freely transferable.

- The issue of warrants must be limited to 20% of the issued equity.

- At least 25% of the shares must be on offer to the public.

- The company must submit three years audited accounts ending not more than 6 months before application for listing.

- There must be continuity of management over a period of three years or more.

- The directors must have appropriate expertise and experience of managing the business.

(ii)
- Price-sensitive announcements must be made through the LSE.

- Dividend announcements must be made through the LSE.

- Full year accounts must be published within six months of the financial year end.

- Half year results must be published within four months of the date of company accounts.

- Additional information must be provided in the company accounts.

(iii)
- There is no minimum size of company.

- There is no minimum percentage of the share that has to be in public ownership.

- A trading record is not required.

- An AIM company must have an appointed nominated broker.

(c) (i)
- T + 3

(ii)
- Frankfurt T+2
- Paris T+3
- New York T+3
- Tokyo T+3

(d) (i)
- The London Gilt-Edged market is a quote-driven market.

- Firms registered with the Bank of England as Gilt-Edged Market Makers (GEMMs) are required to quote prices on enquiry.

    (ii)   •   These are brokers that allow deals to be arranged between GEMMs.

           •   The system enables the transaction to take place on an anonymous basis.

(e) (i)   •   All AIM shares

           •   Listed stocks with less than two market makers

    (ii)   •   Current quotes from member firms

           •   Current quotes from market makers if available

           •   Company information

           •   Past trading activity

           •   The name of the corporate broker

Answers to Quick Quiz questions

Chapter 1

1   When a country has negative growth or a reduction in GDP, (usually for two or more quarters) it is described as being in recession.

2   The level of technological development directly affects economic growth as it impacts on the levels and efficiency of production of that country. Technology also improves the quality and range of goods, making them more desirable, increasing demand.

3   Investors in developed countries can benefit from the growth in emerging countries by buying shares directly or investing in multinational companies with worldwide interests.

4   A strong currency can cause difficulties for domestic companies and exporters competing in overseas markets. Imports will be cheaper where the exchange rate is high. This low cost will increase demand for foreign goods. This has a number of effects. The balance of payments will move against the country and cause other economic problems. Importers and distributors of foreign goods will benefit from the situation, but producers for the domestic market will suffer from competition from cheap imports.

5   As this trend continues, it is likely that there will be more money invested to provide for retirement and healthcare as time goes on. The fresh influx of money is likely to sustain the markets at greater levels.

6   The US system could be described as a 'shareholder value' model of share ownership.

7   Developing economies tend to have large and increasing supplies of labour, which fuels economic growth. Technological advances can rapidly increase production.

8   Interest rates in the UK, since May 1997, are decided by a committee of advisers known as the Monetary Policy Committee, chaired by the governor of the Bank of England, which meets monthly.

9   For many countries the prices of currencies are dependent purely on supply and demand and, as such, float freely on the foreign exchanges. Exchange controls imposed by governments will influence exchange rates to a greater or lesser extent.

10 Fiscal policy is the control of taxation and government spending.

11 In some countries, banks are required to place a proportion of their liabilities as deposits (often non-interest-bearing) with the central bank. The level of this deposit as a proportion of a banks total lending is known as the Reserve Ratio.

12 It will increase money supply.

Chapter 2

1   A share account.

2   These are deposit investments, which must remain invested for a set period of time. The investment is not normally accessible within the fixed rate period.

3   Only if held to maturity.

4   The maximum protection is £31,700 (returned on the first £35,000).

5   An individual who will need to spend their money in a different currency or one who wishes to speculate on changes in exchange rates.

Chapter 3

1   It is a fixed interest security underwritten by an international syndicate sold in currencies of countries other than that in which they are denominated.

2   A bulldog is a foreign fixed interest security issued in Sterling on the London Stock Exchange.

3   It is a derivative of a gilt. The gilt is split onto a number of separate securities representing each interest payment and the final capital repayment. The securities can be purchased separately on the open market.

4   Loan stock will have a normally have a higher risk than debentures as the latter are usually secured by a floating charge over company assets. Debentures will have terms and conditions applied to the assets used as security for the loan.

5   Preference shares pay a fixed interest payment on a regular basis. They would normally return a fixed amount of capital on redemption, but some are convertible into ordinary shares.

6   A repo (a sale and repurchase agreement), a gilt future or an interest rate option.

7   A higher rate taxpayer is more likely to be interested in a gilt trading at below par. On redemption, the investment will be redeemed at par giving a capital gain. Capital gains on gilts are exempt from CGT, which would be beneficial for a higher rate taxpayer.

8   Under these circumstances, the curve is likely to be inverted.

9   The redemption yield would probably be the most useful, as it allows for interest payments and changes in the capital value of a gilt.

10   Gilts or Treasury Bills are the lowest risk fixed interest investments. Gilts can be made even lower risk if held to maturity. Index-linked gilts would stop inflation from eroding the returns from the investment. Such an investment would produce an increasing income and grow very safely in real terms over the term to redemption.

Chapter 4

1   Private investors in the UK are relatively active. A significant proportion of the volume of transactions is driven by private investors.

2   The P/E ratio gives an idea of the way the market rates a share, the higher the P/E the more highly the market rates the share.

3   A counter-cyclical share.

4   Shares of companies that deal with 'essential' goods and services.

5   Dividend yield expresses the dividend as a percentage of the current market value. Although dividend yields do not change much, absolute income levels on equity investments tend to increase over time.

6   The dividend cover calculation (earnings per share/dividend per share) can give an indication of how many times over a company could have paid the dividend. Clearly, the greater this figure is, the more likely the dividend is of continuing.

7   The NAV of a share gives an indication of the money that would be left for the shareholders in the event of the company going into liquidation. It puts a 'worst case scenario' price on the share, although some shares will occasionally trade at below their NAV.

8   Financial gearing is a calculation for the level of a company's borrowing relative to its assets.

9   The required levels of cash flow are specific for each type of business. When comparing the cash flow of a company, it makes more sense to compare it with one operating in the same industrial sector.

10   They are essentially the same, but a merger is a take-over with the agreement of the management of the target company. Where the target company management is not in favour, the term acquisition is used.

11   60 days, within which a minimum of 14 days must be allowed for a vote by the target company's shareholders

12   From cash reserves, by commercial borrowing, using a rights issue or by using shares that have been created but not issued.

13   The P/E figure after the deal will give an indication as to how the market feels about the deal.

14   No, privatisation occurs around the world.

15   The members or policyholders are required to vote on the issue.

16   Mezzanine finance is where money is raised from a number of different sources, each taking a different level of risk and expecting a different level of reward.

17   A 'business angel' is a private individual with risk capital to invest and normally skills or experience to offer to a newly formed company.

18   Via an introduction, a placing, or by an offer for sale.

19   A fixed price offer, a tender offer and a subscription offer.

20   To raise money. This can be to finance a merger or acquisition, to improve liquidity, reduce debt or to generally help a company out when it is having financial difficulties.

21   One with large cash reserves, part of which it wishes to distribute to its shareholders.

22   A share split is effectively a rights issue at no cost to the investor, who does not have to pay for the new shares received.

Chapter 5

1   Exchange traded and over the counter (OTC).

2   Traded options can be traded as a financial instrument in their own right, traditional options can not.

3   The strike price of a traded option is the price at which the option can be exercised. If the option is being settled for cash, the difference between the market price and strike price determines the profit on the contract.

4   They can either deliver the specified shares, or settle for cash.

5   The premium paid.

6   The liability is unlimited.

7   The strike price less the premium.

8   Simply that the value of the derivative is calculated and used to update transactions and holdings data. It means that both parties to a future contract are provided with a daily account of their liabilities/assets.

9   Initial, variation and intra day.

10   Capital gains or losses, but no income.

11   Market risk, liquidity risk and credit risk.

12   To allow them to track an index, to allow them to deal in markets where it is impractical to hold the equities themselves, eg for tax or liquidity reasons, and to anticipate future sums of money.

13   By selling FTSE 100 futures or buying FTSE 100 put options.

14   The option, as the liability is limited to the purchase premium.

Chapter 6

1   An investment which has a limited number of investment units or shares.

2   Companies, as with investment trusts and OEICs, and trusts as with unit trusts.

3   The trustees, but they can get an agent to perform this role on their behalf.

4   Invoking the cancellation notice will return their money without deduction of charges, but the value of the investment could have changed with the value of the underlying investment. There are no limits on the loss in respect of this.

5   10%.

6   At least 80% of the trust's assets must be invested in the geographical area.

7   The manager's box is the stock of units held by a manager to improve liquidity and to reduce the need for creation and cancellation of units.

8   When prices are fixed on a forward pricing basis, buyers and sellers of units will not know the unit price that will apply to their transaction. The reason for this is that the price for transactions up to the valuation point will take place at the next published price.

9   Initial charge, exit charge and annual management charge.

10   A UCITS (Undertakings for Collective Investment in Transferable Securities) certificate.

11   The ACD is broadly responsible for the management of the OEIC and the Depository has a role in the protection of the investor, in a similar capacity to that of a trustee to a unit trust.

12   A dilution levy is an additional charge that can be made to cover the cost of creation or cancellation of units.

13   The main benefit is that the open ended corporate fund structure is the most common type of pooled fund in Europe and the US and will be far easier to market outside the UK.

Chapter 7

1   An investment trust is a closed-ended investment unlike a unit trust. The other main difference is that an investment trust can borrow money to gear up returns for an investor, whereas a unit trust can not.

2   The directors of the investment trust company, although they may contract a third party to perform these duties on their behalf.

3   The level of demand for the share.

4   It would probably be lower.

5   Zero dividend investment trusts.

6   Income and residual capital shares are a highly geared and high-risk class of split capital investment trusts. They offer the potential for high dividends and capital returns.

7   The share with a hurdle rate of 5%, as the underlying assets only need to grow by 5% to repay at the predetermined price.

8   The last one in the priority order for payment. This would usually be capital shares, although if there are any warrants in issue they will be more highly geared. Warrants, however, are not a class of share, but a class of security.

9   A diluted NAV calculation allows for the effects of investors exercising all of their warrants.

10   To compensate the investor for the fact that the investment trust will usually fall to a discount immediately trading starts.

11   A packaged unit is a combination of different classes of Split Capital investment trust shares. The shares are recombined in their original proportions to create a unit with the same investment characteristics as a normal investment trust share.

12   An investment trust manager can borrow to increase gearing.

Chapter 8

1   The units do not produce an income directly, but encashing units can produce an income stream.

2   They are potentially subject to a Market Value Reduction (MVR), which could result in a capital loss.

3   Stock Market Managed.

4   With-profit investment is affected by:

- The performance of the fund's investments
- The underwriting profits of the life assurance company
- The status of the company, mutual or proprietary
- Profit levels of other areas of the business for mutual companies
- The financial strength of the company

5   This is because life companies reserve the right to apply a Market Value Reduction to any pay out they may make. The result of this is a penalty amount added to the increased value of the units, which could reduce the value to less than the original investment.

6   Pound cost averaging affects regular premium investments but not a single-premium investment.

7   Unit-linked life assurance bonds do not produce income at all. The income from the underlying investment is re-invested and represented by an increase in the value of the funds. Encashment of units to simulate income is effectively encashment of a mixture of income and capital.

8   They are both single premium, non-qualifying life assurance policies. Both have access to with-profit investment, but the single premium endowment is 'conventional' and increases in value by a series of bonuses. With profits via a unit-linked life assurance bond will be 'unitised'.

9   The effects of gross roll-up are marginal and will often be cancelled out by the higher charges on offshore policies. The charges are higher for two main reasons: it is more costly to deal in overseas markets, and the life company cannot offset its costs against taxable income.

10   Highly personalised bonds.

11   A life assurance bond is subject to income tax only.

12   The life company usually reserves the right to cancel the issue and return investors' money if there is not sufficient take-up.

13   The minimum is usually a return of the original investment less the income paid out over the term of the policy.

14   The main reason is that with a broker bond there are two layers of investment management to pay for.

Chapter 9

1   Tracker funds are available on a number of indices including some of the world-wide ones. Investing in the index fund will save money over the cost of investing directly and will provide the investor with greater investment diversity. By investing in a world-wide index fund in the UK, an investor can avoid local performance issues.

2   The costs involved in researching and buying suitable equities can be avoided by automatically investing in set equities, in pre-determined quantities.

3   The most accurate method of tracking an index is to fully replicate the index constituents with the tracker fund.

4   Tracker funds eliminate specific or non-systematic risk. This is achieved by the investment in a whole market rather than in a specific share.

5   The key criteria used for the selection of tracker funds are the accuracy with which the fund tracks the relevant index and charges.

Chapter 10

1   Unlisted shares can be bought on the Alternative Investment Market (AIM), OFEX (an independent market in unlisted shares), or, if not available on these markets, directly from other shareholders of the company.

2   Unlisted companies tend to be subject to a number of risks that could affect their business.

   (a)   Many have a lack of diversification with limited products and client base.

   (b)   Most are fully dependant on the UK economy and will suffer if it does.

   (c)   For many, a lack of financial resources can be a problem.

   (d)   Some companies are totally dependant on key individuals for their survival, losing them could prove disastrous.

   (e)   Many companies have limited expertise to deal with business issues such as the legal, financial and marketing side of the business and limited funds to purchase the services from a third party.

3   There are income and capital gains tax incentives for direct investment in unlisted shares. For indirect investment, VCTs and EIS schemes provide a variety of income and capital gains tax breaks.

4   The maximum VCT investment is £200,000 per annum.

5   The maximum VCT investment in quoted investments is 30%.

6   They can become a director of the company and receive a reasonable remuneration and still benefit from the tax breaks if, at the time of the investment, they were not connected with, or employed by, the company.

7   The pooled form of enterprise zone buildings are called Enterprise Zone Trusts.

8   When Enterprise Zone buildings are sold on, the benefit of 100% IBA relief is reduced to 4%, reducing the value of the property to a subsequent investor who will not be prepared to pay as much for it.

9   Physical assets need to be stored and kept secure, both of which will incur costs. Other types of physical asset may require additional specialist attention such as restoration or storage in special conditions.

10   Most physical assets are bought and sold via an auction, or a third party. In either case, this can add significant amounts to the cost through auction house fees or profits for the vendor. It is also possible that VAT will be charged on some transactions purchased from a shop.

11   Direct investment in commodities can cause problems relating to storage and transportation. There may also be a requirement for the purchaser to verify the quality of the commodity, which would require high levels of skill or expertise. Direct investment in commodities is totally unsuitable for most private investors.

12   Commodity options would usually be the lower risk, however put options written on an uncovered basis can be just as risky as futures.

13   Buyers of futures are effectively liable to the extent of the price of the asset at the time it is purchased, or less, if they can close the transaction before expiry at a suitable price.

14   Commodity derivatives are extremely volatile, because the underlying assets are volatile in their own right and the use of derivatives will gear up the price movements.

15   An investment in property usually requires a very large initial outlay which, for many investors, is met by borrowing money. Any increase in the cost of borrowing will increase the outgoings and reduce the overall level of profit.

16   The main problem with property investment is the lack of liquidity. Realising money from the investment can take a long time.

17   The qualification rules allow them to use the property themselves without losing tax concessions.

18   The value of commercial property is considerably more volatile.

19   The lease agreement will cover the term of the lease, the levels of rent, the frequency of rent review and will also identify whether the leaseholder is responsible for maintenance of the building or not.

20   Under normal market conditions, they are as liquid as any other, but many property life assurance and unit trust funds will have a clause allowing a six-month delay on the cancellation of units under certain market conditions.

Chapter 11

1    $$\frac{\text{Long - term loans}}{\text{Capital + reserves}}$$

2   Return on capital employed (ROCE).

3   This gives an indication of the quality of the management of a company, particularly their ability to put capital to the best use.

4 The cash available for investment gives a clear indication as to the extent to which a company could consider capital expenditure or acquisitions without the need to raise finance.

5 • Earnings per share
  • Dividends per share
  • Dividend cover
  • Dividend yield
  • The price/earnings ratio
  • Return on equity
  • Net asset value per share
  • Market to book ratio

6 By examining company accounts, we are looking at the actual value of the company. From this we can tell whether the market has over or undervalued it and we can act accordingly.

Chapter 12

1 Virt-x or OFEX.

2 On the LSE there are markets in gilts, eurobonds and other UK fixed interest securities. Fixed interest securities are also traded on the LSE, AIM and Virt-x.

3 With an order-driven market, buyers and sellers are matched directly by brokers on a trading floor or, more usually, by a computer system. In a quote-driven market, market makers buy and sell the securities to and from the stockbrokers.

4 The main role of the nominated adviser is to guide the directors to ensure they abide by the rules relating to an AIM listing. They are also responsible for the process of obtaining the listing and will be required to advise the directors of their requirement to make the appropriate risk warning statements to existing and prospective investors.

5 For any trade in the shares of an AIM company to take place, they need to be present on the electronic trading system for the AIM, SEATS plus. This can only be done via a sponsoring stockbroker.

6 FTSE 100 shares and a number of others.

7 The prices are not 'firm', ie they could be different to those published. Prices are described as 'indicative' for transactions above NMS.

8 A GEMM is a market maker in gilts. The GEMMs compete on a competitive quotation basis.

9 All orders and the transactions that have been executed are published continuously on the Virt-x stock exchange ticker.

10 Discretionary, advisory and execution only.

11 None unless they have specific insurance to cover the situation.

12 The normal rolling settlement period on the LSE is now T + 3.

13 The cash memorandum account for the money, and the stock account for the shares.

14 The New York Stock Exchange (NYSE).

15 New York, Frankfurt and the UK for transactions via SETS.

16 A central depository must hold shares purchased via the EURONEXT stock exchange.

17 CLEARNET in combination with EUROCLEAR.

Chapter 13

1   Risk and expected returns.

2   Mean, median and mode.

3   The ß of an equity, or any other security, is the volatility of the security as a ratio of the volatility of the market. The β measures the systematic risk of an investment.

4   An asset that is negatively correlated to a specific factor moves in the opposite direction. For example, if the factor increases, the share price reduces and vice versa. This can be used in a portfolio as positively and negatively correlated assets can be paired to cancel out the effects of the factor.

5   Systematic risk is the element of risk attributable to market wide changes. It is often known as market risk.

6   In the CAPM, non-systematic risk is modelled by the β of the asset as a single representation of all the non-systematic factors.

7   The risk free return, is the return that can be achieved on a portfolio without taking any risk.

8   The Capital Market Line runs at a tangent to the efficient frontier from the level of risk free returns. The tangent gives the point for the most efficient portfolio in terms of risk/expected reward, where risk is total risk as measured by standard deviation.

9   As a minimum, two are required.

10   Because most of the assumptions are flawed in some way and the variables are not easy to estimate.

11   The main difference is the number of variables, which is considerably more with APT than with CAPM.

12   They must 'know the customer' and, with them, determine their objectives and needs. They must design an asset allocation strategy to achieve those objectives and need to pick the appropriate assets from each asset class. They need to monitor the portfolio to ensure that the objectives are, and continue to be, achieved and, finally, they must review the customer's circumstances on a regular basis to ensure that the objectives have not changed.

13   No-risk, low-risk, medium or moderate-risk and high-risk.

14   For most private customers, 25-50% of annual income would be required.

15   Suitable investment vehicles might be:
     - ISAs
     - NS&I products
     - EIS or VCT
     - Life assurance bonds, by use of the deferred tax treatment
     - Offshore roll-up funds (also for tax deferral)
     - Use of equities and collective investments up to the annual CGT exemption

16   Diversification within this asset class of gilts can be achieved by investing in a variety of yields and terms to maturity.

17   Business sectors, by market capitalisation and by geographical spread.

18   The three private investor indices published by FTSE International are the Growth Portfolio Index, the Income Portfolio Index and the Balanced Portfolio Index.

Chapter 14

1   The manager has a duty of care to ensure that the customer fully understands the implications of the risk strategy chosen.

2   The underlying financial instrument is quite different and responds to deferent economic and financial influences.

3   Investment objectives could include the following.

- Income
- Growth
- Income and growth
- Term of investment
- Tax reduction
- Environmental friendliness
- Production of cash flow
- Levels of risk

4   They need to adjust their investment strategy to allow for the level of pension fund withdrawals and the eventual encashment of the portfolio to purchase an annuity.

5   Large pension funds often need cash flow to provide transfer values, possibly death benefits (if uninsured) and lump sums to purchase annuities or pay pension benefits.

6   The two main types of portfolio management are: discretionary and advisory. With discretionary management, the fund manager decides on the transactions that will take place, whereas with advisory management, the fund manager contacts the customer with the advice and they choose whether the transaction will take place.

7   The frequency of the generation of the report will vary with the type of investment but it will usually be between monthly and annually.

8   In order to get a reasonable spread of direct equities, a relatively large minimum is required.

9   This is because each pooled fund itself has a wide diversification of assets underlying it.

10   Sixteen.

11   The reason for this is that there are two types of offshore funds. Each are taxed quite differently providing more opportunities for tax planning.

12   Life assurance bonds, as the tax payable is very susceptible to the timing and size of withdrawals. This is an area where the fund manager can have a significant influence on the customer's tax position.

13   A SIPP from a life assurance company may require a minimum sum invested into one or more of the life company's pension funds.

14   Because the investment returns may not be sufficient to overcome the charges and mortality drag.

15   **Permitted SIPP investments**

(a) Quoted shares, including AIM shares
(b) Futures and options (if traded on a recognised exchange)
(c) Collective investments such as unit trusts, OEICs and investment trusts
(d) Insurance company fumds
(e) Traded endowment policies
(f) Commercial property (with up to 75% of purchase financed by borrowing)

Investments not permitted in SIPPs

(a) Residential property (with minor exceptions)

(b) Loans

(c) Unlisted shares

(d) Chattels such as antiques, paintings, fine wines

(e) Gold bullion

(f) NS&I Premium Bonds

16 Between 35% and 100% of the Government Actuary's Department (GAD) rates.

17 The main factors that will affect the fund and hence the pension at the end of the withdrawal period are:

- Charges
- Mortality drag
- Pound cost averaging
- Annuity rates
- Risk/reward

18 It is a term to describe the fact that pension fund withdrawals do not benefit from the same cross subsidy of annuity rates from annuitants who die, as annuities.

19 The more volatile a fund is, the more likely it is that it will be affected by pound cost averaging.

20 £7,000 per tax year.

Chapter 15

1 $PV \times (1 + i)^n = FV$.

2 $FV/(1 + i)^n = PV$.

3 UK indices, overseas equity indices and crossborder indices.

4 Excluding investment trusts, and variations with higher and lower yields.

5 SBF 120 index.

6 Dow Jones, and Standard & Poors.

7 An index where the shares of more than one country are represented.

8 Micropal, HSW (Harvard Stafford Wright), Standard & Poors or Morning Star.

9 Outperform more than half of the other fund managers in their sector.

10 $R = ((V^1 - V^0) + I)/V^0$.

11 A time weighted return allows for movements of cash in and out of a portfolio and does not just look at the overall return.

12 Asset allocation and security selection.

13 A fund with good cash flow has a greater ability to change strategy on an ongoing basis, while one with a poor cash flow must sell assets before they can take a new position.

14 The main considerations are:

- Administration
- Costs and charges
- Experience and skill in the relevant investment area

- Funds under management
- History
- Investment strategy/style
- Past performance
- Quality of service and staff
- Resources

15 Firms that operate a particular style will influence investment returns by the extent to which the company's policies are enforced.

16 The main reason is because they are calculated based on historic data and cannot allow for current or future events.

Chapter 16

1 The Treasury supervises the FSA, while the FSA supervises three categories of regulated body:

- Recognised Clearing Houses (RCHs)
- Designated Professional Bodies (DPBs)
- Recognised Investment Exchanges (RIEs), including Recognised Overseas Investment Exchanges (ROIEs)

2
- To maintain confidence in the UK financial system
- To promote public understanding of the financial system
- To secure the appropriate level of protection for consumers
- To continue to reduce financial crime

3
- Knowingly buying shares in a takeover target before a general disclosure
- Market distortion: dealing on an exchange just prior to the exchange closing with the purpose of positioning the share price at a distorted level in order to avoid having to pay out on a derivatives transaction
- Posting an inaccurate story on an internet bulletin board in order to give a false or misleading impression

4
- Criminal charges
- Contracts becoming voidable
- Claims for damages

5
- Direct authorisation
- Passporting

6 An approved person performing a significant influence function must:

(a) Take reasonable steps to ensure that the business of the firm for which he is responsible is organised so that it can be controlled effectively

(b) Exercise due skill, care and diligence in managing the business of the firm for which he is responsible

(c) Take reasonable steps to ensure that the business of the firm for which he is responsible complies with the relevant requirements and standards of the regulatory system

7
- Where there is a written agreement
- Where best execution is achieved
- Where there is prior and periodic disclosure

- Where goods or services provided are directly relevant to and assist the client

Where the firm acts as principal, commission must cover costs of execution and goods and services provided.

8   A 'Chinese wall' is an internal arrangement, physical or organisational, that restricts the movement of information within a firm eg by a securities firm locating the corporate finance department on a different floor from the sales department.

9   It encompasses a wide range of media including the internet, tip sheets and other publications.

10   - Market counterparties (eg government, other firms)
      - Intermediate customers (eg large businesses, experts)
      - Private customers (eg individuals, small businesses)

11   A two way agreement is signed by the client.

12   There is an obligation to disclose to private customers:

      - The basis or amount of charges
      - Before business is transacted

13   The client must accept the loss. The cancellation allows them to take their money back net of charges, but not net of market movements.

14   It is the requirement to obtain the best price for a transaction of its type and size.

15   Every 25 business days for assets not held by the firm but for which it is accountable and every six months for asset held by the firm.

16   The Financial Ombudsman Service (FOS), £100,000 plus costs and compensation for any distress, suffering, damage to reputation and inconvenience.

17   It is 100% of the first £2,000 and 90% of the next £33,000, making a total of £31,700.

18   Fourteen years' imprisonment.

19   An ISD-authorised firm may offer the following services.

      (a) Reception and transmission of orders, on behalf of investors, in relation to one or more of the relevant instruments or the execution of such orders other than for their own account.

      (b) Dealing in any of the relevant instruments for their own account.

      (c) Managing portfolios of investments in accordance with mandates given by investors on a discretionary, client by client basis where such portfolios include one or more of the relevant instruments.

      (d) Underwriting in respect of issues of the listed instruments and/or the placing of such issues.

20   Having contacted their regulator, a firm must wait up to three months for their decision and wait a further two months for the host regulator to respond.

21   The host state.

Answers to practice questions

PRACTICE QUESTION 1

(a)   This will normally:

- Increase the cost of short-term borrowing

- Increase the cost of long-term borrowing, but by a variable amount

- Reduce equity prices relatively as these will become less attractive than interest bearing assets

- Reduce equity prices also in anticipation of lower demand caused by less disposable income and higher business costs from more expensive borrowing

- Depress growth as a result of more expensive borrowing in business

- Reduce consumer borrowing as a result of higher cost, further reducing demand

(b)   Central banks have different levels of autonomy but are typically responsible for the following.

- Implementing monetary policy (and possibly interest-rate setting, as in the UK)
- Implementing exchange rate policy
- Managing the national debt
- Supervision of the banks (in the UK - passed to the FSA)
- Lenders of money during a financial crisis

(c)   The Bank of England can do the following to implement changes in interest rates.

- Intervene in the repo market. This changes demand for gilts and therefore their price. Interest rates change as a result.

- They can buy or sell short-term treasury bills, changing demand and prices and changing interest rates as a result.

- They could impose a reserve ratio for commercial banks at the Bank of England, which increases the interest rates they need to charge to offset the non-interest bearing reserve.

- In extreme circumstances, the Bank could issue a directive requiring the banking sector to increase rates.

PRACTICE QUESTION 2

Risk

Sterling deposits are typically seen as 'no risk' investments. This is however not strictly true because, in the event of the failure of the bank or building society, the Financial Services Compensation Scheme limits compensation to 100% of the first £20,000 and 90% of the next £33,000, giving a maximum total of £31,700. Deposits may also be at risk from the effects of inflation.   (3)

Return

The return from a Sterling deposit is in the form of interest paid on the capital invested. The interest can be a fixed or a variable amount. For UK bank and building societies, the return is paid net of tax at 20%. Basic rate taxpayers have no further tax to pay. Lower rate and non-taxpayers may reclaim the difference.   (3)

Comparison of return

Typically, the bank or building society will quote both a nominal rate of return and a more accurate rate of return in the form of an AER or Annual Equivalent Rate. The AER would be the appropriate rate to use for comparison purposes. (3)

PRACTICE QUESTION 3

Risk

Gilts held to redemption can be described as no risk, but Gilts traded on the stock market would be more accurately described as low risk. Gilts suffer from inflation risk since the redemption value is fixed in nominal terms. Index-linked gilts overcome inflation risk. The capital value of the Gilts will vary inversely with interest rates, but tend not to fluctuate to the same degree as equities. Once purchased, the income produced by a Gilt will be fixed and is very secure as the British government underwrites it. (3)

Return

A gilt can produce a return in the form of an increase or decrease in capital. This is exempt from capital gains tax. Gilts provide a fixed regular income in the form of a coupon typically paid twice per year. The income is payable to maturity, at which time the capital value is also paid to the holder. The income is paid gross, but is liable to income tax. (3)

Comparison

There are two widely used measurements of Gilt returns, the interest yield and redemption yield. The interest yield can be used to determine the level of income produced, which could be compared to the interest return from a deposit-based investment. However, as we have said there can be movements in the capital value of Gilts. The 'redemption' yield allows for this and provides a yield figure that makes an allowance for the changes in the capital value as well as the income produced. (3)

PRACTICE QUESTION 4

Risk

The level of risk for equities is the higher than with fixed interest investments or cash, although the level of risk varies with the equity chosen. Blue chip shares tend to be relatively low risk, whereas unlisted shares would represent the high-risk end of the spectrum. With equities the higher risks tend to bring higher returns, and the equity markets overall tend to produce higher returns than inflation over the long term. This in itself reduces the inflation risk that savings over the longer term will be eroded by inflation. (3)

Return

Equities provide a return in the form of a dividend payment, typically every six months for UK equities. There is nothing to say that dividends must be paid, but often the share price tends to reflect the size and regularity of the dividend payments. Dividends are paid together with a tax credit of 10% that discharges the shareholder's liability for basic rate tax. The market values of equities also fluctuate and can provide capital gains or losses, which are subject to capital gains tax. (3)

Comparison

The dividend yield of a share can be used to compare it with the income returns from deposits and fixed interest investments. However, as we stated above there can also be changes in the capital values of shares. We can calculate the increase or decrease in the capital values in percentage terms over the period held. This can be added to the dividend income to determine the overall return. It is the overall return that should be compared with the AER for a cash investment and the redemption yields of fixed interest investments. (3)

PRACTICE QUESTION 5

(a) • He could sell sufficient FTSE 100 index future contracts in the market to cover the value of the portfolio.

- The value of the contract will rise if the FTSE 100 index falls and vice versa.

- The profit on the futures contract will offset losses in the portfolio.

- If the market moves in the wrong direction, losses on the future will offset gains in the portfolio.

- The open position could be settled for cash at expiry, or cancelled out by a purchase of FTSE 100 future contracts.

- A loss on the contract will be deducted from the margin payment first and then from subsequent calls for margin variation, the cost of which would need to be met by selling shares in the portfolio.

(b) • In order to calculate the number of contracts, it is first necessary to establish the value of a single contract.

- For each index point the value of the contract will be £10.

- The value of each contract is £10 × 6,500 = £65,000.

- To calculate the number of contracts required the value of the portfolio is divided by the value of one index contract.

- £750,000/£65,000 = 11.5.

- Only whole contracts can be bought or sold.

(c) • The FTSE 100 index future is an actively traded contract, so the margin is likely to be relatively low at £2,500 per contract.

- Each contract will have a margin requirement of £2,500.

- Assuming Mr Jones buys 12 contracts the total initial margin requirement is at £30,000.

(d) • The purchase of FTSE 100 put options.

- Put options increase in value as the underlying asset value decreases.

- The sale (writing) a FTSE 100 call option.

- As the FTSE 100 falls the value of the option from the buyers perspective decreases, the option can either be repurchased at a lower price giving a profit, or left to expire worthless allowing the writer to keep the premium.

PRACTICE QUESTION 6

(a) • Quick entry into the investment market.

- Reduced administration and paperwork for Fred.

- It is easier to value a single portfolio of collective investments than a number of shares.

- Professional investment managers will be making the investment decisions for Fred and they will have access to the latest and most accurate market information.

- In order to diversify the portfolio, Fred would need to buy a least ten different shares if held directly. This number of holdings will reduce but not fully eliminate specific (unsystematic) risk.

- The costs of dealing, accounting and holding the assets are likely to mount up if Fred buys shares, whereas the purchase of a single FTSE 100 index tracker unit trust could be lower.

(b)
- The price at which units are purchased is fixed at the valuation point.

- Where the valuation point used for the purchase and sale of units is the previous one, prices are described as historic.

(c)
- 'Off the page' investors have to take the responsibility for their own investment decisions.

- There is no cancellation notice for this type of investment.

- Investments via an intermediary will get the benefit of a cancellation notice allowing a period to change his mind and cancel his contract without charges.

- Providing that Fred gave full details to the intermediary, he would have a claim against his intermediary if he were given poor advice, ie not suitable for his circumstances.

(d)
- Overseeing the management of the investment company
- Protecting the interests of the investor
- Valuation and pricing of OEIC shares
- Dealing in shares for the OEIC
- The payment of income distributions
- Generally overseeing the ACD
- Ensuring that the ACD is acting in accordance with its investment powers
- Ensuring the ACD is acting in accordance with its borrowing powers

(e)
- Income is subject to tax at 20% on savings income, 22% on rent and 10% on dividends.

- If gilt based a non- or lower rate taxpayer may reclaim the tax deducted, but if equity based they may not. Higher rate taxpayers will be liable for a further 20% with a gilt fund and 22.5% with an equity fund.

- CGT is payable on disposals by the investor (unless exempt).

PRACTICE QUESTION 7

(a) The NBC Trust shares are the lower risk, as the assets on redemption are already covered. The trust would still repay the assets on wind up even if the value of the assets fell by 5% per annum. (Hurdle rate - 5%.)

(b) The CBN trust could produce the best return of 11% over the NBC trusts 7.5%. However, in order to do this, the underlying assets would have to grow at 20% for the remaining five years. This seems unlikely.

(c) The main classes of investment trust are:

- Income shares
- Capital shares
- Stepped preference shares
- Zero dividend preference shares

(d)   The main forms of investment return are:

- Income shares – a combination of income and capital growth

- Capital shares – highly geared capital growth only; no income

- Stepped preference shares – a predetermined, increasing dividend and capital value

- Zero dividend preference shares – capital growth only, at a predetermined rate; no income.

(e)   • The hurdle rate indicates the level of market growth required for capital shares to acquire a value. The lower this hurdle rate, the better the opportunity for returns.

- The asset cover indicates whether a capital share has acquired any value. In the statistics, repayment of the capital shares is assumed at a set price eg 50p. Where the asset cover exceeds one, then the set price has been covered.

PRACTICE QUESTION 8

(a)   Advantages and disadvantages of life assurance managed fund investment are as follows.

Advantages

- The fund is managed by a full-time investment professional.

- The risk is lower as a managed fund invests in cash fixed interest investments and properties as well as equities.

- The minimum investment is likely to be considerably less than with an effective portfolio of shares.

- The managed fund is a pooled fund, considerably reducing the risk by pooling the money of many investors over many more shares than would be possible with a portfolio of shares.

- An 'International' managed fund could have geographical spread, further reducing non-systematic risk.

- The administration and record keeping is much simpler for a life assurance managed fund as there is one set of documents and only one section to fill in on a self-assessment form.

Disadvantages

- Life assurance bonds cannot produce true income as part of a portfolio.

- A managed fund has a limited set of investment objectives, using a range of equities, a far larger range of investment objectives could be achieved.

- A life assurance managed fund has less potential to increase in value than an individual portfolio of shares as it contains cash, fixed interest and property investments which are considerably less volatile than equities.

- It is not possible to use the personal CGT exemption on a life assurance based investment.

- The costs of investing directly in equities is less than with a life assurance bond, which is subject to a bid-offer spread and management charges.

- A life assurance managed fund is subject to internal taxation.

(b) *Multi-manager schemes*

- These can give the benefit of reduced administration.

- They can also give the benefit of full time professional investment management and have access to a very wide range of investment funds.

- They can provide for a wider range of investment objectives by combining life assurance funds in a number of different ways, many providers offer a range of fund portfolios with different objectives.

- It should be possible to improve on normal market returns by active investment, taking advantage of the changes in UK and overseas markets as they happen.

(c) The role of derivatives in guaranteed equity bonds includes the following.

- Derivatives provide the mechanism for a guaranteed equity bond to produce returns in line with one or more stockmarkets over a fixed term for a fixed amount of the original investment.

- The derivative is purchased 'over the counter' and is a specially tailored contract for the life assurance company.

- The derivative typically provides a return linked with the movements in one or more investment market via the indices for those markets, eg FTSE 100, DAX 30.

- The need to purchase the derivative to underwrite the bond issue typically dictates the terms for the issue, eg limited subscription period, fixed tranche of investment.

PRACTICE QUESTION 9

(a) **Advantages of a tracker fund over an actively managed fund**

- The investment performance of the fund is linked to the index and not to the performance of the fund manager. This should make it more consistent than most actively managed funds that often do not outperform the relevant index.

- The risks are lower with a tracker fund as they are on the efficient frontier. They offer the best possible return for the given level of risk. Managers of actively managed funds often take higher risks in order to outperform the index.

- Managed fund managers are subject to specific (non-systematic) risk as well as market (systematic) risk, a tracker fund is not subject to specific risk.

- The charges of an index tracker fund are likely to be less, as there is less need for skilled investment management.

(b) **Advantages of tracker funds over direct investment in shares**

- Tracker funds can be invested quickly with a single transaction.

- Direct investments will be invested in a number of transactions, which are not as quick, and will involve additional charges.

- The administration of a single tracker fund is less than with a number of direct shares.

- With direct investments, investment decisions must be made as to the relevant investments. No decisions are required with a tracker fund except which to choose in the first place.

- A tracker fund covers a wide range of shares in a pooled fund and benefits from the economies of scale, whereas direct investment is constrained by the cost of each share transaction and it is unlikely that a portfolio will be as well spread.

- Money can be invested globally via tracker funds without problems relating to local market condition (eg liquidity) or local taxation laws.

- With a directly invested portfolio, the specific risk is high. With a tracker fund there is none.

(c) Fund performance differences between two different tracker funds.

- The funds may be different financial vehicles, eg unit trusts, OEICs, investment trusts, ISA funds or pension funds. These each have different tax structures.

- They might track different indices, which would give different rates of return.

- They may track the same index in different ways. Full replication of the index is the most accurate, but other methods such as stratification or optimisation may cause tracking errors. This will result in different investment performances.

- The charges may be different on the two funds. This will impact on performance and if the tracking is accurate, the fund with the lower charges will give the better returns.

PRACTICE QUESTION 10

(a) Mr Reynolds describes himself as prudent, or risk-averse. Under these circumstances, it would not be wise to invest in antique fob watches as there will be considerable risks attached. He may end up paying too much or buying copies, or the bottom may fall out of the antique fob watch market.

(b) The main expenses will be:
- The costs of acquisition and sale, for example auctioneers costs
- Dealers profits if purchased from a dealer
- VAT if purchased from a dealer
- The cost of secure storage
- The cost of insurance
- Market intelligence costs, magazines, books, auction reports
- Cost of attending auctions

(c) The problems Mr Reynolds might encounter if he wished to sell his portfolio are as follows.

- Fob watches are a specialist item and are relatively illiquid.

- He would need to get them into the right kind of auction.

- Even in the right auction, buyers will not always be tempted and he may make a loss.

- Auction costs will reduce his investment return.

- If he needs the money very quickly he may have to sell the collection directly to a dealer who may not pay him the full value.

- Fob watches are so specialist that a large collection could flood the market and depress prices.

(d) If Mr Reynolds is a 'prudent' investor then a VCT, which is a very high-risk investment, would not be suitable.

(e)   *Tax benefits of a VCT*

The investment must be held for three years and must not exceed the maximum investment of £200,000 (2005/06) to get the following benefits.

- Tax relief of 40% on the investment as a 'tax reducer'.

- Dividends up to limit are exempt from further taxation.

- Capital gains made on VCTs are exempt from CGT whether or not the qualifying terms or investment limits apply.

(f)   Before going ahead with his scheme, he should consider the following.

- What rental income the property will generate compared to the cost of borrowing, for example a university should be able to tell him what the typical rent figures are

- Is he planning to rent direct or via an agent and, if so, how will that affect the investment return?

- Whether the property is close enough to the university to attract tenants

- If the university is any distance, what are the bus/train routes like?

- Do the deeds of his property allow him to rent the property out?

- Will the buildings insurers take on the liability and, if so, at what cost?

- What will the neighbours think of his scheme and are they likely to take legal action against him for damage caused by his tenants?

PRACTICE QUESTION 11

(a)   Dividend cover shows how many times over the dividend could be paid out of available profit. The greater the dividend cover, the greater the certainty of dividend payments. Companies with lower levels of dividend cover may have to reduce dividends if profits decline. This figure is particularly important for investors seeking income.

(b)   To calculate the dividend cover we need to calculate earnings per share.

EPS = Share price/P/E ratio = 195p/15 = 13p

We also need to know the dividend.

Dividend = Share price × Yield = 195 × 2% = 3.9p

The dividend cover = EPS/Dividend = 13p/3.9p = 3.33

(c)   Where information from company accounts is the only information used to determine whether to invest in a particular share, the limitations are as follows.

The investor is reliant on the information provided and, despite regulations governing the form and content of accounts, a measure of creativity can often be used to disguise problems for some time.

The accounts and report are effectively an historic document and look at the past, with the exception of the chairman's report which will look briefly at the future trading environment.

The accounts cannot predict the future trading environment which can be affected on a number of different levels, global conditions, local conditions and sector conditions. These can all severely impact on profitability and, hence, share price and dividend levels.

They do not and cannot allow for unpredictable factors such as future legislation, litigation from disgruntled customers, take-overs, mergers, employment problems, and raw material cost variations caused by, for example, the weather or changes in fashion.

In extreme market conditions, investor sentiment can move prices significantly with little or no reference to fundamental value, future potential profits or anything else.

PRACTICE QUESTION 12

(a)   Mr Garland is likely to incur the following charges.

- Broker's commission   1-2% or £25 fixed
- Stamp duty   0.5% on purchases
- PTM levy   £1 on deals over £10,000
- FSA charge   at the discretion of the broker

(b)   The costs of buying shares on the AIM are not actually any higher, but the lower turnover volumes and liquidity levels mean the buy/sell spreads can be larger, as much as 10% or more, and this cost will need to be overcome by the movement in the share price.

(c)   Thursday 4 October (three working days after).

(d)   The London Stock Exchange (LSE), Virt-x and OFEX.

(e)   UK and overseas order and quote driven markets:

- UK order-driven – FTSE-100 shares purchased via SETS on the main market
- Overseas order-driven – New York, Tokyo, Frankfurt or Paris
- UK quote-driven, non-FTSE-100 shares on the main market or shares listed on AIM
- Overseas quote-driven – NASDAQ

(f)   *Settlement day via the CREST system*

- The CREST system checks that the stock has been transferred to the seller's broker's stock account.

- The CREST system checks that there is sufficient credit in the buyer's broker's cash memorandum account to cover the cost.

- If these check out, the stock is transferred from the seller's stock account to the buyer's.

- CREST creates a register update request for the registrar of the company's shares to amend the stock register.

- The obligation to make payment by the end of the day is registered with the purchaser's broker.

- The purchaser's broker will instruct their bank to make the payment at the end of the working day.

PRACTICE QUESTION 13

(a) $E(R_i) = R_f + ß_i[E(R_m) – R_f]$

$E(R_i)$ = the expected return from the investment
R_f = the risk free return
$ß_i$ = the beta of the investment
$E(R_m)$ = the expected return from the market

(b)   (i)   Using the formula and substituting the values for Unum we get:

$10\% = R_f + 1[E(R_m) - R_f]$ or $R_f + E(R_m) - R_f$

The $+ R_f$ and $- R_f$ cancel out leaving $10\% = E(R_m)$.

Therefore, the expected return from the market is 10%.

(ii) We can substitute $E(R_m)$ with 10% in the equation using the figures for Quince to tell us the risk free return.

$$25 = R_f + 4[10 - R_f]$$
$$25 = R_f + 40 - 4R_f$$
$$25 - 40 = R_f - 4R_f$$
$$-15 = -3R_f$$
$$-5 = -R_f$$
$$5 = R_f$$

The risk free return is 5%

(c) **Dos**

$$E(R_i) = 5 + 1.5[10-5]$$
$$= 5 + 15 - 7.5$$
$$= 12.5\%$$

The assumption on the return is incorrect. The actual return will probably be 2.5% below the expected return.

Tress

$$E(R_i) = 5 + 2[10-5]$$
$$= 5 + 20 - 10$$
$$= 15\%$$

This is correct for the expected return.

Quattro

$$E(R_i) = 5 + 3[10-5]$$
$$= 5 + 30 - 15$$
$$= 20\%$$

The assumption on the return is incorrect. The actual return will probably be 2.5% above the expected return.

(d) The two main approaches are 'top-down' and 'bottom-up'.

Top-down

With top down management the classes of assets are selected and then individual securities are selected within these to be representative. This approach is the most common for portfolio management and tends to be used when all markets are moving up.

Bottom-up

With a bottom-up approach, the individual securities are selected based on their potential, irrespective of the asset allocation. This method tends to be favoured where markets generally are falling.

PRACTICE QUESTION 14

(a)
- Income portfolios
- Growth portfolios
- Surplus capital (money market investments)
- Investment trusts
- Unit trusts
- Trust investments
- Pension funds
- Charity funds

(b)
- Type of investment return, income or growth or a balance
- The measure of risks they are prepared to accept to achieve it
- Taxation of the investments
- Accessibility to funds
- Personal considerations such as environmental issues etc

(c) With discretionary management, the investment manager is given the right to buy and sell assets without consultation with the investor. The investment strategy is agreed with the client in advance and the manager carries out that strategy without further input.

Discretionary management is on the increase at the expense of advisory management. The system allows the manager to move quickly into situations without too many other people knowing about it. The discretion is limited to the investment strategy (including risk limits) agreed with the client at the start. Discretionary management can be paid for by a flat fee, a higher transaction charge, by allowing the manager to keep commission, or, with some investments, on the performance of the portfolio.

There is a legal requirement for a full client fact find to ensure that the investment is appropriate. It is also a requirement to disclose in detail up front the frequency with which they receive information about their portfolio, which must be clearly laid out in the terms of business letter or client agreement.

(d) (i) Mortality drag is an advantage of an annuity over direct investment.

(ii) It is a term used to describe the cross subsidy given to the surviving members of an annuity by the other annuity holders that do not survive.

(iii) This keeps annuity rates artificially higher than they would otherwise be.

(iv) Effectively the investment return on pension fund withdrawals needs to be higher to over come the effects of mortality drag if clients are to receive a better return.

(e) £7,000 into an ISA.

(f) Gilts, including strips, from any EEA country, with at least five years to run until redemption.

PRACTICE QUESTION 15

(a) If 6.5% is the nominal figure, then if paid half yearly the effective interest rate will be:

$(1 + (6.5\%/ 2))^2 - 1 = 6.606\%$ per annum. Or Nom% = 6.5, P/YR = 2, solve for EFF % = 6.60563.

(b) 5 years at 9% and 5 years at 6% = £10,000 × $(1.09)^5$ × $(1.06)^5$

= 10,000 × 1.5386 × 1.3382 = 20,589.55 (+ or – £1 allowed)

(c) The two main methods for calculating indices are:

- Weighted
- Unweighted

The indices weighted by market capitalisation will be more accurate as the price movement reflects the turnover in the shares as well as the price

Unweighted indices give misleading figures as price changes in small or inactive shares have just the same effect as those in the more active ones

(d) The main benchmarks for the French, German, Japanese and New York stock exchanges are as follows.

- France/Paris – CAC-40 or SBF 120
- Germany/Frankfurt – Dax (30)
- Japan/Tokyo – Nikkei 225, Nikkei 350 or TOPIX
- New York – Dow Jones Industrial Average Index or S&P 500

(e) Money Weighted Return:

Return (R) = (Final Value (V^1) – Initial Value (V^0) + Accrued income (I))/V^0

(f) Time Weighted Returns are more accurate because they allow for the timing and flow of capital in and out of the portfolio.

(g) (i)

UK equities	-	$50\% \times 15\% = 7.5\%$
Overseas equities	-	$40\% \times 10\% = 4\%$
Gilt	-	$5\% \times 7.5\% = 0.375\%$
Fixed interest	-	0%
Property	-	0%
Cash	-	$5\% \times 5\% = 0.25\%$

This gives a total of 12.125%, Patrick's portfolio manager outperformed this by 0.875%

(ii)

UK equities	-	$45\% \times 15\% = 6.75\%$
Overseas equities	-	$45\% \times 10\% = 4.5\%$
Gilt	-	0%
Fixed interest	-	$0\% \times 7.5\% = 0.0\%$
Property	-	0%
Cash	-	$10\% \times 5\% = 0.5\%$

This gives a total of 11.75%, Patrick's portfolio manager outperformed this by 1.25%

PRACTICE QUESTION 16

(a)
- Personal details

- Firm details

- Details of the contractual arrangement between the candidate and the firm, for example whether the candidate is an employee or working under a contract of services

- Controlled functions for which approval is sought

- Confirmation that the candidate meets training and competence requirements

- Ten year employment history

- Answers to question on past convictions, judgement debts etc, to help establish if the candidate is fit and proper

- List of directorships and any additional information offered

- Signed declarations by the candidate and the firm

(b)
- Honesty, integrity and reputation, in the length of employment record and any criminal record, for example

- Competence and capability, based on experience and training

- Financial soundness, relating to court judgements or bankruptcy, for example, rather than a person's financial resources

(c)
- Misleading or attempting to mislead a customer, the firm or the FSA, eg falsification of documents, misleading customer about risks of an investment

- Failing to give a customer, the firm, its auditor or its actuary information which the person knew or should have known they should have provided, eg failing to disclose charges or surrender penalties

- Market abuse, knowingly buying shares in a takeover target before the relevant information has been disclosed.

- Failure to report relevant matters internally, where internal reporting procedures exist in the firm

(d) Financial instruments, to which the terms of the ISD apply, are:
- Financial futures contracts

- Forward interest rate agreements

- Money market investments and related instruments

- Swaps in interest rates, currencies and equities

- Transferable securities, shares, debentures, government and public securities, instruments entitling to shares, and securities and certificates representing shares

- Units in collective investment undertakings

- Options on the above instruments

(e) In order to transact cross border business under the terms of the ISD, the following procedure must take place.
- A firm must apply to their regulator.

- The regulator must consider the application and reply within one month.

- The host regulator is not given a time period within which to respond.

- As soon as the firm receives business from their regulatory authority, they may transact business.

(f) **Non-core services permitted under the ISD**
- Safekeeping and administration in relation to one or more of the listed instruments

- Safe custody services

- Granting loans or credits to an investor to allow him to carry out a transaction in one or more of the listed instruments, where the firm granting the credit/loan is involved in the transaction

- Advice on capital structure, industrial strategy and related matters and mergers and acquisitions

- Services related to underwriting

- Investment advice concerning one or more of the listed instruments

- Foreign exchange services where these are connected with the provision of investment services

(g) In order to qualify for a 'passport' under the terms of the ISD, a firm must comply with the minimum base capital requirements for the services that the individual firm provides, as dictated by the CAD.

Index

REVIEW FORM & FREE PRIZE DRAW

All original review forms from the entire BPP range, completed with genuine comments, will be entered into one of two draws on 31 January 2006 and 31 July 2006. The names on the first four forms picked out on each occasion will be sent a cheque for £50.

Name: _____   Address: _____

_____

Date: _____   _____

How have you used this Text?
(Tick one box only)

☐ home study (book only)

☐ on a course: at _____

☐ with 'correspondence' package

☐ other _____

Why did you decide to purchase this Text?
(Tick one box only)

☐ recommended by training department

☐ recommendation by friend/colleague

☐ recommendation by a lecturer at college

☐ saw advertising

☐ have used BPP Texts in the past

☐ other _____

Your ratings, comments and suggestions would be appreciated on the following areas.

	Very useful	*Useful*	*Not useful*
Introductory section	☐	☐	☐
Main text	☐	☐	☐
Questions in chapters	☐	☐	☐
Chapter roundups	☐	☐	☐
Quizzes at ends of chapters	☐	☐	☐
Practice examination	☐	☐	☐
Structure and presentation	☐	☐	☐
Availability of Updates on website	☐	☐	☐

	Excellent	*Good*	*Adequate*	*Poor*
Overall opinion of this Study Text	☐	☐	☐	☐

Do you intend to continue using BPP Study Texts?   ☐ Yes   ☐ No

Please note any further comments, suggestions and apparent errors on the reverse of this page, or write by e-mail to fpqueries@bpp.com

Please return this form to: AFPC Range Manager, BPP Professional Education, FREEPOST, London, W12 8BR

REVIEW FORM & FREE PRIZE DRAW (continued)

Please note any further comments, suggestions or apparent errors below.

FREE PRIZE DRAW RULES

1   Closing date for 31 January 2006 draw is 31 December 2005. Closing date for 31 July 2006 draw is 30 June 2006.

2   Restricted to entries with UK and Eire addresses only. BPP employees, their families and business associates are excluded.

3   No purchase necessary. Entry forms are available upon request from BPP Professional Education. No more than one entry per title, per person. Draw restricted to persons aged 16 and over.

4   Winners will be notified by post and receive their cheques not later than 6 weeks after the relevant draw date.

5   The decision of the promoter in all matters is final and binding. No correspondence will be entered into.

See overleaf for information on other
BPP products and how to order

AFPC® Order

To BPP Professional Education, Aldine Place, London W12 8AW
Tel: 020 8740 2211. Fax: 020 8740 1184
E-mail: Publishing@bpp.com Web:www.bpp.com

Mr/Mrs/Ms (Full name)

Daytime delivery address

Postcode

Daytime Tel

E-mail

TOTAL FOR PRODUCTS £

POSTAGE & PACKING

	First	Each extra
Texts/Kits		
UK	£5.00	£2.00 £
Europe*	£6.00	£4.00 £
I-Pass		
UK	£2.00	£1.00 £
Europe*	£3.00	£2.00 £

TOTAL FOR POSTAGE & PACKING £

Reduced postage rates apply if you order online at www.bpp.com/afpc

Grand Total (Cheques to *BPP Professional Education*) I enclose a cheque for (incl. Postage)
Or charge to Access/Visa/Switch £

Card Number

Expiry date   Start Date

Issue Number (Switch Only)

Signature

	Study Text £39.95	I-Pass CD-ROM £29.95	Practice & Revision Kit £19.95
ADVANCED FINANCIAL PLANNING CERTIFICATE (7/05 editions, except H15)			
G10: Taxation and Trusts	☐	☐	☐
G20: Personal Investment Planning	☐	–	–
G30: Business Financial Planning	☐	–	–
G60: Pensions	☐	–	☐
G70: Investment Portfolio Management	☐	–	–
H15: Supervision and Sales Management	☐ (1/05)	–	–
H25: Holistic Financial Planning	☐	–	–
Half-credit subjects £32.95			
K10: Retirement Options	☐	–	–
K20: Pension Investment Options	☐	–	–
SUBTOTAL	£	£	£

We aim to deliver to all UK addresses inside 5 working days; a signature will be required. Orders to all EU addresses should be delivered within 6 working days. *Europe includes the Republic of Ireland and the Channel Islands. For delivery to the rest of the world, please call us on +44 (0)20 8740 2211. For information about BPP's study material for the new Certificate in Financial Planning, please call 020 8740 2211.